Configuring Sales and Distribution in SAP® ERP

SAP PRESS is a joint initiative of SAP and Rheinwerk Publishing. The know-how offered by SAP specialists combined with the expertise of Rheinwerk Publishing offers the reader expert books in the field. SAP PRESS features first-hand information and expert advice, and provides useful skills for professional decision making.

SAP PRESS offers a variety of books on technical and business-related topics for the SAP user. For further information, please visit our website: *www.sap-press.com*.

Matt Chudy, Luis Castedo, and Ricardo Lopez
Sales and Distribution in SAP ERP—Practical Guide
2015, 520 pages, hardcover
ISBN 978-1-4932-1054-1

Martin Murray and Sanil Kimmatkar
Warehouse Management with SAP ERP:
Functionality and Technical Configuration (3rd Edition)
2016, approx. 675 pp., hardcover
ISBN 978-1-4932-1363-4

Martin Murray and Jawad Akhtar
Materials Management with SAP ERP:
Functionality and Technical Configuration (4th Edition)
2016, approx. 740 pp., hardcover
ISBN 978-1-4932-1357-3

Chandrakant Agarwal
SAP CRM: Business Processes and Configuration
2015, 737 pages, hardcover
ISBN 978-1-4932-1039-8

Ricardo Lopez, Ashish Mohapatra

Configuring Sales and Distribution in SAP® ERP

Bonn • Boston

Editor Emily Nicholls
Copyeditor Eli Badra
Cover Design Graham Geary
Photo Credit Shutterstock.com/177557252/© Zoom Team
Layout Design Vera Brauner
Production Kelly O'Callaghan
Typesetting III-satz, Husby (Germany)
Printed and bound in the United States of America, on paper from sustainable sources

ISBN 978-1-4932-1260-6

© 2016 by Rheinwerk Publishing, Inc., Boston (MA)

2nd edition 2016

Library of Congress Cataloging-in-Publication Data
Lopez, Ricardo
[Optimizing sales and distribution in SAP ERP] Configuring sales and distribution in SAP ERP / Ricardo Lopez,
Ashish Mohapatra. -- 2 Edition.
pages cm
Revised edition of Optimizing sales and distribution in SAP ERP, 2010.
Includes index.
ISBN 978-1-4932-1260-6 (print : alk. paper) -- ISBN 1-4932-1260-5 (print : alk. paper) -- ISBN 978-1-4932-1261-3 (ebook)
-- ISBN 978-1-4932-1262-0 (print and ebook : alk. paper) 1. SAP R/3. 2. Sales management--Computer programs. 3. Phys-
ical distribution of goods--Management--Computer programs. I. Mahapatra, Asisha. II. Mahapatra, Asisha. Optimizing sales
and distribution in SAP ERP. III. Title.
HF5438.35.L67 2015
658.8'10028553--dc23
2015034410

Contents at a Glance

Dear Reader,

As the economy becomes increasingly international, products are bouncing around the globe at a faster and faster rate. In an era where same-day shipping is the new next-day shipping (and two-day shipping has become commonplace), customers expect their vendors to get them what they want even sooner. To stay competitive, sellers need to ensure that the right goods and services arrive at the right customer at the right time—and that they, in turn, receive prompt and accurate compensation for the wares delivered.

So what is the key to sales and distribution in this brave new world? And how can both incremental and exponential improvements in technology help streamline these processes?

For this, turn your attention to *Configuring Sales and Distribution in SAP ERP* and open the SD toolbox. Learn how to customize SAP ERP to achieve your sales and distribution goals, from fine-tuning your pricing and sales mechanisms to performing critical data analysis with SAP HANA. SD expert Ricardo Lopez joins Ashish Mohapatra for this new edition to show you where SD is going, and how your implementation can keep pace.

What did you think about *Configuring Sales and Distribution in SAP ERP*? Your comments and suggestions are the most useful tools to help us make our books the best they can be. Please feel free to contact me and share any praise or criticism you may have.

Thank you for purchasing a book from SAP PRESS!

Emily Nicholls
Editor, SAP PRESS

Rheinwerk Publishing
Boston, MA

emilyn@rheinwerk-publishing.com
www.sap-press.com

Contents

3   Sales   87

4   Pricing 169

Preface

Any company selling products or services must have the ability to efficiently fulfill orders and deliver their products and services. An integrated sales and distribution system enables them to create contracts and agreements, acknowledge order receipt, fulfill orders, and provide accurate invoices. In today's competitive environment, the ability to employ enterprise software to handle these processes cost-effectively is vital.

The Sales and Distribution functionality in SAP ERP is such a tool—and is one of the most important and most often implemented SAP logistics functionalities. It provides companies tools for managing the different stages of the order-to-cash process, making the information more manageable and accessible.

Who This Book Is For

The book can help the following groups learn how to customize the Sales and Distribution functionality in SAP ERP and how to integrate it with other systems. The target groups are:

- Consultants
- IT administrators
- Project and process leads and key team members

What Will Be Covered Throughout

Sales and Distribution is a mature functionality in SAP ERP. Over the years, SAP has added a lot of new tools to it, and our objective here is to show you how to configure Sales and Distribution using the most recent enhancements and technologies.

The book is written with SAP ERP users in mind, so that you can configure an SD implementation based on their requirements and hand it over to them, ready to fulfill orders and deliver their products and services more effectively. Many of the chapters in this second edition offer SD configuration troubleshooting to help resolve problems discovered during or after an implementation.

In the **Introduction**, we'll take a big-picture look at Sales and Distribution functionality in the context of SAP ERP and look at how it's changing from ten thousand feet. We'll introduce you to recent trends and changes to the functionality and a few project management tools you might consider for your implementation project.

In **Chapter 1**, we'll cover the customization of enterprise structures, and you'll be ready to handle your own organizational units and proper assignments in upcoming chapters.

In **Chapter 2**, Master Data, you'll learn how to do mass maintenance of master data records. We'll cover several kinds of master data records, such as customer master records, material master records, and so on. We'll also cover how to customize master data fields and how to customize layout.

Chapter 3, Sales, is the longest and most important chapter. Most of the processes in the Sales and Distribution functionality in SAP ERP start at this stage and culminate in billing. We'll discuss the customization of orders, items, and schedule line categories, and we'll cover both normal and special business processes such as consignment, or third-party sales. You'll develop a thorough understanding of the copy control technique and use of different routines. This chapter will introduce the condition technique, which is used throughout the SAP system for automatic determination.

In this chapter, we'll also discuss automatic determination of free goods, material exclusion, partners, batches, sales output, and material listing, as well as incompletion control. The chapter will conclude with coverage of returns processing and intercompany sales processing.

Chapter 4, Pricing, will again take you through the configuration of condition techniques. The condition technique used for automatic determination of pricing is considered the complete demonstration of the tool. You'll also learn how to customize rebate agreements, pricing reports, and the SAP interface for external tax software for sales and use tax.

In **Chapter 5**, Credit Risk Management, the primary topic is the configuration of automatic credit control. You'll also learn certain operations in credit management, forms of payment guarantee, and how block and unblock customers. We'll conclude the chapter with some problems and their solutions.

In **Chapter 6**, Logistics Management, we'll discuss the configuration of delivery document types and their item categories. You'll learn about the different processes such as picking, packing, serialization, and goods issue. You'll also learn about the determination process of storage locations, routes, and batches. We'll discuss batch determination, scheduling, and output processing, and conclude with some practical issues and their solutions.

Chapter 7, Billing, covers the configuration of billing types, billing plans, revenue account determination, and the interface with accounting. A list of practical issues and solutions will be provided at the end.

Chapter 8, Cross-Functional Customization, includes coverage of text processing, message control, ABAP tools, and numbering objects. These are topics that are useful but not fully discussed in earlier chapters; they're not exclusive to Sales and Distribution, but are important for you to understand in order to make the most of a new implementation project.

Chapter 9, Reporting and Analysis, starts off with a list of standard reports and analyses and their features. We'll then discuss key tools for creating customized reports and analyses: using ABAP queries, the Sales Information System, and operative reporting tools such as SAP HANA-optimized BI Content for Sales and Distribution.

Chapter 10, Sales and Distribution and SAP CRM, discusses functionality in the SAP CRM module that specifically applies to Sales and Distribution. It highlights the key configuration in customer quotes, sales orders, marketing, and the Customer Interaction Center, and how all of these modules interact with the SAP ERP system.

We'll summarize the book with a summary and conclusion, and offer tips about customizing screen layout and inportant SD transactions in the appendices.

Acknowledgments

I would like to thank Ashish Mohapatra, the author of the first edition of this book, for providing such a solid foundation for me to build upon. I'm also very grateful to my editors, Emily Nicholls and Eli Badra, for their guidance. Finally, I am grateful to my mother, brothers, and sisters, and to my partner, Chris Huygen, for their love and support.

Ricardo Lopez

I would like to sincerely thank all those who bought the first edition of this book. Their feedback was very useful in deciding the content of this edition. I would also like to thank Ms. Emily Nicholls and others at SAP PRESS for their contributions.

I also acknowledge all my teachers, friends, and colleagues who have a big influence on the way I think, learn, and write. I would like to especially thank my boss, Mr. Nikhil Aggarwal, and my mentor, Mr. Atulya Kumar Panda.

I thank my parents, Sri Madhav Chandra Mohapatra and Smt Sarala Mohapatra, and my elder brothers Mr. Amar Ranjan Mohapatra and Mr. Gyan Ranjan Mohapatra, who in spite of all their financial difficulties, provided me with the best education possible. My wife, Namita, daughter, Dikshya, and son, Tejash are a constant source of love and motivation for me. They inspire me to deliver the best.

Finally, I dedicate this book to Him who needs no acknowledgment, but rather acknowledges us by His blessings.

Ashish Mohapatra

Before you can start a new Sales and Distribution project or take advantage of its functionality, you'll want to understand the bigger SAP picture. Let's begin at 10,000 feet.

Introduction

In this chapter, we will establish the groundwork for a new SAP ERP Sales and Distribution implementation by introducing you to the most important SAP software from an optimization point of view, describing the application and its functionalities, and showing how the Sales and Distribution module fits in the context of SAP ERP. We will outline the ways that Sales and Distribution can be improved in an era increasingly driven by real-time data, such as how SAP HANA has influenced project implementation strategies. Finally, we'll conclude with a discussion of the latest in SAP implementation methodologies.

SAP ERP at a Glance

Before we get into Sales and Distribution, we'll discuss the main topics of SAP ERP—its applications and functionalities—to better understand how Sales and Distribution fits in with them. Lastly, we'll look at how SAP ERP—and Sales and Distribution in specific—can be (and have been) improved with new functionality and technological enhancements to Sales and Distribution.

Applications and Functionalities in SAP ERP

Traditionally, SAP ERP delivers its software in modular form, which means it consists of several applications and components, each of which has individual functionalities. This structure helps small and mid-size companies adopt specific portions of SAP software and then gradually integrate other specialized modules as their company grows. Currently, SAP releases modules that require separate installation in order to provide further adaptation and flexibility to its customers.

Table 1 shows the division of SAP ERP applications into three core groups (please note that this list is not exhaustive).

SAP ERP Financials	SAP ERP Operations (logistics)	SAP ERP Human Capital Management
▶ Financial Accounting	▶ Materials Management	▶ Personnel Management
▶ Controlling	▶ Sales and Distribution	▶ Payroll
▶ Funds Management	▶ Warehouse Management	▶ Talent Management
▶ Asset Accounting	▶ Quality Management	
	▶ Production Planning	
	▶ Plant Maintenance	

Table 1 SAP ERP Divisions

To support these applications, SAP recommends separate installation of the following latest technologies:

▶ SAP BusinessObjects BI and SAP Business Warehouse (BW)

▶ SAP Customer Relationship Management (CRM)

▶ SAP Master Data Management (MDM)

▶ SAP Supplier Relationship Management (SRM)

▶ SAP Process Integration (PI)

▶ SAP Global Trade Services (GTS)

Sales and Distribution in the Context of SAP ERP

Sales and distribution is also referred to as *order fulfillment* in the SAP Supply Chain Management (SAP SCM) solution. To handle the order fulfillment process, Sales and Distribution functionality in SAP ERP breaks into the following subcategories, which we'll see throughout the course of this book:

▶ Basic Functions (SD-BF)

▶ Master Data (SD-MD)

- Sales (SD-SLS)

- Foreign Trade (SD-FT)

- Billing (SD-BIL)

- Sales Support: Computer-Aided Selling (SD-CAS)

- Contract Handling for Consumer Product (SD-CH)

- Electronic Data Interchange (SD-EDI)

- POS Interface (SD-POS)

- Information System (SD-IS)

We will also cover the following logistics components:

- Shipping (LE-SHP)

- Transportation Planning and Processing (LE-TRA-TP)

- Batch Management (LO-BM)

Advances in Sales and Distribution

We need to understand what the latest SAP technology is, and what changes and enhancements have occurred across the modules, including Sales and Distribution.

Enhancement Packages

SAP Enhancement Packages (EHPs) provide companies with the flexibility of expanding their SAP software by adding selective functions, along with technical improvements based on their actual needs. EHPs simplify and integrate into the existing system; the idea is to lower costs with less effort and downtime than the typical ERP upgrade, which typically requires significant time and effort to implement. EHPs are usually delivered every two years or so, and include all new and enhanced business functionalities and technical enhancements.

EHP 6, launched during 2013, introduced SAP HANA and SAP Fiori. However, it was only with the launch of EHP 7 in 2014 that most of the existing areas in SAP ERP began to utilize the in-memory and SAP HANA technologies, with one main objective: to help business applications perform better.

SAP HANA

In the last few years, SAP has done immense work to develop and promote SAP HANA, a technology created to enhance data storage and mass analytics. One of the main objectives of SAP HANA is to allow you to perform massive and complex analyses in real time using in-memory data; in other words, to make real use of the server's main memory, not in the hard drive, as was done previously. The use of database memory is not new: it's been around for many years, but only recently has it become economically justifiable and broadly used.

What made this possible? In simple terms, SAP HANA can be described as a combination of database, application platform, and data processing capabilities into a single in-memory platform.

As opposed to a traditional database, which typically writes and reads at the hard-drive, SAP HANA in-memory eliminates the need for disk I/O operations, increasing database performance dramatically. Also, it enables massive data compression by storing and retrieving the data in column-based, as well as row-based, or even object-based, technology, expediting the data retrieval process. Typically, SQL or traditional databases use row-based technology to store and retrieve data. It's important to mention that SAP HANA is not a single component or module as we are traditionally are used to seeing, but rather it's a collection of software and hardware under the same rubric.

SAP now plans for SAP HANA to be the platform for future SAP developments, including analytics and applications. SAP HANA is supported by a new type of architecture and landscape, as depicted in Figure 1. The array of components that form SAP HANA contains an in-memory engine, application engine, modeling studio, real-time replication server, and data services. These are known as the native applications and interfaces. The traditional SAP ERP (part of SAP Business Suite) interacts with SAP HANA via an external interface, in the same way that SAP Business Warehouse (BW) does. On the opposite side, SAP BusinessObjects and other applications interact with SAP HANA via the SQL and BICS technologies.

SAP has created a faster way to process mass data for reporting: SAP HANA-optimized BI Content. It has also added to the Sales and Distribution functionality specifically to significantly expedite the time spent running Sales and Distributions reports and listings. We'll discuss SAP HANA analytics as it relates to Sales and Distribution in Chapter 9.

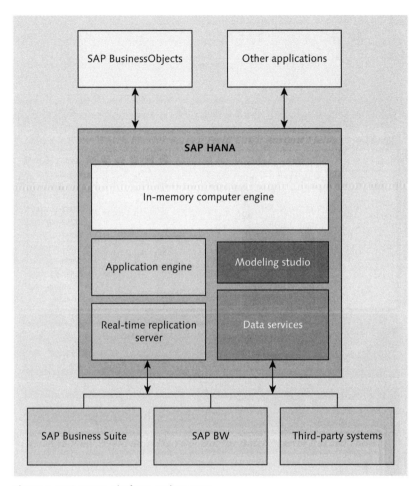

Figure 1 SAP HANA Platform Architecture

SAP Fiori

SAP Fiori is a collection of applications to be used with tablets, smartphones, and mobiles, created by SAP and launched as part of EHP 7. It's intended to be part of the SAP new user experience (UX) paradigm that empowers users with stream-lined, simplified end user screens. SAP Fiori employs the concept of UX 1:1:1:3:N. In other words, a single user can accomplish one task using one line of code in three screens or fewer, and connect to n-platforms. Figure 2 shows a simple comparison of the traditional SAP GUI screens and the new SAP Fiori screens, recently redesigned to provide a better user experience and simplify tasks.

SAP Fiori supports the most common line of business services. It provides applications across all SAP ERP areas, such as HR, finance, manufacturing, CRM, and sales and distribution, among others.

Figure 2 Traditional SAP Screens vs SAP Fiori UX Screens

In order to provide the best UX experience, SAP Fiori enables four distinct types of applications. *Transactional applications* are used for tasks such as changing, creating, or approving information. You can run transactional applications using your existing database and landscape—no migration to SAP HANA is necessary. *Analytical apps* are dedicated to triggering insights and KPIs, or other related analysis. *Fact sheet apps* allow you to search and explore information. Finally, *SAP Smart Business apps* allow you to analyze and evaluate strategic or operation KPIs in real time.

Apps are now being delivered by SAP on a per shipment basis as an array of transactional, analytical, and fact sheet apps. The total number of applications exceeded 500 in 2015, and more are expected to be delivered in the coming years. Unlike the traditional SAP transactions, where several users can access the same transaction, these apps are role-based and personalized to each user. Table 2 represents a list of apps oriented to Sales and Distribution.

Throughout this book, we'll mention related SAP Fiori apps where applicable, but remember that this list is growing constantly. For a more complete list, consult the SAP Fiori apps library.

Transactional Apps	Fact Sheet Apps	Analytical Apps
▶ Create Sales Orders	▶ Customer	▶ Delayed Deliveries (in Transit)
▶ Customer Invoices	▶ Customer Billing Document	
▶ My Contacts		▶ Delayed Deliveries (POD)
▶ My Leave Requests	▶ Goods Issue	▶ Delayed Deliveries (Total)
▶ Track Sales Orders	▶ Material	▶ My Quotation Pipeline
▶ Track Shipments	▶ Sales Contract	▶ Sales Performance
	▶ Sales Group Contract	▶ SAP Smart Business for Sales Order Fulfillment
	▶ Sales Order	
	▶ Sales Quotation	▶ Transportation Cost
		▶ Uncovered Sales Orders

Table 2 Frequently Used Apps for Sales and Distribution

SAP Jam

SAP now integrates with social media for collaboration. In the last quarter of 2012, SAP launched a secured social collaboration solution called SAP Jam. It's set up as an intranet inside a company in order to provide the elements of a social collaboration platform.

Though SAP Jam is predominantly managed by the Human Resources department, this enterprise social network facilitates collaboration at all levels of the business, consequently expediting sales cycles and further engaging customers and employees. We'll look more closely at order management with SAP Jam in Chapter 3.

Implementation Methodology and Resources

Logistics consultants use a variety of methods to manage a new SAP ERP on-premise installation. Let's look at a few methodologies.

ASAP Methodology

As another project management and implementation tool, the objective of ASAP is timely project completion, within budget, at minimal risk (technical or commercial). It accomplishes this objective by providing templates, methods, tools, and accelerators for successful, quick SAP implementations with optimal use of resources.

ASAP consists of six phases:

1. **Project preparation**
   The project team is identified and mobilized, the project standards are defined, and the project work environment is set up.

2. **Blueprint**
   The business processes are defined and documented as the business blueprint.

3. **Realization**
   Configuration, unit testing, user acceptance, knowledge transfer, and data migration plans are key components of this phase.

4. **Final preparation**
   Integration testing, stress testing, and conversion testing are conducted. End users are trained.

5. **Go-live and support**
   Data migration from the legacy system is completed, the new system activates, and post-implementation support is provided.

6. **Operation**
   Operation maturity and daily life situations, maintenance, including helpdesk support, new requirements and upgrade management.

These phases often serve as project milestones, and might also be used for billing purposes. Tracking progress by using established deadlines helps project managers identify issues that threaten the project and resolve them in a timely manner. An ASAP checklist ensures that each phase is complete and documented before moving to the next phase.

Thanks to ASAP, small and mid-sized companies are now often able to implement an SAP system within a couple of months.

Global ASAP Methodology

Global ASAP methodology delivers projects using a process-oriented, clear, and concise methodology, providing step-by-step direction throughout your global or multi-site SAP implementation. An important characteristic of Global ASAP is the construction of a pilot site that is brought live; the pilot solution is then replicated to other sites, locations, business divisions, and even countries. This is archived by creating and maintaining a rollout plan, relating sites, resources, and an overall schedule.

1. **Global program preparation**
   Install and prepare the overall project template and program.

2. **Global business blueprint**
   Document the business requirements for the entire enterprise, sites, or business lines, frequently involving global or overall requirement gathering and solution.

3. **Global realization**
   Develop and implement the business requirements and develop a strong template to implement on rollouts.

4. **Pilot final preparation**
   Finalize cutover preparation and bring pilot site live.

5. **Global template ongoing rollout, support, and maintenance**
   Fine-tune the template, support, and maintenance of the live system, which often involves making adjustments for a strong template and subsequent rollouts.

SAP HANA ASAP Implementation

SAP has created the SAP HANA ASAP Methodology to facilitate the implementation of the new set of SAP HANA solutions and applications. Primarily, this methodology includes the main guidelines following the ASAP methodology, but it also includes the Advanced Delivery Management (ADM) model.

ADM's main objectives are to shorten implementation times and to implement a factory mode (FM). FMs are global in nature and help reduce implementation timelines. ADM introduces a large number of "how-to" guides and accelerators, along with a high level of documentation. It also introduces the advanced delivery models, including the following:

▶ **Expert based**
   This model is driven by experienced consultants to provide a "one-off" solution, such as the case of built-to order projects, services, or customer facing time, and limited remote work.

▸ **Design based**

This model is typically used in traditional projects where blueprinting and about 50% of the onsite customer support are required.

▸ **Assembled to order**

This model is used for projects implemented and assembled using predefined building blocks, or which are pre-constructed. These projects require about 30% of customer facing onsite; remote work is acceptable.

▸ **Industrialized**

This model introduced an all-package implementation, offering fixed price and fixed scope, and therefore requires about 90% of remote delivery.

Rapid-Deployment Solutions (RDS)

The industrialized model includes RDS, which use fixed-price, pre-determined project methodology, with ready-to use accelerators in three main project phases: start, deploy (realization), and run (go-live support).

Agile ASAP Implementation

Agile ASAP is one of the newest methodologies created by SAP with one main objective: archive speed and effectiveness for implementations and deployments. Agile ASAP allows your company to implement functionality in short iterative cycles. You can also establish the priority in which these cycles will be implemented, based on what's more valuable to your organization and priorities. Using this approach empowers you with a more flexible implementation, faster results generation, and therefore immediate insight into the value.

Agile ASAP methodology uses the same project phases as ASAP (project preparation, blueprinting, realization, final preparation, and operation), but it stresses the fact that blueprints should be oriented to determine any variations to the pre-determined solutions. That's why it was renamed as *lean blueprinting*.

Implementation with SAP Solution Manager

As an application management software, SAP Solution Manager aims to help SAP customers manage their solution portfolio. It has the following objectives:

▸ Optimize the SAP solution environment during deployment, operation, and continuous operation phases

▸ Improve return on investment (ROI) by lowering the cost of ownership

▶ Support SAP, non-SAP, and future SAP solutions

▶ Complement ASAP methodology

▶ Transfer knowledge

▶ Reduce risk

SAP Solution Manager provides the following advantages:

▶ **Implementation and upgrades**
ASAP methodology has become a complementary component integrated into SAP Solution Manager. SAP Solution Manager is seen as the successor of the ASAP methodology. It ensures timely implementation by providing useful content, centralized real-time monitoring, and documentation.

▶ **Change management**
SAP Solution Manager controls and tracks all software and configuration changes from the approval stage (for change requests) to the deployment stage. It also allows for post-deployment analysis of changes. Non-ABAP objects are also included in the change and transportation system (for more details on this, refer to SAP Note 1056166. The OSS Note system is explained later).

▶ **Service desk**
The service desk of SAP Solution Manager handles user help requests for forwarding to SAP. The organization of the IT service provider can manage the service desk. This system of issue resolution works efficiently and economically.

▶ **Root cause analysis**
Performance issues may be due to problems in the system, the server, a database, ABAP code, or SAP NetWeaver. Root cause analysis allows you to identify the source of the problem, enabling you to fix it and avoid similar problems in the future.

▶ **Monitoring and notification**
SAP Solution Manager makes possible the centralized, real-time monitoring of the complete SAP landscape (different servers), business processes, intersystem dependencies, and interfaces, which reduces cost and risk. Automatic notification through email, SMS, and other communication methods ensures fast response and lower risk.

▶ **Service-level reporting**
SAP Solution Manager defines and reports service levels, which allows you to have service-level agreements (SLAs) with IT service providers that are based on measurable parameters.

▶ **Background job management**
SAP Solution Manager allows you to schedule background jobs for different components and monitor them for optimal utilization of resources. There is also an enhancement available for this.

▶ **Services and support**
SAP Solution Manager suggests and provides SAP support services. These include SAP Safeguarding (a remote service), which itself includes the SAP GoLive Check service; SAP Solution Management Optimization (an on-site service), which helps you optimize SAP solutions with the help of SAP staff; and SAP Empowering (self service), which helps you manage your solutions.

▶ **System administration**
SAP Solution Manager makes it possible to centrally execute day-to-day administrative tasks.

Two services that you have to pay for—SAP Central Process Scheduling by Redwood and SAP Quality Center by HP—are enhancements in SAP Solution Manager to optimize background job scheduling and testing, respectively.

Customizing Implementation Guide and Resources

The SAP Implementation Guide (IMG) aims to simplify SAP customization by documenting actions that are required with helpful tips and notes. Both online and paper versions of the IMG are available to SAP customers and partners. It's accessed through Transaction SPRO and is present at every node. Both the SAP Standard IMG and Project IMGs are available. A Project IMG may be developed that contains a subset of the Standard IMG.

SAP has grown beyond being a just a company, or just a piece of software. It is now more accurately described as an ecosystem that consists of various entities. These entities include SAP PRESS (*www.sap-press.com*), SAP Education (*http://training.sap.com*), SAP Service Marketplace (*http://service.sap.com*), SAP Community Network (*http://scn.sap.com*) and other community forums such as Americas' SAP Users' Group (*www.asug.com*), SAP HANA (*http://hana.sap.com*), SAP PartnerEdge (*http://partneredge.sap.com*) SAP Store (*www.sapstore.com*) and the SAP Support Portal (*http://support.sap.com*). These sites, together with the SAP Library and the Implementation Guide, are great resources for learning SAP. SAP also issues Online Support System (OSS) Notes, which are also referred to as *SAP Notes* or *S-Notes*.

Summary

In this introduction, we aimed to ground your Sales and Distribution implementation in at least a cursory understanding of the general SAP ERP picture including the latest implementation methodologies.

In the next chapter, we'll discuss what organization structures are needed for Sales and Distribution in SAP ERP, and the tools available for maintaining its organizational components.

This chapter is dedicated to providing perspective on a basic and critical Sales and Distribution functionality: the SD organizational structures. You will learn how to configure them and how to define and assign the units of an enterprise structure that are relevant for Sales and Distribution.

1 Organizational Structure

In any implementation project, the first thing you must finalize is the organizational structure (also called the enterprise structure). In this chapter, we explain the elements in the enterprise structure that are relevant for Sales and Distribution, and outline the four steps involved in customizing an enterprise structure:

1. Defining required organizational units

2. Importing localized sample units

3. Assigning organizational units

4. Checking for consistency

We'll briefly interrupt this workflow to focus on the Sales and Distribution organizational chart.

1.1 Defining Organizational Units

In this phase, the enterprise structure of one organization is mapped in the SAP system. The menu path for this is SAP IMG • ENTERPRISE STRUCTURE • DEFINITION. At the DEFINITION node are options such as FINANCIAL ACCOUNTING, LOGISTICS – GENERAL, SALES AND DISTRIBUTION, MATERIALS MANAGEMENT, and LOGISTICS EXECUTION, where you can define different organizational units. Use the FINANCIAL ACCOUNTING component to define the company code and credit control area; LOGISTICS – GENERAL to define the plant, valuation level, and division; SALES AND DISTRIBUTION to define the sales organization, distribution channel, sales office, and sales group; MATERIALS MANAGEMENT to define the storage location; and

LOGISTICS EXECUTION to define the warehouse number, shipping point, loading point, and transport planning points.

Let's zoom in on each of these organizational units.

Company Code and Company

The *company code* is the level at which balance sheets and profit and loss statements are prepared. The company code is different from the *company*, which itself refers to a group of companies (or a *holding company*) that is composed of all subsidiary companies represented by the company codes. The company is the highest organizational unit from a Financial Accounting point of view, and all company codes are assigned to one or more companies. Financial Accounting integrates Logistics components at the company code level.

In this book, we refer to the company code as a company, and the company organizational unit as a holding company. The organizational unit company is used primarily to consolidate the financial statements of different company codes and is of little importance in Logistics or for Sales and Distribution.

Credit Control Area

Customers or groups of customers are provided with a *credit limit,* which is a set amount in a specific currency. This credit limit is then used for business with the companies (known as company codes) assigned to the credit control area. The update group for the credit control area defines the total credit exposure of a customer or group of customers. Credit control area is the most important organizational unit from a credit management point of view. We discuss credit control areas in more detail in Chapter 5.

Valuation Level

A *valuation level* is the level at which stocks are valuated and is important for inventory management and to determine the cost of a sale. For any specific material, the value is maintained in the material master record (Accounting 1 view). The valuation level is selected only once during customization; once selected, it is available in display mode only. Generally, the recommended valuation area is the plant, as opposed to the company code (a company code valuation level is not even possible in the Production Planning and Controlling components of SAP ERP).

Plant

The *plant* usually represents where goods are manufactured and/or stored, or where services are rendered. In SAP systems, the plant can be defined by copying plant 0001 (which is system delivered).

Division

Companies with several products or services group those products and services into different *divisions*. A material or service in an SAP system can only belong to one division; in other words, divisions are mutually exclusive. Thus, if a product is currently sold in two divisions—for example, a vacuum cleaner in both the home care and automobile divisions of a company—then that product must have a separate material code for each division.

To define a new division, select and copy an existing division and make the appropriate changes.

Sales Organization

Within a company, the organization that is responsible for sales is called the *sales organization*. There can be more than one sales organization in a company (remember, in SAP systems this refers to a company code), but one sales organization cannot be responsible for selling materials or services for two companies. In other words, one sales organization cannot be assigned to multiple company codes.

New sales organizations are defined by copying sales organization 0001 (predelivered) and making the necessary changes.

Distribution Channel

The *distribution channel* is the means through which a company makes its products and services available to its customers; these might include the wholesale distribution channel, the Internet distribution channel, and the direct sales distribution channel.

You create new distribution channels by copying existing ones and making the necessary changes. Only a new key/code and a description of the new distribution channel are required. There is no address or any other field to be maintained for distribution channels.

Sales Office

The *sales office* is the unit responsible for sales to a particular geographical area with one or more customers, and is represented by a four-digit alphanumeric key. The geographical areas for different sales offices can overlap. In a standard SAP system, no restriction is imposed on the plant that can serve a sales office and vice versa, except that both should be in the same company code. Any sales document is usually created for a particular sales area, a sales office, and a sales group; the latter two, though optional, are normally present. One customer can be served by different sales offices, even when a default sales office is maintained in the customer master record.

Sales Group

A *sales group* is a group of employees, attached to one or more sales offices, who are responsible for sales pertaining to orders generated by them. You may attach more than one sales group to a single sales office. The sales group responsible for a sales order appears at the header level.

Storage Location

The *storage location* in a plant refers to either a physical storage location or a logical location. If a New York distribution plant has several warehouses in the city, you might designate them as storage locations (and further assign warehouse numbers in the Warehouse Management functionality in SAP ERP). You can have storage locations such as Sales and Returns to help differentiate goods that can be sold to customers from those that have been returned and thus should not be sold (physically, the different types of stock may be present in the same warehouse). Storage locations are important in delivery and post–goods movement (issue/receipt), because when there is a movement of goods in Sales and Distribution, it's from a storage location. These goods movements have an impact (debit or credit) in Financial Accounting if the material is valuated. You can configure the system to automatically determine the storage location during the sale, return, or stock transfer processes.

Warehouse Number

A *warehouse number* is created when the Warehouse Management functionality of SAP ERP is in place. From an integration point of view, you should know that each warehouse is assigned to a plant–storage location combination. Although storage locations may not necessarily refer to a physical location, warehouse numbers do refer to a specific warehouse that is physically present. It's important to note from a stock valuation standpoint that material valuation occurs at the Inventory Management level (plant-storage location) and not at the Warehouse Management or bin level.

Shipping Point

A plant can have several shipping points, and one shipping point can serve several plants. A *shipping point* refers to the various exit points of the plant where goods are dispatched to customers or other plants. You can configure your system to automatically propose shipping points during different Sales and Distribution processes that include delivery or shipment processing.

Loading Point

Loading points are where goods are loaded and can be automatically proposed in Sales and Distribution. Both loading points and shipping points become very important for the integration of Sales and Distribution with the Transportation Management component in Logistics Execution.

Transport Planning Point

A *transport planning point* is the organizational unit responsible for shipping products. Units responsible for shipments of different types may call for multiple transport planning points; for example, units responsible for rail shipments and air cargo can have two transport planning points.

Let's map the organizational units we've discussed in a Sales and Distribution context. Figure 1.1 shows how each of the components relate to each other throughout a company's organizational model and structure.

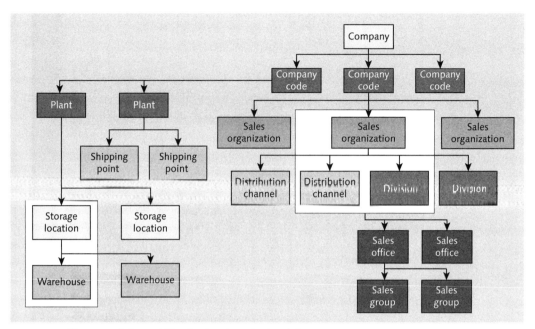

Figure 1.1 Sales and Distribution Organizational Components

We recommend creating an implementation-specific organizational chart to guide every new system configuration. Keep the following three tips in mind:

▸ Always keep the organizational structures as simple as your company requires.

▸ Plan for growth, including projected short-term company growth.

▸ Measure the impact on daily maintenance, especially in master data maintenance. It's best to minimize the complexity of the organizational structure so that the master data and product master will be less impacted by the defined structures.

1.2 Importing Organizational Units

In addition to the organization structure definition we've just described, SAP provides sample organizational units customized according to each country, as shown in Figure 1.2. You can access this screen by following the menu path SAP IMG • ENTERPRISE STRUCTURE • LOCALIZE SAMPLE ORGANIZATIONAL UNITS and then clicking on COUNTRY VERSION.

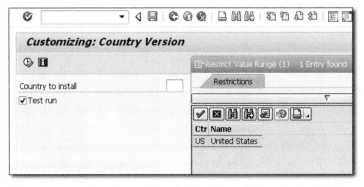

Figure 1.2 Importing Country-Specific Templates of Organizational Units

We recommend the following best practices for importing organizational units:

▸ Run this transaction to install these sample units.

▸ Define the units without preceding zeros. For example, use 100 instead of 001; this is because 001 becomes 1 in Excel, which may cause problems when you transfer data.

▸ Do not delete the sample organizational units in the development clients.

▸ Copy the required customized units from these sample units, not from other customized units. Copying sample units (as opposed to creating them from scratch) not only reduces the time required for customization, but also reduces the chance of errors.

Defining vs. Importing

We recommend defining organizational structures rather than defining country versions because the latest SAP versions come pre-installed with a range of countries that you can refer to.

1.3 Assigning Organizational Units

After you define your organizational units, you need to assign them. SAP offers a few important guidelines for organizational unit assignments; these are listed in Table 1.1.

Step	Assignment	Guidelines
1	Company code to credit control area	You can assign each company code to more than one credit control area.
2	Plant to company code	You can only assign a plant to one company code.
3	Sales organization to company code	You can only assign a sales organization to one company code.
4	Distribution channel to sales organization	You can assign each distribution channel to more than one sales organization.
5	Division to sales organization	You can assign each division to more than one sales organization.
6	Sales area (sales organization, distribution channel, division)	All combinations are possible (maximum possible number of sales areas = number of sales organizations × number of distribution channels × number of divisions), provided all distribution channels and divisions are already assigned to all sales organizations.
7	Sales office to sales area	You can assign each sales office to all sales areas.
8	Sales group to sales office	You can assign each sales group to more than one sales office.
9	Sales organizations, distribution channel, plant	You can assign each plant to all combinations of sales organizations and distribution channels.
10	Sales area to credit control area	You can only assign a sales area to one credit control area.
11	Warehouse number to plant and storage location	You can assign one warehouse number to several combinations of plants and storage locations, but the plant in all of those combinations must be the same.
12	Shipping point to plant	You can assign each shipping point to several plants.

Table 1.1 Guidelines for Organizational Unit Assignments

These assignments of different organizational units are done via SAP IMG • ENTERPRISE STRUCTURE • ASSIGNMENTS. Further down this path, you will find the names of specific functionalities such as FINANCIAL ACCOUNTING and SALES AND

DISTRIBUTION. If you want to know where to assign a particular organizational unit (X) to another organizational unit (Y), you must know the component in which X was defined. That component is where you'll give the assignment. For example, assigning sales organization X to company code Y is done via the menu path SAP IMG • ENTERPRISE STRUCTURE • ASSIGNMENTS • SALES AND DISTRIBUTION, not via SAP IMG • ENTERPRISE STRUCTURE • ASSIGNMENTS • FINANCIAL ACCOUNTING.

1.4 Checking for Consistency

SAP offers a consistency check optimizing tool that allows you to check your customization of the enterprise structure in seconds. You can execute this tool by selecting all of the options shown in Figure 1.3. The menu path is SAP IMG • ENTERPRISE STRUCTURE • CONSISTENCY CHECK • CHECK ENTERPRISE STRUCTURE FOR SALES AND DISTRIBUTION.

This tool checks the following:

- Sales organizations
    - Checks whether addresses exist.
    - Checks whether company codes are assigned.
    - Checks whether master record conversions are maintained.
    - Checks whether sales areas are created.
    - Checks whether plants are assigned.
    - Checks whether texts exist in the logon language.
- Distribution channels
    - Checks whether master record conversions exist.
    - Checks whether sales areas are created.
    - Checks whether texts exist in the logon language.
- Divisions
    - Checks whether master record conversions exist.
    - Checks whether sales areas are created.
    - Checks whether texts exist in the logon language.

- Sales offices
    - Checks whether sales organizations are assigned.
    - Checks whether addresses exist.
    - Checks whether texts exist in the logon language.
- Sales groups
    - Checks whether sales offices are assigned.
    - Checks whether texts exist in the logon language.
- Shipping points
    - Checks whether all plants are assigned.
    - Checks whether shipping points are assigned.
    - Checks whether addresses exist.
    - Checks whether texts exist in the logon language.
- Plants
    - Checks whether the addresses exist and are complete.
    - Checks whether storage locations are available.

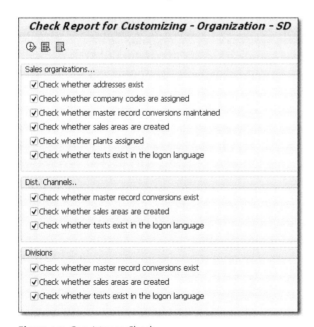

Figure 1.3 Consistency Check

1.5 Summary

Now you know how to configure the structure of a company while leveraging the various elements of the sales and distribution organizational structures; you should be able to define your own organizational units in SAP systems, making use of the provided definitions and the related configuration steps.

In the next chapter, we'll discuss the prerequisites for creating important master records in SAP ERP, and the tools available for maintaining master records.

*After reading this chapter, you should understand how to reduce mainte-
nance efforts by creating common distribution channels and divisions,
how to customize master data fields, how to modify your screen layout,
and how to carry out specific changes to different master records on a
large scale.*

2   Master Data

Master data consists of information that does not change frequently (e.g.,
addresses) and pertains to customers, employees, SAP system users, materials,
batches, condition records, vendors, and more. Master data is composed of individual master records; for example, a single customer will have a customer master
record, and all of the customer master records together make up the customer
master data. Because SAP software aims to meet the needs of almost any company, regardless of size, industry, or country, predefined master data requires
very little customization.

In this chapter, we briefly list the suggested steps for customizing master data
fields, focusing specifically on master data relevant for Sales and Distribution, and
we explain how to manage master data post-implementation. Specifically, we go
into detail about three types of master data:

▶ Customer master data

▶ Material master data

▶ Batch management master data

We then conclude with a brief overview of some of the other types of master
data. Because many of these master data types are created and maintained in
other components, some overarching knowledge is helpful for those interested in
Sales and Distribution.

2.1   Customer Master Data

In SAP systems, we broadly divide customer master records into three parts: general data, company code data, and sales area data. This data is stored in tables, which consist of fields that are important from financial accounting and sales and distribution perspectives.

▶ General data contains the customer's address, communication, control, marketing, payment transaction, unloading point, contact person, and foreign trade-related information. General data is stored in tables KNA1, ADRC, ADR2/3/4/5, and a few other tables.

▶ Company code data is stored in table KNB1, and primarily contains important fields for Financial Accounting.

▶ Table KNVV holds most sales area data, and largely contains fields that are important from a Sales and Distribution perspective. The information about partners defined in the customer master record is stored in table KNVP. Different transactions allow you to create, change, and display customer master data based on the combination of areas to be maintained.

SAP Tables

There are close to a hundred thousand standard tables in SAP ERP. These tables house information (usually in the form of data). Some of these tables do not *store* data, but rather pool information from other tables for use or display.

All tables have columns and rows, and each row is a record. The tables that store data are available in the Oracle® database that SAP uses. These tables can be used by non-SAP components, as well, but the other types of tables (which are not available on the Oracle database) are for exclusive use in SAP systems.

In the upcoming subsections, we will discuss how to optimize customer master record maintenance using common distribution channels and divisions, how to create customer account groups, how to customize customer master record fields, and how to utilize the available tools for mass maintenance.

2.1.1   Reducing Sales Areas

A *sales area* is a combination of sales organizations, distribution channels, and divisions. We represent a sales area with a key that combines all three of these organizational units; for example, a sales area composed of sales organization

1000, distribution channel 10, and division 30 would be referred to as sales area 1000-10-30. The customer master records of one sales area are not available for use by another; thus, if the customer is valid for several sales areas, you must create separate customer records for each individual sales area. Although this task may make the maintenance of customer master records sound difficult, the process is facilitated by the use of a *common distribution channel and division*, which allows you to effectively reduce the number of sales areas for which the customer master record is to be created.

Let's take a look at the process of defining common distribution channels and divisions. At the end of the section, we explain how these configurations result in a reduced number of sales areas, and therefore a reduction in maintenance effort.

Defining Common Distribution Channels

Define common distribution channels using the menu path SAP IMG • SALES AND DISTRIBUTION • MASTER DATA • DEFINE COMMON DISTRIBUTION CHANNEL or via Transaction VOR1, as shown in Figure 2.1. In addition to customer master records, you may also define common distribution channels for material master records. For any distribution channel, you may define a different distribution channel as the common distribution channel. The master data record, or the condition record maintained for a distribution channel, is applicable for all distribution channels for which the record is maintained as the common distribution channel.

To make one distribution channel a common distribution channel for another distribution channel's condition records (what a mouthful), enter the common distribution channel in the DCH-CONDS column. As shown in Figure 2.1, distribution channel 10 is a common distribution channel for distribution channels 10, 12, and 14.

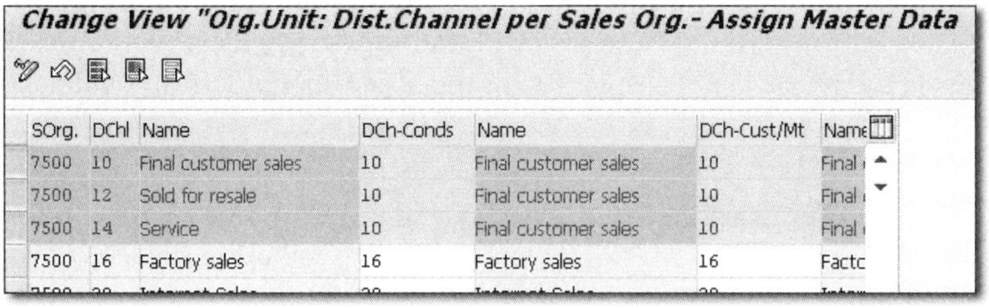

SOrg.	DChl	Name	DCh-Conds	Name	DCh-Cust/Mt	Name
7500	10	Final customer sales	10	Final customer sales	10	Final
7500	12	Sold for resale	10	Final customer sales	10	Final
7500	14	Service	10	Final customer sales	10	Final
7500	16	Factory sales	16	Factory sales	16	Factc

Figure 2.1 Defining a Common Distribution Channel

49

Similarly, you may also make a distribution channel common for other distribution channels, which will allow them to share customer and material master records. Do so by entering it in the DCh-Cust/Mt column. (Keep an eye on the terminology here, since some of these sound very similar!) As a result, the customer master record created for sales area 7500-10-10 (where the sales organization is 7500, the distribution channel is 10, and the division is 10) automatically becomes valid for sales areas 7500-10-10, 7500-12-10, and 7500-14-10.

Common Distribution Channels

In addition to customer master records, you may define common distribution channels for condition records. The common distribution channel for a specific distribution channel defined for reducing the number of required customer master records automatically becomes relevant for material master record creation.

Defining Common Divisions

Define common divisions via the menu path SAP IMG • Sales and Distribution • Master Data • Define Common Division or via Transaction VOR2, as shown in Figure 2.2.

Change View "Org.Unit: Divisions per Sales Org.- Assign Master Data":

SOrg.	Dv	Name	DivCon	Name	DivCus	Name
7500	00	Cross-division	00	Cross-division	00	Cross-division
7500	01	Pumps	00	Cross-division	00	Cross-division
7500	02	Motorcycles	00	Cross-division	00	Cross-division
7500	04	Lighting	04	Lighting	04	Lighting

Figure 2.2 Defining Common Divisions

Common Divisions

In addition to customer master records, you may define common divisions for condition records.

The division in the DivCus column is the common division for the division listed in the Dv column, and is used for creating and sharing customer master records. As shown in Figure 2.2, division 00 is common for divisions 00, 01, and 02, and division 04 is only assigned to division 04. As a result, customer master records created for sales area 7500-00-00 (where the sales organization is 7500, the distribution channel is 00, and the division is 00) becomes automatically valid for sales areas 7500-00-00, 7500-00-01, and 7500-00-02.

If you combine the examples shown in Figure 2.1 and Figure 2.2 without a common distribution channel and division, the total number of possible sales areas is 21. If all sales areas are valid for you, and if a customer is valid for all sales areas, you would have to create that customer 21 separate times. However, with the customization of common distribution channels and divisions, even when all sales area are defined and when a customer is valid for all areas, you can drastically reduce the number of times you must create the customer. In this example, you need only create the customer in two sales areas (7500-00-00 and 7500-00-04).

2.1.2 Defining Customer Account Groups

Customer account groups are created primarily to route financial postings to specific SAP General Ledger (GL) accounts; for example, the sales figures for all domestic retail customers may go to the same reconciliation account. You may create all foreign customers in a different customer account group, and there is a different reconciliation account (GL) for each of them. The menu path for creating a customer account group is SAP IMG • FINANCIAL ACCOUNTING (NEW) • ACCOUNTS RECEIVABLE AND ACCOUNTS PAYABLE • CUSTOMER ACCOUNTS • MASTER DATA • PREPARATIONS FOR CREATING CUSTOMER MASTER DATA • DEFINE ACCOUNT GROUPS WITH SCREEN LAYOUTS (CUSTOMERS). The transaction code is OBD2.

Let's walk through the steps for creating a customer account group:

1. Find the standard SAP template that is closest to what you want to create. Copy the selected template using the COPY AS ([F6]) icon, as shown in Figure 2.3. The screen shown in appears with the message "Specify target entries."

2. Enter basic information. Provide the account group name (which does not have to start with Y or Z) and a description for the account group code in the NAME field. If the account group is for one-time customers, select the ONE-TIME ACCOUNT checkbox. If the output determination procedure is the same for all customers in a group, enter it in the OUTPUT DETERM.PROC. field.

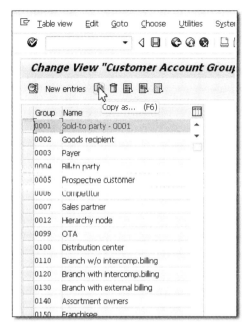

Figure 2.3 Creating a Customer Account Group

3. Maintain field statuses. Customizing account groups also involves maintaining the field status of all customer master fields, also referred to as the maintenance of screen layout.

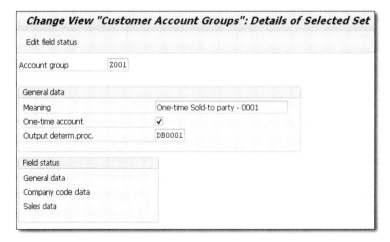

Figure 2.4 Customizing a Customer Account Group

This activity determines how the customer master screens look. Any field can have one of four statuses: *suppressed*, *required entry*, *optional entry*, or *display*. To assign a field status, double-click on GENERAL DATA, COMPANY CODE DATA, or SALES DATA in the screen shown in Figure 2.4. (We have double-clicked on GENERAL DATA in our example.)

4. Double-click on a particular group of fields. In our example, we have double-clicked on ADDRESS (that screen is not shown), which takes you to the screen shown in Figure 2.5.

5. Modify the field status of individual master data fields (again, see Figure 2.5).

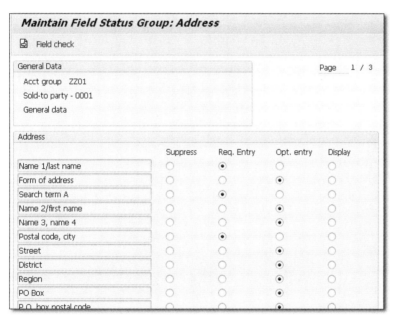

Figure 2.5 Maintain Field Status Group

2.1.3   Customer Mass Maintenance

Maintaining master records after implementation is a big task, and manual updating sometimes becomes impossible. When one field in several thousand master records must be changed without error within a few minutes, mass maintenance tools are the best option. This section discusses several ways to take care of mass maintenance. In the first two subsections, we focus on using Transactions MASS and SE16N (with the SAP edit function). The last section briefly describes a few alternative options.

Transaction MASS

One way to accomplish mass maintenance of customer master data is by using object type KNA1 in Transaction MASS, also accessible via the menu path SAP MENU • LOGISTICS • CENTRAL FUNCTIONS • MASS MAINTENANCE • MASS MAINTE-NANCE • DIALOG PROCESSING, as shown in Figure 2.6.

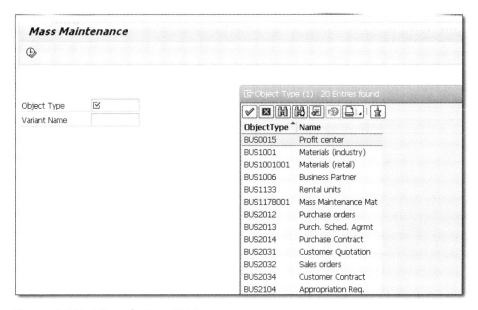

Figure 2.6 Object Types for Mass Maintenance

With Transaction MASS, you can make changes to several fields in several tables simultaneously. By selecting object type KNA1 and executing the transaction, you reach the screen shown in Figure 2.7 (which is the same screen that appears when you execute Transaction XD99, or access the menu path SAP MENU • LOGISTICS • SALES AND DISTRIBUTION • MASTER DATA • BUSINESS PARTNERS • CUSTOMER MASTER MASS MAINTENANCE). The TABLES tab shows a list of tables that can be modified. The FIELDS tab lists both the name of the table and the fields.

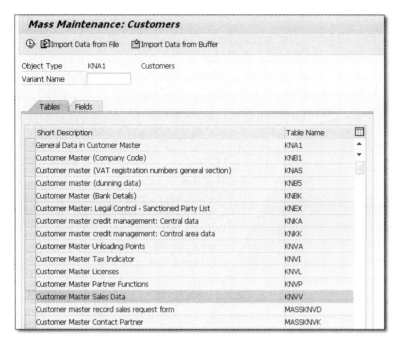

Figure 2.7 Mass Maintenance—Customers

Follow these steps to use Transaction MASS:

1. Select the specific table and field you wish to modify. For example, if the customers belonging to a particular region (KNA1-REGIO) have a new customer pricing procedure (KNVV-KALKS), you would select table KNVV in the TABLES tab, or KNVV-KALKS in the FIELDS tab.

2. Click EXECUTE. This action will take you to the screen shown in Figure 2.8. For our example, because you know that all of the customers of a particular region are to be changed, you can pull up a list of the customers using Transaction SE16 or SE16N, as well as table KNA1. Paste the list, press F8, and select DISPLAY ALL RECORDS. Doing so will produce a list of customers with the existing value in the CUST.PRIC.PROCEDURE field.

You will press the EXECUTION icon (or $\boxed{\text{F8}}$ key) three times while executing Transaction MASS: first, in the first screen after you select the object (KNA1 for customer master); second, after you specify the table and the field (KNVV-KALKS); third, after you enter the list or range of customers (or vendor, GLs, or others as per the object selected) for which you want the mass change.

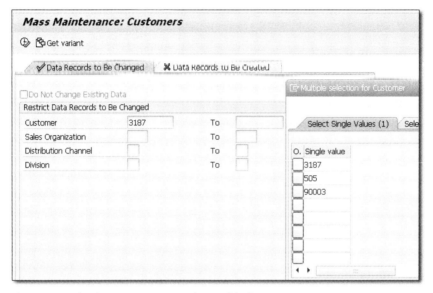

Figure 2.8 Uploading Customer List to be Modified

3. If you used the TABLES tab and not the FIELDS tab in Step 1, click on the SELECT FIELDS icon 📱.

4. A new dialog box opens, shown in Figure 2.9. Select CUST.PRIC.PROCEDURE (KALKS) and bring it to the SELECTION CRITERIA table by clicking on the CHOOSE icon (the black triangle pointing left).

5. Enter the new value ("9", in our example) in the CUST.PRIC.PROCEDURE field.

6. Select the column (CUST.PRIC.PROCEDURE in our example) to which the new value will be applied and click on the CARRY OUT MASS CHANGE icon (⌨ in Figure 2.10).

7. Save.

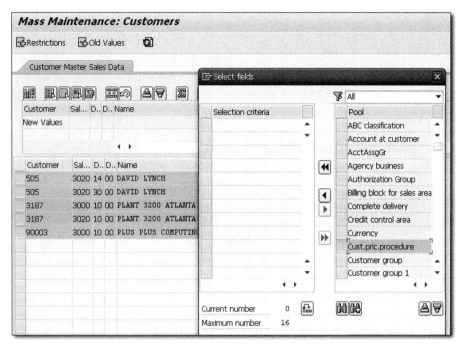

Figure 2.9 Inserting the KNVV-KALKS Field for Mass Maintenance

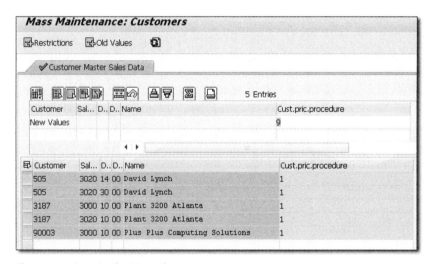

Figure 2.10 Execute the Mass Change

It's possible for a few records to fail mass change if, for example, they are locked by a user. Failed cases appear marked red in the results screen. Because there can be many pages of results, and very few failed cases, you must carefully check the pages of the result screen.

Transaction SE16N with the SAP Edit Function

From SAP ERP 5.0 onward, SAP allows you to directly modify, update, or insert records in any table using Transaction SE16N with the SAP edit function.

Before using Transaction SE16N with the SAP edit function for several records, you should test it with a single record. Also note that if any info structure table is updated when you update the value of a particular field in a table, this will not happen when the field is updated via Transaction SE16N. In order to update the value, you must run an updating program (if such a program is available). We have provided one such example in Chapter 7, Section 7.7, where we discuss how to delete a credit memo request of a cancelled credit memo.

Let's use an example to explain the steps to change (add, delete, or update) table entries using Transaction SE16N with the SAP edit function. In our example, we change the CUST.PRIC.PROC field for all customers in a particular region.

1. Obtain a list of all customers located in the region for which you are implementing a mass change (Transaction SE16N or SE16). For mass changes, you must know the records that need to be modified. You may obtain this list either manually, or by using a report or table. For our example, we pull the list from table KNA1. As shown in Figure 2.11, using Transaction SE16N or SE16, create a list of all customers located in the region for which you are implementing a mass change. Because different countries can have identical region codes, you must specify the country code prior to selecting the region code.

2. Restrict Transaction SE16N. Instead of executing Transaction SE16N for all the records in the table, restrict it to the cases where changes are required. In our example, we have supplied the list of customers obtained in the first step in the CUSTOMER field (KUNNR).

3. Activate the SAP edit function. This is done by typing "&SAP_EDIT" in the transaction window and pressing [Enter] while you are still inside Transaction SE16N.

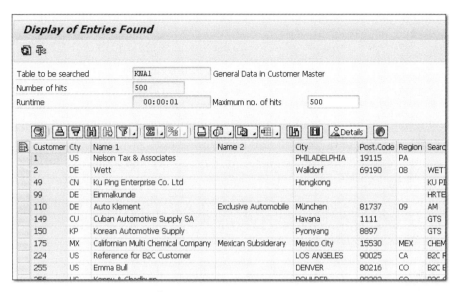

Figure 2.11 Transaction SE16N for KNA1

4. Execute Transaction SE16N with the SAP edit function active. All records appear. Hide all columns except those for which change is required.

5. Using Excel or other suitable software, provide the new values for the list of records. For our example, we have decided to make a new value of 9 for all of the customer pricing procedures (CuPP); currently, the value is B. To do this, we enter the new value "9" in 450 Excel rows (450 is the number of customers to be modified) and then copy it.

6. Open the context menu for the first row of the Customer Pricing Procedure (CuPP) field and select Insert with Overwrite. The new value should appear in all records.

7. Click on the Save icon. Clearly, this process takes less time than using Transaction XD02 or VD02 to change the 450 records one after another.

Other Methods Used in Mass Maintenance

The Legacy System Migration Workbench (LSMW) and Batch Data Communication (BDC) are also used for the mass maintenance of customer master records (and other master records), as well as a variety of other activities (such as creating sales orders and deliveries). In LSMW, you record the steps you follow to modify one record, and then, using the program generated by the LSMW recording, you can make the same modifications for any number of customer master records. We will discuss this as an ABAP tool in Chapter 8. A technical developer writes the BDC, and it takes values from a local file, which it then uses to make changes in different table fields.

> **Transactions SM30 and SM31**
>
> Transactions SM30 and SM31 are also used to modify certain standard tables, especially table views used for customization. These transactions cannot be used to maintain tables that store master data.

2.2 Material Master – Sales Views

The material master data is considered to be the most important master data in SAP systems and features many screens for storing Materials Management, Financial Accounting, Sales and Distribution, Production Planning, Quality Management, and Controlling information. The Sales and Distribution data is stored in three screens: SALES: SALES ORG. DATA 1, SALES: SALES ORG. DATA 2, and SALES: GENERAL/PLANT DATA.

In the next two sections, we will discuss important sales-relevant fields in material master records and provide a few examples of customizing material master fields.

2.2.1 Sales-Relevant Material Master Fields

In the following three subsections, we will examine some of the important fields in the three sales views in the material master records.

Sales: Sales Org. Data 1

The fields that make up this screen are relevant for the combination of plant, sales organization, and distribution channel for which they are created. The following fields are part of this screen:

▸ BASE UNIT OF MEASURE (e.g., KG, liter) is the unit of measurement (UoM) required for maintaining stock.

▸ SALES UNIT is the unit of measurement in which material is sold. It can differ from the base unit of measure.

▸ The SALES UNIT NOT VARIABLE checkbox, when selected, does not allow the user to change the sales unit during document processing.

▸ The UNIT OF MEASURE GROUP field groups different UoMs.

▸ The CROSS-DISTRIBUTION CHAIN STATUS field specifies the status of the material (e.g., under development, discontinued) for all of the distribution chains (combination for sales organization and distribution channel).

▸ The DISTRIBUTION CHAIN-SPECIFIC STATUS field specifies the status of the material for a distribution chain (as per the organizational data of the material master record, or MMR).

▸ The DELIVERING PLANT field stores the information for the plant that will become the default delivery plant when creating a sales document for the material.

▸ The MATERIAL GROUP field is customizable and used to group materials by company- or project-specific criteria.

▸ The CASH DISCOUNT checkbox is selected when a cash discount is allowed for the material.

▸ DIVISION is used to specify the division to which the material belongs.

▸ The TAX CLASSIFICATIONS field stores the material tax classification indicator for different countries. It is one of the criteria that determines the tax charged for a material.

▸ The MINIMUM ORDER QUANTITY field stores the minimum quantity of material a customer must order.

▸ The MINIMUM DELIVERY QUANTITY field stores the minimum quantity of material that can be delivered to a customer.

▸ DELIVERY UNIT specifies a quantity (e.g., 12) within the UoM. Only multiples of the delivery unit (e.g., 12, 24, and 36) are allowed for delivery.

▸ ROUNDING PROFILE is used to derive the delivery quantity for a particular order quantity. For example, when the order quantity is 10 units, the derived delivery quantity can be 12 units based on the rounding profile, especially when the delivery unit is 12.

Sales: Sales Org. Data 2

This screen contains the fields that group material based on various criteria and attributes. Table 2.1 lists the fields and how they group materials.

Field Name	Group Materials Based On
MATERIAL STATISTICS GROUP	How they update the Sales Information System (SIS) or Logistics Information System (LIS)
VOLUME REBATE GROUP	Rebate agreement processing
GEN. ITEM CAT. GROUP	Item category determination
PRICING REFERENCE MATERIAL	Pricing (refer to the following note)
PRODUCT HIERARCHY	Company- and project-specific criteria
COMMISSION GROUP	Commission paid
MATERIAL PRICING GROUP	Pricing
ACCOUNT ASSIGNMENT GROUP	Posting to accounting (GL)
ITEM CATEGORY GROUP	Item category determination
MATERIAL GROUP 1/2/3/4/5	Company- and project-specific criteria
PRODUCT ATTRIBUTES 1 TO 10	Company- and project-specific criteria

Table 2.1 Fields and Group Materials

Pricing
Pricing reference material can be used optimally to reduce the effort required for condition record maintenance. The conditions created for a pricing reference material also become valid for all of the materials that have that pricing reference material.

Sales: General/Plant Data

The values of the fields in this screen are only applicable to the plant for which the material master record is created (base unit of measure and serialization level are two exceptions). For different plants you can assign different values (e.g., availability check or transportation group).

▶ BASE UNIT OF MEASURE (e.g., KG, liter) is the unit of measurement required for maintaining stock.

▶ The GROSS WEIGHT field is used to note the weight of the material including packaging and other weights.

- The NET WEIGHT field notes the net weight (excluding packaging).

- The AVAILABILITY CHECK field is used to group materials for availability checks and transfer to material requirements planning (MRP).

- The BATCH MANAGEMENT checkbox is selected for all materials for which creating batches is mandatory.

- The REPLACEMENT PART indicator specifies whether the material is a replacement part. If it is, then it is specified whether the replacement is mandatory or optional.

- The QUALIFY FOR FREE GOODS DISCOUNT indicator is only used for trading goods. While processing the sales order, this indicator will trigger the functionality to receive the free goods.

- The MATERIAL FREIGHT GROUP field groups materials based on the freight and/ or carrier determination.

- The TRANSPORTATION GROUP field groups materials based on transportation and route determination.

- The LOADING GROUP field groups materials with similar loading requirements and is used in combination with the shipping conditions and delivery plant fields of a sales document to automatically determine the shipping point.

- SETUP TIME is the time required, if any, to prepare for shipping the material. However, it does not include the actual time for processing the shipment.

- PROCESSING TIME is the time required to process a specified base quantity.

- BASE QUANTITY is required to specify the processing time.

- The MATERIAL GROUP PACKAGING MATERIALS field groups materials in order to determine the packaging material.

- The NEGATIVE STOCK checkbox, when selected, allows a temporary negative stock level in the plant.

- The PROFIT CENTER field specifies the profit center to which the accounting posting should go for the material (in the plant for which the MMR is applicable).

- The SERIAL NO. PROFILE field is filled for serialized material.

- SERIALIZATION LEVEL is left blank if the requirement is to make all of the combinations of materials and serial numbers unique. To make serial numbers unique at the client level, set the indicator to 1 for all material master records.

- DISTRIBUTION PROFILE is relevant for IS-Retail.

2.2.2 Customizing Material Master Fields

In this section, we discuss the customization of the product hierarchy; material status; material groups 1, 2, 3, 4, and 5; and material commission groups. However, these are not the only fields that allow for customization, nor are they the most important; we have chosen these fields because they have *a different customization process than normal.*

Product Hierarchy

Product hierarchies come into play when you group materials in a hierarchical manner, such as for pricing and reporting. In the standard system, the product hierarchy consists of up to three levels; the first and second levels have 5 digits, and the third level has 8. The maximum number of digits is 18, and the maximum number of levels is 9. You can define hierarchy nodes at individual levels of the product hierarchy. The menu path for defining product hierarchies is SAP IMG • LOGISTICS – GENERAL • MATERIAL MASTER • SETTINGS FOR KEY FIELDS • DATA RELEVANT TO SALES AND DISTRIBUTION • DEFINE PRODUCT HIERARCHIES, and the transaction code is OVSV.

From this node you can branch to the following steps:

- **Product hierarchy structure**
  In the Data Dictionary, you can change the structure of the product hierarchy (e.g., the number of levels).

- **In/output properties**
  Here, you can customize the product hierarchy's display and the format of its accompanying text.

- **Product hierarchy**
  Here, you define your product hierarchies. Refer to the example shown in Table 2.2 to understand how these hierarchies are defined.

- **Field catalog for pricing**
  Here, you make the product hierarchy available for use in pricing.

- **Field catalog for the Logistics Information System**
  Here, you make the product hierarchy available for use in the Logistics Information System.

Table 2.2 shows an example of a product hierarchy.

Product Hierarchy	Level No.	Description
10000	1	Washing machine
10000 • 10000	2	Washing machine • Semi-automatic
10000 • 10000 • 10000000	3	Washing machine • Semi-automatic • 4 Kg (capacity)
10000 • 10000 • 20000000	3	Washing machine • Semi-automatic • 6 Kg (capacity)
10000 • 20000	2	Washing machine • Automatic
10000 • 20000 • 10000000	3	Washing machine • Automatic • 5 Kg (capacity)
10000 • 20000 • 20000000	3	Washing machine • Automatic • 7 Kg (capacity)
20000	1	Television
20000 • 10000	2	Television • LCD
20000 • 10000 • 10000000	3	Television • LCD • 32"
20000 • 10000 • 20000000	3	Television • LCD • 40"
20000 • 20000	2	Television • Plasma
20000 • 20000 • 10000000	3	Television • Plasma • 52"
20000 • 20000 • 20000000	3	Television • Plasma • 60"

Table 2.2 Example of Product Hierarchy

Material Status

The *material status* (also known as the *sales status*) of any material determines whether the material will be blocked for any particular sales process. The menu path for defining sales statuses is SAP IMG • Logistics – General • Material Master • Settings for Key Fields • Data Relevant to Sales and Distribution • Define Sales Statuses.

To customize the material status, follow these steps:

1. Select any existing entry.

2. Click on the Copy As icon or press F6. This will take you to the screen shown in Figure 2.12, with the message "Specify target entries."

3. Change the two-digit status key and description.

4. Assign a status to each of the processes shown in Figure 2.12. There are 13 Sales and Distribution processes; the statuses of each can be defined as a warning (A)

65

or error (B). It's possible to have no message (when neither A nor B is selected) for some processes. For example, in your company or industry, it may be a standard practice to accept an order for a product when it's still under trial, even though the delivery will occur after trial. Thus, even when the status is listed as *under testing*, there is no warning or error while creating the order; for delivery, however, there can be an error message.

Figure 2.12 List of Sales Activities for Which a Material Can Be Blocked

Assign these statuses to a material in the material master record in the SALES: SALES ORG DATA 1 tab, DCHAIN-SPEC. STATUS field.

Material Groups 1, 2, 3, 4, and 5

Material groups 1, 2, 3, 4, and 5, which appear in the SALES ORG. DATA 2 tab of the material master record, are different from the material group (MARA-MATKL) that appears on the BASIC DATA 1 tab of the material master record. More specifically, material groups 1, 2, 3, 4, and 5 are used for reporting in the Sales and Distribution component, whereas the material group fields of the BASIC DATA 1 tab are used across all components. You may customize the material group (MARA-MATKL) via Transaction OMSF. Material groups 1, 2, 3, 4, and 5 are customized via Transaction OVSU or the menu path SAP IMG • LOGISTICS – GENERAL • MATERIAL MASTER • SETTINGS FOR KEY FIELDS • DATA RELEVANT TO SALES AND DISTRIBUTION • DEFINE MATERIAL GROUPS.

Any of these material groups can contain several three-digit alphanumeric keys with descriptions. While creating a material master record, you can select one of these fields so that a material will receive a value for each material group, from 1 to 5. You can keep one or two of these material groups blank for future usage. These groups can have generic descriptions; you may also use them to address one-time reporting requirements.

Material Commission Groups

Use *material commission groups* to report and price materials. In pricing, you can make a material commission group a key field of a pricing condition table for a condition type (price or surcharge). We'll discuss this more in Chapter 4. Because the field also calculates commission, reports are also prepared using material commission groups in the selection screen for that purpose. We'll discuss reporting in Chapter 9. Define material commission groups using the menu path SAP IMG • Logistics – General • Material Master • Settings for Key Fields • Data Relevant to Sales and Distribution • Define Commission Groups. As shown in Figure 2.13, you define a material commission group by adding a two-digit alphanumeric key and a description.

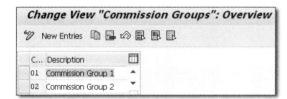

Figure 2.13 Defining Material Commission Groups

Customer Material Info Records

Customer material info records are a form of master data used when the same customers order customer-specific materials. These records provide information about a customer's choice of carrier, delivery priority, specific material codes, and other information that often repeats from one order to the next. Customer material info records also permit the customer to order a material, using their own material number, in situations where their number and yours differ.

During the creation of a sales order for a customer buying a specific material, the information in the customer material info record overwrites the information that would otherwise flow from customer or material master records. These info records are created, changed, and displayed via Transactions VD51/2/3 or the menu path SAP Menu • Logistics • Sales and Distribution • Master Data • Agreements • Customer Material Information • Create/Change/Display. You can create them for a particular sales organization and distribution channel, and can apply them to several materials.

2.3   Batch Master Data

A batch is often used in process industries (oil and gas, concrete, paint, pharmaceuticals, fast-moving consumer goods, and others) or where shelf-life management is a concern (e.g., foods and beverages). A *batch number* is a number associated with the specific storage unit of a material. Products with the same batch number are identical with respect to their most important characteristics, which are often industry-specific (i.e., decided by the industry regulating agency or trade association). These characteristics can vary from company to company; for example, a company dealing with trading goods can decide to assign different batch numbers to identify goods sourced from different vendors. Similarly, a manufacturing company can assign the same batch numbers to goods that go through the same manufacturing process before those goods are placed in different packages.

A batch master record is created, changed, and displayed via Transactions MSC1N, MSC2N, and MSC3N, respectively. Before you create batch master records, you should complete the following customization activities: define batches, customize the system messages relevant to batch management, customize the layout of the batch master record, create and assign number ranges for batches, customize the shelf-life expiration date (SLED), and classify batches. We explain each of these activities now.

2.3.1   Defining Batch Configuration

To define a batch, execute Transaction OMCT or go to menu path SAP IMG • LOGISTICS – GENERAL • BATCH MANAGEMENT • SPECIFY BATCH LEVEL AND ACTIVE STA-

TUS MANAGEMENT. As shown in Figure 2.14, the activity of defining a batch includes defining the batch level, activating batch status management, and defining the initial status of a new batch. We discuss each of these processes in the following subsections.

Batch Level and Batch Status Management

Process the objects in the specified sequence

Batch level

Batch status management

Plants with batch status management

Initial status of a new batch

Batch level -> conversion

Batch status management -> conversion

Figure 2.14 Batch Level and Batch Status Management

1. **Batch level**

   The batch can be unique at the client, plant, and material level. In a standard SAP system, it's at the material level, as shown in Figure 2.15. You reach this screen when you click on the BATCH LEVEL button, or by executing Transaction OMCE.

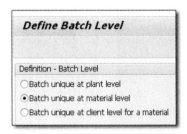

Figure 2.15 Defining the Batch Level

Conversion from one level to another is possible, but may be avoided. The conversion program RM07CHDX creates new batch records in table MCH1 for the new level. If records with the same details already exist in that level, this will create data inconsistency. Refer to SAP Notes 891902 (FAQ: Batch Level) and 533377 (Conversion of Batch Level) if you have to change the batch level. Once you have defined the batch level, you cannot change it through the SAP IMG.

2. **Batch status management**

   After defining the batch level, activate batch status management by selecting the radio button shown in Figure 2.16. You can find the screen for batch status management by executing Transaction OMCS.

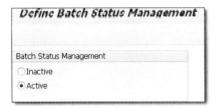

Figure 2.16 Activating Batch Status Management

3. **Plants with batch status management**

   When the batch is defined at the plant level, you must activate batch status management for each plant (see Figure 2.17) using Transaction OMCU.

Change View "Plant Setting: Batch Status Management": Overview

Plnt	Name 1	Batch status management	Converted
1000	Hamburg	✓	☐
1100	Berlin	☐	☐
1200	Dresden	✓	☐
1300	Frankfurt	☐	☐
1400	Stuttgart	✓	☐
1500	München	☐	☐
1600	Köln	☐	☐
2000	Heathrow / Hayes	✓	☐
2010	DC London	✓	☐
2100	Porto	☐	☐
2200	Paris	☐	☐
2210	Lyon	✓	☐
2220	Centre de Distribution Nantes	✓	☐

Figure 2.17 Plant Setting: Batch Status Management

4. **Initial status restricted for material type**

   As shown in Figure 2.18, you can set the initial status of a new batch for a specific material type to RESTRICTED by selecting the checkbox in the INITIAL STATUS column. The screen shown in Figure 2.18 appears when you click on the INITIAL STATUS OF A NEW BATCH button, or when you execute Transaction OMAC.

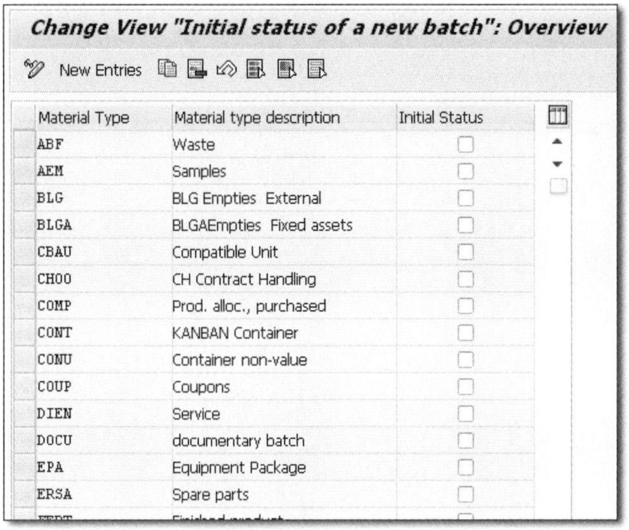

Figure 2.18 Initial Status Restricted for Material Type

When a batch level is defined as a plant, a new batch is made available for restricted or unrestricted use for a combination of plants and material types (Figure 2.19) via Transaction OMAC.

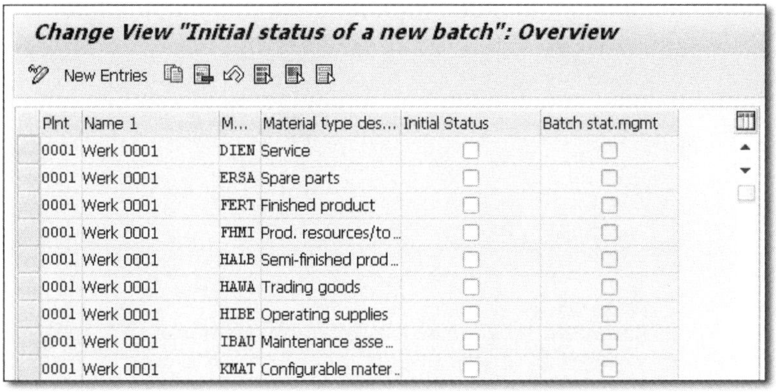

Figure 2.19 Initial Status Restricted for Plant and Material Type

2.3.2 Configuring System Messages

You can modify system messages related to batch management to appear when required. The transaction code for configuring system messages is OCHS (also accessible via the menu path SAP IMG • Logistics – General • Batch Management • Define Attributes of System Messages • System Messages), and is shown in Figure 2.20.

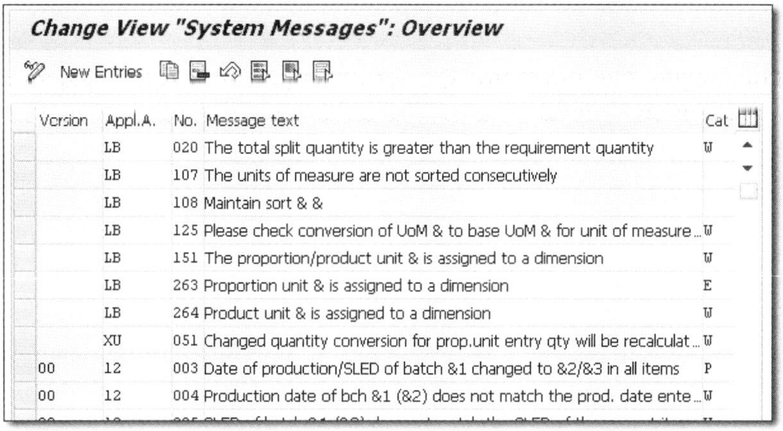

Figure 2.20 Modify System Messages

The first column shows the version, the second shows the application area, and the third shows a number specific to the message text you see when you encounter it during a transaction.

You should be very sure about the category to which any particular message should belong, because messages can enhance or hamper the users' productivity. For example, if a warning appears when it shouldn't (based on the business policy), it might confuse the user; new users may even stop working until the implications become clear.

2.3.3 Configuring the Layout of Batch Master Records

You create, modify, and display batch master records using Transactions MSC1N, MSC2N, and MSC3N, respectively. All fields of batch master records are assigned to a field group, as shown in Figure 2.21. Follow the menu path SAP IMG • Logis-

TICS – GENERAL • BATCH MANAGEMENT • BATCH MASTER • FIELD SELECTION BATCH MASTER • ASSIGN FIELDS TO FIELD GROUPS.

Make the field group mandatory, required, display-only, or hidden by selecting the appropriate radio button (Figure 2.22). Defining a new field group is neither possible nor required.

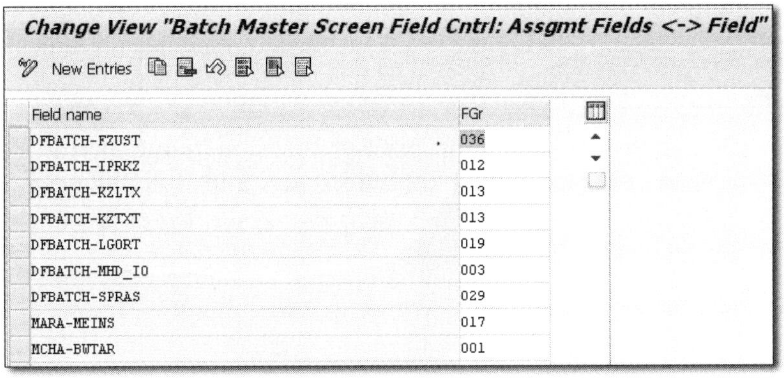

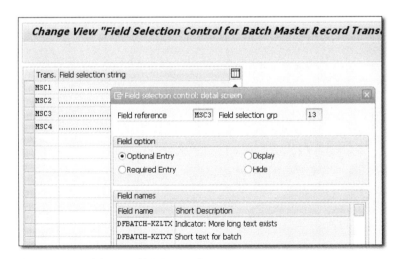

Figure 2.21 Assigning Fields of Batch Master Records to Field Groups

Access the FIELD SELECTION group via menu path SAP IMG • LOGISTICS – GENERAL • BATCH MANAGEMENT • BATCH MASTER • FIELD SELECTION BATCH MASTER • EDIT FIELD SELECTION CONTROL, as shown in Figure 2.22.

Figure 2.22 Modifying Field Selection Groups

2.3.4 Activating the Document Management System

It's also possible to activate the *document management system* (DMS) for batch master records. You can access this screen via Transaction ODOC, or via menu path SAP IMG • Logistics – General • Batch Management • Activate Document Management for Batches. When DMS is activated for the batch master record, a new tab for the document management system appears in the batch master record to the right of the existing tabs.

2.3.5 Configuring Batch Numbers

Batch numbers, which you may print on product labels, are customizable for internal and external number ranges. Select Internal when the batch number is controlled by SAP in sequence, and select External if the batch number is imported from an external vendor or system.

You maintain the numbering object for a batch (BATCH_CLT) using Transaction SNRO or OMAD. As shown in Figure 2.23, the number range 01 is for an internal batch number assignment, and the number range 02 is for an external number assignment, shown by the checkbox in the last column. (You can also have several other number ranges.) Whether the number is generated externally and then fed into the SAP system or generated in the SAP system and then printed on the label doesn't matter: what matters is that the batch number maintained in the SAP system and the one printed on label are the same.

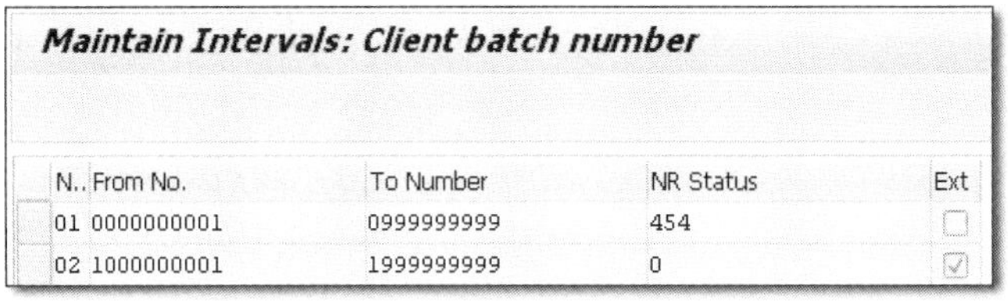

Maintain Intervals: Client batch number

N..	From No.	To Number	NR Status	Ext
01	0000000001	0999999999	454	☐
02	1000000001	1999999999	0	☑

Figure 2.23 Maintaining Number Ranges for Batches

2.3.6 Configuring Shelf-Life Expiration Date

The unit of measurement for counting the expiration date in batch master records can be days, weeks, months, or years, and its format is determined by the *period indicator*. One or more of the four available period indicators can be activated via Transaction O02K, or menu path SAP IMG • Logistics – General • Batch Management • Shelf-Life Expiration Date (SLED) • Maintain Period Indicator. For example, if the period indicator is in days, the dates are maintained as MM.DD.YYYY; if it's in years, the dates are maintained as YYYY only. If the period indicator is left blank, it defaults to days. Table 2.3 lists the internal period indicators and their corresponding external period indicators in English and German, as well as the description in English.

Internal Period Indicator	External Period Indicator		Description
	German	English	
	T	D	Day
1	W	W	Week
2	M	M	Month
3	J	Y	Year

Table 2.3 Standard SAP Period Indicators

The expiration date restricts the movement of goods, such as stock transfers, goods returned from customers, and goods received from external vendors; the system defines these movement types by different keys. It's also possible to keep certain plants free of expiration date checks. As shown in Figure 2.24, plant 0001 has no check for an expired material for a goods receipt. This means the expired material can be received at these plants without any check. You perform this by using Transaction OMJ5, or via menu path SAP IMG • LOGISTICS – GENERAL • BATCH MANAGEMENT • SHELF-LIFE EXPIRATION DATE (SLED) • SET EXPIRATION DATE CHECK, and then selecting the plant.

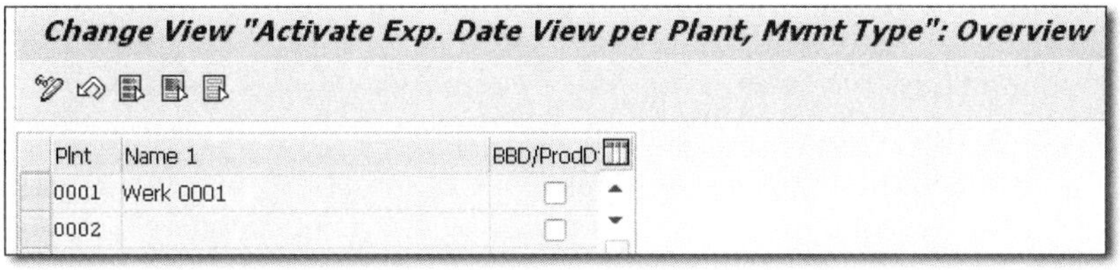

Figure 2.24 Expiration Date Check at the Plant Level

For the receiving plants where the SLED is active, the restrictions are further refined to particular movement types. As shown in Figure 2.25, you define the nature of the check for each movement type by using Transaction OMJ5, or via menu path SAP IMG • LOGISTICS – GENERAL • BATCH MANAGEMENT • SHELF-LIFE

EXPIRATION DATE (SLED) • SET EXPIRATION DATE CHECK, and then selecting the
MOVEMENT TYPE option. Movement type defines the nature of the movement
when there is any change in the stock. For example, one movement type may
make the stock returned by a customer immediately available for sale (unrestricted type), while another will block it for sale (return type) until quality checks
are carried out.

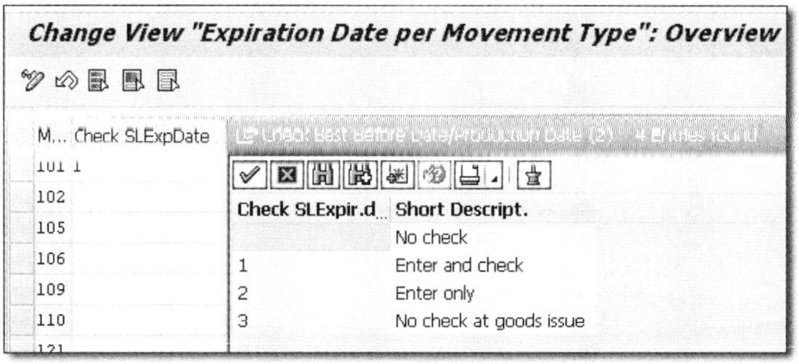

Figure 2.25 Expiration Date Check for Different Movement Types

2.3.7 Configuring Batch Classification

The classification system is a feature not unique to batch management, but rather
it is part of cross-application components (another example of a cross-application
component is DMS). The classification system consists of *classes* and *characteristics,*
and can also be used to classify materials. It's also used in several components
other than Logistics. SAP provides a list of objects for which the class type is predefined, for example, class type 023, Batch. Use this class type to create classes
that classify batches based on various characteristics, such as manufacturing location (if the same material is manufactured at several plants). You can create the
class in the production client using Transaction CL02 or by following the menu
path SAP MENU • CROSS-APPLICATION COMPONENTS • CLASSIFICATION SYSTEM • MAS-
TER DATA • CLASSES. As shown in Figure 2.26, you must use class type 023 to create a class for batch classification.

Characteristics like classes are also considered master data, which means that they
are not transported from the development to the production client, but are
instead created in the production client itself using Transaction CT04, or menu
path SAP MENU • CROSS-APPLICATION COMPONENTS • CLASSIFICATION SYSTEM • MAS-
TER DATA • CHARACTERISTICS.

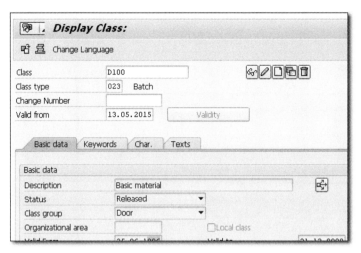

Figure 2.26 Create Class

More than one characteristic is often used to define a batch. In Figure 2.27 and Figure 2.28, we show how to define the date of manufacturing (or date of production) as a characteristic of the batch. Because we express the date of manufacturing is in terms of a date, the data type is the DATE FORMAT; other possible data formats are CHARACTER, NUMERIC, and CURRENCY. The status should be released, to make the batch available for use.

In the CHARS GROUP field, you can group different characteristics together and assign them to one characteristics group in the list available. Characteristics groups are defined using the menu path SAP IMG • CROSS-APPLICATION COMPONENTS • CLASSIFICATIONS SYSTEM • CHARACTERISTICS • DEFINE CHARACTERISTICS GROUPS. If you plan to restrict the characteristic to specific users, use the AUTH.GRP field.

If you wish to create a batch in which entering the value for the characteristic is required, select the ENTRY REQUIRED checkbox. The value requested can be a single value (as in case of DATE OF MANUFACTURING), but you can also allow users to enter multiple values by selecting the MULTIPLE VALUES radio button. The INTERVAL VALUES checkbox, when selected, allows numeric characteristics to use intervals as values. The RESTRICTABLE checkbox, when selected, allows the characteristic to have a value from a predefined set of values.

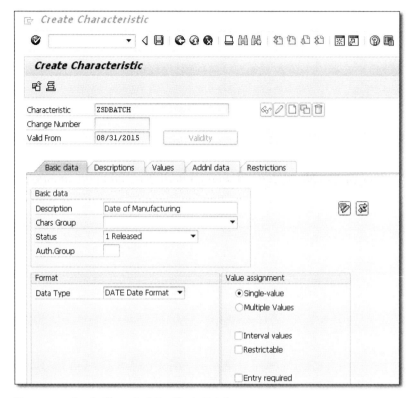

Figure 2.27 Create Characteristics (Basic Data)

The description entered in the Basic Data tab is also automatically supplied in the Descriptions tab (in the logon language). If a description in another language is required, it can also be stored in that view. The Values tab is used to define values that the characteristics can have when creating a batch. The Addnl Data (Additional Data) tab is especially useful if the value of the characteristic is to be automatically filled, as shown in Figure 2.28.

Automatically filled fields require no input from you, so the more characteristics you can add here, the more time you will save. Here, for example, we have made the MCH1-HSDAT field a default value for the date of manufacturing, meaning that the date on which the batch is created (MCH1-HSDAT) is also the value for the Date of Production field. (This is generally a good assumption to make, and a very good assumption if you're creating the batch automatically.)

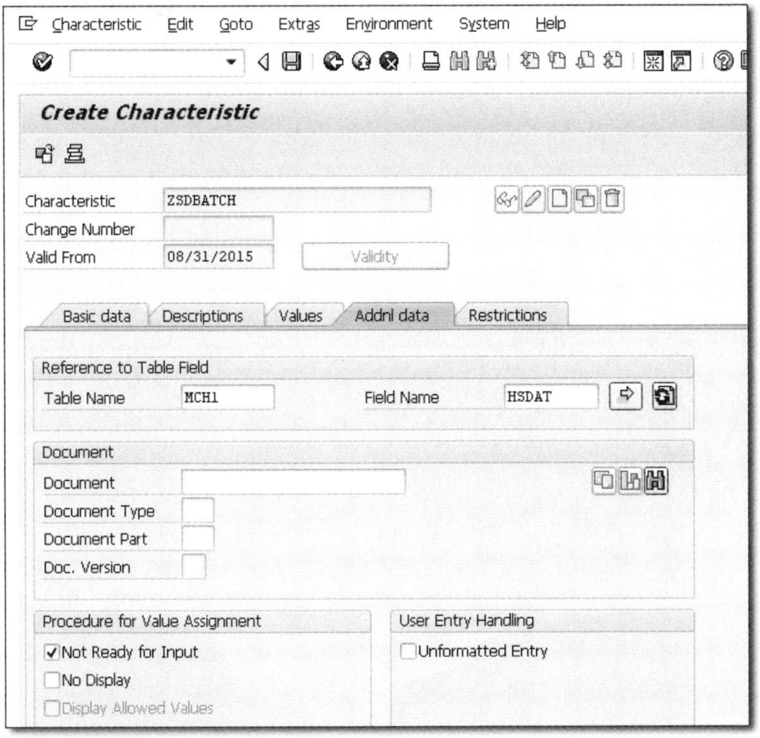

Figure 2.28 Create Characteristics (Additional Data)

> **Foreign Trade Master Data**
>
> Foreign trade-related master data is accessed through a single point (the General Foreign Trade Processing Cockpit) but is part of four separate master records: vendor master record, purchasing info record, material master record, and customer master record. The menu path to access the General Foreign Trade Processing Cockpit is SAP EASY ACCESS • LOGISTICS • SALES AND DISTRIBUTION • FOREIGN TRADE/CUSTOMS • GENERAL FOREIGN TRADE PROCESSING • GENERAL FOREIGN TRADE PROCESSING • COCKPIT – GENERAL FOREIGN TRADE PROCESSING, and the transaction code is EN99. All of the master data fields relevant for foreign trade processing are accessible and maintainable via this cockpit transaction. We'll discuss some of the important foreign trade master data fields in Chapter 3.

2.4   Other Important Master Data

Before closing this chapter on master data, there are a few more types to discuss that are especially relevant for Sales and Distribution: vendor master data, employee master data, general ledger master data, and user master data. We'll discuss condition records (e.g., pricing, output) in subsequent chapters.

The more time you spend on master data (and on organizational structure), the better you'll understand the different processes and how master data impacts them.

2.4.1 Vendor Master Data

Vendors are individuals or organizations that sell goods and/or services to you or your organization. Carriers or transporters are the most important group of vendors for us to understand from a sales and distribution perspective. This is because transportation is very closely integrated to delivery, which we'll discuss later. We create transporters or carriers as partner functions for customers and attach them to their customer master record. For the purposes of reimbursement of travelling expenses, treat employees as vendors, as well. If you understand the customer master data well, you can visualize the vendor master data as a mirror image of it.

Transactions XK01/2/3 are used to centrally create/change/display vendor master data. Transactions FK01/2/3 are used to create/change/display vendor master accounting data, and Transactions MK01/2/3 are used to create/change/display vendor master purchasing data. You can customize message control, industry sector, the minority indicator (whether the vendor is a minority or owned by a minority), number range, and text IDs in the Financial Accounting module for the vendor master record. In menu path SAP IMG • MATERIAL MANAGEMENT • PURCHASING • VENDOR MASTER or via Transaction OLME, you can customize the terms of payment, incoterms, vendor hierarchy, contact person, and so on. If you want customers who are also vendors to belong to particular customer account groups, you can define that here. As for customer master records, we advise creating vendor master records with reference to an existing vendor.

As with customer account groups, you create vendor account groups in the Financial Accounting module using Transaction OBD3, or menu path SAP IMG • FINANCIAL ACCOUNTING (NEW) • ACCOUNTS RECEIVABLE AND ACCOUNTS PAYABLE • VENDOR ACCOUNTS • MASTER DATA • PREPARATIONS FOR CREATING VENDOR MASTER DATA • DEFINE ACCOUNT GROUPS WITH SCREEN LAYOUT (VENDORS). You also decide the field statuses of different vendor master records here. As for the customer account group, you can customize field statuses to vary depending upon the company code and the transaction used.

Each vendor master record exists for a particular company code and a purchasing organization. The vendor master record has three major areas: GENERAL DATA, COMPANY CODE DATA, and PURCHASING ORGANIZATION DATA. There are nine screens, which you access when you select the checkboxes and press [Enter]. We discuss each of these areas in the subsections to come.

General Data

As for customer master records, the vendor master record General Data area consists of three screens that are used by both the accounting and purchasing departments. The ADDRESS screen stores address fields found in tables ADRC and ADR2/3/4/5, which themselves are linked to the tables for vendor master data general data (e.g., table LFA1) by the field address number (e.g., LFA1-ADRNR and ADRC-ADDRNUMBER). The CONTROL screen stores various tax-related information, authorization objects that restrict users who can modify the master record, and customer numbers (if the vendor is also a customer). The PAYMENT TRANSACTION screen stores the vendor's bank details.

Company Code Data

The four screens of the COMPANY CODE DATA area store, among other things, the reconciliation account for the vendor, payment terms, payment methods, and withholding tax details.

The reconciliation account is a general ledger account for several vendors who are similar in nature: it is a balance sheet item. When employees are created as vendors in the ACCOUNTING INFO screen, the PERSONNEL NUMBER field determines the employee for which this vendor master record is created.

Purchasing Organization Data

The purchasing department maintains this data. In the PURCHASING DATA screen, you'll find the ordering currency, terms of payment, incoterms, schema applicable for the vendor (which is equivalent to the customer pricing procedure), minimum order value, account number for the organization in the sales department of the vendor (LFM1-EIKTO), shipping conditions, planned delivery time, and other vendors attached to the vendor master through partner functions. In the PARTNER FUNCTIONS screen, different partner functions are attached to the vendor master record.

2.4.2 Employee Master Data

SAP ERP 6.0 allows you to create employee master records without implementing HR components. Import the tables of HR components via the menu path SAP IMG • Sales and Distribution • Master Data • Business partners • Use Sales Employee without HR. Use Transactions VPE1/2/3 or menu path SAP Menu • Logistics • Sales and Distribution • Master Data • Business Partners • Sales Personnel • Create/Change/Display to create/change/display employee master records. As shown in Figure 2.29, you will see a minimum of six filled screens (or, as they are called in the HR components, *infotypes*) for a particular employee.

The sales data maintained for sales employees includes the sales organization, sales office, sales group, and search term. The data is stored in table PA0900.

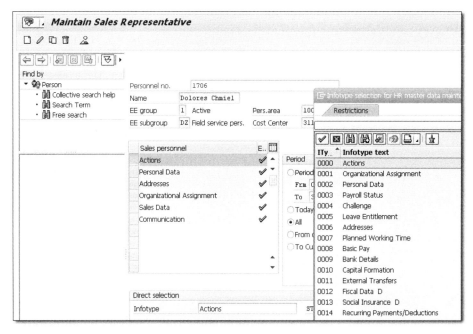

Figure 2.29 Maintain Sales Employee for Different Infotypes

2.4.3 General Ledger Master Data

Much of what you do in your SAP system is eventually reflected in either a profit and loss statement or a balance sheet. For example, the creation of a standard sales order in Sales and Distribution has no direct impact on either the profit and loss statement or the balance sheet, but when you look at the complete process of creating a sales order (delivery of the materials requested, invoice creation, and payment receipt), each of the steps do. Similarly, when you deliver or post goods issue (explained in Chapter 6), the stock or inventory reduces (a balance sheet item), and the cost of goods sold account increases (a profit and loss account item); when you create an invoice, your sales revenue account increases and your customer reconciliation account reduces. In any accounting document, when you credit one or more accounts, you simultaneously debit one or more accounts. These accounts are called *general ledger accounts*. Even in a small organization, there can be thousands of general ledger accounts.

You centrally create, modify, and display general ledger accounts are centrally created, modified, and displayed using Transaction FS00, or via menu path SAP MENU • ACCOUNTING • FINANCIAL ACCOUNTING • GENERAL LEDGER • MASTER RECORDS • G/L ACCOUNTS • INDIVIDUAL PROCESSING • CENTRALLY. To perform these actions at the chart of accounts or company code levels, use Transactions FSP0 or FSS0, respectively. You can also collectively process GL accounts. Maintenance of GL accounts, however, is the responsibility of finance team.

The important data stored in GL master records is the account group to which the GL belongs, whether a GL is a profit and loss statement or balance sheet account, the account currency, the field status group that determines the status of each field, whether only automatic posting is allowed, the authorization group, and whether a reconciliation account is for a customer, vendor, or asset.

2.4.4   User Master Data

Although user master data is the last thing we're discussing, it's the first thing you need to log on to an SAP system. Maintaining user master records is primarily a Basis activity, and involves creating and maintaining user IDs via Transaction SU01. The user master record mainly stores roles, profiles, and authorization-related data, but the user can maintain certain aspects of the record using Transaction SU3. The three things the user should maintain are found in the ADDRESS, DEFAULT, and PARAMETERS tabs, all of which we discuss next.

Address Tab

In the ADDRESS tab, you'll find the name, title, address, phone numbers, fax numbers, mobile numbers, email address, language, function, and department of the user.

Defaults Tab

In the DEFAULTS tab, as shown in Figure 2.30, you can save your preference for the area menu with which your SAP system opens. Most of the area menus behave like transaction codes. You can save the logon language, decimal notation, and date format based on your own preferences. The SPOOL CONTROL section indicates the name of the output device, whether output is to be issued immediately, and whether it is deleted after output. In the PERSONAL TIME ZONE section, you can maintain a personal time zone in addition to the system time zone.

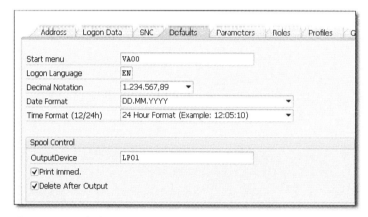

Figure 2.30 Default Tab

Area Menus

Area menus are alphanumeric strings (for example, VA00), just like transaction codes (for example, VA01). When executed, an area menu opens a new SAP menu and transaction list. In the DEFAULT tab (of the user master record), you can maintain area menus in the START menu field, but not the transaction code.

Parameters Tab

In the PARAMETERS tab, you can include several different parameter IDs with specific values in the PARAMETER VALUE column. If the company code parameter ID (BUK) with a specific parameter value (e.g., 1000) exists in a particular user profile, the COMPANY CODE field always automatically fills with this default value (1000) for the user. You can save parameter IDs for many important organizational units and other fields in your own user master record using Transactions SU2 and SU3. Doing so will save you a lot of time.

There are other uses for parameters, as well. For example, the value of parameter ID SCL with possible values X or blank determines whether the text you type in a program will be uppercase or lowercase. Another parameter, MMPI_READ_NOTE, which takes a value in YYYYMMDD format, allows the user to use Transaction MMPI for initializing the MM period for the day mentioned in the YYYYMMDD format. Finally, in the current version of SAP ERP, the Services for Object icon is, by default, not available in Transactions VA02 and VA03. Use this icon to attach Word, Excel, or PDF documents from your laptop or desktop to a particular SAP document. To make this icon available for Transactions VA02 and VA03, add parameter ID SD_SWU_ACTIVE with a value of X in the user master record. As you can see, parameter IDs and parameter values can be quite versatile in their purposes.

2.5 Summary

In this chapter, we discussed customer master data, material master data (SD views), and batch management master data in detail. You received an overview of customer-material info records and foreign trade master data. We also offered a brief introduction to other types of master data, specifically, vendor master data, employee master data, general ledger master data, and user master data. Though we didn't discuss every field of the master data records in this chapter, we'll introduce you to other fields as they become relevant in subsequent chapters.

Thus far, we have dealt with static elements such as organizational structure and master data. Beginning with the next chapter, we'll discuss dynamic elements such as sales, deliveries, goods issues, billing, and more.

In this chapter, you'll learn about the different types of sales documents, including sales orders, outline agreements, and complaints. You'll discover how to optimize the automatic determination of partners, free goods, material determination, Global ATP, and much more, and learn how to customize consignment sales, third-party sales, and others when necessary.

3   Sales

Sales is the process of exchanging of goods and services—and in modern economies, this process is quite complex.

Consider, for example, the last shirt you purchased from a store. It may have been manufactured in another country. The manufacturer may have outsourced the design of the shirt. The fabrics and threads used in it may have been from different manufacturers. The cotton used could have come from several growers. The cotton growers had probably purchased seeds and other inputs for their crops from different companies. The man-made fiber used for blending could be from different sources. When you paid for your shirt, you also paid for the hundreds of goods and services that went into its making.

Economies of scale, competitive advantage, and the division of labor have all made us produce many very specific, specialized goods or services, and led us to consume a huge number of goods and services. It's also important to recognize that sales can occur between an individual and an organization, and vice versa. As an individual, you don't require an SAP ERP system to optimize your earnings and spending, but it makes sense for a large organization. For any organization, sales is the process of earning revenue that results in profit (or loss). It's important for the organization that customers find it easy to order from them, and that they are able to fulfill those orders. The *fulfillment* matches the *specifications* of the customer requirement. When a customer makes a purchase order, he specifies his requirements. The customer's purchase order is your sales order.

In this chapter, we'll primarily discuss sales documents. We'll start by explaining the basic principle of sales document processing, and proceed into configuring the many elements that impact sales: partner determination, availability checks, special business transactions, incompletion control batch determination, returns, and intercompany processes. Let's get started.

3.1 Processing Sales Documents

Customizing the sales process depends on the purchasing process that your customers follow. You also group your customers differently if there is significant difference in their purchasing processes. The Sales and Distribution functionality in SAP ERP is necessary if sales processes are complex, such as if you want the system to accomplish the following:

▶ Check availability and transfer the requirements for production planning

▶ Evaluate and block certain orders based on their credit worthiness assessment

▶ Pick the oldest batch for delivery

▶ Print the order confirmation automatically when it's complete

▶ Automatically post the elements of the invoice value (e.g., freight) to the correct GL

A typical sales process starts with a customer making an *inquiry* and *request for quotation* (RFQ), which are nonobligatory in nature. Your response is voluntary. If you do submit a quotation, your customer may decide to buy from you, in which case they would issue a purchase order that is either based on the quotation, or on an agreement or contract. Therefore, the content of a quotation can be legally binding for you.

A purchase order issued by your customer is recorded as a sales order in your system. The order is processed according the details described within it. Once the goods and services have been delivered to the customer, you create an invoice based on the terms and conditions detailed in the sales order. The customer, upon receiving the invoice, verifies it and makes the payment. During invoice verification, the customer may find your goods or services deficient when compared to their purchase order, and subsequently request a sales return or credit memo. For sales returns, you take back the supplied material (or part of it) and issue a credit memo. For a credit memo request, no physical return of material is involved, and the customer issues the credit memo. In certain cases, the invoice price may be, by mistake, less than the price agreed upon by you and your customer, and you have to issue a debit note. The debit note is similar to an invoice from a financial accounting point of view.

In the SAP system, there are several types of sales documents. All sales documents have a header level and an item level, and certain types of sales documents have a schedule line, if physical movement is involved. Normally, the documents that are referred to as sales documents are as follows:

- Presales documents (e.g., inquiry and quotation)
- Sales orders (e.g., order, cash sale, and rush order)
- Outline agreements (e.g., value contract and scheduling agreement)
- Complaints (e.g., credit memo request, debit memo request, and return)

Now that you understand sales documents on a general level, let's move on to the different types.

Several standard sales document types come preconfigured in SAP ERP. You can create your own document types using Transaction VOV8, or by going to SAP IMG • Sales and Distribution • Sales • Sales Documents • Sales Document Header • Define Sales Document Types. This essentially allows you to configure the header level of the sales document. Transaction VOV8 is very important and has been divided into multiple illustrations: from Figure 3.2 to Figure 3.10, we highlight the important features of this screen.

Every sales order type must be assigned to a sales document category, listed in Table 3.1. If selected, the Sales Document Block will prevent the user from accidentally using order types that are not required or are outdated. It's also possible to only allow automatic creation by choosing A: Only Automatic Creation Allowed. This Block field can be maintained in the initial screen of Transaction VOV8, as shown in Figure 3.1.

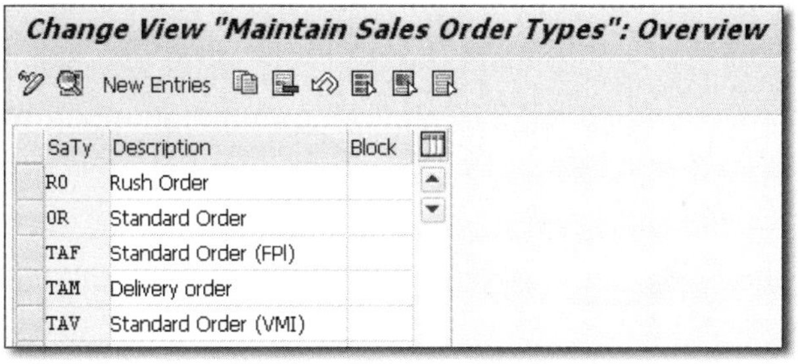

Figure 3.1 Sales Order Types

> **Order Types**
>
> You should block the standard SAP order types and the customized order types that aren't in use, rather than deleting or modifying them for new requirements.

Table 3.1 lists the SD document categories that appear in the Transaction VOV8 screen and their descriptions.

Code	SD Document Category
A	Inquiry
B	Quotation
C	Order
D	Item proposal
E	Scheduling agreement
F	Scheduling agreement with external service
G	Contract
H	Returns
I	Order without charge
K	Credit memo request
L	Debit memo request
W	Independent requirements plan
0	Master contract

Table 3.1 SD Document Categories

To create a customized sales order by copying the standard order (OR), the first step is to give it a name, starting with Y or Z, and a description. The SD DOCU-MENT CATEGORY field can take a value, as listed in Table 3.2. The SALES DOCUMENT BLOCK indicator can take a value of X or A. When blank, the document type is not blocked for use. A value X indicates that the document type cannot be used for creating any new order, while a value A means this type of document will only be created automatically.

The numbering object for sales documents is BV_BELEG. The number range for internal assignment is 01 (000000001 to 599999999), which means that if you save a document without an external document number, it will take the next available number in that range. The number range for an external assignment is 02 (6000000 to 99999999), meaning you're allowed to pick any available number from this range for a new document. The item number increment determines how the items are numbered. If the value is 10, as shown in Figure 3.2, the items will be numbered as 10, 20, 30, and so on. The subitem increment determines how the subitems are numbered (e.g., BoM).

Several order types can have the same number range. Separate number ranges are often required for one order type, depending on the sales office or sales group. This is not possible in the standard SAP system. You can achieve this by adding new number ranges in the RV_BELEG numbering object, creating a z-table that will determine the appropriate number range for each situation. Next, you can write your code in Transaction SE38, using the form USEREXIT_NUMBER_RANGE of the include program MV45AFZZ. For a different sales office, sales group, or customer account group, you may require different number ranges, even when the order type is the same. You can define a separate number range for orders belonging to different sales offices, even when the sales order type is the same.

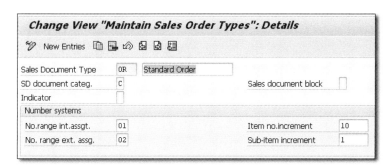

Figure 3.2 Standard Sales Order

Located in the GENERAL CONTROL section, the REFERENCE MANDATORY field is generally left blank; it makes references to other sales documents such as quotation, inquiry, or invoice, optional.

Mandatory References

In certain types of sales documents, such as the sales return or request for credit or debit memo, we recommend making references mandatory. Oftentimes, the order types that aren't mandatory for the reference are in the system at the time of go-live, because referencing legacy invoices isn't possible or recommended.

When the CHECK DIVISION field is left blank, the system will not check whether the division of the sales document header and the items are the same. When you select ITEM DIVISION, the division of the material recorded in the material master record is copied to the sales document. If you enable the CHECK PURCHASE ORDER No checkbox, the system will display an error (or information) message when there is already a sales order with same purchase order number from the same customer.

The fields in the TRANSACTION FLOW group (shown in Figure 3.3) determine how the different screens in Transactions VA01, VA02, and VA03 behave. SCREEN SEQUENCE GRP. determines which screens for the document header and item will appear while creating, changing, and displaying an order, as well as the sequence in which the screens appear. To modify the screens and sequence, you can create a screen and transaction variant using Transaction SHD0. The transaction variant will apply to the particular document type only you enter it in the VARIANT field, as shown in Figure 3.3. Use the document pricing procedure (DOC. PRIC. PROCEDURE) field to determine pricing procedure.

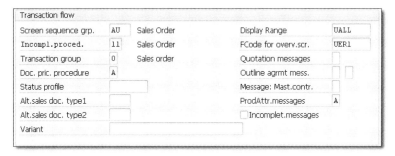

Figure 3.3 Standard Sales Order (Transaction Flow)

Incompletion Procedure

The incompletion procedure assigned to this document type is in disabled mode, because it's not assigned here. We'll discuss this later in Section 3.10.

Alternate sales document types 1 and 2 are used to change the documents created using one document type to another. Suppose there are two document types, YOR and ZOR, and the document created using one document should be changed to the other type. In this situation, you maintain both as the alternate sales document type for each other. In other words, you maintain ZOR in the ALT.SALES.

DOC. TYPE1 field for YOR, and maintain YOR in the ALT.SALES. DOC. TYPE1 field in the customization of the ZOR document type (in Transaction VOV8). As you can see in Figure 1.4, if alternate sales document types are maintained, then the alternate document type will appear as a radio button in the SALES tab of the SALES OVERVIEW screen, which allows you to change the document type and save the document using Transaction VA02. You can use this functionality when you won't know the exact document type until the order is saved (for example, if your order type depends on the plant from where you will supply the material).

Figure 3.4 Alternate Sales Document Type in Sales Tab in Transaction VA02

You will use the QUOTATION MESSAGES field to check and copy the open quotation to the sales order. Use OUTLINE AGREEMENT MESSAGE to check open contracts and make them available for copying to the sales document. The MESSAGE: MASTER CONTRACT field will check and copy the master contract data to the contract. PRODUCT ATTRIBUTE MESSAGES checks the product attributes of only those items that are manually entered. For product attributes that are not acceptable to the ship-to party, you may issue an error or warning message. If selected, the INCOMPLETE MESSAGE checkbox will not allow a user to save a document of this type if it's incomplete.

The fields shown in Figure 3.5 are used for the document types of document category E (SCHEDULING AGREEMENTS). Customize the usage indicator (USE) field via Transaction OVA4 or by following the menu path SAP IMG • SALES AND DISTRIBUTION • SALES • SALES DOCUMENTS • SALES DOCUMENT HEADER • DEFINE USAGE INDICATORS. The DELIVERY BLOCK set automatically applies to the scheduling agreements created using this document type. In the CORR.DELIVERY TYPE field, you can specify the delivery type that will be used for this purpose. The MRP FOR DLVSCHTYPE field defines whether forecast delivery schedules or just-in-time (JIT) delivery schedules (of the scheduling agreement) are relevant for material requirements planning (MRP) and/or delivery. JIT is a concept where the buyer receives the material exactly when he requires it so that he doesn't have to stock it for long time.

Figure 3.5 Standard Sales Order (Scheduling Agreement)

Figure 3.6 illustrates the SHIPPING group, which determines the delivery type that processes the sales document type. The IMMEDIATE DELIVERY indicator allows you to automatically create a delivery as soon as the order is saved, such as for cash sales (BV) or rush orders. The DELIVERY BLOCK and SHIPPING CONDITIONS values specified here become the default values for all documents of this type. The shipping condition overwrites the value that flows from the customer master record.

Figure 3.6 Standard Sales Order (Shipping)

Figure 3.7 illustrates the BILLING group, which determines the billing document type that will process the sales document for delivery-related billing, order-related billing, or intercompany billing. If the BILLING BLOCK field is filled, its content will automatically move to all orders of this type, and those orders will be blocked for billing. For example, you may want to automatically block (for billing) all credit memo requests when they're created. The block is to be removed by an approving authority before the credit memo is issued.

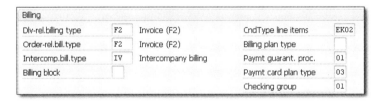

Figure 3.7 Standard Sales Order (Billing)

In the CNDTYPE LINE ITEMS field, you enter the cost condition type (e.g., EK01, EK02) that will determine the cost of the items in a make-to-order scenario. Condition type EK01 transfers the actual production cost of the controlling functionality, including different overheads, to order as price. Condition type EK02 does the same thing, but is statistical, and the actual price is compared to it to determine the profit margin. For further details, refer to SAP Note 155212. In the BILLING group, you can specify whether a periodic or milestone type of plan will be used. We'll discuss this in Chapter 7. The PAYMT GUARANT. PROC., PAYMT CARD PLAN TYPE, and CHECKING GROUP fields will be discussed in Chapter 5.

When there's a value in the LEAD TIME IN DAYS field (see Figure 3.8), the system adds that value to the current date (also referred to as system date, SYDATUM field) in order to propose the requested delivery date. You have the option of specifying the date type (1 = day, 2 = week, 3 = month, 4 = posting period, and 5 = planning calendar period) for the schedule line that's created for a particular document type. The PROPOSED PRICING DATE (options here are: blank = system date, A = requested delivery date, B = valid from date, and C = contract start date) is the modifiable default value for automatic pricing determination. The PROPOSED VALID-FROM DATE (options are: blank = no proposal, A = system date, B = beginning of next month) becomes the default valid-from date (which can be changed) when you create a document of this type. The PROPOSED DELIVERY DATE and PROPOSED PO DATE checkboxes, when selected, propose the current date as the delivery date and PO date, respectively.

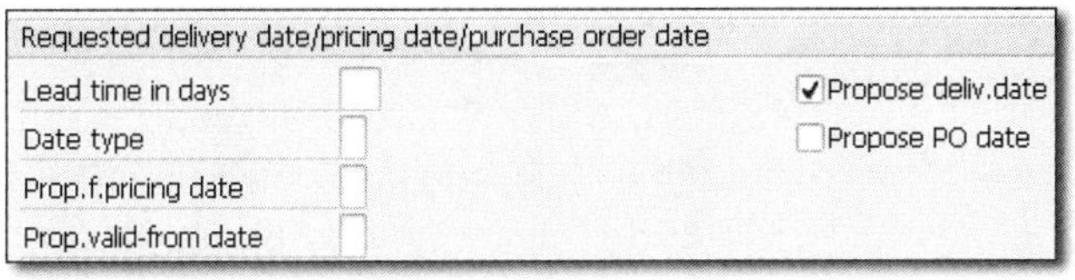

Figure 3.8 Standard Sales Order (Dates)

We'll discuss the fields under the CONTRACT group, shown in Figure 3.9, in Section 3.8, Outline Agreements.

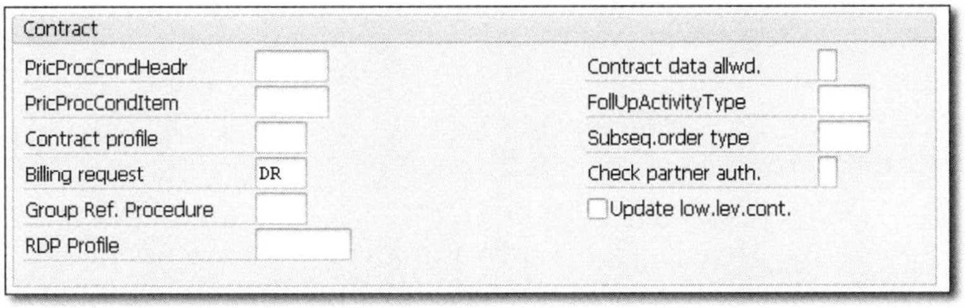

Figure 3.9 Standard Sales Order (Contract)

Use the BUSINESS TRANSACTION field shown in Figure 3.10 if the SAP Advanced Planning and Optimization system will perform availability checks. Refer to the text box in Section 3.7 for more information.

Figure 3.10 Standard Sales Order (Availability Check)

In addition to defining the sales document type, which we just discussed, you have to assign different sales areas to that sales document. When you assign a sales area (combination of sales organization, distribution channel, and division) to an order type, other sales areas cannot use the order. This assignment is not required for sales document types, which are valid for all sales areas. Make the assignment via Transaction OVAZ, or by going to menu path SALES AND DISTRIBUTION • SALES • SALES DOCUMENTS • SALES DOCUMENT HEADER • ASSIGN SALES AREA TO SALES DOCUMENT TYPES.

Another important step is to define the order reason. This is important for reporting, and sometimes pricing, purposes. It's done via Transaction OVAU or by following the menu path SAP IMG • SALES AND DISTRIBUTION • SALES • SALES DOCUMENTS • SALES DOCUMENT HEADER • DEFINE ORDER REASONS. Each reason is an alphanumeric key with a description.

Table 3.2 lists important standard sales document types. We have also provided the subsequent standard document types used for delivery and billing. A close look at this table can reveal a lot of information. For example, an inquiry can be neither delivered nor invoiced, whereas you can create a pro forma invoice (F5) with reference to a quotation.

Sales Document Type		Del. type	Billing Type		
			Dlv.	Ord.	Interco.
IN	Inquiry				
QT	Quotation			F5	
B1	Rebate credit memo request			B1	
B2	Rebate correction request			B2	
B3	Part rebate settlement request			B3	

Table 3.2 Important Sales Document Types

Sales Document Type		Del. type	Billing Type		
			Dlv.	Ord.	Interco.
B4	Rebate request for manual accruals			B4	
CS	Cash sale	BV		BV	IV
CR	Credit memo request			G2	
GK	Master contract				
CP	Consignment pick-up	LR			
CF	Consignment fill-up	LF			
CI	Consignment issue	LF	F2	F2	IV
FD	Delivery free of charge	LF			
QC	Quantity contract				
SDF	Subsequent delivery free of charge	LF			
CONR	Consignment returns	LR		RE	
DR	Debit memo request			L2	IV
PV	Item proposal				
RE	Returns	LR	RE	RE	IG
RK	Invoice correction request			G2	
RSA	Returns scheduling agreement	LR	F2	RE	
SO	Rush order	LF	F2	F2	IV
OR	Standard order	LF	F2	F2	IV

Table 3.2 Important Sales Document Types (Cont.)

3.2 Item Categories and Schedule Line Categories

A sales document is divided into two or three levels.

At the header level, you specify who the sold-to-party is for the order or the sales office processing the order. The order type controls how the document will behave with respect to a credit check, or which subsequent document type of delivery or invoice can process it.

In addition to the header level, all sales documents have an item level. This level determines whether the item is relevant for delivery (or billing). Item categories control behavior at the item level. An item category, for example, may automatically generate a purchase order for that item. The schedule lines are not present in all types of order. For example, credit memo requests do not have schedule lines. Schedule line categories control the behavior of schedule lines. Typically, a schedule line appears when the item's schedule for delivery depends on an availability check. Schedule lines also transfer the stock requirement to production planning.

In the following two sections, we discuss how to customize item categories and schedule line categories.

3.2.1 Item Categories

The steps for customizing item categories are given below.

1. The first step is defining the item category using Transaction VOV7 or by going to the menu path SAP IMG • Sales and Distribution • Sales • Sales Documents • Sales Document Item • Define Item Categories. The fields that you'll need to define for customizing an item category are shown in Figure 3.11.

2. The Item category group is a key field that determines the material type (e.g., raw material, finished goods, trading goods, and so on). It determines the item category for a material at the item level. All of the materials that will share the same item category at the item level should also have the same item category group in their material master records. You can define item categories groups via Transaction OVAW, or the menu path Sales and Distribution • Sales • Sales Documents • Sales Document Item • Define Item Category Groups. Assign the item category group to a material using material master record.

3. You assign item category groups to different material types using Transaction VOVA or by going to Sales and Distribution • Sales • Sales Documents • Sales Document Item • Define Default Values For Material Type. All of the materials created in the particular material type will have the default item category group in their material master records, which can subsequently be modified.

4. Item category usage is an additional field used to determine the default value of an item. Normally, a new entry is not required, but if it is required, you can add it using Transaction OVVW or by going to the menu path SAP IMG • Sales and Distribution • Sales • Sales Documents • Sales Document Item • Define Item Category Usage. If you want to use the indicator in the item category determination, it is stored in the customer material info records for a specific combination of material and customer.

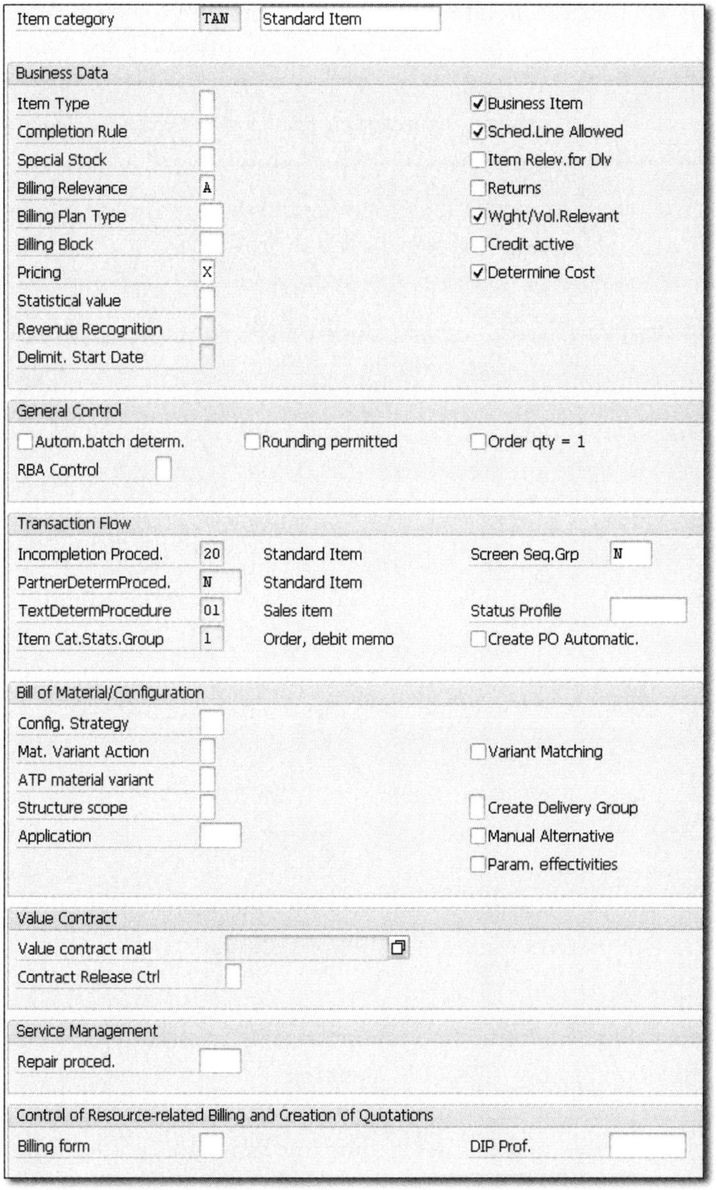

Item category	TAN	Standard Item

Business Data

Item Type		☑	Business Item
Completion Rule		☑	Sched.Line Allowed
Special Stock		☐	Item Relev.for Dlv
Billing Relevance	A	☐	Returns
Billing Plan Type		☑	Wght/Vol.Relevant
Billing Block		☐	Credit active
Pricing	X	☑	Determine Cost
Statistical value			
Revenue Recognition			
Delimit. Start Date			

General Control

☐ Autom.batch determ.	☐ Rounding permitted	☐ Order qty = 1
RBA Control ☐		

Transaction Flow

Incompletion Proced.	20	Standard Item	Screen Seq.Grp	N
PartnerDetermProced.	N	Standard Item		
TextDetermProcedure	01	Sales item	Status Profile	
Item Cat.Stats.Group	1	Order, debit memo	☐ Create PO Automatic.	

Bill of Material/Configuration

Config. Strategy			
Mat. Variant Action		☐	Variant Matching
ATP material variant			
Structure scope		☐	Create Delivery Group
Application		☐	Manual Alternative
		☐	Param. effectivities

Value Contract

Value contract matl		🗗
Contract Release Ctrl		

Service Management

Repair proced.	

Control of Resource-related Billing and Creation of Quotations

Billing form		DIP Prof.	

Figure 3.11 Define Item Category

5. The item category group, the item category of the higher-level item, and the item category usage all determine the item category in a sales document. The

default values for all possible combinations are maintained in Transaction VOV4 or via the menu path SAP IMG • SALES AND DISTRIBUTION • SALES • SALES DOCUMENTS • SALES DOCUMENT ITEM • ASSIGN ITEM CATEGORIES. The higher-level item plays a role in determining the item category of subitems—for example, when you use a bill of materials (BoM) or free goods.

6. Create reasons for rejecting an item using Transaction OVAG or following the menu path SAP IMG • SALES AND DISTRIBUTION • SALES • SALES DOCUMENTS • SALES DOCUMENT ITEM • DEFINE REASONS FOR REJECTION. While processing a sales document, you may have to reject some items and continue to process others. For example, a customer may request to supply some items immediately and delay other items for a month. As such, those that are to be supplied later are rejected, using the CUSTOMER REQUEST reason for rejection. When you process the order for delivery, in the delivery itself you will not find the items that were rejected. Subsequently, you can remove the reason for rejection and process it in another delivery. As you can see, this functionality can be used to manually split an order into two or more deliveries.

3.2.2 Schedule Line Categories

In addition to the item category, some order types (for example, where delivery is involved) can have schedule lines. You define the schedule line types using Transaction VOV6. To reach the screen shown in Figure 3.12, double-click on any schedule line category already created by copying an existing one. The default schedule lines are maintained for all combinations of item categories and MRP type via Transaction VOV5 or the menu path SAP IMG • SALES AND DISTRIBUTION • SALES • SALES DOCUMENTS • SCHEDULE LINES • ASSIGN SCHEDULE LINE CATEGORIES.

Material requirements planning (MRP) is a very important functionality in production planning and purchasing. All of the requirements for a material are transferred to this functionality based on MRP type. Consider the following examples of MRP types used to determine schedule line categories (and transfer requirements):

▶ V1: Manual reorder point with external requirements

▶ V2: Automatic reorder point with external requirements

▶ VB: Manual reorder point planning

- VI: Vendor-managed inventory

- VM: Automatic reorder point planning

- VS: Seasonal MRP

- VV: Forecast-based planning

- ND: No planning

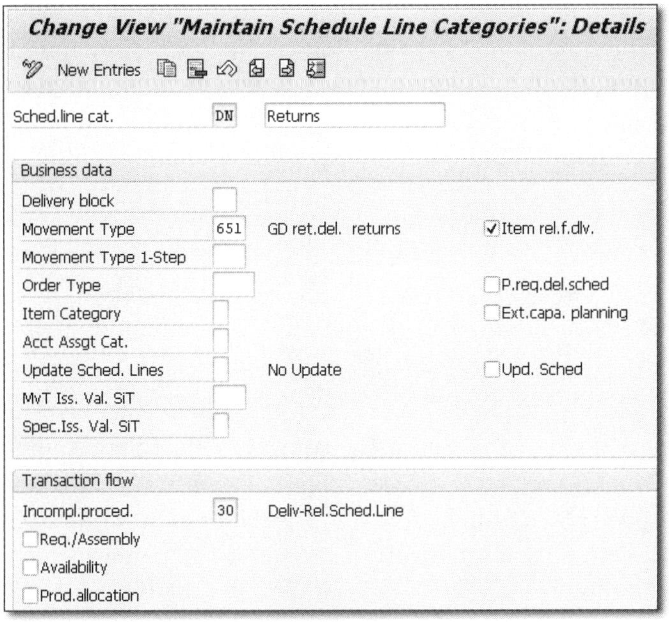

Figure 3.12 Define Schedule Line Category

Default Values

When assigning item categories and schedule line categories, you have the option of maintaining one default value. You can maintain eleven and nine other values, respectively, for item categories and schedule line categories, for possible manual entry at the time of document processing. In the configuration overview screen, only three values are visible. Double-click on the particular row to define more than three manual values, if required.

Now that you have a thorough understanding of item and schedule line categories, let's move on to creating a sales document with a reference.

3.3   Create with Reference

You can create a sales document with reference to another document. When you do this, you exert less effort and minimize the possibility of errors. That is optimization. Common examples are sales orders created with reference to a quotation, and credit or debit memo requests created with reference to a billing document. This process reduces the redundancy of data entry and error in data entry. You can also add a validation or check, decide which data should be copied, and manipulate data. Use VOFM routines to perform these functions. SAP ERP offers several VOFM routines, which are ABAP programs that are called when you create one document with reference to another:

- Copying requirements
- Data transfer
- Requirements
- Formulas

Figure 3.13 shows how the routines relevant for the Sales and Distribution functionality in SAP ERP are further classified. When you create sales documents with reference, only the first two types play a role. The copying requirement routine checks if certain prerequisites are fulfilled. Data transfer routines decide which data to transfer from the reference document to the target document. In addition to the standard routines, you can create your own using allowed name spaces 600 to 999 for your specific requirement. You should not modify the standard routines. The standard routines are used in several situations in SAP ERP that you may not know about. Modifying them may solve your problem in one process but simultaneously create trouble in another.

There are five types of copying requirements:

- Orders copying requirements routines
- Deliveries copying requirements routines
- Billing documents copying requirements routines
- Sales activities copying requirements routines (no standard routine is available, but you can create your own)
- Texts copying requirements routines

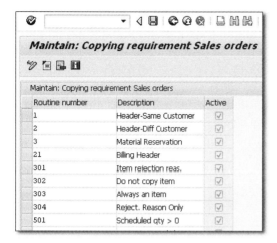

Figure 3.13 Routines Used in Sales and Distribution Processes

The first four types of routines execute before the creation of order, delivery, invoice, or sales activity, respectively. The texts copying requirement routine is checked to determine if text will transfer from the reference to the target document. Table 3.3 lists the different standard order copying requirement routines, and what they check for in creating the target document.

Order Copying Requirement	Checks
1 (header – same customer)	Sold-to and sales areas are same in target and reference document.
2 (header – different customer)	Sold-to can differ, but sales areas are same for target and reference document.
21 (billing header)	Same sold-to, sales area, and currency. Valid header division in the reference billing document.
301 (item rejection reason)	Rejected items are not copied.
302 (do not copy item)	Item categories with this routine assigned are not copied to target document.
303 (always an item)	Item categories with this routine assigned are always copied to target document.
304 (rejection reason only)	Only the rejected items are copied.
501 (schedule quantity > 0)	Only the schedule lines with some quantity are copied.
502 (do not copy schedule line)	Schedule lines are not copied.

Table 3.3 Order Copying Requirement Routines

Your requirement can be the same as the order copying requirement 1 (header – same customer; the first entry in Table 3.3), but with some additional requirements. For example, in addition to sold-to party and sales area, you may want the ship-to party of both the target and source documents to be the same. You can create a new routine 601 by copying the ABAP code in routine 1 and adding your requirements to it. After activating the new program, you can assign it to the copy rules for some document types.

There are three types of delivery copy requirement routines. The first type checks the reference sales document, and includes the standard routines 1, 2, 3, 101, and 102. The second type determines if several reference documents can be combined into one delivery, and includes routines 51 and 151. The third type validates the manual addition of items into an existing delivery, and includes routines 201 and 202.

You can create a billing document with reference to an order, delivery, billing (such as invoice cancellation), or external EDI document. Thus, there are four types of billing copy requirement routines. The first group (which includes 1, 2, 7, 8, 12, 20, 21, 23, 26, and 28) validates the reference order document. The second type checks the reference order document (including 3, 4, 9, 10, 11, 14, 15, 18, 19, and 24). The third type checks the reference billing document (including 5, 6, 16, 17, 27, and 29). The fourth type checks the external EDI document (13, 22, and 25).

The text copy requirement routine 1 (which references the document header) checks if the reference document header has a text entry. If it finds a text entry, the routine can copy that entry to the target document. Text copy requirement routine 50 (reference document item) does the same for items.

The copying requirements routines only check if the target document can be created from the source document; the data transfer routines are what make the actual data transfer. These routines can transfer data to targets from the source document, or from customization, with or without manipulation. The different types of these routines include orders, deliveries, billing documents, sales activities, handling units, texts, text names, and shipments.

When a newly created order references another sales or billing document, contract, or billing plan, the order data transfer routines can transfer the data. For example, data transfer routines for transferring data from a bill to an order (e.g., with reference return) are 3, 4, 52, 53, 103, 104, 153, and 403.

The delivery data transfer routines transfer data from the reference document to the delivery. The routines delivered by SAP ERP are 1, 2, 3, 101, 102, 110, 201, 202, 301, 302, 303, 500, and 510.

Billing transfer routines, on the other hand, transfer data from the reference document to the billing document. The billing data transfer routines delivered by SAP ERP include 1, 2, 3, 5, 6, 7, 8, and 10. The sales activity data transfer routines transfer data from a reference sales document to a sales activity. The SAP ERP–delivered standard routines are 1 and 2. The handling unit data transfer routines perform their role when a newly created delivery references to a scheduling agreement. The standard routine is 1.

Text data transfer routines transfer text when you create one document that references another. Standard texts are automatically copied from the reference to the target document, and don't require these data transfer routines, which only come into play for the user-defined routines.

Text name data transfer routines 1 to 11 are not used for data transfer. Rather, they are hard-coded into different programs, and determine how the texts are stored in different tables, such as tables STXH and STXL.

Shipment data transfer routines 1 to 12 transfer data from the delivery to the shipment.

In the post-implementation phase, process improvement often requires the replacement of these routines, sometimes with customized routines. We'll see those soon.

SAP Fiori for Sales

At the time of writing, there are several important SAP Fiori apps for sales and quotes to keep in mind.

Description	Requirements
Using the *My Quotations* transactional app, you can generate quotations or modify them using a tablet or laptop—directly at the customer's location.	SAP EHP 7 for SAP ERP 6.0 SP 02
You can use the *Sales Order* fact sheet app to display sales quotations and navigate to related business objects and transactional apps. You can access header/item and business data along with sold-to/ship-to data.	SAP EHP 7 for SAP ERP 6.0 SP 02

Description	Requirements
You can create or display sales orders in the field using the *Create Sales Order* transactional app. Display or reorder products, browse and search for sales orders and products, check customer price and availability, select ship-to, and determine multiple or single orders.	SAP ERP 6.0 SP 15 or higher
You can change or display sales orders in the field interactively using the *Change Sales Orders* transactional app. Browse and search for orders, change the ship-to, and access sales order details.	SAP ERP 6.0 SPS 15 or higher
The *Change Shipping Address* transactional app lets you to change a shipping address. Browse and search for a list of orders and sales orders details with this app.	SAP EHP 7 for SAP ERP 6.0 SP 08
You can use the *Sales Contract* fact sheet app to display sales contracts and navigate to related business objects and transactional apps. Header/item, status, and business data are accessible along with sold-to/ship-to data.	SAP EHP 7 for SAP ERP 6.0 SP 02
Sales group contractual information is accessed via the *Sales Group Contract* fact sheet app. You can get header/item, sold-to, and contracts data, along with material info, when this app is activated in the backend.	SAP EHP 7 for SAP ERP 6.0 SP 02
You can use the *Track Sales Orders* transactional app to track and display sales orders, view sales orders or purchase orders by customer, search sales orders, and display deliveries.	SAP ERP 6.0 SP 15 or higher
The *Sales Order Fulfillment Issues* analytical app is part of the SAP Smart Business cockpit in the backend. This app allows you to detect issues on sales orders fulfillment by showing you a sales orders list with any items that cannot be completed highlighted.	SAP Smart Business 1.0 for SAP ERP

3.4 Order Management with SAP Jam

SAP now integrates with social media and collaboration, and SAP Jam is a new vehicle for order management with Sales and Distribution, expediting sales cycles and further engaging customers and employees.

EHP 7 delivered the SAP Jam integration for Sales and Distribution and SAP CRM sales processes (business function LOG_SD_JAM_INTEG and component SD-BF-JAM). EHP 7 also provides enhancements to use the SAP Gateway notifications in order for the Sales and Distribution messages to reach SAP Jam groups and subscriptions. Once SAP Jam is enabled, the services for objects will show the SAP Jam FOLLOW/UNFOLLOW options in each of the Sales and Distribution documents, as shown in Figure 3.14. The main configuration steps are listed below. Make sure that, on the ABAP side, the Social Media ABAP Integration component (BC_SRV_STW_03) is activated.

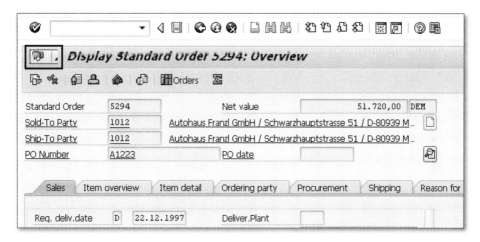

Figure 3.14 Sales Order Services for Object Menu

Table 3.4 lists the Sales and Distribution business objects relevant for SAP Jam notification. Each SAP user can decide which level of notification he or she should receive. If the FOLLOW option is selected, the user will receive notifications every time the Sales and Distribution object changes or updates. The notifications are received in the SAP Jam page. With the UNFOLLOW option, on the other hand, you can turn off the notifications received per Sales and Distribution object.

Sales and Distribution Business Objects	Follow	Unfollow
Sales orders	X	X
Invoices	X	X
Quotations	X	X
Customers business objects	X	X
Outbound deliveries	X	X

Table 3.4 SAP Jam Follow/Unfollow Supported for Sales and Distribution Business Objects

You can find detailed configuration steps and the components needed for SAP Jam Integration via the SAP Jam integration with Sales and Distribution in SAP Note 2071934. However, there are two main prerequisites for the SAP Jam integrator: a valid SAP Jam license registered and installed in your system, usually provided by the account executive of your company, and the configured interface to the Social Media ABAP Integration Library (SAIL). SAP Note 2067682 provides you with the necessary configuration if you require Sales and Distribution-Jam integration for outbound deliveries.

1. **Subscriptions in SD**

   One important prerequisite on the ABAP side is to activate the Social Media ABAP Integration (BC_SRV_STW_03). Documentation is available under the name Enable Social Media ABAP Integration 3.

2. **Generic Object Service (GOS)**

   This can only be displayed if the SET/GET PARAMETER ID field and value SD_SWU_ACTIVE are associated to the user profile. Use Transaction SU3 and enter such parameters in the PARAMETERS TAB. In the PARAMETER VALUE field, make sure that you enter "x" or "*" and save. You should be able to see GOS in each change, and display transactions for each business object.

   The business function ESJI_NOTIF_RECEIVERS enables the business objects and customer objects described below, allowing SAP Jam Follow/Unfollow notifications, and it will also allow you to enable the Business Configuration (BC set) ESJI_NOTIF_RECEIVERS. Customer and Quotations business object notifications are activated via this BC set.

3. **SAP Gateway Server**

   This is the configuration of the ESJI+SD_SRV OData Services (See OData in following section). Basically, you register the ESJI+SD_SRV OData Services in the SAP Gateway system.

4. **SAIL on the SAP Gateway Server**

   In this step, you activate the ESJI+SD_SRV OData Services in SAP Gateway.

5. **SAIL in the application Back End**

   Provides an ABAP API to help use external service providers, including SAP Jam. SAIL provides an OData service registry as a reuse component for SAP applications.

You can find the full SAP Gateway configuration guide in sections 3, 4 and 5 of the provided documentation, called "SAP Gateway Server of the SAIL Configuration Guide Distributing SAP Gateway Notifications to SAP Jam."

3.5   Copy Control

In the post-implementation phase, copy control is one of the few tools in the Sales and Distribution functionality in SAP ERP that you will frequently revisit. Once your implementation is live, and it's very difficult to visualize the finer details of the copy control rules. Another complicating factor is that companies change (or improve) their business processes, which may also require changes in copy control rules. For example, you may need to determine the following:

▶ Whether the invoice will have the same price as the order or whether it will recalculate the price

▶ Whether one sales return document contains items delivered from a different plant

▶ Whether the manual addition of a line item in a delivery is allowed

As you know, you can create an order can with reference to another sales document (order, quotation, inquiry), or billing document. When a new sales document references another sales document, Transaction VTAA defines the copy control rules. Similarly, when a new sales document references a billing document, Transaction VTAF defines the copy control rules. Table 3.5 provides a complete list of the copy control transaction codes and their corresponding target and source documents.

Transaction	Target Document	Source Document
VTAA	Sales (A)	Sales (A)
VTAF	Sales (A)	Billing document (F)
VTLA	Delivery document (L)	Sales (A)
VTFA	Billing document (F)	Sales (A)
VTFL	Billing document (F)	Delivery document (L)
VTFF	Billing document (F)	Billing document (F)

Table 3.5 Copy Control Transactions

To create any order document type with reference to another order document type, you must maintain the copy control rules using Transaction VTAA. In this example, we're creating the document type OR (standard order) with reference to document type QT (quotation). Observe the data transfer (DATAT) and copying requirement routines in Figure 3.15, Figure 3.16, and Figure 3.17. As mentioned earlier, you can have your customized routines replace these standard routines.

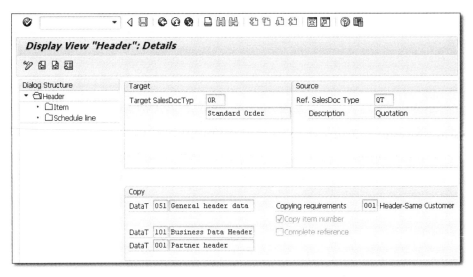

Figure 3.15 Copy Control for QT to OR Document Type at Header Level

At the header level of copy control (see Figure 3.15), the COPY ITEM NUMBER checkbox copies the item number of the source document to the item number of the target document. When you select the COMPLETE REFERENCE checkbox, you are unable to delete items copied from the source document in the target document.

Once you've defined the copy control rules at the header level, you have to define the copy control rule for all applicable item categories. In this example, item category AGN (standard item in quotation) is shown in Figure 3.16. The FPLA field is simply a field for the copy requirement routine that checks whether certain requirements have been fulfilled when data transfers from the BILLING PLAN field. Apart from the data transfer and copy requirement routines, the following fields are defined:

▸ The COPY SCHEDULE LINES field is selected when the schedule lines are to be copied.

▸ The POS./NEG. QUANTITY field is left blank (or option 0) when the quantity field in the target document will have neither a positive (option +) nor negative (option -) effect on the source document. (For example, a pro forma invoice created with reference to a delivery.) If the target document reduces the available quantity for another source document, the effect is positive. When the target document quantity increases the available quantity in the source document for other target documents, the effect is negative. For example, if you have a quantity contract for 100 units, a sales order created for 20 units will reduce the available quantity in the contract for other order to 80 units (positive effect), and a return of 10 units will increase it to 90 units from 80 unit (negative effect).

▶ Even when the Copy Quantity field is blank, the system will still copy the quantity based on the routines used. Because of this, we recommend leaving the field blank.

▶ The Pricing Type field determines the pricing in the target document. Table 3.6 lists the possible pricing types. For example, pricing type G keeps the value of all of the condition types the same in the target document as it was in the source document, except for the tax. The condition types defined as tax are redetermined. If there is a change in condition records, then the value of the condition type automatically changes when the target document is created.

▶ The Update Document Flow field updates the FBVA table. Document flow is the link that connects the target and source documents. The information is stored in table VBFA. The document flow icon, available in orders, deliveries, and invoices (application tool bar), can be display the document flow. There is a header-level document flow, and for each item, an item level document flow may also exist. If the document flow is required, then select option X. If it is not required, simply leave the field blank. To create document flow records, except for delivery and goods issue and billing documents, select option 2. This option improves system performance. Unlike the standard document flow that tracks all of the documents linked to a billing, delivery, or goods issue (GI) document, here you have to track the document flow from the target to the source document where the target is a billing, delivery, or GI document, and track the source of the sales order. The source can be a quotation or a contract. So, you avoid the redundant link between the quotation or contract and the billing or delivery document.

▶ If the Do not copy batch checkbox is selected, the items copy without batches.

▶ The Configuration field can be blank (no particular control), A (copy configuration/do not fix), B (copy/fix configuration), or C (copy configuration/automatically fixed). If the configuration is fixed, then the bill of materials for the item does not re-explode.

▶ The REEXPLODE STRUCTURE/FREE GOODS checkbox, when selected, reexplodes the bill of materials or free goods structure in the target document.

▶ The CONT. ITEM COPY MODE indicator is useful when the source document is a value contract.

▶ The COPY PRODUCT SELECT. indicator determines if product selection should be redone in the target document or copied. Again, if you're in the target document, you can cancel the copied product selection.

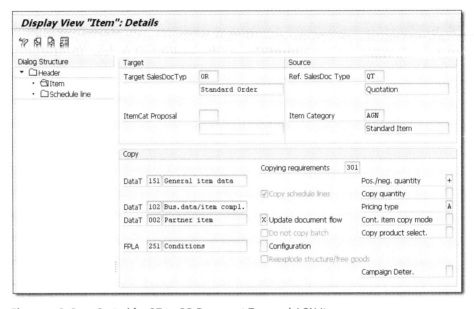

Figure 3.16 Copy Control for QT to OR Document Type and AGN Item

Pricing Type	Description
A	Copy price components and redetermine scales
B	Carry out new pricing
C	Copy manual pricing elements and redetermine the others
D	Copy pricing elements unchanged
E	Adopt price components and fix values
F	Copy pricing elements, turn value and fix
G	Copy pricing elements unchanged and redetermine taxes

Table 3.6 Examples of Pricing Types

Pricing Type	Description
H	Redetermine freight conditions
I	Redetermine rebate conditions
J	Redetermine confirmed purchase net price/value (KNTYP=d)
K	Adopt price components and cost and redetermine taxes
M	Copy pricing elements, turn value
N	Transfer pricing components unchanged, new cost
O	Redetermine variant conditions (KNTYP=O)
Q	Redetermine calculation conditions (KNTYP=Q)
U	Redetermine precious metal conditions (KNTYP=U)

Table 3.6 Examples of Pricing Types (Cont.)

Finally, as shown in Figure 3.17, you can customize copy control rules for the schedule line. In this case, we have shown the schedule line category BP. The Proposed Schedule Line Category (SCHDLNECATPROPOSAL) field is left blank so that it will take a value as per the configuration setting. Copy requirement 501 means only the schedule lines with some quantity will transfer to the source document.

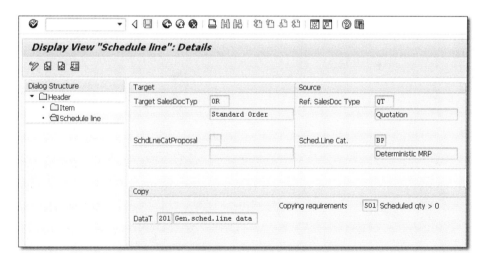

Figure 3.17 Copy Control for QT to OR Document Type and BP Schedule Line

In this section, we discussed the copy control Transaction VTAA (remember—there are five other transactions) for copy control from quotation (QT) to standard order (OR). There are usually several source documents and several target documents for item category AGN (again, several item-level categories are possible). The copy control for schedule line level is only relevant when the target document is an order (i.e., Transactions VTAA and VTAF). At all levels there are data transfer and copying requirement routines, either standard or customized, which can fine-tune the system. We also discussed the data transfer and copying requirement routines in Section 3.3, and you now know where to assign them in configuration. This is the most important activity in projects at the post-implementation stage. We don't go into the details of the ABAP code of the standard routines and how you can insert your own code, because that is a subject for technical developers.

In the next section we discuss the partner determination functionality that SAP ERP offers.

3.6 Partner Determination

In Sales and Distribution documents, you can configure the system to automatically determine partners. The customers, employees, and vendors have different *partner functions*. Sometimes the same customer can be a sold-to party (AG/SP), ship-to party (WE/SH), bill-to party (RE/BP), and payer (RG/PY). Sometimes a sold-to party can have several ship-to parties, a different payer, and a bill-to party. Normally the sold-to party issued the purchase order, the ship-to party received the delivery, the bill-to party's name appears on the invoice, and the payer issued the payment. As the business becomes more complex, the number of partner functions can increase.

The partner determination procedure can be individually assigned to the following objects:

▸ Customer master

▸ Sales document header

▸ Sales document item

▸ Delivery

▸ Shipment

▸ Billing header

▸ Billing item

▶ Sales activities (CAS)

To access these objects for partner determination, follow the menu path SAP IMG • SALES AND DISTRIBUTION • BASIC FUNCTIONS • PARTNER DETERMINATION • SET UP PARTNER DETERMINATION or use Transaction VOPAN.

The steps for partner determination are as follows:

1. **Execute partner function conversion.**
   In this step the partner function keys are maintained for different languages.

2. **Create partner functions**.
   Several standard partner functions are available, and you can create your own partner functions if required.

3. **Assign partner function to customer account groups.**
   Partner functions are assigned to different customer account groups.

4. **Create partner determination procedure.**
   For each type of object, such as the customer master, sales document header, and others already mentioned, you can create a new partner determination procedure, or modify the standard SAP-delivered procedures. In the partner determination procedure, you can list all of the allowed partner functions and indicate whether the partner function is NOT MODIFIABLE. If you select this checkbox, it means that once the Sales and Distribution document or the customer master record is created, the partner function cannot change. Similarly, if the MANDATORY checkbox is selected, then in order to create the Sales and Distribution document or CMR, you must enter the specific partner function or functions selected.

5. **Assign partner determination procedure.**
   After their creation, partner determination procedures are assigned to customer account groups for the customer master, to sales document types for the sales document header, and to item categories for the sales document item. Deliveries and shipments receive assignments to the delivery types and shipment types, respectively, the billing header and billing item receive assignments to billing type, and the sales activities receive assignments to sales activity type.

3.7 Availability Check and Transfer of Requirements

When the customer gives you an order, he expects a confirmation that the ordered material will arrive on time and in the quantity specified. You, in turn, expect the SAP ERP system to check the availability and find out if the material is available in sufficient quantity, or if it will be available to promise (ATP).

Because this quantity is also transferred as a confirmed requirement, ATP is very important, not only as a customer service, but also for production planning. An availability check in a sales document or delivery and a transfer of requirements to MRP from Sales and Distribution are two independent processes, though they normally go together. The transfer of requirements can happen for an individual schedule line of an order (individual requirement), or all quantities in the schedule lines of all orders of a day or week can be combined (collective requirement), based on following criteria:

▶ Plant

▶ Batch

▶ Storage location

▶ Date

▶ Transaction

▶ Requirements class

The availability check and transfer of requirement are specific to a plant. When you check a material for availability you do so for one plant, regardless of whether it is available in another. So, in the transfer of requirements, the requirements are generated and transferred to the plant listed in the sales order or stock transfer order as the delivery plant.

Availability

Transaction CO09 provides the availability overview for a specific material in a particular plant. You can also use Transactions MB52, MB5T, MMBE, MB5B, and others used in Inventory Management for further information on availability. A material master record (PLANT STOCK and STORAGE LOCATION STOCK tabs) gives you another way to manually check the availability (using Transaction MM03). Remember, manual checking and transfers are not what an ERP system is for. Regardless, this information will be useful while you test your settings for availability check and transfer of requirements.

The steps for activating the availability check and transfer of requirements (TOR) are provided as follows:

1. Activate the availability check and transfer of requirements using Transaction OVZG or by following the menu path SAP IMG • SALES AND DISTRIBUTION • BASIC FUNCTIONS • AVAILABILITY CHECK AND TRANSFER OF REQUIREMENTS • DEFINE REQUIREMENTS CLASSES, as shown in Figure 3.18. You can create your own requirement class if the available ones are not suitable. Selecting the first two checkboxes (AVAILABILITY CHECK (AvC) and TRANSFER OF REQUIREMENTS (Rq)) activates the availability check and transfer of requirements functions, respectively.

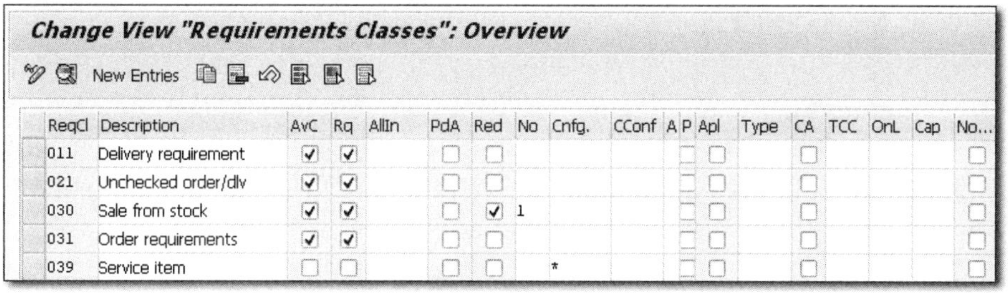

Change View "Requirements Classes": Overview

ReqCl	Description	AvC	Rq	AllIn	PdA	Red	No	Cnfg.	CConf	A	P	Apl	Type	CA	TCC	OnL	Cap	No...
011	Delivery requirement	✓	✓		☐	☐						☐		☐				☐
021	Unchecked order/dlv	✓	✓		☐	☐						☐		☐				☐
030	Sale from stock	✓	✓		☐	✓	1					☐		☐				☐
031	Order requirements	✓	✓		☐	☐						☐		☐				☐
039	Service item	☐	☐		☐	☐		*				☐		☐				☐

Figure 3.18 Define Requirement Classes

2. Use Transaction OVZH to assign the requirement class to the requirement type or follow the menu path SAP IMG • SALES AND DISTRIBUTION • BASIC FUNCTIONS • AVAILABILITY CHECK AND TRANSFER OF REQUIREMENTS • DEFINE REQUIREMENT TYPES.

3. Assign the requirement type to the possible combinations of item categories and MRP types using Transaction OVZI or following the menu path SAP IMG • SALES AND DISTRIBUTION • BASIC FUNCTIONS • AVAILABILITY CHECK AND TRANSFER OF REQUIREMENTS • DETERMINATION OF REQUIREMENT TYPES USING TRANSACTION. You maintain the MRP type in the material master record (MRP 1 tab) of the material.

4. The previous three steps will make the availability check and TOR active (or inactive) at a global or requirement class level. When it's active for a requirement class, you can make it inactive at the schedule line category level using Transaction OVZ8 or OVZ8X.

5. Using Transaction OVZK, you can make the availability check inactive for any delivery item category when the global setting in the preceding step ensures that the availability check is active. Please note that for this step and the preceding ones, the reverse case is not valid. That is, when the global setting makes the availability check and/or TOR inactive, you cannot activate it for a specific schedule line category or delivery item category.

Now let's discuss the specific customization requirements for availability checks and transfer of requirements.

3.7.1 Availability Check

When a customer makes an order, he specifies the materials, quantity, and delivery date. The order for the customer and for the particular material is generally filled from a specific delivery plant, so long as the customer is not blocked because of a credit limit or another reason. When an order enters the SAP system, the following information defines how the availability check carries out a few key items:

▶ Date of delivery: whether you can change the date.

▶ Part delivery: whether the customer will accept partial delivery.

▶ Stock blocked by other processes: whether you can use stock that is currently blocked or reserved by other processes.

▶ Delivery from a different plant: whether stock available at another plant should be considered available.

▶ Credit and other block: whether you'll carry out the check even when the order will not be delivered due to credit or another mitigating factor.

▶ Requested batch: whether you'll ignore the requested batch while checking availability.

▶ Replenishment lead time: the average time required to make any quantity of stock available, either by procurement or production. You have to decide whether to use replenishment lead time during an availability check.

▶ Safety stock: the stock that should always be available for an emergency. Your stock level should never fall short of this level for the particular material. You have to decide whether to use it for the availability check.

▶ Stock in transit: material that has been dispatched by a plant, but not yet received at the destination plant. You have to decide whether it is available for availability check.

Three types of availability checks are possible:

1. **Available to promise (ATP)**
   The availability check checks against the ATP quantity, which calculates according to your configuration. We'll discuss this later in this chapter.

2. **Planning**
   The availability check is carried out for planned independent requirements, which is expected sales independent of individual orders.

3. **Product allocation**
   The materials are allocated to different customers or -customer groups (in a week, month, or year). Materials become available to the customer until the allocated quantities are used (or consumed).

For the first two types of availability check (ATP and planning), follow these customization steps:

1. **Define checking groups.**
   Define checking groups using Transaction OVZ2 or following the menu path SAP IMG • Sales and Distribution • Basic Functions • Availability Check and Transfer of Requirements • Availability Check • Availability Check with ATP Logic or Against Planning • Define Checking Groups.

   Using checking groups, you can club (or add up) the requirements for individual orders on a daily or weekly basis. For example, you receive thousands of orders for Material A, and there are several hundred in stock. While creating a weekly production plan, it would be better if the production department could see the requirements from last few weeks.

   It addition, it would also be helpful for your production department to know the weekly requirements during the same timeframe last year. You can use standard checking group 02 (individual requirements) when the clubbing is not required. While creating the material master record for a material, you specify the checking group to which it applies in the Sales: Sales Org.2 tab. You can define the default values for each plant and material type combination using Transaction OVZ3, which will automatically feed into the material master record when it's created.

As shown in Figure 3.19, when defining the checking group, you specify the following:

- The TOTALSALES and TOTDLVREQS fields specify whether an individual record (A) or all records of a period are to be considered for sales orders and deliveries, respectively.
- When selected, the BLOCK QTRQ checkbox blocks the material for use by any other user, during an availability check by one user in a document. The block, and whether a material is available to multiple simultaneous users, can be further fine-tuned using Transaction OVZ1.
- The NO CHECK checkbox, when selected, prevents an availability check.
- The ACCUMUL. field defines how and whether the quantities are cumulated during order processing.
- The RESPONSE field defines whether there will be a response if the availability check results in a shortfall.
- The RELCHKPLAN field defines whether the checking is performed against a planned quantity.

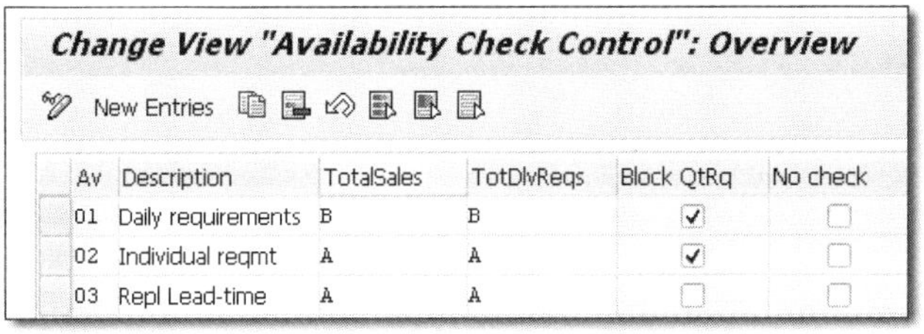

Av	Description	TotalSales	TotDlvReqs	Block QtRq	No check
01	Daily requirements	B	B	☑	☐
02	Individual reqmt	A	A	☑	☐
03	Repl Lead-time	A	A	☐	☐

Figure 3.19 Checking Group for Availability Check

2. **Modify the checking rule.**
   Using Transaction OVZ9 or following the menu path SAP IMG • SALES AND DISTRIBUTION • BASIC FUNCTIONS • AVAILABILITY CHECK AND TRANSFER OF REQUIREMENTS • AVAILABILITY CHECK • AVAILABILITY CHECK WITH ATP LOGIC OR AGAINST PLANNING • CARRY OUT CONTROL FOR AVAILABILITY CHECK, you will see the list of checking rules preconfigured and preassigned to the checking groups. When you select any entry and click on the DETAILS icon, you find the screen shown in Figure 3.20, where you can modify the rule (though it is not recommended).
3. **Maintain the requirements class.**
   The requirement class, along with requirements type, checking group, and schedule line category, determine the availability check and transfer of

requirements. You identify the standard requirements classes that you can use or create your own using Transaction OMPO or by following the menu path SAP IMG • PRODUCTION • PRODUCTION PLANNING • DEMAND MANAGEMENT • PLANNED INDEPENDENT REQUIREMENTS • REQUIREMENTS TYPES/REQUIREMENTS CLASSES • MAINTAIN REQUIREMENTS CLASSES. Examples of requirement classes are make-to-stock production, gross requirement planning, and so on.

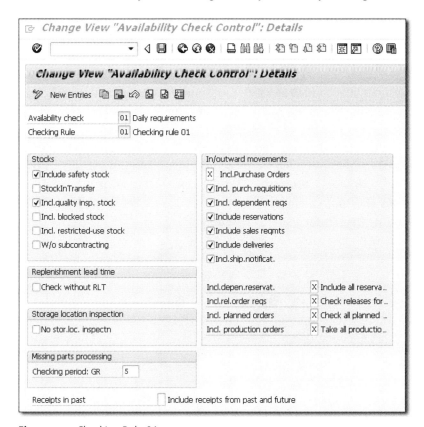

Figure 3.20 Checking Rule 01

Availability Check and TOR

The combination of requirement class, requirements type, checking group, and schedule line category (or delivery item category) determine the availability check and transfer of requirements. This means you have the flexibility to keep certain materials (e.g., material that is available to you on a consignment basis) out of the availability check and/or transfer of requirements. This is typically done by using the checking group key for the material in the material master record.

4. **Define the requirements type**.

   You create requirement types using Transaction OMP1 or following the menu path SAP IMG • Production • Production Planning • Demand Management • Requirements Types/Requirements Classes • Define Requirements Types and Allocate Requirements Class.

5. **Create a strategy group.**

   You customize the strategy group (in the MRP 3 tab of the material master record) using Transaction OPPT or by following the menu path SAP IMG • Production • Production Planning • Demand Management • Planned Independent Requirements • Planning Strategy • Define Strategy Group. A strategy group, as shown in Figure 3.21, will have one main planning strategy and seven other possible strategies. At the document level, you can change from the default strategy without changing the strategy group to any one of the above-listed strategies. Before defining the strategy group, you can define the strategy using Transaction OPPS or by following the menu path SAP IMG • Production • Production Planning • Demand Management • Planned Independent Requirements • Planning Strategy • Define Strategy. As you can see in Figure 3.22, the setting for standard strategy group is 40.

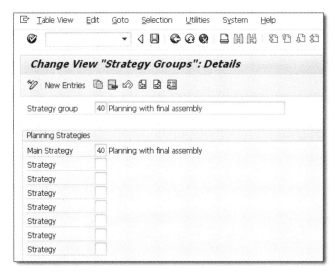

Figure 3.21 Strategy Group 40

6. **Assign a strategy group to a material.**

   There are two options for assigning a strategy group to a material.

▸ You can directly assign the strategy group to the material in the MRP 3 tab of the material master record.

▸ You can assign the strategy group to the MRP group using Transaction OPPU or following the menu path SAP IMG • PRODUCTION • PRODUCTION PLANNING • DEMAND MANAGEMENT • PLANNED INDEPENDENT REQUIREMENTS • PLANNING STRATEGY • ASSIGN MRP GROUP TO STRATEGY GROUP. The MRP group is then assigned to the material master record MRP 1 tab.

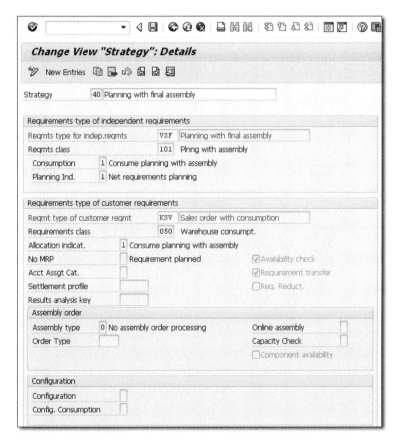

Figure 3.22 Strategy 40

Product allocation means automatically making a material available to a group of customers. The allocated quantity to each group is subsequently allocated to each customer of that group. In other words, there is a fixed quantity of material available to a customer during a particular period of time (a day, week, or month), which itself is a fixed fraction of the total available quantity. In this scenario, the availability check follows a different set of rules. A key element of the product allocation is the standard information structure (info structure) S140, which stores the allocated quantities and is updated by each incoming order.

Additional Resources

Refer to SAP Notes 64636 (Procedure for Statistical Data Setup in LIS) and 651162 (Reorganization of S140: Additional Information) if the sales orders are not properly updating the info structure S140.

To customize an availability check based on product allocation, follow these steps:

1. Create product allocation determination procedure using Transaction OV1Z or following the menu path SAP IMG • SALES AND DISTRIBUTION • BASIC FUNCTIONS • AVAILABILITY CHECK AND TRANSFER OF REQUIREMENTS • AVAILABILITY CHECK • AVAILABILITY CHECK AGAINST PRODUCT ALLOCATION • MAINTAIN PROCEDURE. Assign the new procedure to the material master record of a material in the PRODUCT ALLOCATION field in the BASIC DATA 1 tab.

2. Define product allocation object using Transaction OV2Z or following the menu path SAP IMG • SALES AND DISTRIBUTION • BASIC FUNCTIONS • AVAILABILITY CHECK AND TRANSFER OF REQUIREMENTS • AVAILABILITY CHECK • AVAILABILITY CHECK AGAINST PRODUCT ALLOCATION • DEFINE OBJECT.

3. Specify hierarchy. In this step, you assign an info structure to the product allocation determination procedure using Transaction OV3Z or following the menu path SAP IMG • SALES AND DISTRIBUTION • BASIC FUNCTIONS • AVAILABILITY CHECK AND TRANSFER OF REQUIREMENTS • AVAILABILITY CHECK • AVAILABILITY CHECK AGAINST PRODUCT ALLOCATION • SPECIFY HIERARCHY.

4. Assign an allocation object to the product allocation determination procedure using Transaction OV4Z or following the menu path SAP IMG • SALES AND DISTRIBUTION • BASIC FUNCTIONS • AVAILABILITY CHECK AND TRANSFER OF REQUIREMENTS • AVAILABILITY CHECK • AVAILABILITY CHECK AGAINST PRODUCT ALLOCATION • CONTROL PRODUCT ALLOCATION.

5. Define past and future consumption periods using Transaction OV5Z or following the menu path SAP IMG • SALES AND DISTRIBUTION • BASIC FUNCTIONS • AVAILABILITY CHECK AND TRANSFER OF REQUIREMENTS • AVAILABILITY CHECK •

AVAILABILITY CHECK AGAINST PRODUCT ALLOCATION • DEFINE CONSUMPTION PERI-ODS.

6. For collective product allocation, enter the info structure of the planning hierarchy using Transaction OV7Z or following the menu path SAP IMG • SALES AND DISTRIBUTION • BASIC FUNCTIONS • AVAILABILITY CHECK AND TRANSFER OF REQUIREMENTS • AVAILABILITY CHECK • AVAILABILITY CHECK AGAINST PRODUCT ALLOCATION • PERMIT COLLECTIVE PRODUCT ALLOCATION IN INFO STRUCTURES.

7. Perform a consistency check for each combination of product allocation determination procedure and product allocation object using Transaction OV8Z or following the menu path SAP IMG • SALES AND DISTRIBUTION • BASIC FUNCTIONS • AVAILABILITY CHECK AND TRANSFER OF REQUIREMENTS • AVAILABILITY CHECK • AVAILABILITY CHECK AGAINST PRODUCT ALLOCATION • CHECK SETTINGS IN PRODUCT ALLOCATION.

Availability Check Using SAP APO

If you're using SAP APO, you can define business transactions using the menu path SAP IMG • SALES AND DISTRIBUTION • BASIC FUNCTIONS • AVAILABILITY CHECK AND TRANSFER OF REQUIREMENTS • AVAILABILITY CHECK • RULE-BASED AVAILABILITY CHECK • DEFINE BUSINESS TRANSACTION. It should same as the business transactions defined in SAP APO using the menu path GLOBAL ATP • SETTINGS • RULE-BASED ATP • CONDITIONS • ASSIGN RULE STRATEGY. In Transaction VOV8, the business transaction attaches for each type of order.

3.7.2 Transfer of Requirements

There are no additional steps beyond those previously mentioned for activating the TOR. However, you can do some fine-tuning using routines that utilize Transactions OVB8 and OVB5, respectively, for transfer of requirements and for preventing the creation of a purchase requisition for TOR. For example, VOFM routine 102, shown in Listing 3.1, prevents a transfer of requirements in the event of credit check.

```
*-------------------------------------------------------------*
* FORM BEDINGUNG_PRUEFEN_102 *
* User checks for subsequent functions from a sales document*
* *
* Purchase requisition *
*-------------------------------------------------------------*

FORM BEDINGUNG_PRUEFEN_102.
```

```
* if there is not in simulation mode
 IF SIMUL_MODE EQ SPACE.
* No purchase requisition if a credit block exists.
 IF VBUK-CMGST CA 'B'.
* Read the subsequent function information for the message
 PERFORM FOFUN_TEXT_READ USING GL_FOFUN
 CHANGING FOFUN_TEXT.
 DA_SY-MSGID = 'V1'.
 DA_SY-MSGNO = '849'.
 DA_SY-MSGV1 = FOFUN_TEXT.
 ERROR_EXCEPTION = TRUE.
 ENDIF.
 ENDIF.
ENDFORM
*eject
```

Listing 3.1 VOFM Routine 102

Transfer of Requirements

The transfer of requirements displays at the sales or delivery document item level using the menu path ENVIRONMENT • AVAILABILITY from the overview screen. At the material level for the plant, you can use Transaction MD04.

Using Transactions VA02 or VA03, press [F4], select the SALES DOCUMENTS – NOT FULLY CONFIRMED tab, and press [Enter] to pull up the list of unconfirmed orders.

3.7.3 Global ATP

Let's now discuss about an important part of the SAP APO application: the Global Available-to-Promise (GATP). GATP is an enhancement to the regular ATP functionality we've already discussed. GATP's primary use in the Sales and Distribution module is as a means of improving the accuracy of product availability offered to customers, particularly in sales order processing. ATP checks at the customer sales orders use two main methods: basic and advanced ATP.

Figure 3.23 illustrates how the sales order sends the requirements to SAP APO, which in turns runs the GATP settings to check for availability based on the rules defined across multiple plants and levels. Once its requirements are verified, the sales order returns to SAP ERP with either a full confirmation, a partial confirmation, or no confirmation.

In contrast to regular ATP checks, GATP represents the look of your customer's requested product at the requested time, and the required quantity.

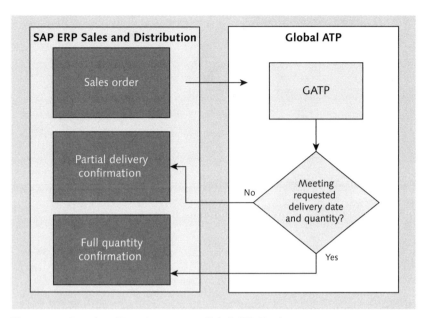

Figure 3.23 Transfer of Requirements to Global ATP Checks

You can configure GATP scenarios based on your company's specific configuration using either the basic or advanced methods among the plants and available locations, as shown in Table 3.7. Even though the det
ailed discussion in each of the ATP methods is outside the scope of this book, it's important for you to be familiar with these terms and methods.

Basic Methods	Advanced Methods
▶ Product availability check	▶ Combination of basic methods
▶ Product allocation	▶ Production (CTP or MATP)
▶ Check against forecast	▶ Rules-based ATP
	▶ Rules-based ATP and/or production

Table 3.7 Availability Check Methods

Table 3.8 describes the most commonly used documents in GATP and Sales and Distribution. You can run GATP for the sales orders or deliveries in addition to being able to execute availability checks during stock transfers. These two scenarios are commonly configured across multiple industries. On the other hand, you can also run GATP as a component of the production orders or the inventory good issue, serving then for availability checking done in Sales and Distribution and Materials Management.

Document	Samples
SD documents	Sales orders or deliveries
Stock transfers	Stock transfer requisitions, in-plant stock transfer reservations
Component check	Production orders, planned order, subcontract procurement
Inventory management	Good issue, check MM, reservation

Table 3.8 Global ATP Commonly Used Documents

If you want to implement GATP into your system, you have to configure the following main steps. Depending on your particular needs, you may still require additional configuration in both SAP APO and GATP.

1. **Global settings for availability check**
   Configure the global settings to allow an availability check. Follow the menu path Transaction SPRO • Advanced Planning and Optimization • Global Available-to-Promise (Global ATP) • General Settings • Maintain Global Settings for Availability Check.

2. **Maintain ATP group**
   The ATP group configuration should match and comply with the checking group in SAP ERP. Follow the menu path Transaction SPRO • Advanced Planning and Optimization • Global Available-to-Promise • Product Availability Check • Maintain ATP Group.

3. **Maintain check control**
   Check control is commonly configured to control the checking horizon. Non-checking horizon needs to be deactivated. Follow the menu path Transaction SPRO • Advanced Planning and Optimization • Global Available-to-Promise • Product Availability Check • Maintain Check Control.

4. **Maintain check mode**
   Verify that the check mode has transferred to SAP SCM. Follow the menu path Transaction SPRO • Advanced Planning and Optimization • Global Available-to-Promise • General Settings • Maintain Check Mode.

5. **Maintain check instructions**
   Definition of the instructions of the ATP scenarios. Follow the menu path Transaction SPRO • Advanced Planning and Optimization • Global Available-to-Promise • General Settings • Maintain Check Instruction.

6. **Maintain distribution definition**

This option outlines how to distribute the planning results to the backend system. Follow the menu path Transaction SPRO • Integration with SAP Components • Integration via APO Core Interface (CIF) • Basic Settings for Data Transfer • Publication • Maintain Distribution Definition.

3.8   Outline Agreements

In this section, we'll discuss customer contracts and scheduling agreements. There are four types of customer contracts: master contract, quantity contract, value contract, and service contract.

We will also look at scheduling agreements. Whereas the contract displays the materials and services sold during a particular period, the scheduling agreement refers to the quantities scheduled for delivery on different dates. All outline agreements are sales document types, and we'll give the standard document types shortly. The functions related to sales documents, such as price determination, partner determination, incompletion log, availability check, and other functions, also apply to outline agreements. You can create one document with reference to another based on copy control rules. Like many other sales documents, the essential parts of the outline agreements are price, quantity, sold-to party, and schedule lines. In scheduling agreements, there can be different schedule lines for forecasting (and subsequent production or purchase) and shipping.

In the next two sections, we'll discuss the customization requirements for contracts and the scheduling agreement.

3.8.1   Customer Contracts

You create contracts using Transaction VA41 or following the menu path SAP Easy Access • Logistics • Sales and Distribution • Sales • Contract • Create. The following are standard sales document types for scheduling agreements:

▸ GK: Master contract

▸ KM: Quantity contract

▸ MV: Rental contract

▸ WK1: Value contract – general

▸ WK2: Material-related value contract

▸ WV: Service and maintenances contract

Contracts do not contain any schedule lines, delivery dates, or delivery quantities. Release orders, which are similar to sales orders, are created with reference to the contract. The release orders have schedule lines and are processed like standard orders. Release orders created with reference to a contract will update that contract. For example, suppose a contract is for 100 units of one material. When a release order is created for 40 units, the updated quantity available for other release orders is 60 units. This action is governed by a copy control functionality. When customizing sales document type VOV8, you should specify for the release orders how the system will behave for the open outline agreements, choosing from among the following options:

▸ Blank: Do not check

▸ A: Check at header level

▸ B: Check at item level

▸ C: Check at header level and copy if unique

▸ D: Check at item level and copy if unique

▸ E: Check at header level and branch directly to selection list

▸ F: Check at item level and branch directly to selection list

When no option is selected (blank) there is no check. For options A and B, the outline agreements available for customers and materials are checked, and a dialog box appears to display the list. For options C and D, if just one outline agreement is available, it's automatically copied to the order. For options E and F, when one outline agreement is available, it behaves like options C and D. When more than one outline agreement is available, the system behaves like options A and B, but moves directly to the list without the intermediate dialog box.

The sales document types used to create a contract and the document types used for release orders are controlled by the fields shown previously in Figure 3.9, in Transaction VOV8. The PRICPROCCONDHEADR and PRICPROCCONDITEM fields are used to specify the pricing procedure of the contract at the header and item levels, respectively. In the billing request field, you specify the order type that will be used as the release order. The CONTRACT DATA ALLOWED indicator dictates whether the contract data is allowed for such document types and, if so, whether it's applicable to both the header (X) and item (Y) levels. The FOLLOW UP ACTIVITY TYPE field is for service contracts. If the order type of the subsequent process is fixed, it's entered in the SUBSEQ.ORDER TYPE field. The CHECK PARTNER AUTHORIZATION field checks if the user has the authorization to create a release order for the contract. When selected, the UPDATE LOWER LEVEL CONTRACT checkbox updates the lower-level contract for changes in the master contract. For this, you also have to activate the workflow for master contract using Transactions SWE2 and PFTC.

The contract profile is customized via Transaction VOVR or following the menu path SAP IMG • SALES AND DISTRIBUTION • SALES • SALES DOCUMENTS • CONTRACTS • CONTRACT DATA • DEFINE CONTRACT PROFILES. The profile is attached upon defining the sales document type. You can select the standard contract profile (i.e., 0001) and click on the COPY AS (F6) icon to reach the screen shown in Figure 3.24.

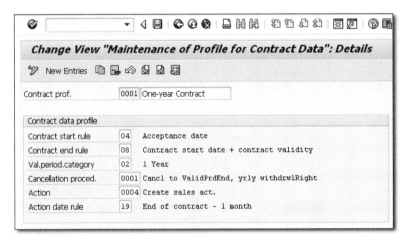

Figure 3.24 Customizing Contract Profile (Transaction VOVR)

You customize the options for the contract start and end rule and action date rule using Transaction OVBS or VOVP or following the menu path SAP IMG • SALES AND DISTRIBUTION • SALES • SALES DOCUMENTS • CONTRACTS • CONTRACT DATA • DEFINE RULES FOR DETERMINING DATE. The VALID PERIOD CATEGORY (e.g., 30 days, 3 months, or 2 years) field is customized via Transaction VOVO or following the menu path SAP IMG • SALES AND DISTRIBUTION • SALES • SALES DOCUMENTS • CONTRACTS • CONTRACT DATA • DEFINE VALIDITY PERIOD CATEGORIES. The cancellation reasons, procedure, and rules are defined via Transactions VOVQ, VOVM, and VOVL, respectively. You assign rules to the procedure using Transaction VOVN.

The GROUP REFERENCE PROCEDURE field, maintained in the screen shown in Figure 3.9, is customized via Transaction VORS or following the menu path SAP IMG • SALES AND DISTRIBUTION • SALES • SALES DOCUMENTS • CONTRACTS • MASTER

CONTRACT • DEFINE REFERENCING PROCEDURES. By selecting the existing procedure and clicking on the COPY AS icon ([F6]), you create a new procedure.

Before defining the reference procedure, you must define the master and target contracts using Transaction VORB or following the menu path SAP IMG • SALES AND DISTRIBUTION • SALES • SALES DOCUMENTS • CONTRACTS • MASTER CONTRACT • DEFINE REFERENCE SALES DOCUMENT TYPES. As shown in Figure 3.25, document type GK is the master contract for different contacts.

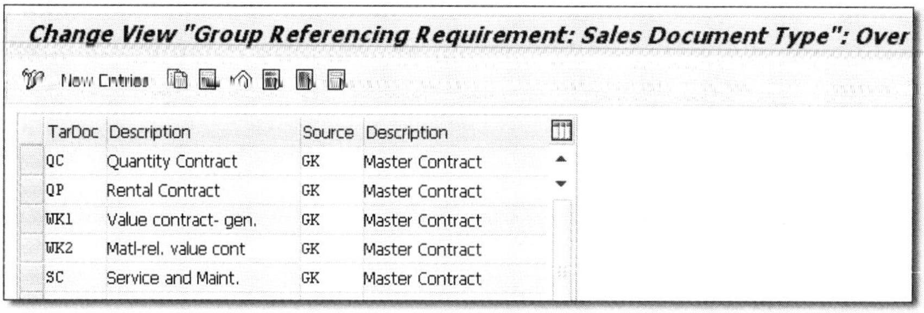

Figure 3.25 Defining Master Contract for Different Contract Types

By selecting the already created procedures and clicking on the FIELDS folder, you find a list of table fields with copy rules and message checkboxes, as shown in Figure 3.26.

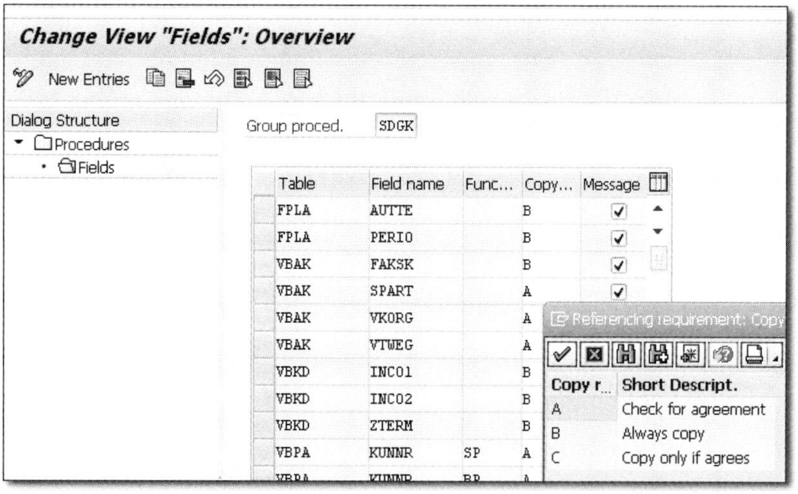

Figure 3.26 Group Reference Procedure for Contracts and Scheduling Agreements

In the group reference procedure, you specify the list of table fields that must be identical (copy rule A) for referencing a target document to a master document, while referencing one contract to a master contract, or copied to (copy rule C) the target from the master contract or copy as default values to the target contract. This, subsequently, can be modified (copy rule B).

3.8.2 Scheduling Agreement

A scheduling agreement is like a quantity contract, but with specific dates for the delivery of specific quantities of product. You create a schedule agreement using Transaction VA31 or following the menu path SAP EASY ACCESS • LOGISTICS • SALES AND DISTRIBUTION • SALES • SCHEDULING AGREEMENTS • CREATE. There can be several schedule lines for an item in a scheduling agreement. The scheduling agreement uses the delivery due list (Transaction VL10 or VL10A) or Transaction VL01N to create different deliveries and subsequent billing using a billing plan. The following are the standard sales document types for scheduling agreements:

▶ LK: Scheduling agreement external agency

▶ LP: Scheduling agreement

▶ LZ: Scheduling agreement w/rel.

▶ LZM: Scheduling agreement w/ dly ord.

▶ LZS: Scheduling agreement: self-bill w/inv.

3.9   Special Business Transactions

Some sales processes differ significantly from normal sales processes, in which material is procured or produced and stored. In this section, we'll discuss consignment sale processing, returnable packaging, make-to-order production, bills of materials, third-party order processing, and configurable materials in sales documents. In these processes, orders are delivered and then billed.

3.9.1   Consignment Sale Processing

Consignment sale is primarily used for industrial or trade sale, where the seller stocks the material at the buyer's premises or warehouse. When a seller has very few buyers, this option becomes beneficial to both buyer and seller. This is primarily done to increase sales, but there can be other reasons as well (e.g., a contract).

The transfer of ownership for stock does not change at the time of physical stock movement. This situation is called a *consignment process*. The seller keeps the stock at the customer's warehouse (consignment fill-up process), and the customer takes the material from the filled-up stock for his own use (consignment issue process). The consignment fill-up is subsequently delivered, but not invoiced. The standard delivery type LF (outbound delivery) or NK (consignment replenishment delivery) can be used to process consignment fill-up orders. The consignment issue, on the other hand, should be invoiced either directly (order relevant) or after delivery (normal delivery document type is to be used).

For returns, you have two possible processes: either you can take returns as you do in a standard return process, or you can return the material, already billed, to the consignment stock, using delivery type NKR (consignment replenishment return delivery). That stock may now return to the company warehouse, or be used for future customer orders. Note that you can use delivery type NKR even if the material is not sold as part of a consignment sale process. The stock that's physically present with the customer, either by consignment fill-up or consignment return process, and not yet issued using the consignment issue process, can return to the seller (consignment pick-up process). The consignment pick-up follows up with a return delivery, but not a credit memo (because an ownership change did not occur). An issue of credit memo must follow the consignment return, with or without delivery. If the customer wants a replacement, use a free-of-charge order (SD) or free-of-charge delivery order (FD). Table 3.9 summarizes the different consignment processes.

Order Type	Process	Goods Movement	Ownership Change?
KB	Consignment fill-up	Company to customer	No. Company is the owner.
KE	Consignment issue	No physical movement	Company to customer
KA	Consignment pick-up	Customer to company	No. Company is the owner.
KR	Consignment return	No physical movement	Customer to company

Table 3.9 Standard Consignment Order Types

3.9.2 Returnable Packaging

In certain industries, returnable packaging material is the norm, especially when the packaging material is costly and reusable. Sometimes, packaging can include specialized equipment for installing the product sold. After installation, this equipment should be returned. If the customer does not return the equipment for any reason, he must pay for it.

There are two prerequisites for this process:

1. Create the returnable package in the relevant material type. The standard material type for returnable packaging is LEIH (returnable packaging).

2. Ensure that the item category group for the packaging materials to be returned is LEIH in the material master record.

The returnable packaging material is included in the normal order/delivery/billing process and is not billed as other material. After the billing is complete, an order with document type LA (return packaging pick-up) is created. The new order is fundamentally similar to the document type RE (return). LA documents are further processed by delivery type LR (return). Normally, a credit memo for a return is not issued. If the customer does not return the material, then you invoice him by the return packaging issue process. The order type is LN. Further processing is done using standard delivery document LF (outbound delivery) and invoice type F2.

3.9.3 Make-to-Order Production

The distinctive feature of the *make-to-order items* of a sales order is that when you save such an order, it will automatically create production orders. After completing the production cycle, the stock will be available only to the original order that triggered the production process. Delivery and billing is same as that of the standard order-delivery-billing cycle. The make-to-order items are those materials for which the item category group maintained in the SALES: SALES ORG 2 view of the material master record is 0001 (make-to-order) or 0004 (make-to-order/assembled).

3.9.4 Bill of Materials

The *bill of materials* (BoM) is another tool to automatically populate the sales order with subitems. The BoM of a top-level item consists of all of the material that constitutes that item. In production planning, the BoM is used extensively. In sales, it's not used as extensively, but in few industry sectors, it's required. The BoM is used in sales, for example, in sectors such as aerospace and defense. Create a BoM for the top-level material using Transaction CS01 or following menu path SAP EASY ACCESS • LOGISTICS • SALES AND DISTRIBUTION • MASTER DATA • PRODUCTS • BILLS OF MATERIAL • BILL OF MATERIAL • MATERIAL BOM • CREATE with BoM usage 5 (sales and distribution). The item category group maintained in the SALES: SALES ORG 2 view of the material master record is ERLA or LUMF, depending on whether you want to process the pricing, inventory management at header-item level (ERLA) or at the constituent materials level (LUMF).

3.9.5 Third-Party Order Processing

When the item category group of an item in the sales order is a third party item (BANS, or a customized version of it), a purchase requisition is automatically generated when the order is saved. The purchase requisition will also create a purchase order for the vendor. The vendor receives instructions to supply the material directly to the customer. The vendor then sends the material to your customer, and sends the invoice (vendor invoice) to you. Thus, the customer receives an invoice by you, and not your vendor. You pay your vendor, and your customer pays you. Even when the item category is not BANS, manual purchase requisitions can be created, and the process for third-party order processing can be completed. Trading companies use this process extensively.

3.9.6 Individual Purchase Order

In individual purchase order processing, the sales order creates the purchase order. However, unlike third-party order processing, the vendor does not send the goods directly to the customer. The company receives the goods and dispatches them against the specific sales order. It cannot be sold to other customers. The item category for such materials is BANC (individual purchase order). Even when the item category is not BANC, you can manually create a purchase order for the individual items in the sales order.

3.9.7 Configurable Material

Configurable material is a functionality that SAP ERP offers when a material can have several possible bills of materials (BoMs), especially in a make-to-order scenario. The material is only assembled upon receipt of an order. Typically, the price is determined by the components and operations used in assembling the final material. Configure the material using material type KMAT (configurable material). Maintain the item category group in material master record (SALES: SALES ORG 2), where it should either be 0002 (configuration) or 0004 (make to order/assemble).

3.10   Incompletion Control

Incompletion control defines precisely what makes a specific document incomplete for specific subsequent processing. For example, you may consider a sales order complete for delivery processing, but incomplete for billing. Incompletion control achieves the following objectives:

1. The incompletion log is created for each document so that the user knows which fields are incomplete and still require action.

2. The incomplete documents appear in different reports to list such documents (e.g., V.00 – incomplete SD documents, V_UC – incomplete outbound deliveries).

3. It avoids further processing of documents without necessary and sufficient data.

4. The STATUS tab of the document shows the status of completeness based on the configuration in incompletion control.

5. During processing, a variety of fields fill with the default values from different master records, determination procedures, or customization settings. These fields can also be defined as incompletion fields. Because they usually fill automatically, the user rarely checks them manually.

6. If the customer-expected price is too low, the price can be determined in a sales item, and the document can be processed as incomplete until deciding whether to continue with the sale, reduce the price, or stop the sale.

7. Before doing any customization in the user exit, you can check if the objective for the user exit is achievable using the incompletion procedure. Because the incompletion control checks the value that will be present in a certain table field, this allows you to define incompletion, because the table field needs not be present in a particular screen. It can be a field from a customized Z-table.

The following are the general steps for customizing incompletion control:

1. Define status groups to control the specific subsequent process that cannot complete if the document is incomplete, as per the incompleteness procedure assigned to it (error group).

2. Identify the incompletion group from the seven groups that the incompleteness procedure is to define.

3. Define the incompleteness procedure for different incompletion groups.

4. Assign an incompleteness procedure to the different document types that belong to different incompletion groups.

Let's look at each step in more detail.

3.10.1 Define Status Groups

Status groups define precisely what subsequent activities (e.g., billing, pricing, packing, and so on) can be carried out, even when a sales document is incomplete. These status groups are further used in the incompleteness procedure. A field not filled in the sales document item may make it incomplete for bill processing, but it should not prevent the order from being delivered.

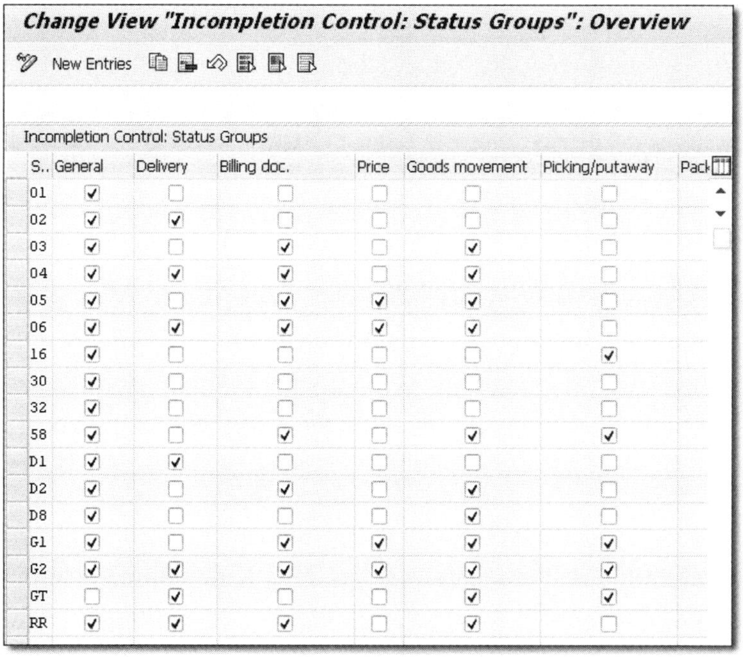

Change View "Incompletion Control: Status Groups": Overview

New Entries

Incompletion Control: Status Groups

S..	General	Delivery	Billing doc.	Price	Goods movement	Picking/putaway	Pack
01	✓						
02	✓	✓					
03	✓		✓		✓		
04	✓	✓	✓		✓		
05	✓		✓	✓	✓		
06	✓	✓	✓	✓	✓		
16	✓					✓	
30	✓						
32	✓						
58	✓		✓		✓	✓	
D1	✓	✓					
D2	✓		✓		✓		
D8	✓				✓		
G1	✓		✓	✓	✓	✓	
G2	✓	✓	✓	✓	✓	✓	
GT		✓			✓	✓	
RR	✓	✓	✓		✓		

Figure 3.27 Status Groups for Incompletion Control—Incompletion Groups

As shown in the Figure 3.27, you can use several predefined status groups, Transaction OVA0, or the menu path SAP IMG • SALES AND DISTRIBUTION • BASIC FUNCTIONS • LOG OF INCOMPLETE ITEMS • DEFINE STATUS GROUPS.

3.10.2 Identify Incompletion Groups

There are seven standard predefined incompletion groups that you can use to define the new incompleteness procedures. You can assign the incompleteness procedure defined in a particular incompletion group to the document types of that incompletion group. For example, the new incompleteness procedure, starting with Y or Z, created in incompletion or error group A (SALES – HEADER) can be assigned to the sales document type or sales header types such as OR or CR document types, but not to sales item categories such as TAN or REN. Figure 3.28 shows the seven incompletion groups (A, B, C, D, F, G, and H) and their descriptions. Adding to this list is not required, or even possible. Think of the incompletion groups as the option to group the different incompletion procedures.

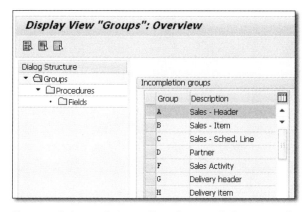

Figure 3.28 Incompletion or Error Groups—Define Incompleteness Procedure

3.10.3 Define Incompleteness Procedure

You define the incompleteness procedure using Transaction OVA2 or following the menu path SAP IMG • SALES AND DISTRIBUTION • BASIC FUNCTIONS • LOG OF INCOMPLETE ITEMS • DEFINE INCOMPLETENESS PROCEDURES. Several predefined incompleteness procedures exist in different incompletion groups, but if you need a new one, follow these steps:

1. Identify the suitable status groups required or create new ones using Transaction OVA0.

2. Identify the incompletion group that the new procedure is created for, using Transaction OVA2.

3. Select the incompletion group and double-click on the PROCEDURE folder. In Figure 3.28, we have selected incompletion group A (SALES – HEADER).

4. You'll get a list of all existing incompleteness procedures in the group (in this case, we selected A). Pick the one that's closest to the one you want to create.

5. Click on the CHANGE-DISPLAY (pencil and spectacles) icon.

6. Select the procedure you want to copy and click on the COPY AS (F6) icon.

7. An intermediate screen will ask you if you want to copy all dependent entries. Select COPY ALL.

8. A dialog window will show the number of dependent entries copied to the new incompleteness procedure. Press Enter and proceed.

9. Select the newly created incompleteness procedure and click on the FIELDS folder. You'll see the screen shown in Figure 3.29.

The new procedure shown in Figure 3.29 is the copy of the standard incompleteness procedure 11 (standard order). You can delete the table and fields already defined as *incompletion fields* and/or add a new table-field combination to it. The incompletion field on the screen (see the SCR. column in Figure 3.29) for which the status group is defined in the STATUS column is the field that, if not filled during processing, will make the document incomplete for the subsequent processes defined in the applicable status group.

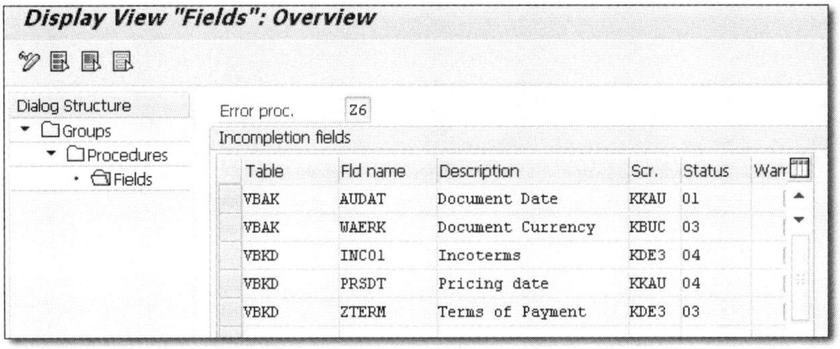

Figure 3.29 Defining Fields for Incompleteness Procedure

You can have a number of incompletion fields in an incompleteness procedure. The WARNING checkbox will issue a warning at the time of saving the document, and the SEQUENCE column determines the sequence when multiple entries are present in the incompletion log .

3.10.4 Assign Incompleteness Procedure

You assign the incompletion procedures to specific document types using Transaction VUA2 or following menu path SAP IMG • SALES AND DISTRIBUTION • BASIC FUNCTIONS • LOG OF INCOMPLETE ITEMS • DEFINE INCOMPLETENESS PROCEDURES. As we already mentioned, there are seven standard incompletion groups for which incompleteness procedures are created. Based on the group for which they're created, there are seven options at the previously mentioned menu path. For example, if you have created the procedure for group A (SALES – HEADER), you have to select the option ASSIGN PROCEDURES TO SALES DOCUMENT TYPES. You assign allowed procedure to different document types, as shown in Figure 3.30.

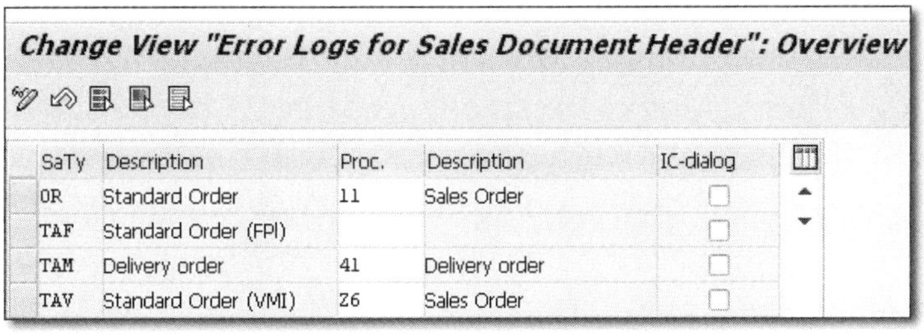

Change View "Error Logs for Sales Document Header": Overview

SaTy	Description	Proc.	Description	IC-dialog	
OR	Standard Order	11	Sales Order	☐	
TAF	Standard Order (FPI)			☐	
TAM	Delivery order	41	Delivery order	☐	
TAV	Standard Order (VMI)	26	Sales Order	☐	

Figure 3.30 Assigning Incompleteness Procedure

> **Incomplete Text**
>
> Even when there is no defined text ID in the incompletion control, it can still appear on the incompletion log if it's defined as mandatory in the text determination procedure.

3.11 Free Goods and Items

Free goods are part of pricing strategy. As a promotional campaign, a company gives free goods when a customer purchases a specific quantity of some material. An apparel company can offer you one shirt, free of cost, when you buy three shirts or a pair of pants. If you buy three shirts, they have to further clarify whether you will get an additional shirt free or if one of the three that you bought will be free.

You configure the automatic free goods determination with the following steps. It uses the condition technique.

1. Define a number range for FREE GOODS CONDITIONS using Transaction WC07 or SNRO (numbering object KONN).

2. Maintain the field catalog using Transaction OMA5 or following menu path IMG • SALES AND DISTRIBUTION • BASIC FUNCTIONS • FREE GOODS • CONDITION TECHNIQUE FOR FREE GOODS • MAINTAIN FIELD CATALOG. This is the list of all available fields for condition records.

3. Maintain the condition table using Transaction V/N2 or following the menu path IMG • SALES AND DISTRIBUTION • BASIC FUNCTIONS • FREE GOODS • CONDITION TECHNIQUE FOR FREE GOODS • MAINTAIN CONDITION TABLE. SAP ERP provides two default condition tables: 010 (CUSTOMER-MATERIAL) and 017 (CAMPAIGN ID – MATERIAL). If you want more, you can create tables with numbers between 500 and 999.

4. Maintain the access sequence using Transaction V/N1 or following the menu path IMG • SALES AND DISTRIBUTION • BASIC FUNCTIONS • FREE GOODS • CONDITION TECHNIQUE FOR FREE GOODS • MAINTAIN ACCESS SEQUENCE. When multiple condition records exist for the same condition type in different condition tables, the access sequence determines which of these is relevant.

5. Maintain the condition type using Transaction V/N4 or following the menu path IMG • SALES AND DISTRIBUTION • BASIC FUNCTIONS • FREE GOODS • CONDITION TECHNIQUE FOR FREE GOODS • MAINTAIN CONDITION TYPE. The SAP EPR standard-delivered condition type for free goods is NA00. If you need additional condition types, you can create them by copying from it.

6. Maintain the pricing procedure using Transaction V/N5 or following the menu path IMG • SALES AND DISTRIBUTION • BASIC FUNCTIONS • FREE GOODS • CONDITION TECHNIQUE FOR FREE GOODS • MAINTAIN PRICING PROCEDURE. The pricing for free goods is quite different from the pricing steps, and depends on whether the free goods create a separate item or, as in some cases (free goods category 3), are part of the main item. For inclusive free goods without item generation, use condition type NRAB (free goods), which uses the VOFM requirement routine 59 and formula routine 29. Condition type R100 (100% discount), used in other cases, uses requirement routine 55 and formula routine 28 in the pricing procedure.

7. Activate free goods determination using Transaction V/N6 or following the menu path IMG • SALES AND DISTRIBUTION • BASIC FUNCTIONS • FREE GOODS • CONDITION TECHNIQUE FOR FREE GOODS • ACTIVATE FREE GOODS DETERMINATION.

8. Assign item categories following the menu path IMG • SALES AND DISTRIBUTION • BASIC FUNCTIONS • FREE GOODS • DETERMINE ITEM CATEGORY FOR FREE GOODS. For the standard order OR and the standard item category TAN (item category group NORM), the free goods item category to assign is TANN (free of charge item).

9. Maintain condition records for free goods using Transaction VBN1 or following the menu path SAP EASY ACCESS • LOGISTICS • SALES AND DISTRIBUTION • MASTER DATA • CONDITIONS • FREE GOODS • CREATE. Select the default free goods condition type NA00 and the required key combination, and click on the EXCLUSIVE tab. In Figure 3.31, you'll see the EXCLUSIVE view; the tab appears as INCLUSIVE. When you're giving 1 unit free with 10 units of material A, for an order of 10 units in the case of inclusive free goods, you sell 9 units and give 1 unit as free. With exclusive free goods, you sell 10 units and give 1 unit as free, thus delivering 11 units.

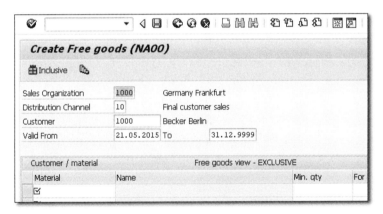

Figure 3.31 Create Condition Record for Free Goods (Exclusive Type)

To create a condition record for free goods, you have to maintain the following for a date range:

▸ **Material**
Enter the material for which free goods are given.

▸ **Minimum quantity**
The minimum quantity of the material that must be ordered to get free goods.

- **For**

  The quantity for which free goods start. If for every 100 units of material A, 1 unit of material B is free, you would enter 100 here. It becomes "from" in the inclusive case.

- **Unit of measure** (UNITFG)

  The unit of measure of the material for which free goods are given.

- **Additional free goods** (ADD.FG)

  The quantity of free goods to be given to the customer. It becomes "are free goods" in the inclusive case

- **Unit of measurement** (ADDQTYUNIT)

  The unit of measurement of the additional quantity.

- **Calculation rule**

  In the standard SAP system, there are three rules used for calculating the free goods quantity when the order quantity is more than the minimum quantity:

  - Select 1 (pro-rata) for a quantity that is above the minimum quantity, in which the customer gets free goods on proportional basis. So, using the pro-rata rule, if 10 units are free with a 100 unit purchase, the customer would get 12 free units with an order of 120.

  - Select 2 (unit reference) when no additional free goods are supplied for an order more than the minimum order.

  - Select 3 (whole unit) when no free goods are supplied for an order more than the minimum order. For example, if 100 units of material A are ordered, 10 units of material B are given as free. So, with an order of 110 units, the customer will receive 11, 10, and 0, respectively, for calculation rules 1, 2, and 3.

  These rules are simply VOFM routines and can be modified. New routines can also be created using Transaction VOFM in the allowed range of 600 to 999.

- **Free goods**

  The FREE GOODS field can take 1, 2, or 3 as input. When the free goods rebate is exclusive, then the material given as additional free goods will always create a new line item in the order, and you will need to select free goods category 2. But when the free goods rebate is inclusive, you have the option of generating another line item (option 1) or including the additional quantity in the main item without creating an additional line item in the order (option 3).

▶ **Additional material free goods** (ADDMAT FRGD)
This field is not present in the inclusive type of free goods because the additional material cannot be different from the material for which free goods are given. For the exclusive type, you can maintain the same material as exclusive, or you can have a different material. For example, for 10 units of material A, you can give 1 unit of material B as free goods, or you can give 1 unit of material A as free goods.

▶ **Free goods delivery control** (FGDELYCONT)
This controls delivery of the free goods with respect to the delivery of the main item.

▶ **Scale**
You can use scale when you have to give a different quantity of free goods for different quantities ordered. For example, if for 100 units, 10 units are free; for 200 units, 25 units are free; for 300 units, 40 units are free; and so on, then it's maintained in scales.

3.12　Material Determination, Listing, and Exclusion

Material determination replaces one material with another in the sales document. Swapping can be done one-to-one, or manually by selecting from a proposed list. You would use this in a situation such as nonavailability, product discontinuation, or promotional packaging during a specific period.

Material listing and exclusion is the procedure for giving a customer or group of customers a predefined list of products by either listing the allowed material, listing the not allowed material (exclusion), or both.

Both material determination and material listing/exclusion use the condition technique. The steps to automatically determine a material and material listing/exclusion are as follows:

1. Add the field required in the condition table to the field catalog, if not already available.

   ▷ For material determination, this is menu path SAP IMG • SALES AND DISTRIBUTION • BASIC FUNCTIONS • MATERIAL DETERMINATION • MAINTAIN PREREQUISITES FOR MATERIAL DETERMINATION • MAINTAIN FIELD CATALOG.

> ▷ For material listing/exclusion, this is menu path SAP IMG • SALES AND DISTRIBUTION • BASIC FUNCTIONS • LISTING/EXCLUSION • MAINTAIN ALLOWED FIELDS FOR LISTING/EXCLUSION.

2. Create condition tables using fields available in the field catalog, or identify the standard SAP condition tables that are suitable for storing condition records.

> ▷ For material determination, this is menu path SAP IMG • SALES AND DISTRIBUTION • BASIC FUNCTIONS • MATERIAL DETERMINATION • MAINTAIN PREREQUISITES FOR MATERIAL DETERMINATION • CREATE CONDITION TABLE.

> ▷ For material listing/exclusion menu path, this is menu path SAP IMG • SALES AND DISTRIBUTION • BASIC FUNCTIONS • LISTING/EXCLUSION • MAINTAIN CONDITION TABLE FOR LISTING/EXCLUSION.

3. Create an access sequence and assign condition tables for the system to access the condition tables in correct sequence.

> ▷ For material determination, this is menu path SAP IMG • SALES AND DISTRIBUTION • BASIC FUNCTIONS • MATERIAL DETERMINATION • MAINTAIN PREREQUISITES FOR MATERIAL DETERMINATION • MAINTAIN ACCESS SEQUENCES.

> ▷ For material listing/exclusion, this is menu path SAP IMG • SALES AND DISTRIBUTION • BASIC FUNCTIONS • LISTING/EXCLUSION • MAINTAIN ACCESS SEQUENCES FOR LISTING/EXCLUSION.

4. Create condition types with the correct access sequence assigned to them.

> ▷ For material determination, this is menu path SAP IMG • SALES AND DISTRIBUTION • BASIC FUNCTIONS • MATERIAL DETERMINATION • MAINTAIN PREREQUISITES FOR MATERIAL DETERMINATION • DEFINE CONDITION TYPES.

> ▷ For material listing/exclusion, this is menu path SAP IMG • SALES AND DISTRIBUTION • BASIC FUNCTIONS • LISTING/EXCLUSION • MAINTAIN LISTING/EXCLUSION TYPES.

5. Create a determination procedure and assign it to the condition types.

> ▷ For material determination, this is menu path SAP IMG • SALES AND DISTRIBUTION • BASIC FUNCTIONS • MATERIAL DETERMINATION • MAINTAIN PREREQUISITES FOR MATERIAL DETERMINATION • MAINTAIN PROCEDURE.

> ▷ For material listing/exclusion, this is menu path SAP IMG • SALES AND DISTRIBUTION • BASIC FUNCTIONS • LISTING/EXCLUSION • PROCEDURES FOR MAINTAINING LISTING/EXCLUSION.

6. Assign a determination procedure to sales document types.

▸ For material determination, this is menu path SAP IMG • SALES AND DISTRIBUTION • BASIC FUNCTIONS • MATERIAL DETERMINATION • ASSIGN PROCEDURES TO SALES DOCUMENT TYPES.

▸ For material listing/exclusion, this is menu path SAP IMG • SALES AND DISTRIBUTION • BASIC FUNCTIONS • LISTING/EXCLUSION • ACTIVATE LISTING/EXCLUSION BY SALES DOCUMENT TYPE.

7. Create condition records.

▸ For material determination, this is menu path SAP EASY ACCESS • LOGISTICS • SALES AND DISTRIBUTION • MASTER DATA • PRODUCTS • MATERIAL DETERMINATION • CREATE (VB11).

▸ For material listing/exclusion, this is menu path SAP EASY ACCESS • LOGISTICS • SALES AND DISTRIBUTION • MASTER DATA • PRODUCTS • LISTING/EXCLUSION • CREATE (VB01).

8. In addition to the steps for material determination, you can define substitution reasons using Transaction OVRQ or following the menu path SAP IMG • SALES AND DISTRIBUTION • BASIC FUNCTIONS • MATERIAL DETERMINATION • DEFINE SUBSTITUTION REASONS.

3.13 Batch Determination

In addition to the Sales and Distribution functionality in SAP ERP, batch determination is also used in the Material Management, Production Planning, and Warehouse Management functionalities in SAP ERP. Batch determination also uses the condition technique; that is, it uses the condition tables, access sequence, condition type, and a search procedure.

▸ **Condition tables**

The transaction code for creating condition table in the Sales and Distribution functionality in SAP ERP for batch determination is V/C7. The menu path for condition tables is SAP IMG • LOGISTICS – GENERAL • BATCH MANAGEMENT • BATCH DETERMINATION AND BATCH CHECK • CONDITION TABLES • DEFINE SALES AND DISTRIBUTION CONDITION TABLES. There are six standard condition tables and their corresponding fields used:

- 001: Material (MATNR)
- 002: Customer (KUNNR) – material (MATNR)
- 003: Customer (KUNNR) – plant (WERKS) – material (MATNR)
- 004: Destination country (LAND1) – material group (MATKL)
- 005: Destination country (LAND1)
- 006: Material group (MATKL)

If you want to create your own condition tables, the number should be between 501 and 999, and the fields to be used should be in the field catalog. You can use all fields in the field catalog by using the option Conditions: Allowed Fields (Sales and Distribution) at the end of this menu path.

▶ **Access sequence**

Access sequences attach to the batch strategy and control the sequence in which the condition tables are accessed. The menu path is SAP IMG • Logistics – General • Batch Management • Batch Determination and Batch Check • Access Sequence • Define Sales and Distribution Access Sequences. The access sequence determines the order in which the condition tables are accessed. SD01, SD02, and SD03 are SAP-delivered access sequences. You can create your own with a code starting with Z.

▶ **Strategy type**

Strategy types are condition types that use the access sequence for automatic determination. Figure 3.32 displays the standard strategy type SD01. Enter the values for class and sort sequence in the production client itself, after transport of the strategy type.

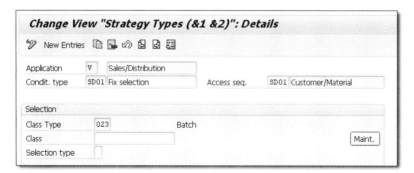

Figure 3.32 Strategy Type SD01

▶ The selection type determines how the batches are selected at the start of batch determination. The four available options are:

- Blank: Batches are immediately displayed for selection that matches the selection criteria.

- N: Batches are not selected, even when the selection criteria exists. The user has the option to change selection criteria.

- 0: All batches are displayed for selection, irrespective of selection criteria. The selection carries out after finalization of selection criteria.

- F: Selection criteria cannot be changed for batch determination.

▶ SORT SEQUENCE determines how the search results are sorted.

▶ NO. OF SPLITS determines how many batch splits are allowed. Because this field can take any three-digit number, the highest number (999) is the maximum batch split allowed.

▶ CHANGES ALLOWED determines if changes in the number of splits are permitted during batch determination.

▶ OVERDEL ALLOWED is not relevant for Sales and Distribution.

▶ DISPLAY UOM determines whether the unit of measurement (UoM) is document UoM (option B) or stock-keeping UoM (option A) during batch determination.

▶ The DIALOG BATCH DETERMIN. checkbox determines if the batch determination is carried out in the background (not selected) or foreground (selected).

▶ QTY PROPOSAL can be any of the four standard routines or customized routines that fine-tune the way quantities are proposed in the batch determination.

▶ **Batch search procedure**
The batch search procedure lists the sequence of strategy types that the system tries to access for valid condition records (or strategy records) during batch determination. The standard batch search procedure is SD0001, defined using Transaction V/C3 or following the menu path SAP IMG • LOGISTICS – GENERAL • BATCH MANAGEMENT • BATCH DETERMINATION AND BATCH CHECK • BATCH SEARCH PROCEDURE DEFINITION • DEFINE SALES AND DISTRIBUTION SEARCH PROCEDURE. You can create your own search procedure beginning with Z by clicking on the NEW ENTRY tab. You can then add the strategy types you want in the appropri-

ate sequence (steps and counter decide the sequence) by opening the CONTROL folder and selecting NEW ENTRY.

Once you define the search procedure, it's assigned to the combination of sales area and document type, as shown in Figure 3.33 and the menu path SAP IMG • LOGISTICS – GENERAL • BATCH MANAGEMENT • BATCH DETERMINATION AND BATCH CHECK • BATCH SEARCH PROCEDURE DEFINITION • ALLOCATE SD SEARCH PROCEDURE/ ACTIVATE CHECK. Finally, you create the batch search strategy records using Transaction VCH1 or following the menu path SAP EASY ACCESS • LOGISTICS • SALES AND DISTRIBUTION • MASTER DATA • PRODUCTS • BATCH SEARCH STRATEGY • CREATE.

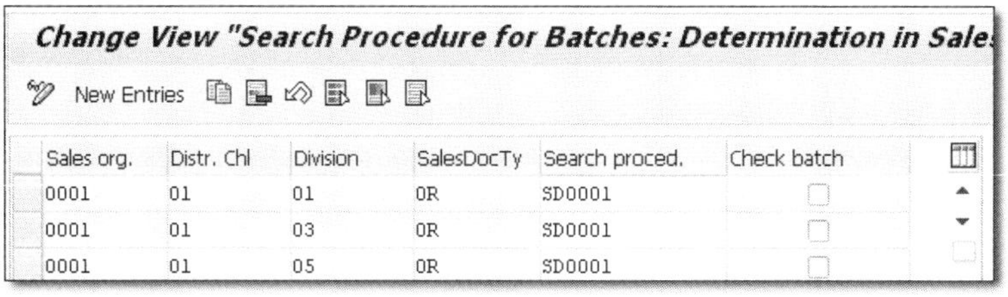
Change View "Search Procedure for Batches: Determination in Sale

New Entries

Sales org.	Distr. Chl	Division	SalesDocTy	Search proced.	Check batch
0001	01	01	OR	SD0001	
0001	01	03	OR	SD0001	
0001	01	05	OR	SD0001	

Figure 3.33 Batch Search Procedure Determination

For batch determination to occur in a delivery created without reference to a sales order, you must define the default order type for the delivery type using Transaction OVLK or following the menu path SAP IMG • LOGISTICS EXECUTION • SHIPPING • DELIVERIES • DEFINE DELIVERY TYPES. From here, you must assign the default order type to a batch search procedure. Batch determination at the delivery level is also required when it's not possible to determine the batch at the order level.

3.14 Returns (Complaints) Processing

If a customer registers a complaint, the company may decide to take back the material, which is handled by a returns process, issue a credit memo (without taking back the material), or send additional material without charges. These processes are called returns or complaint processing. Table 3.10 lists the sales order types that are used in complaint processing.

Order Type	Description	Physical Stock Movement?	Reference
FD	Deliv.Free of Charge	Yes, outward	Not mandatory
SD	Subs.Dlv.Free of Ch.	Yes, outward	Mandatory
CR	Credit Memo Request	No	Not mandatory
DR	Debit Memo Request	No	Not mandatory
RK	Invoice Correct. Req	No	Mandatory
RE	Returns	Yes, inward	Not mandatory

Table 3.10 Standard Order Types for Complaint Processing

Reference to Complaint

It's always important to create the order documents with reference to the original invoice that the complaint was received in. So SD and RK are better suited. To use the types RE, CR, and DR, we recommend that you create a copy of these order types and make reference mandatory in the customized order types.

3.14.1 Free-of-Charge Delivery and Subsequent Delivery

The free-of-charge delivery (FD) type is primarily used to issue a sample free-of-charge, but can also be used as part of a complaint handling or return process. This standard order type has the document pricing procedure (DoPP) C (free of charge). The system determines pricing procedure using the combination of sales area, document pricing procedure, and customer pricing procedure (CuPP), which we'll discuss in Chapter 4. The pricing procedure for any combination that contains the DoPP as C is to make the item free of charge. The free-of-charge subsequent delivery (order type SD) is the same as FD, except that reference to an existing order is mandatory for it. You can create order type FD without reference. The free-of-charge pricing in an invoice is ensured by the copy control.

3.14.2 Invoice Correction without Return

When the company receives a complaint (or a request to take back the material), they may decide to compensate the customer by modifying the invoice without taking back the material or supplying additional material. The three standard sales document types are CR (credit memo request), DR (debit memo request), and RK (invoice correction request). They're used for complaint handling. It's important to note that for the CR and DR documents, reference to a billing document is not mandatory, whereas for RK, a reference is mandatory. While copying the billing document to the RK type order, the system creates two line items: one for credit and one for debit. For CR and DR orders, the relevant standard billing types (G2 and L2) can issue credit memos and debit memos, respectively. RK type orders are also processed by the G2 type invoice. The total value of an RK type order and the G2 invoice for it can be negative, so you should refer to it as a credit memo with negative value, and not as a debit memo.

Multiple References

When reference is mandatory, enter the reference document number in the first screen; you may only enter one document number here, and the complete document will then copy to the order. To add items from another reference document, use the menu path SALES DOCUMENT • CREATE WITH REFERENCE from the overview screen to enter the second referred document and copy its items. Repeat the process until all reference documents are included. Note that there are a few standard limitations. For example, sold-to must be the same with reference to each document.

3.14.3 Returns

Companies often take back stock that has been sold to customers when there's a complaint and return the price the customer had paid for it. This is done to retain customer loyalty, improve brand image, and avoid legal costs or for social responsibility.

Customers always appreciate an unambiguous and clear-cut sales return policy. Many times, customers are allowed to return the material under specific conditions (e.g., within 15 days for any reason), and a credit memo for the return is issued to that customer. The sales document type, item category, and schedule line category used for return processing in a standard system are RE, REN, and DN, respectively. If the goods are received as unrestricted stock, then in the schedule line category, you need to use the movement type 653 (GD returns unrestricted), whereas if the goods are received as return, you can use the movement type 651 (GD ret.del returns). When you use movement type 653, the stock received from a customer return can be sold to another customer like any other unrestricted type stock. When you use movement type 651, the stock after receipt becomes return type stock and has to be further processed to make it available for sale (by changing it to unrestricted type using Transaction MIGO). When you use movement type

651, the stock arrives at your warehouse, but as blocked stock (because it has yet to be inspected and given the green light to be released as unrestricted or scrapped). The returns stock is not considered for valuation. This is surprising because the stock in quality inspection or restricted uses is considered for valuation.

Movement Type
Movement type comes into play when there's a physical or logical movement of stock. Stock moving from one plant to another is an example of physical movement, and stock being blocked for delivery is a logical movement. Movement type also determines the GL that will post for the stock movement. Also note that stock or inventory is an asset and is a balance sheet item. The consumption accounts, such as cost of raw material, are expenses and are profit and loss account items. Movement types typically debit one asset/consumption account and credit another. Movement types that are configured in Material Management and used elsewhere, including Sales and Distribution, should be checked very closely, especially for the automatic account posting that the movement types do.

3.15   Intercompany Sales Processing

When a sales organization sells stock to the plant of another company code, the process is called *intercompany sales processing*. When a customer orders stock that can be supplied by a plant that belongs to another company code, you have two options:

1. Transfer the stock to a plant belonging to the same company code as that of the sales organization, and complete the normal sales processing procedure. We'll discuss the inter-company and intracompany stock later in this chapter.

2. Sell the product directly to the customer from the plant belonging to another company code. Issue a normal invoice to the customer from the company code of the sales organization and issue an intercompany invoice from the company code of the supplying plant to the company code of the sales organization.

3.15.1   Intercompany Billing

If you choose the second option, you need to follow these steps:

1. Using Transaction OVV8 or following menu path SAP IMG • SALES AND DISTRIBUTION • BILLING • INTERCOMPANY BILLING • DEFINE THE ORDER TYPES FOR

INTERCOMPANY BILLING, assign the intercompany credit memo (billing type IG) to all order types that will be issued for intercompany credit memo requests, and assign intercompany billing (billing type IV) to all order types that be issued for intercompany debit memo request or billing.

2. Using Transaction OVV9 or following menu path SAP IMG • SALES AND DISTRIBUTION • BILLING • INTERCOMPANY BILLING • ASSIGN ORGANIZATIONAL UNITS BY PLANT • ASSIGN ORGANIZATIONAL UNITS TO THE PLANTS, assign sales organizations, distribution channels, and divisions (the combination is called a sales area) to the plants which require intercompany billing. After the assignment of the intercompany billing from a plant to the sales areas, intercompany billing becomes possible.

3. Using Transaction OVVA or following the menu path SAP IMG • SALES AND DISTRIBUTION • BILLING • INTERCOMPANY BILLING • DEFINE INTERNAL CUSTOMER NUMBER BY SALES ORGANIZATION, you assign customers created for offsetting entries in the intercompany billing process to the respective sales organizations. You can perform this step directly in the production server, because it involves customer master records that are not transported. A typical accounting entry in the selling company will look like this:

    CR REVENUE (intercompany sales): 100 USD

    DR CUSTOMER (internal customer for intercompany sale): 100 USD

    In the purchasing company the entries will be like this:

    CR PURCHASE (intercompany purchase): 100 USD

    DR VENDOR (plant created as vendor): 100 USD

    These entries are eliminated at the time of consolidation at the group level, or by actual payment processing. Refer to SAP Note 308989 for more information on cross-company billing.

4. You must maintain all of the steps for pricing for intercompany billing. The steps in pricing will involve creating condition tables, access sequences, condition types, pricing procedures, and condition records. You can use the two standard condition types mentioned below for billing the dummy customer created for the sales organization in step 3.

    ▸ PI01 INTERCOMPANY: fixed amount per material unit (e.g., 10 USD/Kg)

    ▸ PI02 INTERCOMPANY: percentage of the net invoice amount (e.g., 10% of maximum retail price, 4% of PI01 condition type)

5. Create a sales order using Transaction VA01. The default value for the plant comes from either a customer-material info record, a material master record (when there's no default plant for the customer, a material combination is found in any customer material info record), or a customer master record (when the above two options do not return any default value for the plant). You can manually change this plant.

6. When the plant and the sales area (or sales organization) belong to different company codes but are permitted for intercompany billing (per step 2), necessary pricing is done either manually or automatically to complete the process of intercompany sales. (When the plants involved in stock transfer belong to same company code, it is intracompany stock transfer.)

7. After order processing, the delivery and goods issue is completed. The customer (or receiving plant) receives a bill and an offsetting intercompany bill is raised simultaneously, or at the time of consolidation of financial statements at the holding company level. (Typically, actual payments are not involved.)

3.15.2 Stock Transfer

What happens when stock moves around? When you receive a purchase order from a customer, it's called a *sales order*. When you receive requirements from a plant within the seller's group company, they are usually fulfilled by a *stock transfer order*. You can think of a plant like an internal customer, since a customer master record is created and assigned to the plant for this purpose. The ordering plant creates the stock transfer order for materials it requires. When the ordering plant and the supplying plant belong to the same company code, we call the process *intracompany stock transfer*; when they belong to different companies, the process is *intercompany stock transfer* (or cross-company stock transfer).

You may adopt either a one-step or two-step stock transfer process for both intra- and intercompany stock transfers:

▸ The one-step process, called the *transfer posting,* normally comes into use when no physical movement is involved. For example, stock identified for quality inspection or stock blocked for sale may not involve any physical movement. For cases involving physical movement, a two-step process is recommended.

▸ The two-step process is a better representation or model for the actual physical process that occurs in a stock transfer.

Figure 3.34 illustrates the difference between the one-step and two-step stock transfer.

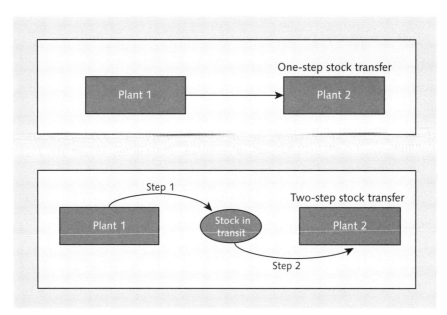

Figure 3.34 One-Step versus Two-Step Stock Transfer

Follow these steps to execute customizing stock transfer processes:

1. **Define the number range for stock transfer orders**.

   The number range for stock transfer orders specifies all of the numbers you can use to identify individual documents of a particular type of stock transfer order. You define the number range for stock transfer orders using Transaction OMH6 or Transaction SNRO (object EINKBELEG).

   Please note that this is not the usual number range object (RV_BELEG), and you cannot maintain it using Transaction VN01, which itself is used in the Sales and Distribution functionality in SAP ERP. This number range object (EINKBELEG) provides numbers to different types of purchase orders. For different types of stock transfer orders, you can assign different number ranges to distinguish between them. For example, you can use different document types (and number ranges) to differentiate between forward-moving stock transfers and returns, as illustrated in Table 3.11.

Stock Transfer Order	STO Type	Number Range
Transfer from plant 1 to plant 2	ZST1	46000000 to 46999999
Return from plant 2 to plant 1	ZST2	47000000 to 47999999

Table 3.11 Different Number Ranges Assigned to Different STO Types

2. **Define the document type for stock transfer orders.**

You can define the document types for a stock transfer order using Transaction S_ALR_87002197 or following the menu path SAP IMG • MATERIAL MANAGEMENT • PURCHASING • PURCHASE ORDER • DEFINE DOCUMENT TYPES. Use the standard document type UB for intracompany stock transfer, and NB for intercompany stock transfer, as shown in Figure 3.35. You can copy these standard document types to create several document types as needed. You may assign different number ranges, which were created in the previous step, to different document types them. Leave the CONTROL field blank if you will use the document types for intercompany stock transfer, or enter the value T if you'll use them for an intracompany stock transfer.

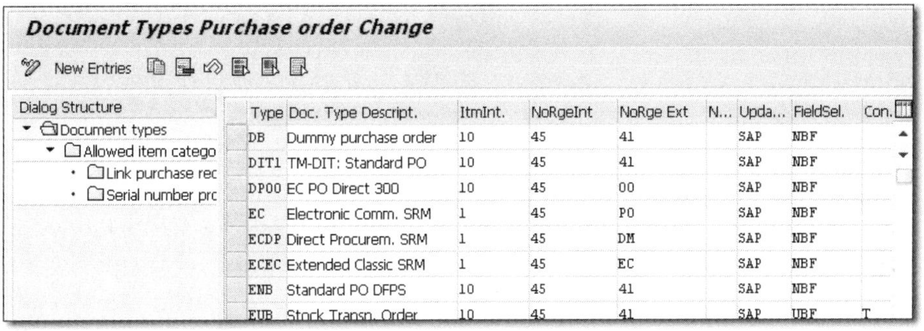

Figure 3.35 Define Document Types for Stock Transfer Orders

3. **Create internal customers for receiving plants.**

You can define internal customers for the receiving plants using Transaction XD01. You should create the customer in the company code of the receiving plant. The sales area (which is a combination of sales organization, distribution channel, and division) should be the same as the shipping data for the receiving plant, which we'll explain in the next section. For these internal customers, you can define a different customer account group.

4. **Define shipping data for receiving plants.**

Use Transaction S_ALR_87002189 to define shipping data for the ordering plant or follow the menu path SAP IMG • MATERIAL MANAGEMENT • PURCHASING • PURCHASE ORDER • SET UP STOCK TRANSFER ORDER • DEFINE SHIPPING DATA FOR PLANTS. As shown in Figure 3.36, simply double-click on any particular plant in the overview screen. This is where you assign the customer created in the step before the ordering/receiving plant. You should also define the sales area applicable for the plant. This should be the same as the sales area defined for the internal customer.

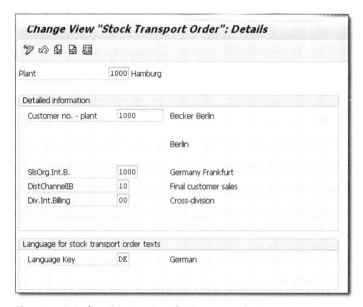

Figure 3.36 Define Shipping Data for Receiving Plants

Master Data Creation

This step is performed directly in the production server, as opposed to the normal practice of transporting changes from development via the quality server. This is because you cannot transport the customer master data from one server to another, and the customer created for the plant cannot be available in the development client.

Another best practice is to avoid creating any master data in the *golden client*. The golden client is one of the many clients in development servers used exclusively for final customization and transport to production via the quality server. By not creating any master data record, you prevent any transactions in this client. Other clients of the development server, which the system uses as sandboxes for trial and testing, may contain master data—but the golden client should be a mirror image of the production client of the production server, except for the master data and transactional data.

Also note that the ABAP reports are not developed in the golden client, because the developer requires some master and transactional data during preliminary testing while developing the report. However, because all ABAP programs are cross-client developments, they become available in the golden client immediately.

5. **Assign document type to plants**.

Assign the document types created in Step 2 to the combination of delivering plant and supplying plant via the menu path SAP IMG • MATERIAL MANAGEMENT • PURCHASING • PURCHASE ORDER • SET UP STOCK TRANSFER ORDER • ASSIGN DOCUMENT TYPE, ONE-STEP PROCEDURE, UNDERDELIVERY TOLERANCE. Clicking on the IMG ACTIVITY icon at the end of this menu path will take you to the screen shown in Figure 3.37. The first two columns show the supplying and receiving plants, and the third column displays the default document type.

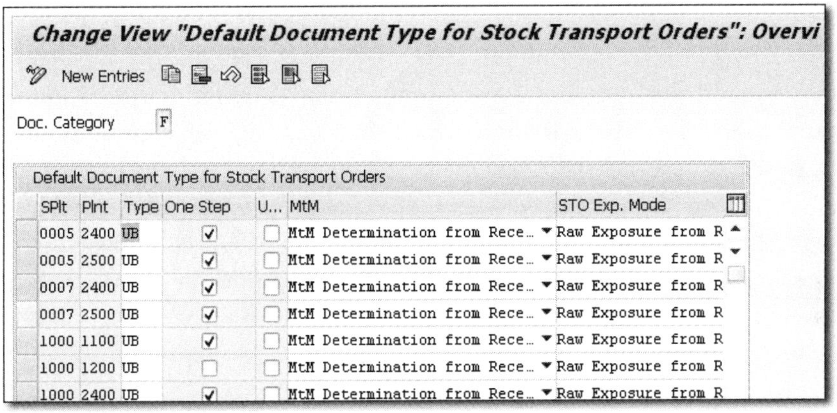

Figure 3.37 Default Document Type for STOs of Different Plants

If you're following the one-step process, select the checkbox in the fourth. If you select the fourth column, underdelivery tolerance becomes allowed. If tolerance is allowed, the delivery completion indicator (EKPO-EGLKZ) in the stock transfer order is set automatically, even when the delivery is less than the order quantity but still within the tolerance limit. The tolerance limit is the limit at which delivery quantity can be less than the order quantity (as a percentage of order quantity). This functionality significantly reduces the total number of incomplete deliveries, so you don't waste time with deliveries that are "practically" complete.

6. **Assign delivery type and checking rule to STO document type.**

You assign the delivery type and checking rules to the document types for a stock transfer order you follow the menu path SAP IMG • MATERIAL MANAGEMENT • PURCHASING • PURCHASE ORDER • SET UP STOCK TRANSFER ORDER • ASSIGN DELIVERY TYPE AND CHECKING RULE. If you click on IMG ACTIVITY at the end of this menu path, you'll see the screen shown in Figure 3.38. For the STO document type and the supplying plant, you specify a delivery type in the DELIVERY TYPE (DLTP) column and a checking rule in the CHECKING RULE (CKR) column. You can also activate shipment scheduling and route scheduling functionalities by selecting the checkboxes in SHIP. SCH. ROUTE SCH. columns, respectively.

If you specify a delivery type in the DELIVERY TYPE (DLTP) column and nothing in the last three columns, then the delivery type becomes relevant for intercompany stock transfers, intracompany stock transfers, and transfers to consignment stock. If for these three processes, you want to assign separate delivery types (which is normally the case), you can specify the delivery type's intracompany stock transfer in the DELIVERY TYPE 1 column, intracompany stock transfer in the DELIVERY TYPE 2 column, and transfer to consignment stock in the DTCONS. column. Different users may be responsible for these processes, so you can use the delivery type (and STO type) as the basis for managing authorization. The standard delivery types for the intra- and intercompany stock transfers are NL and NLCC, respectively. If you need more than one delivery type for these processes, you can copy the standard document types to create your own.

Change View "Stock Transfer Data": Overview

New Entries

Ty.	DT Dscr.	SPl	Name 1	DlTy.	Description	CRl	Description o...	S...	R...	De...	De...	DT...
UB	S.T.O	0005	Cavite Depot	NL	Replenishment ...02		Checking rule ...	☐	☐			
UB	S.T.O	0006	New York	NL	Replenishment ...A		SD order	☐	☐			
UB	S.T.O	0007	Werk Hamburg	NL	Replenishment ...02		Checking rule ...	☐	☐			
UB	S.T.O	0008	New York	NL	Replenishment ...A		SD order	☐	☐			

Figure 3.38 Assign Delivery Type and Checking Rule to STO Document Types

Further Customization

We do not describe the customization for the checking rule, delivery document type, shipping point determination, output determination for stock transfer order, and other related customizations for stock transfer orders here, because we've either already covered them or will cover them shortly. You can also refer to SAP Note 498143 for FAQs on the stock transfer process. We also don't discuss the two-step stock transfer without delivery process where goods receipt is done with reference to the stock transfer order instead of the delivery or return scenario that's relevant for intercompany transfer processes. These are out of the scope of this book.

3.15.3 Create Vendor Master Record for Receiving Plant

In an intercompany stock transfer scenario, you create a vendor master record for the receiving plant via Transaction XK01. The company code for the record is kept the same as the company code to which the supplying plant is assigned. The purchasing organization remains the same as what is valid for the receiving and ordering plant. Note that the vendor master record we're creating is that of the supplying plant, but it's created for the receiving plant. All vendors are created for a particular plant. For purchasing, a plant (receiving plant here) can use any vendor (supplying plant here) associated with it.

Standard Schedule Line Categories

The standard schedule line categories for stock transfer are NN (intracompany) and NC (intercompany). The movement types attached for one-step and two-step processes are 645 and 643, respectively, for schedule line category NC. For schedule line NN, the movement types are 647 (one-step) and 641 (two-step). The problem you may have is how to determine these schedule line categories for the stock transfer delivery type. We know that a sales order automatically determines the schedule line category.

The delivery is also determined per the delivery type mentioned in the customization of order type. So during the goods issue of the delivery, the schedule line for the item determines the movement type. But in stock transfer, this is done by the default order type field and requirement routine 202 maintained in the customization of the delivery types for intra- and intercompany stock transfer.

3.16 Outputs in Sales

The client 000 contains outputs as they come out of a standard system. You can copy the outputs from client 000 if they are not available in your system. You receive the information you want in print-outs, email, SMS, and several other possible forms. In sales, the output of the sales order serves various purposes, such as order confirmation and material safety data sheets (MSDSes). The MSDSes exist for each item or material and are required if the material is to cross the border into another country. So, in a given condition, the type of output issued and to whom it's issued is determined using a condition technique in SAP ERP called the output determination process. The menu path is SAP IMG • BASIC FUNCTIONS • OUTPUT CONTROL • OUTPUT DETERMINATION – OUTPUT DETERMINATION USING CONDITION TECHNIQUE • MAINTAIN OUTPUT DETERMINATION FOR SALES DOCUMENTS. Even when you don't require the automatic determination of output, you must have an output type and output determination procedure to manually select the output.

Follow these steps for output determination in sales:

1. Add the field required in the condition table to the field catalog if it's not already available. The menu path is SAP IMG • BASIC FUNCTIONS • OUTPUT CONTROL • OUTPUT DETERMINATION – OUTPUT DETERMINATION USING CONDITION TECHNIQUE • MAINTAIN OUTPUT DETERMINATION FOR SALES DOCUMENTS • MAINTAIN CONDITION TABLES. Select FIELD CATALOG: MESSAGES FOR SALES DOCUMENTS.

2. Create condition tables using fields available in the field catalog or identify the standard SAP condition tables that are suitable for storing condition records. The menu path is same as above. Select MAINTAIN OUTPUT CONDITION TABLE FOR SALES DOCUMENTS. Table 3.12 lists the standard available condition tables.

Condition Table	Description	Fields Used
001	Sales Organization/Customer Number	VKORG, KNDNR
005	Sales Organization/Order Type	VKORG, AUART
006	SOrg./Distrib.Ch/Division/Customer	VKORG, VTWEG, SPART, KNDNR
007	Order Type	AUART
013	Sales Org.	VKORG
015	Credit Control Area/Credit Repr. Group/ Risk Category	KKBER, SBGRP, CTLPC

Table 3.12 Standard Condition Tables for Output Determination in Sales

Condition Table	Description	Fields Used
150	Doc.Type/Sales Org./Customer	AUART, VKORG, KUNNR
200	Overall Credit Status	CMGST

Table 3.12 Standard Condition Tables for Output Determination in Sales (Cont.)

3. Create an access sequence and assign condition tables for the system to access in correct sequence. You can create the assess sequence using the menu path SAP IMG • BASIC FUNCTIONS • OUTPUT CONTROL • OUTPUT DETERMINATION – OUTPUT DETERMINATION USING CONDITION TECHNIQUE • MAINTAIN OUTPUT DETERMINATION FOR SALES DOCUMENTS • MAINTAIN ACCESS SEQUENCES. The access sequence can contain several accesses or access numbers, and each access can contain one condition table. You can display the fields of the condition table by selecting the access number and opening the FIELDS folder. The key for the access sequence must start with a Z. The access sequence determines the search sequence for condition type records and output type records (in this case), in order to find the appropriate condition type record (output type record).

4. Create output types with the correct access sequence assigned to them. The condition types are called *output type* here. Defining output types is key in the output determination process. The list of important standard output types is as follows:

   ▶ AF00: Inquiry

   ▶ AN00: Quotation

   ▶ BA00: Order confirmation

   ▶ BAIN: Output type for manual processing

   ▶ BAV0: Order confirmation VMI

   ▶ ESYM: Internal output

   ▶ K000: Contract

   ▶ KRML: Credit processing

   ▶ LP00: Scheduling agreement

   ▶ MAIL: Internal output

   ▶ RD03: Cash sale

   ▶ SDB: Material safety data sheet (MSDS)

As an example, let's take order confirmation (BA00) to understand how you can modify the standard output type or create a Z-output type. In Transaction V/30, OUTPUT TYPES (Sales Document)—this is same as executing Transaction NACE and selecting the application V1 and double-clicking on the OUTPUT TYPE tab, as shown in Figure 3.39—when you double-click on any output type, in this case BA00, you go to the screen shown in Figure 3.40.

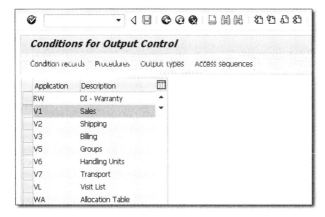

Figure 3.39 Application V1 (Sales) in Transaction NACE

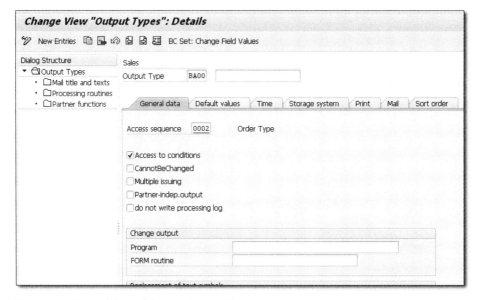

Figure 3.40 General Data of Output Type BA00

The menu path for Transaction V/30 is SAP IMG • BASIC FUNCTIONS • OUTPUT CONTROL • OUTPUT DETERMINATION – OUTPUT DETERMINATION USING CONDITION TECHNIQUE • MAINTAIN OUTPUT DETERMINATION FOR SALES DOCUMENTS • MAINTAIN OUTPUT TYPES. You maintain the access sequence in the GENERAL DATA tab. In the DEFAULT VALUES tab, you can maintain the values for DISPATCH TIME, TRANSMISSION MEDIUM, PARTNER FUNCTION, and COMMUNICATION STRATEGY that will become the default values when you create condition records.

In the processing routine, you can replace the form (RVORDER01 as shown in Figure 3.41 for output type BA00) with customized forms created using SAP Smart Form (Transaction SMARTFORMS).

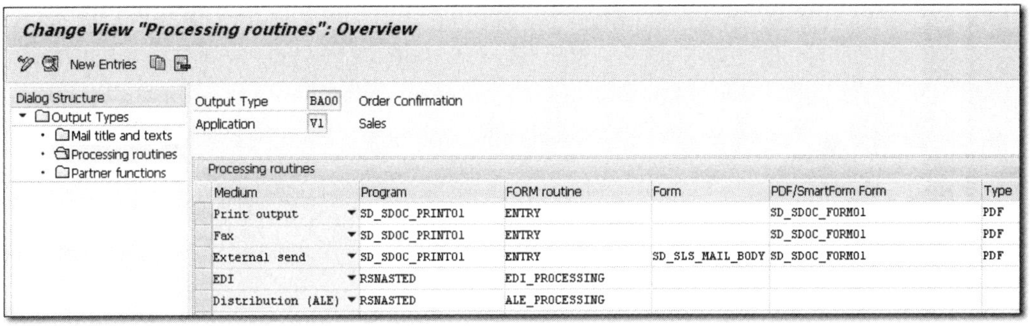

Figure 3.41 Processing Routines for Output Type BA00 (Order Confirmation)

After creating the output types, they are assigned to partner functions. You may only issue the output to the partners assigned to it. This basically depends on the preference (and technical feasibility) of the partner.

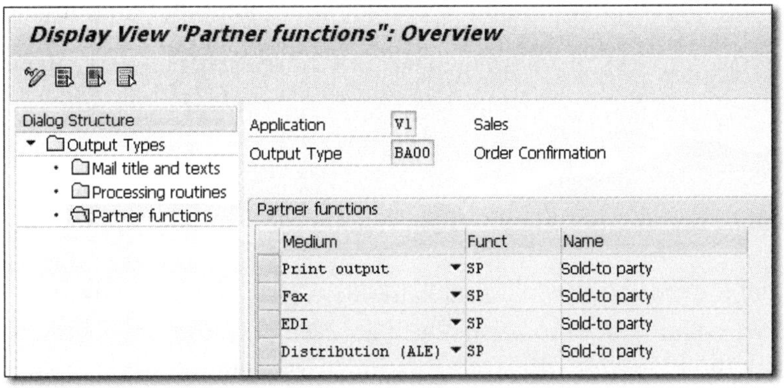

Figure 3.42 Partner Functions for Output Type BA00 (Order Confirmation)

A customer may like to receive the output by courier, while another may prefer by fax (if they have fax machine, which is technically feasible). In Figure 3.42, you can see the assignment of the OUTPUT TYPE BA00 to the partner function sold-to party for different mediums.

1. Create the determination procedure and assign to it the output types. Follow the menu path SAP IMG • BASIC FUNCTIONS • OUTPUT CONTROL • OUTPUT DETERMINATION – OUTPUT DETERMINATION USING CONDITION TECHNIQUE • MAINTAIN OUTPUT DETERMINATION FOR SALES DOCUMENTS • MAINTAIN OUTPUT DETERMINATION PROCEDURE to define the output determination procedure. Different output types receive assignment to each step of the procedure. The requirement routines improve performance by skipping steps that are irrelevant because of the specific requirement mentioned for a step. The EXCLUSIVE checkbox also improves performance by not allowing the system to search for other condition records upon finding a condition record.

2. Assign a determination procedure to sales document types and item categories. You assign output determination by following the menu path SAP IMG • BASIC FUNCTIONS • OUTPUT CONTROL • OUTPUT DETERMINATION – OUTPUT DETERMINATION USING CONDITION TECHNIQUE • MAINTAIN OUTPUT DETERMINATION FOR SALES DOCUMENTS • ASSIGN OUTPUT DETERMINATION PROCEDURES and then selecting ALLOCATE SALES DOCUMENT HEADER. In addition to the procedure, you can specify the default output type here. The option ASSIGN SALES DOCUMENT ITEMS can assign the determination procedure, defined for a sales document item, to the item categories.

3. Create condition records using Transaction VV11 or following the menu path SAP EASY ACCESS • LOGISTICS • SALES AND DISTRIBUTION • MASTER DATA • OUTPUT • SALES DOCUMENT • CREATE. Select the output type for which condition records are to be maintained and then click on KEY COMBINATION. Select the appropriate key combination. PARTNER FUNCTION, PARTNER, TRANSMISSION MEDIUM, TIME, and LANGUAGE values maintain for all condition records.

3.17 Solving Common Sales Problems

Find here a list of the most common errors found soon after you configure, modify, or add a new system to your solution. There are several ways to troubleshoot a problem, including revising the configuration, debugging via ABAP, and researching for SAP notes that can resolve your specific needs.

▸ **Problem**

The sales area is not defined for customer. This problem arises when a new or existing customer is maintained when selecting sales area.

Solution

Make sure that the customer is extended to the sales area in question or configure a new sales area. Review the organizational structure configuration in Chapter 1 about sales areas.

▸ **Problem**

The company code does not exist. It's common to find this type of error during the material master creation.

Solution

Is the material properly extended to the company code in question? If not, extend the material. Is this a new company code? If so, review organizational structure configuration in Chapter 1 and Chapter 2.

▸ **Problem**

The order type is not defined for sales area. This error happens during the sales order creation or Transaction VA01.

Solution

Make sure that the sales area combination entered is valid and the order type exists. You can also verify the sales document type assignment against sales area (see Section "What Will Be Covered Throughout" of this chapter).

▸ **Problem**

No pricing procedure could be determined—which is relatively common during sales order creation.

Solution

Verify determination in configuration for the sales area, as shown in Chapter 4.

▸ **Problem**

No business area can be determined. During sales order creation, you may face a business area error.

Solution

Verify the configuration of business area by sales area, via the menu path IMG • BASIC FUNCTIONS • ACCOUNT ASSIGNMENT/COSTING • BUSINESS AREA ACCOUNT ASSIGNMENT • ASSIGN BUSINESS AREA BY SALES AREA.

3.18 Summary

In this chapter, we discussed how to configure the header, item, and schedule line levels of sales documents. We discussed different sales documents, such as orders, outline agreements, and complaints. We discussed the use of condition techniques in automatic determination of partners, free goods, material determination, material listing and exclusion, batch, and output. We also discussed incompletion logs, availability checks, and transfer of requirements. With this knowledge, you'll be able to optimize both routine and special sales processes.

In next chapter, we'll discuss pricing, where the condition technique is demonstrated at its best.

This chapter discusses routines, pricing, and the improvement of system performance by configuring the condition technique for pricing. After reading this chapter, you should be able to customize rebate agreements and SAP interfaces for external tax software.

4   Pricing

Condition techniques are one of the most important functionalities in SAP ERP. In Chapter 3, you saw the use of condition techniques in automatic determination. In this chapter, we'll see its use in pricing. We'll discuss rebate agreements and tax processing, which are also part of pricing in a broader sense. The customization of pricing reports discussed in this chapter will be, perhaps, the first step in developing your own reports.

Price is what a customer pays you for your goods and/or services. In modern economies, several factors have made price a very complex functionality. Tax is one such factor. Almost all countries tax goods and/or services. Keeping in mind national interest and social objectives, some goods are taxed more than others. For example, the tax rate on cigarettes may be much higher than the tax rate for fresh fruit. You may have to pay a higher tax on an imported car than on a domestically manufactured one.

Discounts, freight, and surcharges are also considered part of your price, in addition to tax. Discounts are given to encourage customers to buy more, propose purchasing decisions, to pay in advance, or for a variety of other reasons. For surcharges, the objective is similar, but the execution is different. You add a surcharge to a customer's purchase for not buying a minimum quantity, for delaying payment, or for not buying before an agreed-upon date.

Rebates are similar to discounts but are subject to certain conditions (e.g., buying a certain quantity within a time period). Only when the condition is fulfilled is the rebate paid to the customer. Unlike discounts, rebates are not paid to a customer up front. A deduction from the invoice value is also considered a payment.

These are all conditions. In this chapter, we'll start by introducing condition techniques and then move on to condition records. We'll then discuss the application of the condition technique in pricing. The section on optimizing pricing determination will teach you how to carry out pricing and how you can optimize its performance. From there, we'll discuss the rebate agreement process and show you how to customize a pricing report. Finally, you'll learn about commonly available external tax software and how to integrate it with your SAP system. So, let's get started.

4.1 Condition Techniques

In SAP ERP, condition techniques automatically determine output, batches, material listing and exclusion, text, and revenue accounts, and are used many other components. It's not confined to the Sales and Distribution functionality in SAP ERP, and in fact may also be used in many other SAP ERP components that require where automatic determination. In Section 4.2 we'll list the general steps for customization of condition techniques, which will give you an overview of how the elements of this type of technique are integrated. But first, let's describe these elements.

- ▶ **Field catalog**
  A field catalog is simply the collection of all fields that are or can be used in a condition table. The field catalogs for different determination functionalities (e.g., pricing, revenue GL) differ. You can add new fields to this catalog if required.

- ▶ **Condition tables**
  Condition tables store the condition records. There can be several condition tables for the determination of the same object (e.g., price). A company can have one price for a material (e.g., 100 USD), another for a particular sales organization (e.g., 90 USD for sales org 1000), and another for a customer, for example, XYZ Inc. of the sales org 1000 (e.g., 85 USD). These three prices require three kinds of condition tables to store them. The table that stores prices based on material will store the price 100 USD/unit. The table that stores prices based on material and sales organization will store the price 90 USD/unit. We require a third type of table to store the price based on material, sales organization, and customer.

  Some of these tables may be available in the standard system. When they're not available, you have to create them using fields available in the field catalog. A field that is unavailable in the field catalog (e.g., customer code) must be added to the field catalog first, to make it available for use as a key field in the condition table.

▶ **Access sequence**
This is a list of condition tables given in a specific sequence. Take the example that we gave for condition tables. The difficulty in the system is to decide on the price for the customer XYZ Inc. All three prices are valid. But based on the access sequence, the price 85 USD/unit, which is valid for the material, sales org, and customer, may be accessed first. When the system finds a valid condition record, it (depending on the exclusive indicator and routines used) searches for records in other tables or accesses.

▶ **Condition type**
For each element (e.g., price, discount) that is to be determined, you define a condition type. The condition type also specifies the access sequence to be used, among many other things. We'll revisit this when we discuss the step for defining the pricing condition type.

▶ **Determination procedure**
A determination procedure lists the condition types. It's assigned to a combination of objects (e.g., sales area, document pricing procedure, and customer pricing procedure in the case of pricing) for which determination will carry out using the condition technique.

▶ **Condition records**
Each row in a condition table represents a condition record. This is a master data element. Its value is the result of the determination process that used the condition technique. This result moves to the document (or other object) that used the condition technique.

Now let's see how these elements are used in the customization of condition techniques, starting with the recommended sequence in pricing configuration:

1. Add the field required in condition table to the field catalog if it's currently unavailable.

2. Create condition tables using the fields available in the field catalog, or identify the standard SAP condition tables suitable for storing condition records.

3. Create an access sequence and assign condition tables for the system to access in the correct sequence.

4. Create condition types with the correct access sequence assigned to them. You cannot assign an access sequence if the condition type is not meant for automatic determination.

5. Create a determination procedure.

6. Assign the determination procedure.

7. Create condition records.

We'll look at these in more detail in Section 4.2.1.

SAP Fiori for Pricing

Before we get too far into pricing, a quick reminder: at the time of writing, there's one important SAP Fiori app for pricing to keep in mind.

Description	Requirements
The *Check Price and Availability* transactional app allows you to check price and availability. It lists products based on sales orders, detailed info of the material master, classification on configurable products, and related price availability.	SAP ERP 6.0 SP 15 or higher

---

4.2   Setting Up Condition Records

The production client maintains pricing condition records, such as other master records, and accesses them during sales document processing. When we say "price," we're referring to the gross price, the various types of discounts that are deducted from it, additional surcharges, included freight (based on incoterms), and additional tax.

Of these price elements, some are applicable to all goods and services and are difficult to allocate to individual items, such as freight or processing fees. These are *header conditions*. Others are clearly meant for individual items, called *item conditions,* such as tax. However, the method for calculating these conditions determines whether it's a header or item condition. For example, if you charge 10 USD for any invoice as a processing fee, then it becomes a header condition. When the processing fee is 1 USD per item, it becomes an item condition.

Pricing condition records are usually created for a particular sales organization and distribution channel. The transaction code for creating pricing condition record is VK31, or you can go to SAP EASY ACCESS • LOGISTICS • SALES AND DISTRIBUTION • MASTER DATA • CONDITIONS • CREATE. Then you select the folders on the left, as shown in Figure 4.1, depending on the type of condition record you want to create. The transaction codes to change, display, and create with reference are VK32, VK33, and VK34, respectively. The selection using the condition type or the menu path SAP EASY ACCESS • LOGISTICS • SALES AND DISTRIBUTION • MASTER DATA • CON-

DITIONS • SELECTION USING CONDITION TYPE can also create (VK11), change (VK12), display, (VK13) and create with reference (VK14) condition records.

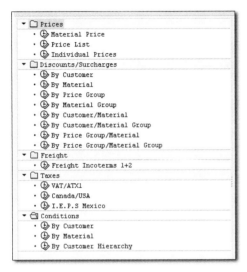

Figure 4.1 Create, Change, Display, and Create with Reference Pricing Condition Records (Transactions VK31, VK32, VK33, and VK34)

When creating a condition record using Transaction VK11, as seen in Figure 4.2, you enter the condition type and select the key combination. Depending on the key combination, different condition tables will contain the condition record. In addition to the fields mentioned in the key combination, you also enter the sales organization and distribution channel when creating the condition record. This means the condition record is valid only for the relevant sales organization and distribution channel.

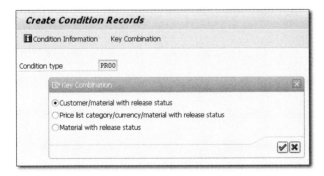

Figure 4.2 Create Condition Record Using Transaction VK11

In the FAST ENTRY mode shown in Figure 4.3, you can create the condition records for all materials for one customer. You can copy the list from other applications (e.g., Microsoft Excel) and paste it.

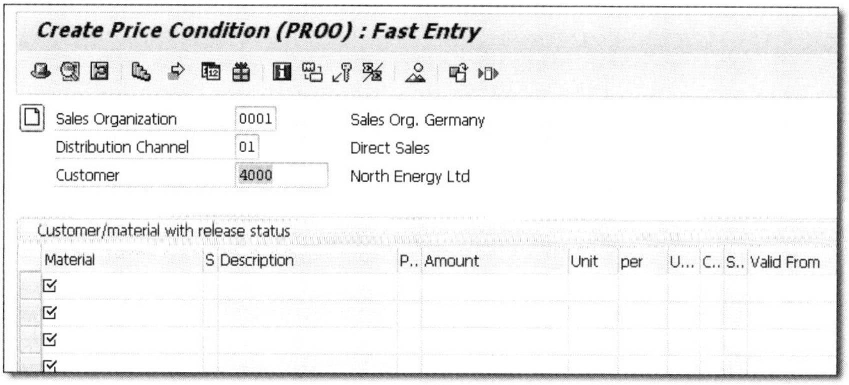

Figure 4.3 PR00 Condition Record with the Customer/Material with Release Status Key Combination

The condition record can have more than one amount stored in the condition value field. This is possible because of the *scales* functionality, which allows for different values for the condition record depending on the *scale basis*. For example, the price of a material can be 10 USD/unit when the order is for five or fewer units, and 9 USD/unit when the order is for six or more units. Table 4.1 lists the different standard scale bases.

Scale Basis (Key)	Scale Basis (Text)
B	Value scale
C	Quantity scale
D	Gross weight scale
E	Net weight scale
F	Volume scale
G	Scale based on a formula
L	Point scale
M	Time period scale – month
N	Time period scale – years
O	Time period scale – days

Table 4.1 List of Scale Bases

Scale Basis (Key)	Scale Basis (Text)
P	Time period scale – week
R	Distance
S	Number of shipping units
T	Reserved (IS-OIL, time prices)
X	Reserved (IS-OIL, day prices)

Table 4.1 List of Scale Bases (Cont.)

There are three possible types of scales:

▶ **From scale**
The quantity 100, price 100 USD means that when the quantity is more than 100, the price per unit is 100 USD (as shown in Figure 4.4).

▶ **To scale**
The quantity 100, amount 100 USD means that when the quantity is less than 100, the price per unit is 100 USD.

▶ **Interval scale**
You can't use a graduated-to interval scale for group conditions, and this can't be modified at the condition record level, which restricts its use.

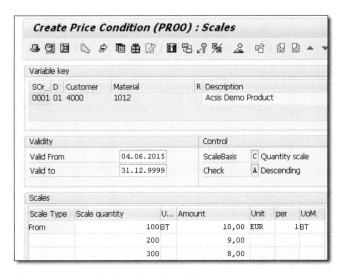

Figure 4.4 Use of Scale in Condition Type

You can modify the scale type by going to GOTO • DETAILS, as shown in Figure 4.5, except when the scale type is fixed as D (graduated-to interval) for the condition type in the customization.

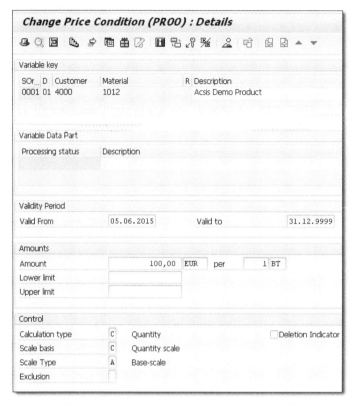

Figure 4.5 Detail Screen of Condition Record (Program SAPMV13A Screen Number 300)

When the processing status (as shown in Figure 4.5) of a condition record is blank, the condition record becomes active, or in use. Your other options are A (blocked), B (released for pricing simulation), and C (released for planning and pricing simulation).

Condition Tables, Date Ranges, and Statuses

The important thing to note is that you can have condition records in the same condition table with the same or overlapping date ranges, provided the status is different. For pricing, only those records with a status of released are available for processing, but some of the customized status types can be made available for use in pricing.

Depending on customization, the condition's value can be modified manually in the sales document. It's better to have an upper limit or lower limit (or both) for the condition type in the condition record. These fields are also available in the DETAILS screen. If, for example, there's is a percentage-type discount and someone manually changes it to 200% in a document, the system should generate an error or warning message.

Supplement conditions are allowed in certain condition types, and can be accessed using the SUPPLEMENT CONDITION icon or the menu path GOTO • CONDITIONS SUPPLEMENT. As shown in Figure 4.6, you can add additional condition types with values to a condition record. So, when any sales document picks up this condition record, that sales document automatically picks up the supplement conditions attached to it. For example, you can set a pricing policy of giving a 10% discount for customers who will bear the freight cost. So when you select the condition type (e.g., Z10P) for a 10% discount, the condition type to add a surcharge for freight (e.g., ZFRT) automatically joins the pricing procedure. This is made possible by making ZFRT a supplement condition of Z10P.

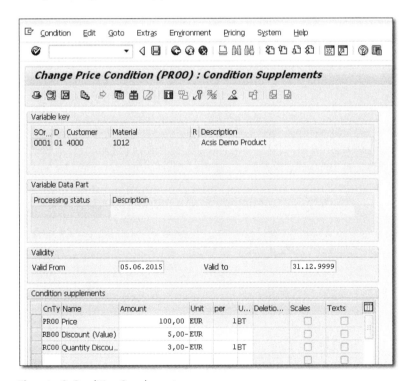

Figure 4.6 Condition Supplement

Maintaining condition records involves deleting records, changing the validity period, and changing the amount. You can delete condition records from the database with archiving functionality (Transaction SARA, object SD_COND). The system archives only those condition records already marked for deletion. A record marked for deletion can be reversed before the archiving program deletes it from the database. That is, you can make a condition record that's marked for deletion available for use again. To change the validity period of multiple condition records, select all of the records using Transaction VK12. Click on the CHANGE VALIDITY icon for changing the validity period, shown in Figure 4.7 (fifth icon from the left). A dialog screen will appear (not shown in Figure 4.7). All of the selected condition records contain the new VALID FROM and VALID TO dates in the pop-up screen.

Figure 4.7 Condition Maintenance Icons

To change the amount, you click on the CHANGE AMOUNT icon, shown in Figure 4.7 (the sixth icon from the left, which looks like a calculator). The pop-up gives you two options. The PERCENTAGE option allows you to enter a value (e.g., 5) in the PERCENTAGE field. When you click on the COPY button, all of the selected records will increase by 5%. Figure 4.8 shows the intermediate screen for log display. The ABSOLUTE AMOUNT field (refer to Figure 4.7) allows you to enter a value (e.g., 10) and currency unit (e.g., USD), and all of the records will increase by that amount (e.g., 10 USD). Typically, price change rules are very complex, so you'll rarely use this functionality.

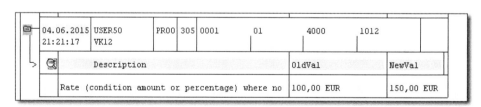

Figure 4.8 Log for 5% Price Increase (PR00 Condition Type) for All Material

You can report changes to the condition records via the menu path ENVIRONMENT • CHANGES • PER CONDITION RECORD (for a single record) or CHANGE RECORD (for multiple records). You can copy and modify the `RV16ACHD` program for change record reports.

The terms of payment and additional or fixed value days can be part of the condition record (see Figure 4.3, last three columns), and when they are, they take priority over customer master records or data from other customization settings. This information is used for processing a cash discount at the time of payment receipt, based on the terms of payment. You attach this information to the condition record using the ADDITIONAL DATA icon. In the same screen (shown in Figure 4.9), when the functionality for cumulating the values for the condition record, UPDATE CONDITION, is active, limits for pricing, such as maximum condition value, maximum number of orders, and maximum condition base value (quantity), are also entered. Cumulation can happen for the sales value, number of sales orders, or sales quantity. The additional advantage of cumulation (or the update condition function) is that you can view the usage or cumulation up to a particular time by selecting EXTRA • CUMULATIVE VALUE.

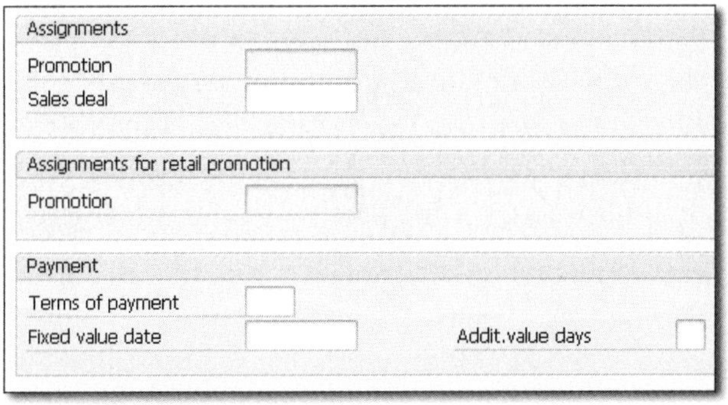

Figure 4.9 Additional Data for Condition Record

You would normally maintain condition *exclusion* for condition types in customization, but you can also maintain it for the condition record level (as you can see in the fourth column from the right in Figure 4.3). The important thing is that the condition supplement has priority over exclusion. So, you can use the combination of condition supplement (at the condition record level) and exclusion (at the condition type level) when one condition doesn't normally go with another, unless there are exceptions.

Now that you understand condition records, let's move on to condition techniques.

4.2.1 Addressing Basic Configuration

The basic pricing configuration consists of the definition of basic elements such as pricing fields and tables, and then associates them to the related pricing procedure determination. Follow these steps:

1. **Add fields to field catalog.**
   Add the fields required in condition table to the field catalog if they aren't already available. The menu path is SAP IMG • SALES AND DISTRIBUTION • BASIC FUNCTIONS • PRICING • PRICING CONTROL • DEFINE CONDITION TABLE • CONDITIONS: ALLOWED FIELDS.

2. **Create condition tables.**
   Condition tables store condition records. Several different condition tables can store the records of same condition type. For example, you can have a price for a material based on material type (applicable to all sales organizations, divisions, and so on).

   Another price for the same material can exist for a particular sales organization. These two condition records remain in different condition tables. Create condition tables using fields available in the field catalog. You can also identify and use the standard SAP condition tables suitable for storing condition records. The menu path for creating condition tables is SAP IMG • SALES AND DISTRIBUTION • BASIC FUNCTIONS • PRICING • PRICING CONTROL • DEFINE CONDITION TABLE • CREATE CONDITION TABLES; you can also use Transaction V/03.

3. **Create access sequence.**
   An access sequence is assigned to the condition types that require automatic determination, and consists of a sequence of condition tables. You create an access sequence and assign the condition tables for the system to access in the correct sequence. The menu path is SAP IMG • SALES AND DISTRIBUTION • BASIC FUNCTIONS • PRICING • PRICING CONTROL • DEFINE ACCESS SEQUENCE; you can also use Transaction V/07. Figure 4.10 shows the standard access sequence PR00. Note the use of requirement routine 3 in access number (AcNo) 30. This means that if the conditions specified in requirement routine 3 are not met, then the system skips the step (AcNo 30). Also, with the EXCLUSIVE checkbox selected, once a condition record is available, the system will not go to the next table in the access sequence.

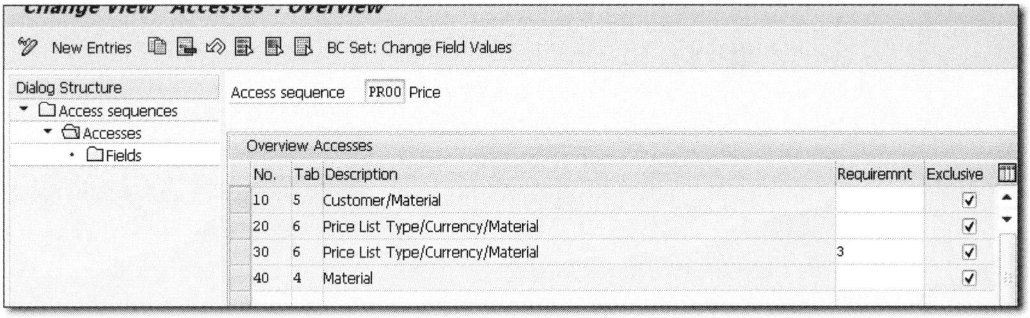

Figure 4.10 Access Sequence PR00

4. **Create condition types.**

You create condition types for each type of price. Prices, surcharges, discounts, and taxes are general types of prices. There can be several types of discounts for a material or item, such as trade discount, off-season discount, and so on, and for each of them you need a condition type. In the condition type, you also specify how to calculate the discount (e.g., percentage or quantity based), among other things that we'll discuss. You create condition types with the correct access sequence assigned to them. You cannot assign an access sequence if the condition type is not meant for automatic determination (header conditions, for example). The menu path for defining condition types is SAP IMG • SALES AND DISTRIBUTION • BASIC FUNCTIONS • PRICING • PRICING CONTROL • DEFINE CONDITION TYPE; you can also use Transaction V/06. The screen used for defining condition type, shown in Figure 4.11, is an important one.

There are a few important fields that define the condition type:

▷ The CONDITION CLASS determines whether the condition type is a price, discount or surcharge, or tax. The CONDITION CATEGORY is another way of classifying the condition type. The CALCULATION TYPE restricts the selection of the unit of measure for the AMOUNT field of the condition record. You can also change this at the condition record level. If you expect the value of a condition will always be either positive or negative, then, using the PLUS/MINUS field, you can change the value and prevent any errors, even with manual entry. The ROUNDING RULE can be commercial (1.51 becomes 2 and 1.49 becomes 1), round up (both 1.51 and 1.49 become 2), or round down (both 1.49 and 1.51 become 1). The STRUCTURE CONDITION field determines how the condition type behaves in an order containing a bill of materials or configurable material.

▷ When you select the GROUP CONDITION checkbox, the condition record of the condition type should include the material group as a field. Items belonging to same material group are grouped to receive the benefit of scale, which otherwise is not available to individual items. The GROUP CONDITION ROUTINE influences the group condition, or how the values of the condition type in different items are grouped. If you select the ROUNDING DIFFERENCE COMPARISON checkbox, it will compare the difference at the header and sum of items (difference can occur due to rounding at the item level) and settle the difference by adding or subtracting it to the largest item. Please note that both item and header level condition types can be a group condition, so rounding the difference comparison applies to it.

▷ The option selected for MANUAL ENTRIES determines whether the condition type can be added at the document processing time and whether it will take priority over the automatically determined condition record. The HEADER CONDITION is the condition type that applies to a document as whole, and cannot be made applicable to items. ITEM CONDITIONS, as opposed to header conditions, apply to items of a document, and cannot be added manually at the header level, although the total of individual items is displayed at the header level. Please note that you may define a condition type as a header and an item condition at the same time, and assign an access sequence to such a condition type. But this does not mean the condition can be determined automatically using the access sequence, condition table, and condition record maintained for it. The header conditions are still added manually at the document level, and a condition type that is exclusively a header condition can't have an access sequence. The DELETE checkbox determines if the condition record inserted manually or determined automatically can be deleted manually from a document. The AMOUNT/PERCENTAGE, QTY RELATION, VALUE, and CALCULATION type checkboxes determine if these fields of a condition record inserted in a document are changeable.

▷ The VALID FROM and VALID TO data entered in the condition type automatically populates the condition record, unless these fields are filled manually in the condition record. For the rebate and condition update function, the date range assumes more significance. The REFERENCE CONDITION TYPE and REFERENCE APPLICATION (Sales and Distribution is V, Purchasing is M) helps you reduce the additional master data maintenance. The PRICING PROCEDURE field stores condition supplements. The DELETE FROM DATABASE field determines if any master data will be deleted from the database or marked for deletion. The CONDITION INDEX checkbox allows you to update some of the condition indices automatically when you create a condition record. The CONDITION UPDATE checkbox makes the condition record cumulate the condition value, number of documents using the condition record, or condition base value (quantity) in the valid date range. When you select this checkbox, you can also add a maximum condition value, maximum number of documents, and maximum condition base value (quantity) in the additional data screen of a condition record. So when you have to give a few customers a 2% discount for a year, subject to the condition that their total discount will not be more than 100 USD, you know what the setting will be.

▸ For maintaining scales in a condition record, you maintain SCALE BASIS, CHECK VALUE, SCALE TYPE, SCALE FORMULA, and UNIT OF MEASURE in the customization of the condition type.

▸ The CURRENCY CONVERSION checkbox converts the currency of the condition record before inserting it into the condition record. If you select this checkbox, it will convert the condition record currency to the document currency after multiplying with the quantity of the document item. The ACCRUALS checkbox, if selected, makes the value of the condition in the sales document statistical and posts that value in subsequent accounting documents, if any, as accrual. The INVOICE LIST CONDITION checkbox makes the condition type relevant for the invoice list. The INTERCOMPANY BILLING checkbox, if selected, applies to condition types used for intercompany billing. When you select the VARIANT CONDITION checkbox for any condition type, only the key for the condition type appears in the conditions screen of the sales document. When the calculation type for a condition type is C (quantity), then the unit of measure of the document quantity can differ from the unit of measure for which the condition record is maintained. In such a situation, the QUANTITY CONVERSION checkbox specifies if the base value for calculating the condition should be determined after converting it to the stock-keeping unit of measure. The EXCLUSION checkbox excludes the condition types from a document. The PRICING DATE field determines the date that's relevant for deciding the condition record. The RELEVANT FOR ACCOUNT ASSIGNMENT field determines if the accounting indicator should be added at the time of account assignment.

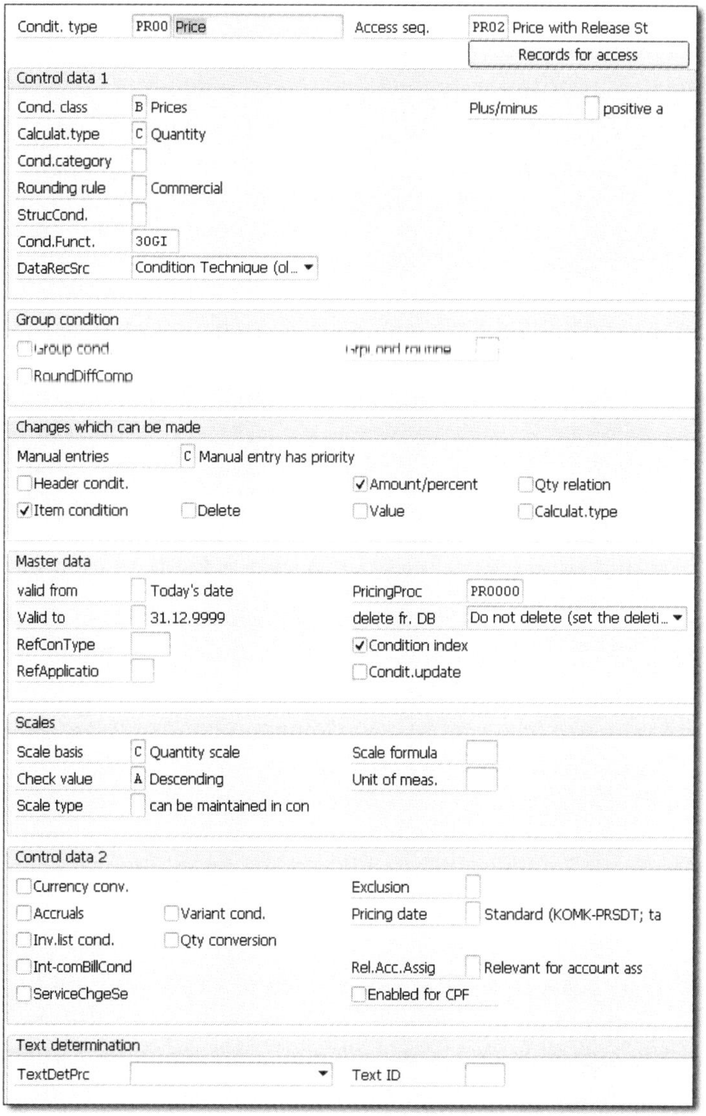

Figure 4.11 Customizing Condition Types

Condition Type Limits

It's easier to maintain the upper and lower limit value for the condition type here than at the condition record level. Use Transaction VCHECKT685A to check the customization setting for all of the pricing condition types in your system.

4.2.2 Creating Pricing Procedure

The menu path to create a pricing procedure is SAP IMG • SALES AND DISTRIBUTION • BASIC FUNCTIONS • PRICING • PRICING CONTROL • DEFINE AND ASSIGN PRICING PROCEDURE • MAINTAIN PRICING PROCEDURE (Transaction V/08). A pricing procedure is a set of condition types that can be prices, discounts, surcharges, taxes, and freights. Figure 4.12 illustrates standard pricing procedure RVAA01.

Let's walk through the different columns shown in Figure 4.12 and their role in pricing procedure:

▶ The condition types are specified in each of the steps.

▶ For one step, you can have different counters. This becomes relevant if you already have a pricing procedure and want to insert new condition types between two steps that have no gaps (that is, the existing steps are already consecutive numbers). The steps and the counter determine the sequence in which the condition types are determined.

▶ The FROM and TO columns pull the total value of certain condition types, as seen in step 300, where the total discount is calculated.

▶ The MANUAL (MAN.) checkbox makes the condition type available to a pricing procedure only if the user adds it manually.

▶ When the MANDATORY checkbox is selected for any condition type, it checks if the condition type is present in a document, inserted either automatically or manually, to decide if the document is complete for further processing.

▶ The STATISTICAL checkbox makes the value of a condition type statistical, derived during pricing. Statistical condition types (e.g., maximum retail price [MRP]) in a pricing procedure can calculate other pricing conditions (e.g., discount is 5% of MRP).

▶ The amount entered in the SUBTOTAL (SUBTO) column copies or carries the value to the specified table field (KOMP-CMPRE when SubTo is B or KOMP- KZWI1 to KOMP-KZWI6). These fields are important for reporting and further processes, such as credit management or costing. The values of different items in KOMP-CMPRE, for example, determine the value of a document in the credit management submodule.

▶ The REQUIREMENTS (REQT) column allows you to enter a requirements type VOFM routine that checks if specific conditions are met before processing the step against which the VOFM routine is mentioned.

Step	Co	CTyp Description	Fro	To	Ma...	R...	St...	P	SuTot	Reqt	CalTy...	BasT...	Acc...	Acc...
8	0	EK01 Costs			✓								KP1	
11	0	PR00 Price								2			KP1	
13	0	PB00 Price (Gross)			✓					2			KP1	
14	0	PR02 Price Increased								2			KP1	
15	0	ZK01 Variant Costs						x		2			KP1	
20	0	VA00 Variants						x		2			KP1	
21	1	ZA00 General variants						x		2			KP1	
100	0	Gross Value						x	1		2		KP3	
101	0	KA00 Sales Promotion						x		2			KP3	
102	0	K032 Price Group/Material						x		2			KP3	
103	0	K005 Customer/Material						x		2			KP3	
104	0	K007 Customer Discount						x		2			KP3	
105	0	K004 Material						x		2			KP3	
106	0	K020 Price Group						x		2			KP3	
107	0	K029 Mat.Pricing Group						x		2			KP3	
108	0	K030 Customer/Mat.Pr.Grp						x		2			KP3	
109	0	K031 Price Grp/Mat.Pr.Grp						x		2			KP3	
110	1	RA01 % Disc. from Gross	100		✓			x		3			KP3	
110	2	RA00 % Discount from Net			✓			x		2			KP3	
110	3	K020 Quantity Discount			✓			x		2			KP3	
110	4	KB00 Discount (Value)			✓			x		2			KP3	
110	5	K029 Weight Discount			✓			x		2			KP3	
111	0	HI01 Hierarchy						x		2			KP3	
112	0	HI02 Hierarchy/Material						x		2			KP3	
115	0	PI41 Product Hierarchy						x		2			KP3	
120	0	Markt. variants or						y		-			KP3	
121	0	ZWU Discount/contract	100					8		2			KP3	
300	0	Discount amount	101	299						-	7	3	KP3	
305	0	ab.00 Price			✓			x		2	6		KP1	
310	0	PN00 Net Price			✓			x		2	6		KP1	
320	0	PMIN Minimum Price						x		2	15		KP1	
399	0	R100 100% discount						x		55		28	KP3	
400	0	Rebate Basis						y						
600	0	Net Value for Item						x	2		2			
601	0	NRAB Free goods						x		55		29	KP3	
605	1	KP00 Pallet Discount								2		22	KP3	
605	2	KP01 Incomp.Pallet Surch.								2		24	KP3	
605	3	KP02 Mixed Pallet Disc.								2			KP3	
605	4	KP03 Mixed Pallet Surch.								2			KP3	
610	1	KA00 Percentage Discount			✓								KP3	
610	2	HB00 Discount (Value)			✓								KP3	
610	3	KF00 Freight			✓			4					KPF	
615	0	KF00 Freight						4					KPF	
616	0	FX00 Cust. shipment(IDES)			✓									
617	0	AMIW Minimum SalesOrdVal					✓	B		2				
618	0	AMIZ Minimum ValueSurchrg								2	11		KP3	
620	0	BO00 Order Value			✓								KP3	
830	0	ARM1 ARM - Return Reason	800											
831	0	ARM2 ARM - Refund Code	800											
890	0													
895	0	PDIF Diff.value (own)			✓								KP3	
900	0	Net Value 2						3			2			
901	0	B001 Group Rebate	400							24			ERB	ERU
902	0	B002 Material Rebate	400							24			ERB	ERU
903	0	B003 Customer Rebate	400							24			ERB	ERU
904	0	B004 Hierarchy Rebate	400							24			ERB	ERU
905	0	B005 Hierarchy rebate/mat	400							24			ERB	ERU
906	0	ZB07 Cust. hier./p-group	400							24			ERB	ERU
908	0	Net Value 3												
910	0	PI01 Intercompany Price			✓	✓		D		22			KP1	
911	0	AZWR Down Pay./Settlement								2	48		KP1	
914	0	SKTV Cash Discount					✓	D		14	2			
915	0	MWST Output Tax								10	16		MW5	
919	0	DIFF Rounding Off			✓					13	16	4	KP3	
920	0	Total						A			4			
930	0	SKTO Cash Discount					✓			9	11			
932	0	PL00 Factoring Discount								23	2		KP3	
933	0	MW15 Fact.Discount Tax	932			✓	✓			21			MW5	
935	0	GRWR Statistical Value					✓	C		8	2			
936	0	ZREA REA Conditions					✓	C						
940	0	VPRS Cost					✓	B	4					
941	0	EK02 Calculated costs			✓		✓	B						
942	0	EK03 Calculated ship.cost			✓		✓							
950	0	Profit Margin									11			
970	0	EDI1 Cust.expected price			✓		✓				9			
971	0	EDI2 Cust.expected value			✓		✓				8			

Figure 4.12 Control Data of Pricing Procedure RVAA01

▸ Use the ALTCTY and ALTCBV columns to enter the formula type VOFM routines that manipulate the condition record and/or the condition base value. The ALTCTY field stores the condition formula for the alternative calculation type, and ALTCBV is for the condition formula for the alternative condition base value. For example, instead of using the order quantity as a condition base value, you can use a standard available routine to use the gross weight as the base value.

▶ The ACCOUNT KEY (ACTKEY) automatically posts the value to a specific general ledger (GL) maintained in SAP ERP Financial Accounting. The accrual key does the same thing, except that the posting is an accrual type.

Transaction VCHECKT683

You can use Transaction VCHECKT683 to check the customization setting for all the pricing procedures in your system.

4.2.3 Assigning Pricing Procedure

The menu path to assign the pricing procedure is SAP IMG • SALES AND DISTRIBUTION • BASIC FUNCTIONS • PRICING • PRICING CONTROL • DEFINE AND ASSIGN PRICING PROCEDURES • DEFINE PRICING PROCEDURE DETERMINATION (Transaction OVKK). The pricing procedure is assigned to the relevant combinations of the following:

▶ Sales area, which is the combination of following three units:
  ▸ Sales organization
  ▸ Distribution channel
  ▸ Division
▶ Customer pricing procedure
▶ Document pricing procedure

4.2.4 Creating Condition Records

The menu path to create the condition record is SAP EASY ACCESS • LOGISTICS • SALES AND DISTRIBUTION • MASTER DATA • CONDITIONS • CREATE; you can also use Transaction VK31. We already discussed this in a previous section.

Now let's move on to the principle of processing pricing.

4.3 Optimizing Price Determination

Before learning any tips on optimizing condition techniques for pricing, you should know how it works.

The system reads the document pricing procedure (DoPP), customer pricing procedure (CuPP), and sales area (which is a combination of sales organization, distribution channel, and division) of the document to determine pricing procedure maintained for such a combination. Once the system knows the pricing procedure applicable for a particular document, it goes step by step through the pricing procedure. When the system encounters the condition type, it checks if any access sequence has been assigned to it. It also checks if there's an applicable VOFM routine (requirement and formula type). If there is an access sequence assigned to the condition type and the applicable requirement routine is satisfied, then the system goes to the row with the lowest access number and searches for the condition record in the condition table listed in that row. If it finds a record, it stops there and transfers the value to the document, as long as the EXCLUSIVE checkbox is selected. Otherwise it goes to the next access number and repeats the process until it finds a condition record. The value for the price then transfers to the document. Once all of the steps in the pricing procedure are complete, the pricing is complete. All of the mandatory condition types in the pricing procedure must have some value for the pricing to be complete. The document fields that used for searching and deciding the condition record can be from customer or material master records, from customization, or entered manually. Figure 4.13 shows the fundamentals of processing pricing.

In an optimal system, the following applies:

▸ You can use multiple pricing procedures.

▸ Each of these pricing procedures should have fewer steps and fewer "automatic" condition types. Manually inserted condition types don't affect performance, but such condition types should not have an access sequence assigned to them.

▸ The access sequence should have minimal steps or access numbers with the EXCLUSIVE checkbox selected at each step (except when it's intentional).

▸ The condition table should not contain "related" fields. If any two or more fields in the condition records relate through a customer master record or material master record, then it becomes redundant for both to be present in the condition table. A condition table with CUSTOMER, MATERIAL GROUP and MATERIAL as key fields is redundant because the material group relates to the material via the material master record. Therefore, the condition table should have either CUSTOMER – MATERIAL GROUP or CUSTOMER – MATERIAL, as key fields.

▸ You don't maintain unnecessary condition records.

▸ You use the condition exclusion and condition supplement when possible.

▸ You use VOFM routines (requirement and formula type) in the pricing procedure and access sequence to avoid unnecessary table searches that reduce the performance. We'll discuss a few such routines to explain their importance in performance tuning.

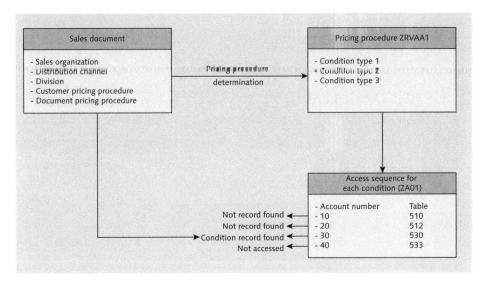

Figure 4.13 Processing Pricing

You assign the requirement routines to the condition type in the REQUIREMENT column of the pricing procedure. If the conditions coded in the requirement routine are fulfilled, then only the access sequence and subsequently, the condition table search is done.

▸ The ROUTINE ITEM with PRICING requirement (2) checks if the item category is relevant for pricing and no previous access in the access sequence has set the condition exclusion flag.

▸ The COST PRICING requirement (4) is met when there is a plant for the item in the document, when the valuation area company code and company code of the sales organization are same, and the item is not a down payment. You should assign this requirement routine to the cost condition type (VPRS in the standard system).

- Pricing requirement 10 (PLANT IS SET) is met when the plant in the item or departure country in the document exists. You can use this requirement for the tax condition type, or condition types for which require the above condition.

- The NOT IN RETURNS pricing requirement (57) is met if the item category is not a return type. We recommend that you use different, but similar, pricing procedures for return processing. However, when the pricing procedure is the same as the one used for sales, you can use this routine to avoid certain condition types in return processing.

- Pricing requirement routine 24 (ONLY IN BILLING DOCUMENT) normally assigns to the rebate condition types. This requirement allows the rebate condition types that have been determined or calculated in invoices, credit and debit memos, and returns, but not in sales orders or pro forma invoices.

- Pricing requirement 25 (ONLY IN REBATE DOCUMENTS) is met only when the document is a rebate settlement document or a rebate correction document. This normally assigns condition types not based on sales volume to the rebate.

We've listed just a few important requirements. You should also have a look at other standard VOFM requirement routines to see if they are relevant for a specific condition type. Alternatively, you can customize your own for optimizing pricing.

In the pricing procedure, formula routines manipulate or determine the scale, condition base value, and condition value. An example to help you understand these routines from a functional point of view is as follows: the scale base formula 23 (PARTIAL QUANTITY) is assigned to the condition type KP03 (MIXED PALLET SURCHARGES), which converts the whole number (the number that comes before the decimal place) to zero. Thus, 10.56 becomes 0.56. The pricing procedure can include two condition types (surcharges). One of them calculates the surcharge by rounding 10.56 to 10, and the other, KP03 (or a copy of it), with formula 23 for 0.56.

Normally, the same document line item has a quantity and a sales unit. The condition records exist as value per sales unit. After determining the condition record, the quantity multiplies by the value of the condition record. If the order quantity is 10 kg and the price is 5 USD per kg, then the total value is 50 USD. But the condition record can express itself in terms of volume or gross weight, so 10 kg can be 5 cubic meters in terms of volume, or have a gross weight of 12 kg when you add the weight of packaging materials. You can find this information in material master records. To calculate the freight (condition type), you can either use condition base value formula 1 (volume) or 12 (gross weight). The condition base value formulas also distribute the header condition value among the items. Another example is formula `28` (100% discount), which is assigned to condition type `R100` and sets the rate of the condition to a 100% discount. The condition value formula routine `11` (profit margin) makes the value of a condition type equal to net price minus cost. It's a good idea to show the profit margin if you already have the net value calculated and are using condition type `VPRS`.

Now that you understand how to optimize pricing, let's move on to rebates and rebate agreements.

4.4   Rebate Agreement

A rebate is simply a discount that's subject to certain conditions. Until the conditions are met, the system will only calculate the accrued rebate. Accrual value is calculated based on the assumption that the customer will achieve the sales volume specified in the rebate agreement within the time specified. Once the customer reaches his targets, he receives the accrued value as a cash payment, or as a credit memo. If the customer does not achieve the target, he does not receive the rebate. Instead of one target, typically there are multiple targets (some achievable, some not), and the customer receives the rebate based on the target level achieved. The following is a typical example.

If the total purchase in the date range specified in rebate agreement is:

▸ 100 units, you receive 5% of your total invoice as rebate.

▸ 200 units, you receive 7% of your total invoice as rebate.

▸ 300 units or more, you receive 10% of your total invoice as rebate.

In SAP ERP, the prerequisites for rebate processing are as follows:

▸ Sales organization is relevant for rebates.

▸ Payer is relevant for rebates.

▸ Document type is relevant for rebates.

▸ When material is not involved, there should be a material master record for a dummy material called the material for settlement.

All of the steps for the customization of rebate processing are accessible through AREA MENU OLS1, shown in Figure 4.14.

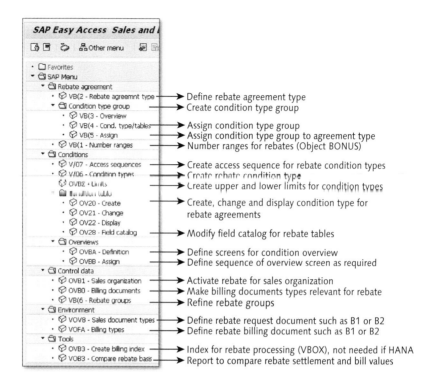

Figure 4.14 Area Menu OLS1 Listing the Customization of Rebate Processing Steps

When you try to create a rebate agreement (which is like a condition record), you need to specify the *rebate agreement type* (which is like a condition type). Figure 4.15 shows the screen where you customize rebate agreement type. The following data of a rebate agreement type apply for all condition records that you create within it:

- Validity period
- Status
- Rebate recipient
- Currency
- Method of payment
- Condition type group (the rebate condition types is assigned to the condition type group, which is then assigned to the rebate agreement type)

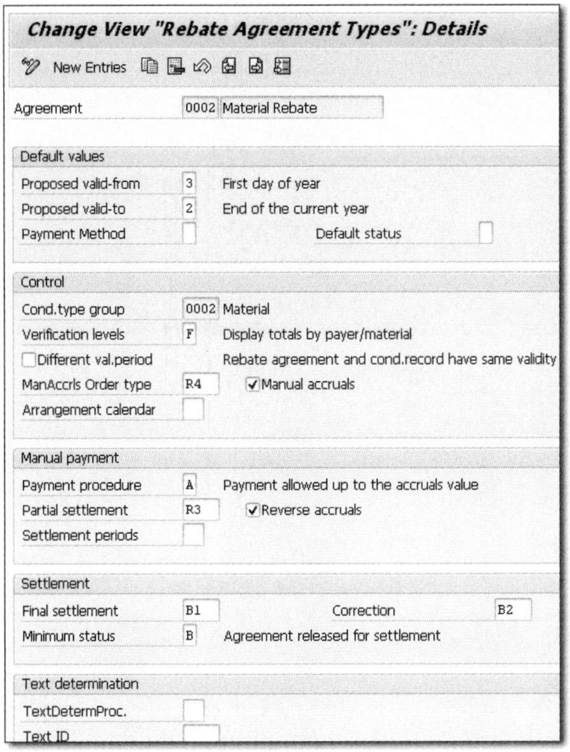

Figure 4.15 Rebate Agreement Type 0002 (Material Rebate)

Create the condition record for a rebate agreement, as shown in Figure 4.16, using Transaction VBO1 or following the menu path SAP EASY ACCESS • LOGISTICS • SALES AND DISTRIBUTION • MASTER DATA • AGREEMENTS • REBATE AGREEMENT • CREATE.

In order to create a rebate condition record, you need to gather the following elements, as they all are needed and associated in this record:

- Rebate agreement type (see Table 4.2)
- Basis for the rebate (e.g., customer, customer/material)
- Validity period (same as the rebate agreement or within the validity range)
- Condition rate
- Material for settlement
- Accrual rate
- Pricing scale details

Agreement Type	Basis of Rebate	Calculation Type	Condition Type
0001	Customer/material	Quantity based	BO01
	Customer/rebate group	Quantity based	BO01
0002	Customer/material	Quantity based	BO02
0003	Customer	Percentage	BO03
0004	Customer hierarchy	Percentage	BO04
	Customer hierarchy/material	Percentage	BO05
0005	Sales volume independent	Fixed amount	BO06

Table 4.2 Standard Rebate Agreement Types

Figure 4.16 Condition Record for Rebate Agreement

Several standard rebate condition types are available for use. When required, you can create your own using Transaction V/06, which also creates pricing condition types. In the initial screen, you can select any standard rebate condition type (we've selected BO02) and click on the COPY AS icon to go to the screen shown in Figure 4.17. The customization that you've done here controls how the condition type behaves.

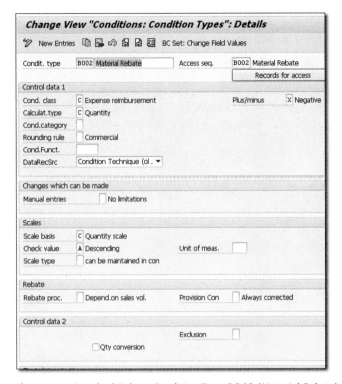

Figure 4.17 Standard Rebate Condition Type BO02 (Material Rebate)

You can customize the sequence of screens of the overview of rebate conditions using Transactions OVBA and OVBB. Table 4.3 lists some of the standard screens.

View	Description	Screen Number
0001	Condition rates	3001
0002	Administrative data	3002
0003	Sales promotion	3003
0004	Terms of payment	3004
0005	Validity periods	3005
0008	Planned values	3008

Table 4.3 Rebate Condition Overview Screens

The customization of the rebate condition type, access sequence, and condition table are similar to that of pricing.

Tables

The tables that store the condition records for pricing are different from the tables that store the same for rebate agreements. The database table for storing pricing condition records has the same name as the pricing table with the added prefix A. So pricing table 001 becomes A001, and 501 becomes A501. For the rebate table, the prefix is KOTE. So rebate table 001 becomes KOTE001 and 501 becomes KOTE501.

Programs RV15C001 and RV15C002 are very useful for the mass processing of rebate agreements as a background job. You can process rebates at night, or some other time when system usage is low. This optimizes your system performance and usage. By using the Issue Verification Level option in report RV15C001, you can use the same report for listing the rebate agreements.

After the final settlement of a rebate agreement, you can modify the credit memo request for rebate (order types) using Transaction VA02 before you issue the credit memo for rebate.

Depending upon the valid-from date, you can make a rebate agreement active or valid from a date in the past. This is called a *retroactive rebate*. The usual problem with retroactive rebates is that the subtotal you need for calculating the rebate may not be available in the pricing procedure used in old documents. You can overcome this problem by executing program RV15B003 and by restructuring the billing index by running program RVV05IVB. We'll discuss program RVV05IVB in the problem and solution section in Chapter 7. The billing index is simply additional tables that SAP provides (e.g., VKDFS for the billing initiator) to store information for a specific purpose, billing in this case.

Rebate Agreement Check

You can use Transaction VCHECKBONUS to check customization for all of the rebate agreement types in your system.

Now that you understand rebate agreements in the SAP system, let's move on to customized pricing reports and lists.

4.5 Customized Pricing Report and Price List

A customized pricing report is normally the first report that Sales and Distribution functional developers create without the help of technical developers. Transaction V/LA creates the report, Transaction V/LB modifies it, Transaction V/LC displays it, and Transaction V/LD executes it. Several standard pricing reports are available for you to use, as listed in Table 4.4.

Pricing Report	Pricing Report Name
14	Taxes
15	Material Price
16	Individual Prices
17	Discounts and Surcharges by Customer
18	Discounts and Surcharges by Material
26	Canada/USA
28	Conditions by Customer

Table 4.4 Examples of Standard Pricing Reports Available in Transaction V/LD

The first step in creating your own pricing report is to give a name and description/title to the list. In the example shown in Figure 4.18, we've selected Y1, but the name can be any alpha-alpha or alphanumeric code (except LE, LI, and UP). The next step is to give a suitable title to your report (e.g., "Report by Country ID") and click on the SELECTED FIELD icon (or press F5).

Figure 4.18 Creating Price Report Y1

Select the fields that you want to display in the report. In this example, we've selected COUNTRY ID (Figure 4.19). If you want to select more than one field, you have the option of using the OR or AND tabs on the top. OR means the selected tables contain at least one of the selected fields, whereas AND means the selected table contains all of the selected fields. Because we've selected only one field in this example, no matter which option we select, we'll get table `002` and `003`. If we select Bill to Party and Batch, the AND option may not give us any table, whereas OR will give us a few tables in addition to `002` and `003`. This option is also important when you're using a single field, because it decides how the tables will be joined (left-outer join or inner join). We'll discuss the difference between these joins in Chapter 9.

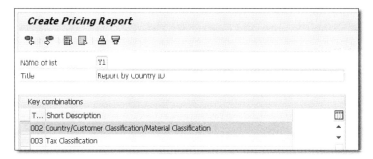

Figure 4.19 Selecting Fields for the Report

Once you reach the next screen, you can select the tables you want and then click on Continue to List Structure (F5) to go to the screen shown in Figure 4.20.

All of the fields of the selected tables will appear in a list, as shown in the Field name column in Figure 4.20. In the Positioning column, you have three options:

▶ Position 1 (Page Header)

▶ Position 2 (Group Header)

▶ Position 3 (Item Level)

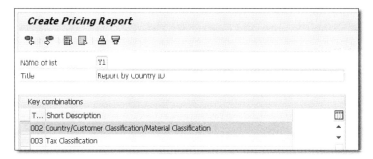

Figure 4.20 Customizing Pricing Report

You can use these positioning fields to make the report more presentable. As shown in Figure 4.23, you'll find the fields that aren't likely to change often (i.e., sales organization, distribution channel, and company code) at this level. This prevents these fields from appearing on all items. Fields such as material code and material group are normally assigned to the group header level. The group-level fields are the fields that group the items in the report, whereas the item-level fields appear as items it the report.

It's important for a report to be presentable. In SAP ERP, any field can have a limited number of characters and may have to start with Y or Z. The key or code for the field may not be long enough to describe it, so in the report, you need to include the description as well. There are three options available in a text column for display in the report:

▸ 1 (only key field)

▸ 2 (key field + its text)

▸ 3 (only the text of the key)

The selection of any field will make it available to use in the selection screen. If you select a field in the REQUIRED ENTRY column, then you must enter a value for the field before executing the report.

The default values for the screen field have five checkboxes, which are also present in the selection screen of the report. So if you select any of these, they will appear in the selection screen of the report. When you select any of these options, they will add additional columns, including SCALE TYPE, SCALE QTY, and UoM, and so on.

When you save the setting, it generates a transport request and makes the change effective for all other clients in the development server. The transport request then moves to the product server after testing in the quality server.

To use the pricing report created using Transaction V/LA, you can use Transaction V/LD. It the first screen, select the report (Y1), and execute it to go to the reports selection screen shown in Figure 4.21.

After entering the required values in the input fields, you can execute the report to receive its output, as shown in Figure 4.22. Note the change (pencil) and display (spectacles) icons in the output. You can keep your cursor on any particular line and use these icons to display or change the actual condition record (subject to authorization).

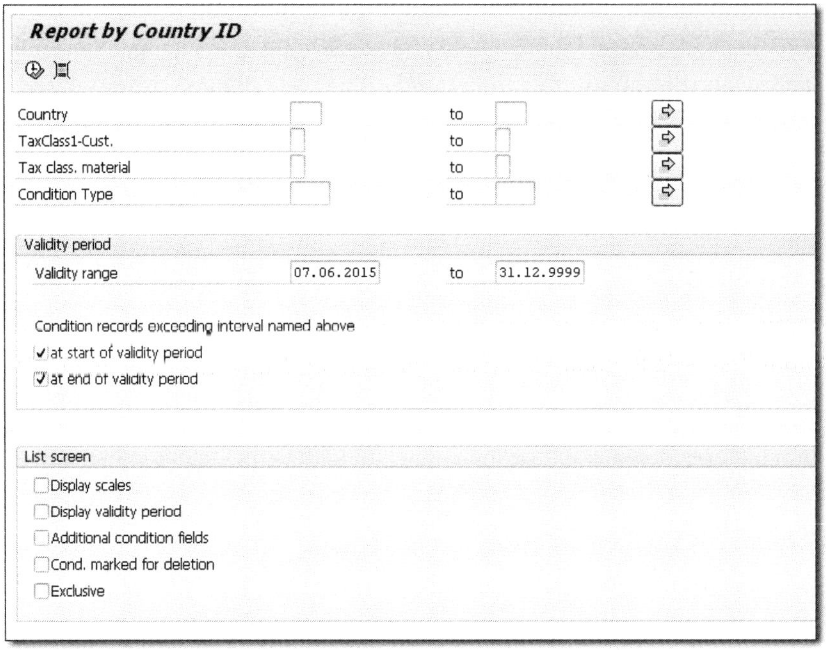

Figure 4.21 Selection Screen of Pricing Report Y1

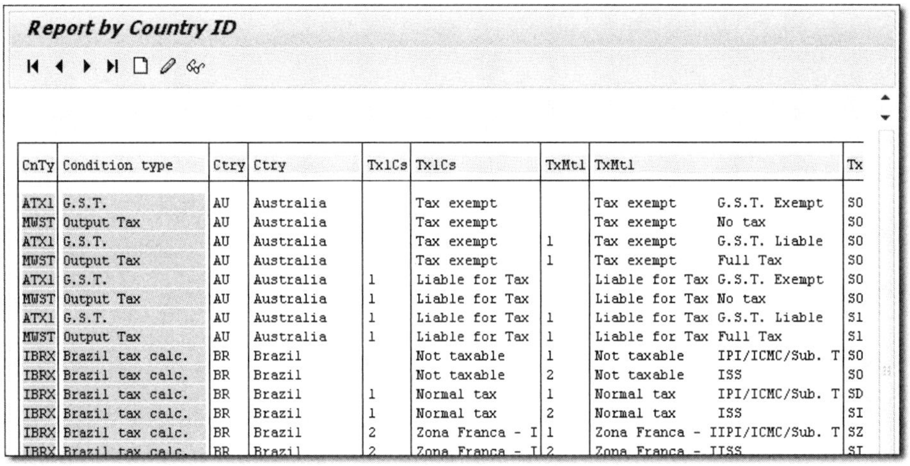

CnTy	Condition type	Ctry	Ctry	TxlCs	TxlCs	TxMtl	TxMtl	Tx
ATX1	G.S.T.	AU	Australia		Tax exempt		Tax exempt G.S.T. Exempt	S0
MWST	Output Tax	AU	Australia		Tax exempt		Tax exempt No tax	S0
ATX1	G.S.T.	AU	Australia		Tax exempt	1	Tax exempt G.S.T. Liable	S0
MWST	Output Tax	AU	Australia		Tax exempt	1	Tax exempt Full Tax	S0
ATX1	G.S.T.	AU	Australia	1	Liable for Tax		Liable for Tax G.S.T. Exempt	S0
MWST	Output Tax	AU	Australia	1	Liable for Tax		Liable for Tax No tax	S0
ATX1	G.S.T.	AU	Australia	1	Liable for Tax	1	Liable for Tax G.S.T. Liable	S1
MWST	Output Tax	AU	Australia	1	Liable for Tax	1	Liable for Tax Full Tax	S1
IBRX	Brazil tax calc.	BR	Brazil		Not taxable	1	Not taxable IPI/ICMC/Sub. T	S0
IBRX	Brazil tax calc.	BR	Brazil		Not taxable	2	Not taxable ISS	S0
IBRX	Brazil tax calc.	BR	Brazil	1	Normal tax	1	Normal tax IPI/ICMC/Sub. T	SD
IBRX	Brazil tax calc.	BR	Brazil	1	Normal tax	2	Normal tax ISS	SI
IBRX	Brazil tax calc.	BR	Brazil	2	Zona Franca - I	1	Zona Franca - IIPI/ICMC/Sub. T	SZ
IBRX	Brazil tax calc.	BR	Brazil	2	Zona Franca - I	2	Zona Franca - IISS	SI

Figure 4.22 Output of Report Y1

Figure 4.23 shows the output of the same report, but this time with an identifiable output structure.

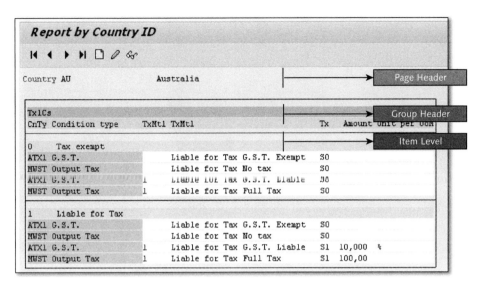

Figure 4.23 Structured Output

Now that we've discussed pricing reports and lists, let's move on to external software packages for taxes.

4.6 Common External Tax Software Packages

A variety of external tax software packages are on the market today. Sabrix-Thomson Reuters, Sovos Compliance, and Vertex are common software package vendors that support the process for sales and use tax in the U.S. and Canada. Table 4.5 lists a few reference details about the company and the name of the software that integrates to SAP for US, Canada, and global tax needs—but do some research to figure out what works best for you.

Company	Tax Software Name
Sabrix-Thomson Reuters 12647 Alcosta Blvd, Suite 155 San Ramon, CA 94583	ONESOURCE Indirect Tax Integration. ONESOURCE Global Next Integration

Table 4.5 SAP Certified External Tax Software for Sales and Use Tax (U.S. and Canada)

Company	Tax Software Name
Sovos Compliance (Taxware) 200 Ballardvale St. Wilmington, MA 01887	Sales and Use Tax (SUT)
	Taxware Enterprise (TWE) Adapter 8.4 for SAP
	Tax Content Solution (TCS)
Vertex, Inc. 1041 Old Cassatt Road Berwyn, PA 19312	Indirect tax SAP solution
	Direct tax SAP solution

Table 4.5 SAP Certified External Tax Software for Sales and Use Tax (U.S. and Canada) (Cont.)

The suggested steps for customization are as follows.

1. Define and test the physical destination for external tax calculation.

2. Activate the SAP tax interface.

3. Configure the external tax document.

4. Define the tax jurisdiction code.

5. Define the tax category for different countries.

6. Define the customer tax classifications.

7. Define the material tax indicators.

8. Set the tax codes.

9. Maintain the tax condition records and master data records.

In the following sections, we'll discuss each of the steps listed above.

4.6.1 Defining and Testing the Physical Destination for External Tax Calculation

In this first step, you define the location of the server on which the external tax software is installed. The menu path for defining the physical destination is SAP IMG • FINANCIAL ACCOUNTING (NEW) • FINANCIAL ACCOUNTING BASIC SETTINGS (NEW) • TAX ON SALES/PURCHASES • BASIC SETTINGS • EXTERNAL TAX CALCULATION • DEFINE PHYSICAL DESTINATION; you can also use Transaction SM59. You can navigate to the screen shown in Figure 4.24 by clicking on the CREATE button in the RFC DESTINATION screen, and provide a name for the new connection (e.g., VERTEX). From here, select CONNECTION TYPE T (TCP/IP). If the tax software and SAP system are on the same server, select the START ON APPLICATION SERVER radio button and specify the path for the executable program name in the PROGRAM field. If the tax software is on a different server, select the START ON EXPLICIT HOST option and specify the path of the executable program and target host. Click on the TEST CONNECTION button to test the connection. If the test is successful, go on and test the four function modules using Transaction SE37 or following the menu path SAP EASY ACCESS • TOOLS • ABAP WORKBENCH • DEVELOPMENT • FUNCTION BUILDER. The following four function modules should be tested, one at a time, using Transaction SE37:

▶ RFC_DETERMINE_JURISDICTION

▶ RFC_CALCULATE_TAXES_DOC

▶ RFC_UPDATE_TAXES_DOC

▶ RFC_FORCE_TAXES_DOC

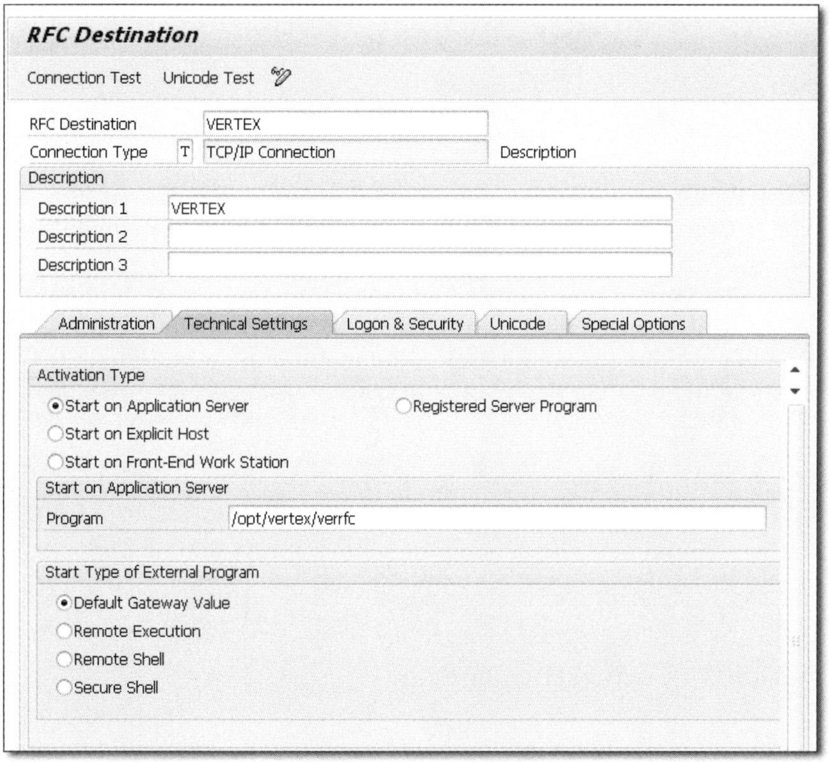

Figure 4.24 Physical Connection to External Tax Software

4.6.2 Activating the SAP Tax Interface

Activate the SAP tax interface to use the external tax software. Two steps are required to activate the SAP tax interface:

1. Assign the tax calculation procedure to the country. You may only assign one procedure to a country, using Transaction OBBG or following the menu path SAP IMG • FINANCIAL ACCOUNTING (NEW) • FINANCIAL ACCOUNTING BASIC SETTINGS (NEW) • TAX ON SALES/PURCHASES • BASIC SETTINGS • ASSIGN COUNTRY TO CALCULATION PROCEDURE. TAXUSX is the tax procedure in this case, because you want to use the external tax software. You can modify the tax calculation procedure by selecting it and double-clicking on the CONTROL DATA folder.

2. Activate the external tax calculation by following the menu path SAP IMG • FINANCIAL ACCOUNTING (NEW) • FINANCIAL ACCOUNTING BASIC SETTINGS (NEW) • TAX ON SALES/PURCHASES • BASIC SETTINGS • EXTERNAL TAX CALCULATION • ACTIVATE EXTERNAL TAX CALCULATION.

4.6.3 Configuring External Tax Documents

In this step, you give a number range for the external tax documents that SAP ERP will receive, and instruct your system to use the external tax documents only for tax purposes. There are two steps for configuring the external tax documents:

1. Define the number ranges for external tax documents using Transaction OBETX or following the menu path SAP IMG • FINANCIAL ACCOUNTING (NEW) • FINANCIAL ACCOUNTING BASIC SETTINGS (NEW) • TAXES ON SALES/PURCHASES • BASIC SETTINGS • EXTERNAL TAX CALCULATION • DEFINE NUMBER RANGE FOR EXTERNAL TAX DOCUMENTS.

2. Activate the external tax document by following the menu path SAP IMG • FINANCIAL ACCOUNTING (NEW) • FINANCIAL ACCOUNTING BASIC SETTINGS (NEW) • TAXES ON SALES/PURCHASES • BASIC SETTINGS • EXTERNAL TAX CALCULATION • ACTIVATE EXTERNAL UPDATING.

4.6.4 Defining Tax Jurisdiction Codes

Use Transaction OBCO to define the structure for the tax jurisdiction code or follow the menu path SAP IMG • FINANCIAL ACCOUNTING (NEW) • FINANCIAL ACCOUNTING BASIC SETTINGS (NEW) • TAXES ON SALES/PURCHASES • BASIC SETTINGS • SPECIFY STRUCTURE FOR TAX JURISDICTION CODE. You can define the structure for

TAXUSX as (2,2,5,5) for Sabrix, (2,5,2) for Taxware, and (2,3,4,1) for Vertex. When the TxIn checkbox is selected, the system calculates tax based on line items. When you use external tax software with the TxIn checkbox selected, there can be some error, so be sure to check SAP Notes 605829, 643273, 798372, 976780, and 972253, found at *service.sap.com*, via Transaction SNOTE, or by following the menu path Goto • Download SAP Note from the initial screen.

4.6.5 Defining the Tax Category for Different Countries

Tax determination rules determine the tax categories to be used for different countries. Define the tax determination rule using Transaction OVK1 or following the menu path SAP IMG • Sales and Distribution • Basic Functions • Taxes • Define Tax Determination Rules. In the tax determination rule, you assign different tax categories to different countries. When using external tax software, you should assign only one tax category to the U.S. and Canada (UTXJ for the U.S. and CTXJ for Canada against sequence 1). No additional sequence 2 or 3 and UTX1, UTX2, CTX1, CTX2, or CTX3 tax categories should be maintained against them. You should delete all rows that come predefined in the standard system.

4.6.6 Defining Customer Tax Classifications

A customer tax classification is a customer master record field. A customer operating in different countries can have different classifications in different countries. For example, their operations can be tax-free in one country and taxable in another. You can use Transaction OVK3 to define the tax classifications for tax categories (e.g., UTXJ, CTXJ) that will be maintained for the customer in the customer master record; you can also use the menu path SAP IMG • Sales and Distribution • Basic Functions • Taxes • Define Tax relevancy of Master records • Choose : Customer Taxes. For different tax categories, tax classifications such as 0 (tax exempt) and 1 (liable for taxes) are defined.

4.6.7 Defining Material Tax Indicators

The material tax indicator is a material master record field. A material can be taxable or tax-free. This indicator stores that information. In combination with the customer tax indicator, it determines the tax status (taxable or tax-free). The possible list of tax classifications or indicators for the material for a particular tax category (e.g., UTXJ, CTXJ) are maintained in Transaction OVK4 or accessed via the menu path SAP IMG • Sales and Distribution • Basic Functions • Taxes • Define Tax relevancy of Master records • Choose: Material Taxes. Different indicators such as 0 (exempt) and 1 (taxable) are maintained as possible selections in the material master record.

4.6.8 Setting Tax Codes

In a tax code, you specify the tax percentage. You also specify whether it is to be collected from the customer (accounts receivable [A/R]) or paid to the vendor (accounts payable [A/P]). You create the tax codes using Transaction FTXP or following the menu path SAP IMG • Financial Accounting (New) • Financial Accounting Basic Settings (New) • Taxes on Sales/Purchases • Basic Settings • Define Tax Codes for Sales and Purchases. Tax codes 00 (A/R sales tax, 0%) and 01 (A/R sales tax, 6% state, 1% county, 1% city) come predefined in the standard system and are copied to create new tax codes for use in the Sales and Distribution functionality in SAP ERP. To use the tax code in Sales and Distribution, the tax type must be A. For the six condition types (XR1, XR2, XR3, XR4, XR5, and XR6) of tax calculation procedure TAXUSX, all of the tax codes relevant for Sales and Distribution (e.g., 00, 02) maintain the tax percentage as 100.

After you maintain the tax code, the following step ensures automatic posting to a specific general ledger. In the tax procedure (e.g., TAXUSX), you maintain the accounting key for a specific condition type. In Transaction OB40 or SAP IMG • Financial Accounting (New) • Financial Accounting Basic Settings (New) • Taxes on Sales/Purchases • Posting • Define tax Accounts, double-click on the Transaction for which the different account should be maintained for the different tax codes, and specify the chart of account. This takes you to the screen shown in Figure 4.25, where you maintain the different accounts for different tax codes. You can use Transaction OBCN or follow the menu path SAP IMG • Financial Accounting (New) • Financial Accounting Basic Settings (New) • Taxes on Sales/Purchases • Basic Setting • Check and Change Settings for Tax Processing to create a new account key or process key if required. Note that the posting indicator for processing/accounting key NVV is 3 (distribute to relevant expense/revenue items) and all other accounting keys used in the TAXUSX procedure, the posting indicator is 2 (separate line item). The transaction keys used for determining tax accounts are the same as the accounting keys maintained in the tax procedure, which themselves are the same as the process key when the posting indicator is 2.

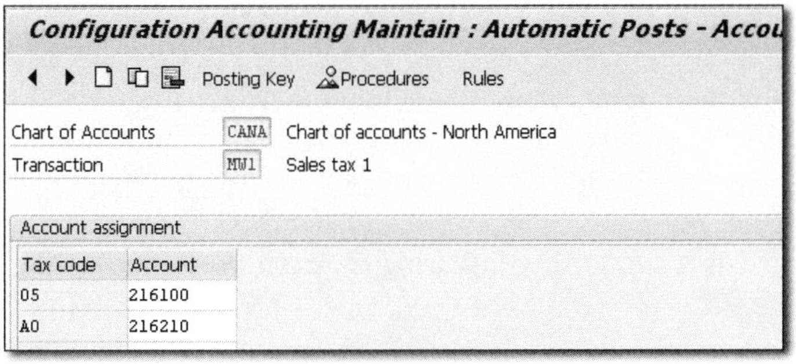

Figure 4.25 Different Accounts for Different Tax Codes for Transaction/Accounting Key MW1 Specified Using Transaction OB40

4.6.9 Maintaining Tax Condition Records and Master Data Records

Using Transaction VK11/12, you maintain the condition records for tax category UTXJ and CTXJ for the U.S. and Canada, respectively, for all possible combinations of customer tax classification (e.g., 0, 1) and material tax classification (e.g., 0, 1). There are other key combinations for export and other scenarios for which you can maintain condition records.

Using Transactions XD01 or XD02, you can maintain the customer tax classification in the BILLING DOCUMENT tab (SALES AREA DATA). A customer can have different tax classifications in different countries (e.g., 0 for U.S., 1 for Canada). Using Transactions MM01 and MM02, you maintain the material tax classification in the SALES: SALES ORG. 1 tab. Because a material taxable in one country can be exempted in another, you should maintain the tax classification accordingly.

> **Max Tax**
>
> SAP systems support calculating tax for a document instead of computing it for an individual line and aggregating. Instead of pricing procedure RVAXUS, you use procedure RVAXUD when you have to calculate tax per document. We recommend this because it makes fewer remote function calls (RFCs) to external systems, compared to when each line requires one RFC, which means better performance. Formula routine 300, assigned to tax condition UTXJ in procedure RVAXUS, and routine 500, assigned to tax condition UTXD in procedure RVAXUD, call the SAP tax interface. While modifying the pricing procedure, you should not change the formula. Use program RFYTXDISPLAY to display an error (marked red) during tax processing when using external tax software.

4.7   Solving Common Pricing Problems

In this section you will find a list of the most common pricing errors you may encounter soon after installing, modifying, or adding a new system to your solution. There are several ways to troubleshoot a problem, including revising the configuration, debugging via ABAP, and researching for OSS notes that can resolve your specific needs; consider the following common problems and frequent solutions.

▶ **Problem**
The billing document is not released to accounting/accounts determination or the billing document cannot be released to accounting.

Solution
Review the account determination at Transaction VF02. You'll often find that an account key is missing or wrongly assigned at the pricing procedure. See Section 4.2.3.

▶ **Problem**
Pricing cannot be determined at sales order creation.

Solution
First check the customer pricing procedure assigned at the SOLD-TO and SHIP-TO fields, and then check the customer pricing procedure assigned to the sales order.

▶ **Problem**
The condition type is not in procedure, or there is an error in sales order pricing. Occasionally, you need to enter a condition not recognized or not part of the determined pricing procedure on a particular document. This error can occur whether manually entering the pricing condition or via an uploading program.

Solution
Verify that the right pricing procedure is determined and then revise the customer master pricing procedure and order type combination.

If a new condition is needed, add the condition in question following configuration for Transaction V/08.

▶ **Problem**
An entry already exits with the same key (Configuration: pricing procedure determination). While making a new entry on pricing procedure determination,

Transaction OVKK, you will see this error, which typically means you are trying to make an entry with similar existing key combinations of SORG, DISTCHANNEL, DIVISION, DOC PRICING PROC, and CUSTOMER PRICING PROCEDURE.

Solution

Make sure the key combination is unique, or create more entries for customer or document pricing procedure.

▶ **Problem**

The field assignment has not yet been made (Configuration: Saving the pricing access sequence). This problem typically arises when adding new tables to the pricing access sequence and immediately saving it. It could also happen when working anywhere where the condition technique is used, and attempting to add new tables.

Solution

After adding the new table to the access sequence, such as in Transaction V/07, select the FIELDS tab. Each field of the table will automatically be displayed and proposed. Make sure you confirm those fields by hitting Enter and then clicking SAVE. The proposed fields will be confirmed for the access sequence.

▶ **Problem**

Invoice cannot be posted (pricing error). This error will commonly show that certain mandatory pricing conditions are not maintained.

Solution

Verify that all pricing procedure mandatory access sequence are fulfilled. You may want to create a condition record for those (i.e., tax code).

4.8 Summary

This chapter focused on pricing. We touched on condition techniques, routines, and the seven steps used in condition techniques. We also highlighted the importance of routines, requirements, and formula types for optimizing the pricing process, and then looked at rebate agreements. We discussed the steps required for creating the pricing report and the price list. Finally, we focused on customizing external tax software in the U.S. and Canada.

With this knowledge you should be able to implement and maintain customization for pricing. The system should not only determine the correct prices, but do so in less time. You should be able to create your own reports for prices and use the rebate agreement functionality that SAP ERP offers. You should also be able to customize your system to use the external tax software, which helps the system determine the correct tax amount faster. We hardly need to emphasize that both pricing and taxes are vital elements to any business.

In the next chapter, we'll will look at credit management and touch on financial accounting in SAP ERP Financials.

This chapter will teach you how to customize automatic credit control, which is the fundamental functionality of credit management in the SAP system. You'll also be able to customize your system to block customers for different sales and distribution processes. Finally, you'll learn about the latest technology in credit management and how it integrates with the sales processing.

5   Credit Risk Management

Eliminating risk from business is neither possible nor desirable; in fact, risk should be managed such that you minimize it, while maximizing profit. Generally speaking, a business that involves more risk has the potential to generate more profit.

In the Sales and Distribution functionality in SAP ERP, risk arises primarily due to credit extended to the customer. You sell material to customers and then bill them, expecting payment within a certain time period—but if the bills are not paid within this time, it's a loss for you. Of course, this is not a risk if you sell only after receiving the total payment. But for goods and services that you have to sell without receiving the total payment up front, you can opt for one of two options to minimize or manage your risk:

▶ A payment guarantee, which ensures your payment, subject to certain conditions, such as a goods receipt in good condition

▶ Credit management, wherein there is neither payment nor any guarantee

In this chapter we'll discuss credit management and how it reduces risk, and then move on to customizing for blocking and unblocking a customer, which is not directly linked to either credit management or payment guarantee but is often used to minimize risk. Finally, we'll discuss the steps for customizing different forms of payment guarantees and their automatic determination during document processing.

5.1   Credit Management

Credit management involves managing the credit, and associated risk of default, that a company extends to its customers. From a narrow operational point of view, it involves deciding when to stop sales. From a broader perspective, credit management involves the accurate credit rating of customers (and grouping them with customers with similar risk), follow-up for receiving payment, fast action in response to customer complaints, improved communication, regular internal review, and so on. We won't discuss many of these in this book and will instead confine our discussion to what SAP ERP offers for credit management.

The general steps for configuring credit management are as follows:

1. Set prerequisites for automatic credit control.

2. Maintain customer credit master records.

3. Define automatic credit control.

Now, let's walk through the first step.

5.1.1   Prerequisites for Automatic Credit Control

You should complete most of the steps as part of customization for other processes, before you perform the automatic credit control customization. If this book discusses a step elsewhere, we'll review it here, so you can use this section as a checklist. If the step has not been discussed so far in the book, we'll discuss it here. We will also emphasize the role of each step in the final setting. The following steps are the prerequisites for activating automatic credit control. Most of these steps are already configured at the time of defining and assigning the enterprise structure, or at the time of customizing the customer credit master record.

1. Define credit control areas. As discussed in Chapters 1 and 2, the important fields you need to define in the credit control area are UPDATE GROUP, CURRENCY, the rule for DSO, and accounts receivable.

2. Assign the sales area and company codes to the credit control area. As discussed in Chapter 1, use Transaction OVFL or follow the menu path SAP IMG • ENTERPRISE STRUCTURE • ASSIGNMENT • SALES AND DISTRIBUTION • ASSIGN SALES AREA TO CREDIT CONTROL AREA, and use Transaction OB38 or follow the menu path SAP IMG • ENTERPRISE STRUCTURE • ASSIGNMENT • FINANCIAL ACCOUNTING • ASSIGN

COMPANY CODE TO CREDIT CONTROL AREA, to assign the sales area and company code, respectively, to the credit control area.

3. If needed, assign the additional company codes to the credit control area, as discussed in Chapter 1. In addition to assigning an initial company code to a credit control area, you can assign that code to additional credit control areas, using Transaction OBZK or following the menu path SAP IMG • FINANCIAL ACCOUNTING (NEW) • ACCOUNTS RECEIVABLE AND ACCOUNTS PAYABLE • CREDIT MANAGEMENT • CREDIT CONTROL ACCOUNT • ASSIGN PERMITTED CREDIT CONTROL AREAS TO COMPANY CODE.

4. You can define the customer credit groups using Transaction OB12 or following the menu path SAP IMG • FINANCIAL ACCOUNTING (NEW) • ACCOUNTS RECEIVABLE AND ACCOUNTS PAYABLE • CREDIT MANAGEMENT • CREDIT CONTROL ACCOUNT • DEFINE GROUPS. The customer credit group groups customers for reporting purposes; assign it to the customer in the STATUS screen of the customer credit master record. The CUSTOMER GROUP field is also found in the STATUS screen. This field is different from the customer credit group, but you'll also use it for grouping and reporting purposes, and it is freely definable (that is, in the credit master record, you can assign any value to it). This step is optional from a credit management point of view. As shown in Figure 5.1, you create a credit group for a particular credit control area (CCAR) with a meaningful description.

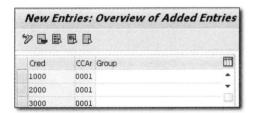

Figure 5.1 Define Customer Credit Groups

5. Define the document credit group that groups documents via Transaction OVA6 or the menu path SAP IMG • SALES AND DISTRIBUTION • BASIC FUNCTIONS • CREDIT MANAGEMENT/RISK MANAGEMENT • CREDIT MANAGEMENT • DEFINE CREDIT GROUPS. As shown in Figure 5.2, the three standard groups for orders, deliveries, and goods issue are sufficient for practical purposes. You can create a new group by selecting any existing group, copying it, and providing a new key or

code and description. Because different settings for different document groups are possible for automatic credit control, this field is very important.

Figure 5.2 Document Credit Groups

6. Risk categories group customers with the same levels of risk. You can have, for example, one risk category for all new customers. Risk categories, as shown in Figure 5.3, are defined via Transaction OB01 or the menu path SAP IMG • FINANCIAL ACCOUNTING (NEW) • ACCOUNTS RECEIVABLE AND ACCOUNTS PAYABLE • CREDIT MANAGEMENT • CREDIT CONTROL ACCOUNT • DEFINE RISK CATEGORIES. In the STATUS screen of the customer credit master record, you can enter the customer's risk category. Because different settings for different risk categories are possible for automatic credit control, this field is very important.

Change View "Credit Management Risk Categories": Overview

New Entries

Risk category	CCAr	Name
001	0001	Risk category
001	3000	Low risk
002	0001	Medium category
003	0001	Low category
100	1000	New customers

Figure 5.3 Define Risk Categories

Use Transaction OB02 to define credit representative groups or follow the menu path SAP IMG • FINANCIAL ACCOUNTING (NEW) • ACCOUNTS RECEIVABLE AND ACCOUNTS PAYABLE • CREDIT MANAGEMENT • CREDIT CONTROL ACCOUNT • DEFINE CREDIT REPRESENTATIVE GROUPS. As shown in Figure 5.4, this key both defines credit representative groups for particular credit control areas (CCAR) and groups customers. You enter the credit representative group of the customer in the STATUS screen of the customer credit master (see Figure 5.8).

Change View "Credit Management: Credit Representative Groups":

New Entries

Credit rep.group	CCAr	Name of the credit rep.group
100	7000	Credit Representative 100
200	7000	Credit Representative 200
300	7000	Credit Representative 300

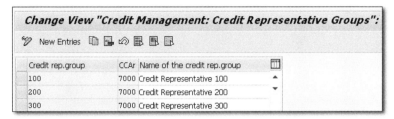

Figure 5.4 Define Credit Representative Groups

7. You define credit representatives with Transaction OB51 or the menu path SAP IMG • Financial Accounting (New) • Accounts Receivable and Accounts Payable • Credit Management • Credit Control Account • Define Credit Representatives. In this step, you can specify which employee is responsible for a credit representative group, as shown in Figure 5.5.

New Entries: Overview of Added Entries

New Entries

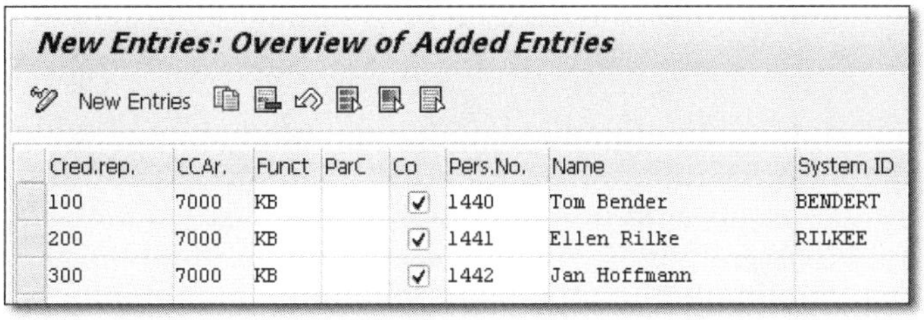

Cred.rep.	CCAr.	Funct	ParC	Co	Pers.No.	Name	System ID
100	7000	KB		✓	1440	Tom Bender	BENDERT
200	7000	KB		✓	1441	Ellen Rilke	RILKEE
300	7000	KB		✓	1442	Jan Hoffmann	

Figure 5.5 Define Credit Representative

8. Document credit groups and credit checks are assigned to the sales and delivery document types. Using Transaction OVAK or following the menu path SAP IMG • Sales and Distribution • Basic Functions • Credit Management/Risk Management • Credit Management • Assign Sales Documents and Delivery Documents • Credit Limit Check for Order Types or SAP IMG • Sales and Distribution • Basic Functions • Credit Management/Risk Management • Simple Credit Limit Check, you can assign different types of credit checks and credit groups to different order types, as shown in Figure 5.6. The various types of credit checks possible are also shown in Figure 5.6.

   When the Check credit field in the third column is left blank, there will be no credit check for the document type. The options A, B, and C are called *simple credit limit checks* and check the customer's document pertaining to the document type when the total receivable is more than the credit limit. (The update group for the credit control area further defines whether in addition to open accounting documents, open order, delivery, and billing are to be considered.) When a document fails to clear a simple check, the system can issue a warning (option A) or an error message (option B) or block the document for creation of delivery (option C). When you select option D (CREDIT MANAGEMENT: AUTOMATIC CREDIT CONTROL), you have to further specify the document credit group that we defined in the Step 5. Simple credit checks can be used effectively when you only want to check a single criterion (credit limit) against the total receivable to decide about blocking a document. Automatic credit check gives you the option of specifying the credit check for delivery types, which you do with Transaction OVAD or menu path SAP IMG • SALES AND DISTRIBUTION • BASIC FUNCTIONS • CREDIT MANAGEMENT/RISK MANAGEMENT • CREDIT MANAGEMENT • ASSIGN SALES DOCUMENTS AND DELIVERY DOCUMENTS • CREDIT LIMIT CHECK FOR DELIVERY TYPES.

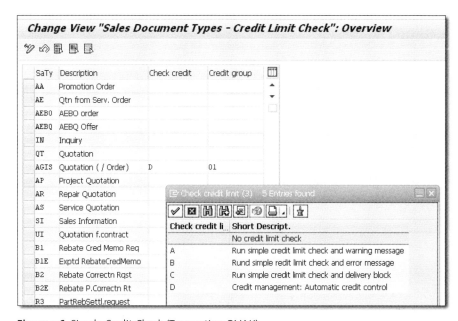

Figure 5.6 Simple Credit Check (Transaction OVAK)

9. You assign partner function KB (credit representative) and KM (credit manager) to the partner determination procedure of the customer master record, sales document header, and delivery document using Transaction VOPAN.

10. You can use Transaction OVB9 to modify requirement routine 104, which prevents a document from appearing in the delivery due list when there's a credit

block. Alternatively, you can use the menu path SAP IMG • SALES AND DISTRI-BUTION • BASIC FUNCTIONS • CREDIT MANAGEMENT/RISK MANAGEMENT • CREDIT MANAGEMENT/RISK MANAGEMENT SETTINGS • ENTER SETTINGS • REQUIREMENT FOR CREATING DELIVERY DUE INDEX FROM ORDER.

11. You can use Transaction OVB7 to modify requirement routine 113, which doesn't allow a goods issue if a credit block exists. Alternatively, you can use the menu path SAP IMG • SALES AND DISTRIBUTION • BASIC FUNCTIONS • CREDIT MANAGEMENT/RISK MANAGEMENT • CREDIT MANAGEMENT/RISK MANAGEMENT SETTINGS • ENTER SETTINGS • REQUIREMENT FOR GOODS ISSUE FROM A DELIVERY.

12. Using Transaction OVA7 or following the menu path SAP IMG • SALES AND DISTRIBUTION • BASIC FUNCTIONS • CREDIT MANAGEMENT/RISK MANAGEMENT • CREDIT MANAGEMENT/RISK MANAGEMENT SETTINGS • DETERMINE ACTIVE RECEIVABLES PER ITEM CATEGORY, you can specify all of the item categories that are relevant for credit checks and updates. The item categories (for example, the one used for stock transfer) are not specified here and are not relevant for credit management. These items don't update tables S066 and S067, which store the open order and open delivery values

13. You define document value classes using Transaction OVBC and assign them to the credit control area and different credit values using Transaction OVBD or following the menu path SAP IMG • SALES AND DISTRIBUTION • BASIC FUNC-TIONS • CREDIT MANAGEMENT/RISK MANAGEMENT • CREDIT MANAGEMENT/RISK MANAGEMENT SETTINGS • MAINTAIN AUTHORIZATION • ASSIGN DOCUMENT VALUE CLASSES. These document value classes further restrict the authorization object for releasing the documents blocked by the credit check. For example, a credit representative with authorization to release a blocked document can be authorized only for documents with values less than 200,000 USD by assigning document value class A01 (as shown in Figure 5.7) to his profile.

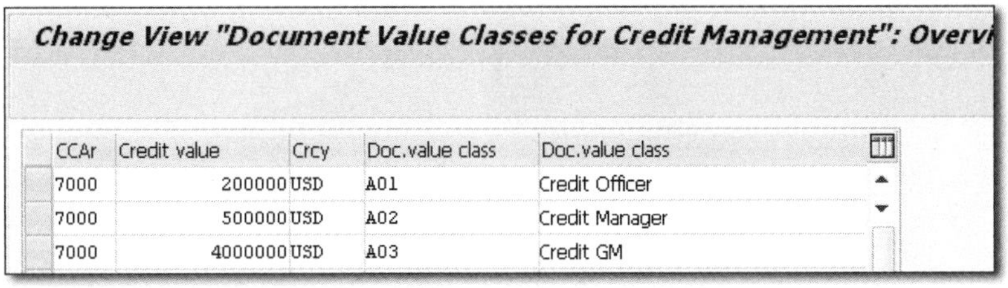

CCAr	Credit value	Crcy	Doc.value class	Doc.value class	
7000	200000	USD	A01	Credit Officer	
7000	500000	USD	A02	Credit Manager	
7000	4000000	USD	A03	Credit GM	

Figure 5.7 Document Value Classes (A01, A02 and A03) Assigned to Credit Control Area (7000) and Credit Values

5.1.2   Customer Credit Master Records

As we've discussed, you can set the credit master record to automatically generate by specifying the default credit limit, risk category, or credit representative group in the credit control area for any new customers. To find to the screen where you define the credit control area, as shown in Figure 5.8, execute Transaction OB45, or follow the menu path SAP IMG • ENTERPRISE STRUCTURE • DEFINITION • FINANCIAL ACCOUNTING • DEFINE CREDIT CONTROL AREA and double-click on the specific credit control area, which is created by copying an existing one.

With this method, there's little chance that you'll have a customer without a customer credit master record, and no customer credit master record means no credit check for that customer. For new customers, this means exposing yourself to a higher risk. Therefore, it's recommended that you create the customer credit master record automatically and then modify it using Transaction FD32 or following the menu path SAP EASY ACCESS • ACCOUNTING • FINANCIAL ACCOUNTING • ACCOUNTS RECEIVABLE • CREDIT MANAGEMENT • MASTER DATA • CHANGE.

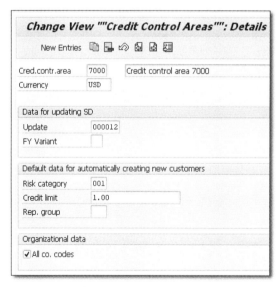

Figure 5.8 Credit Control Area

You can create the customer credit master record directly using the above transaction. You enter the customer code (obtained after creating the customer master record using Transaction XD01, FD01, or VD01) in the CUSTOMER field and credit control area (as you saw previously). Select only the CENTRAL DATA and STATUS screens for data entry. The other fields will fill automatically from the customer master records (e.g., the ADDRESS screen), transactions pertaining to the customer (e.g., PAYMENT HISTORY, shown in Figure 5.12), or the other screens of the customer's credit master record (e.g., the OVERVIEW screen, shown in Figure 5.9).

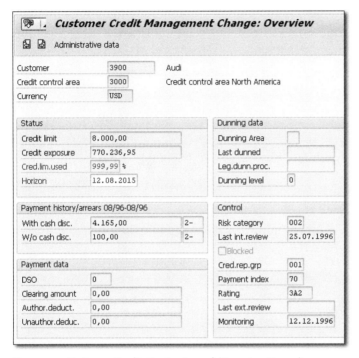

Figure 5.9 Customer Credit Master Record (Overview Screen)

In the CENTRAL DATA screen, you can enter the TOTAL LIMIT and INDIVIDUAL LIMIT. This applies when you assign a customer to several credit control areas (via different company codes), and there is a total limit for the customer for all of the credit control areas and an individual limit for the specific credit control area. The currency becomes important, because different credit control areas can have different currencies.

The STATUS screen (refer Figure 5.13) has the credit limit field and credit horizon date. By default, the credit horizon date is the current system date. You can define in the automatic credit control setting (shown in Figure 5.13) if it is to be system date plus a specific number of days (T), week (W), month (M), or year (I).

Note that in the setting shown in Figure 5.13 (automatic credit control) the unit for credit horizon is in months (M), and the value is not modifiable. In fact, it's the same as the update unit for info structure S066. To change it to days (T) or any other period, use Transaction OMO1 or follow the menu path SAP IMG • LOGISTICS – GENERAL • LOGISTICS INFORMATION SYSTEM (LIS) • LOGISTICS DATA WAREHOUSE • UPDATING • UPDATING CONTROL • ACTIVATE UPDATE • SALES AND DISTRIBUTION. Upon execution, you'll get a list of all info structures of Sales and Distribution. If you double-click on S066, you'll see a dialog box where you can change the period unit (e.g., from months to days). After selecting for the radio button you want, click on the SAVE icon.

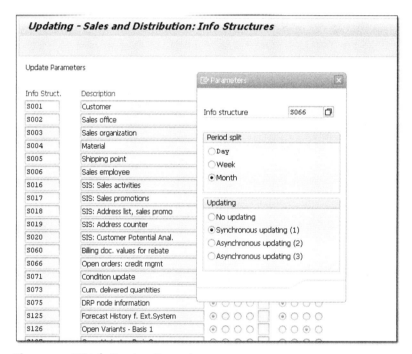

Figure 5.10 LIS Info Structure Parameters

Additionally, Figure 5.13 shows that there is no way to specify the currency, so the currency of the credit control area automatically becomes the currency for the customer's credit limit. The fields defined for the group customer (e.g., RISK CATEGORY, CREDIT REP. GROUP, CUST. CRED. GROUP) are also specified for the customer. You can block the customer by selecting the BLOCK checkbox. This blocking is different from blocking the customer for sales, delivery, billing, or other operations that we'll discuss in the next section.

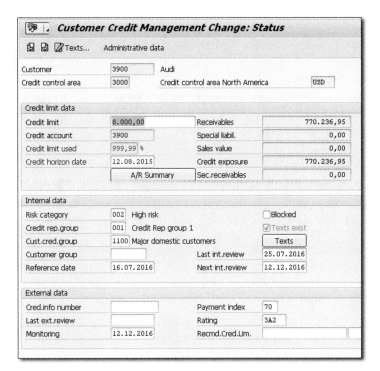

Figure 5.11 Customer Credit Master Record (Status Screen)

In this screen, you can also enter information about the last internal review date, next internal review date, and customer obtained from an external rating organization.

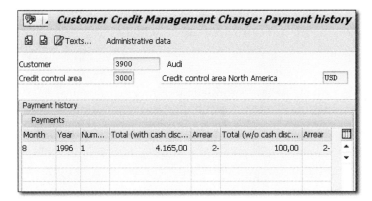

Figure 5.12 Customer Credit Master Record (Payment History Screen)

5.1.3   Automatic Credit Control

For each combination of credit control area, risk category, and credit group, you maintain different rules for automatic credit control. The update group and currency maintained for the credit control area become the default for each credit strategy. The credit control can be done during the order, delivery, or post goods issue (PGI). Once the goods issue is complete, the credit control is no longer relevant because the material is no longer physically under company control. Depending on the setting, the system may not allow the creation of order, delivery, or material documents (created at the time of PGI). Order and delivery documents can be created with credit block, in order to prevent further processing. This way, you proactively reduce your credit risk. Once material is with the customer, your risk increases. Risk and cost involved in recovering the stock or payment goes up.

You can release the blocked documents for further processing using Transaction VKM1 or VKM2 or following the menu path SAP Easy Access • Logistics • Sales and Distribution • Credit Management • Sales and Distribution Documents • Blocked. Instead of releasing individual documents, your company can decide to change the customer credit master records (i.e., credit limit) or credit strategy (setting for an individual combination of credit control area, risk category, and credit group) or delete other open documents that currently block the credit limit. These actions will not automatically release the documents that are already blocked. To release the documents that should be blocked, as per the new setting, you can run the program RVKRED08.

In automatic credit management you, decide the following:

1. Whether there will be a static check (blocking document if the credit limit is exceeded) or a static and dynamic check (blocking documents if the credit limit or some other criteria specified in customization are fulfilled).

2. The other criteria mentioned in step 1 can include the document value, change in critical fields of the document, next review date, open items (percentage and days open), oldest open item, highest permitted dunning level, or any other criteria defined in the user exits LVKMPTZZ, LVKMPFZ1, LVKMPFZZ2, and LVKMPFZZ3.

   ▹ When the sales document value exceeds a predefined value (in Figure 5.13, it is 100,000.00 in the credit control area currency), the document is blocked. The process can be specially adopted for high-value order processing.

   ▹ The critical fields for credit management are Order Quantity, Unit of Measurement, Pricing Condition, Terms of Payment, INCO Term, and Plant.

If these fields change, even to the original value or to a value that makes the total document value less than the original value, the credit check process reoccurs, and the released document is blocked. We recommend that you make the check for CRITICAL FIELDS active, as shown in Figure 5.13.

▶ The next internal review date (NEXTREVIEW date) is maintained in the customer credit master for internal review of the customer for credit management and for changing the customer credit master. If this date is in the past, it means the review and change of the customer credit master is overdue. You can use Transaction FDK43 or S_ALR_87012218 to receive a report for this purpose. In this type of situation, it may be company policy to stop sales to such customers.

▶ To make the open items active, you have to fill in the additional fields of MAX.OPENITEM% (X) and NO DAYS OPEN ITEM (Y). The system checks all of the items open for more than Y days and finds its percentage of the total customer balance. If the percentage calculated is more than X, the document is blocked.

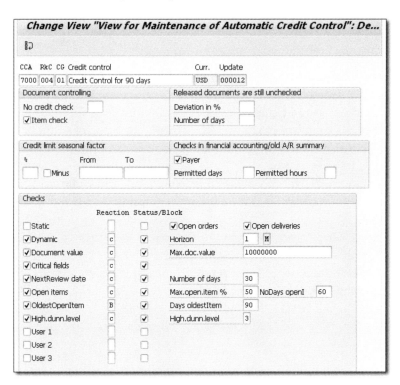

Figure 5.13 Automatic Credit Control

- ▶ OLDESTOPENITEM can be referred to as credit limit in days. If the oldest open invoice or debit note is above a specific age (e.g., 90 days), it may be company policy to stop sale, irrespective of the fact that the total overdue outstanding is within the credit limit. So, while activating this setting, you have to additionally specify the day limit (as you can see in Figure 5.13, it's 90 days). Note that if open invoices are not knocked off (or settled) by the payment received in the Financial Accounting component, the process won't work as intended.

- ▶ The accounting department issues dunning letters to customers. If the dunning reaches a specific level (HIGH DUNN LEVEL, which is 3 in Figure 5.13), the document is blocked for the specific customer.

- ▶ The prerequisite for activating users 1, 2, and 3 is to specify the details for credit checks in the user exits LVKMPTZZ, LVKMPFZ1, LVKMPFZZ2, and LVKMPFZZ3. A *user exit* is the program where a user can add his own ABAP codes to influence a standard SAP business process or transaction.

- ▶ The credit horizon refers to a date that's normally a future date maintained in the customer credit master. All of the documents that are to be delivered within this date are considered relevant for the credit check.

For automatic credit control to be effective, you must decide on the relevant documents for credit management and document value. *Update groups* decide which documents are valid for a credit check. There are three update groups: 000012, 000015, and 000018. Each update group's open invoices (invoices not yet posted to accounting) and open financial documents are taken into account. In addition, group 000012 takes into account open deliveries and open orders, group 000015 takes into account open deliveries only, and group 000018 takes into account open orders only. Update group 000012 is the most comprehensive and is frequently used. When it's a practice not to delete or reject very old open orders for any valid reason, update group 000015 is more suitable. Update group 000018 is suitable for items that are billed directly, without delivery. You'll find the updated open orders in table S066, and open deliveries in table S067. Found in the document's pricing procedure, subtotal A decides the value of the document in credit management, and is stored in the VBAP-CMPRE table field, which subsequently updates tables S066 and S067. Once an order is delivered, the relevant entry in table S066 moves to table S067.

The update can fail, though this is very rare. You can schedule and run program RVKRED08 in the background so that these odd cases are also taken care of. Table 5.1 lists the other useful programs.

Program	Description
RFDKLI10	Customers with missing credit data
RFDKLI20	Reorganization of credit limit for customers
RFDKLI30	Short overview of credit limit
RFDKLI40	Overview of credit limit
RFDKLI41	Credit master sheet
RFDKLI42	Early warning list (of critical customers)
RFDKLI43	Master data list
RFDKLI50	Mass change of credit limit data
RVKRED06	Checking blocked credit documents
RVKRED08	Checking credit documents that reach the credit horizon
RVKRED09	Checking the credit documents from the credit view
RVKRED77	Reorganization of Sales and Distribution credit data
RFDKLI10	Customers with missing credit data
RFDKLI20	Reorganization of credit limit for customers
RFDKLI30	Short overview of credit limit
RFDKLI40	Overview of credit limit

Table 5.1 Useful Programs for Credit Management

SAP Fiori for Credit Risk Management
At the time of writing, there's one important SAP Fiori app for credit risk management to keep in mind.

Description	Requirements
The *Credit Limit Utilization* analytical app is used to report on business partners' credit limit exposure, credit segment, country, and region. You define your own threshold for comparison.	EHP 7 for SAP ERP 6.0 SPS 09

5.1.4 SAP FSCM Credit Management

So far in this chapter, we have detailed how the Sales and Distribution credit risk management works and how it integrates into SAP ERP Sales and Distribution during order and delivery processing. Now is time to discuss a very important new feature in the SAP Financial Supply Chain Management (FSCM) module, and how credit management is also part of it.

Nomenclature

SAP recently renamed its FSCM module as Receivable Management (RM), so you'll find literature referring to both names.

SAP FSCM integrates closely with credit management as a sophisticated tool that is faster and more reliable. Figure 5.14 shows how SAP FSCM Credit Management (FSCM-CR) compares to the Sales and Distribution module. In fact, SAP FSCM-CR integrates the most to the Sales and Distribution module, because it's a new way to check for customer credit and perform credit checks. You may find FSCM-CR to be a powerful tool, due to its integration to both SAP and non-SAP systems. This way, you can verify the customer's credit along with external sources, such as any bureau of credit. Additionally since SAP FSCM-CR offers credit limits and a credit rules engine, you can perform a deeper and richer customer analysis. You can maintain credit scoring both internally and externally via SAP FSCM-CR.

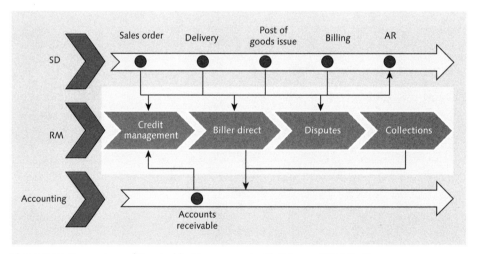

Figure 5.14 Comparison of Receivable Management with Sales and Distribution

SAP FSCM-CR interacts with Sales and Distribution and Accounts Receivable via credit checks during ordering, delivery, and billing.

Figure 5.15 shows how SAP FSCM-CR integrates with the rest of SAP modules, along with external sources of credit. We expect the traditional credit checks in SAP to merge into SAP FSCM Credit Management, and eventually fully replace it in coming SAP releases.

If your company wants to use these new features, you need to plan ahead with regard to the architecture and SAP components required. It's very common to define your external vendors and credit bureaus along with the internal SAP integration. It's also important to understand to what extent you'll be integrating business intelligence (BI) into your SAP FSCM-CR implementation. SAP has provided the main method of exchanging information between components and external interfaces via SAP Process Integration (PI), which was formerly known as the Exchange Infrastructure (XI).

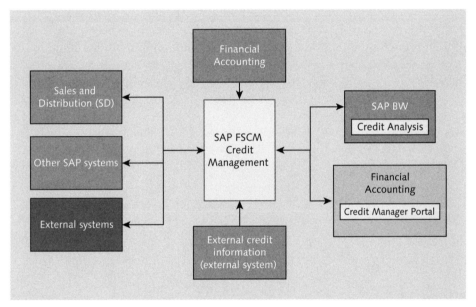

Figure 5.15 FSCM Component Architecture and Interaction with Sales and Distribution

You can find help on architecture, as well as a good source of information for the configuration of Business Intelligence integrated to SAP FSCM-CR, at the SAP Help portal under this path: DOCUMENTATION • SAP ERP CENTRAL COMPONENTS • ERP CENTRAL COMPONENT (RELEASE 6.0) • SAP NETWEAVER LIBRARY • SAP NETWEAVER BY KEY CAPABILITY • INFORMATION INTEGRATION BY KEY CAPABILITY • BI CONTENT • FINANCIALS • SAP FINANCIAL SUPPLY CHAIN MANAGEMENT • SAP CREDIT MANAGEMENT.

Similarly, a good source for the configuration of SAP PI (XI) for FSCM-CR is provided at SAP HELP DOCUMENTATION • SAP ERP CENTRAL COMPONENTS • ERP CENTRAL COMPONENT (RELEASE 6.0) • SAP NETWEAVER LIBRARY • SAP NETWEAVER BY

KEY CAPABILITY • PROCESS INTEGRATION BY KEY CAPABILITY • SAP NETWEAVER EXCHANGE INFRASTRUCTURE.

Component/System	Related SAP Releases and SAP Notes	Description
FIN-FSCM-CR	▶ Financial Basis 6.0 ▶ SAP Notes 967611 and 969190	This is a mandatory requirement for the FSCM-CR. Please follow the SAP notes for details on technical prerequisites.
SAP NetWeaver Application Server	▶ Required release 7.0	This is a mandatory component
SAP NetWeaver Exchange Infrastructure	▶ Minimum required release is 3.0 preferably higher. Highly recommended 7.0	This is a mandatory component
Account Receivable (FI-AR) and/or Contract Account Receivable (FI-CA)	▶ The FI-AR integration minimum release should be 4.6C Plug-in 2004.1 ▶ FI-CA ▶ Industry release 4.72 or later ▶ SAP Note 1096883	Although these components are suggested as optional, it's highly advisable to install them.
Sales and Distribution	▶ Same as in FI-AR integration, the minimum release should be 4.6C Plug-in 2004.1 ▶ SAP Note 1096882	This integrator is highly suggested.
External Credit Information	▶ External System	Install any external credit information as required by your company.

Table 5.2 Minimum Required Components and Systems in FSCM-CR

Based on your company's requirements, you can decide to what extent you want to the control the customer credit, and what reaction is required. Once the SAP FSCM-CR installation is completed, including internal and external interfaces, you can proceed to configure it. The basic configuration relates to four main areas: business partners, credit risk monitoring, events, and integration with accounts receivable accounting and sales and distribution. Let's look closer at each of these.

Business Partners

One of the main objectives of this specific configuration is to adapt the business partners (BP) component. The BP component was created with the purpose of maintaining the customer's credit profile, as well as other internal credit data, including credit information from external sources and credit bureaus. Figure 5.16 shows Transaction UKM_BP for business partner's credit views.

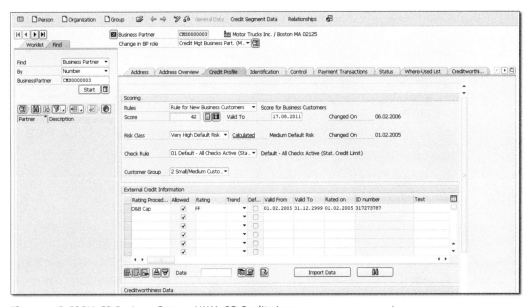

Figure 5.16 FSCM CR Business Partner UKM_BP Credit views

One of the most important configurations to make is the BP roles configuration. Use the menu path SPRO • CROSS-APPLICATION COMPONENTS • SAP BUSINESS PARTNER • BUSINESS PARTNER • BASIC SETTINGS • BUSINESS PARTNER ROLES • DEFINE BP ROLES. The UKM00 (CREDIT MGT BUSINESS PART) role selected in Figure 5.17 is the standard role delivered by SAP to activate the CREDIT PROFILE tab and credit segment data. This will help you to personalize a customer's credit limits and checks.

Additionally, you can define your customized role by making your own copy and then selecting a title and description. You must select a category role under the attributes of the BP role category. This will allow your roles to update via internal

SAP tables. Also, be sure to define BP roles groupings and roles exclusion groups, as required by your company's specific needs.

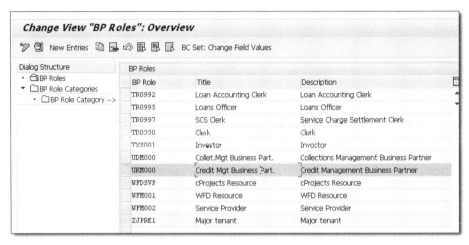

Figure 5.17 FSCM BP Role Category Configuration

Credit Risk Monitoring

First, you need to configure the master data. As you can see in Figure 5.16, the BP credit profile has the following main components:

▶ Scoring rules and credit limit calculation must be configured in order to determine how the credit score will be calculated. Use menu path SPRO • FINANCIAL SUPPLY CHAIN MANAGEMENT • CREDIT MANAGEMENT • CREDIT RISK MONITORING • MASTER DATA • CREATE RULE FOR SCORING AND CREDIT LIMIT CALCULATION, as shown in Figure 5.18. As a prerequisite for this configuration, you need to review and configure credit segments. You can configure credit segments via menu path SPRO • FINANCIAL SUPPLY CHAIN MANAGEMENT • CREDIT MANAGEMENT • CREDIT RISK MONITORING • CREATE CREDIT SEGMENTS. A credit segment normally represents your own company, or even its branches. They also calculate the credit limit, and are associated with a specific currency.

▶ You can assign the rules for scoring to the score formula under the SCORE folder; you can also assign them to a credit limit. In turn, you can assign the credit limit to a validity date, so as to specify the number of days the calculated results will be valid. If your credit checks include an external credit information, you can select the external rating procedure under RATING PROCEDURE SELECTION.

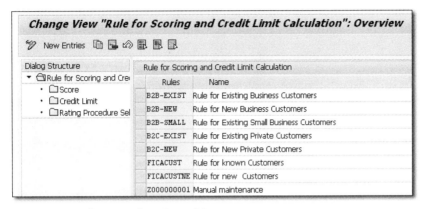

Figure 5.18 Configuration for Rules and Scores

▸ You can create credit formulas and rating procedures by assigning a new entry formula name and a result type (calculation to be part of the credit score or the credit limit), as shown in Figure 5.19. Use menu path SPRO • FINANCIAL SUPPLY CHAIN MANAGEMENT • CREDIT MANAGEMENT • CREDIT RISK MONITORING • MASTER DATA • DEFINE FORMULAS.

By selecting FORMULA EDITOR to the right of the icons, you can enter your own formula for calculation and expected results.

Change View "SAP Credit Management: Formulas": Overview

New Entries 🗋 🗔 🖎 🗐 🗐 🗐 BC Set: Field Value Origin 🖼Formula Editor

SAP Credit Management: Formulas

Formula	Formula Name	Result
FICABONITÄT	Creditworthiness FI-CA	Calculati
FICABONITÄTNEW	Creditworthiness FI-CA for new customers	Calculati
FICALIMIT	Credit limit FI-CA	Calculati
FICALIMIT0000	Credit limit FI-CA for segment 0000	Calculati
FICALIMIT_NEW	Credit limit FI-CA for new customers	Calculati
FICALIMIT_NEW0000	Credit limit FI-CA segment 0000 new customers	Calculati
LIMIT_B2B	Credit Limit for Business Customers	Calculati
LIMIT_B2B_100	Credit Limit for Business Customers	Calculati
LIMIT_B2B_MAIN	Global Credit Limit	Calculati
LIMIT_B2C	Credit Limit for Private Customers	Calculati
LIMIT_B2C_MAIN		Calculati
SCORE_B2B	Score for Business Customers	Calculati
SCORE_B2C	Score for Private Customers	Calculati

Figure 5.19 Configuration on Credit Formulas

- The configuration of the risk class is also part of the master data settings of SAP FSCM-CR. You can configure your required risk classes and determine if any manual changes made may overwrite the class, which has been determined automatically. Use menu path SPRO • FINANCIAL SUPPLY CHAIN MANAGEMENT • CREDIT MANAGEMENT • CREDIT RISK MONITORING • MASTER DATA • CREATE RISK CLASSES. As shown in Figure 5.20, you can include the SCORE FROM and SCORE TO fields to delimit each risk class. The risk class has a direct connection to the Sales and Distribution Risk Category. Make sure your configuration matches both, accordingly.

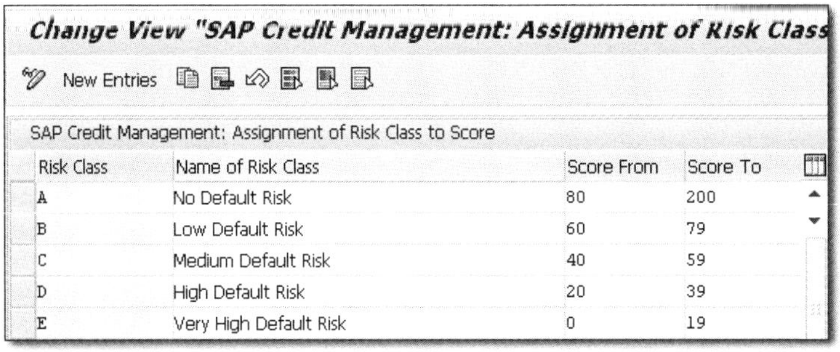

Risk Class	Name of Risk Class	Score From	Score To
A	No Default Risk	80	200
B	Low Default Risk	60	79
C	Medium Default Risk	40	59
D	High Default Risk	20	39
E	Very High Default Risk	0	19

Figure 5.20 Risk Class Configuration

Finally you need to define the customer credit group. You can define your own customer groups via menu path SPRO • FINANCIAL SUPPLY CHAIN MANAGEMENT • CREDIT MANAGEMENT • CREDIT RISK MONITORING • MASTER DATA • DEFINE CUSTOMER CREDIT GROUP.

Credit Limit Check

One of the most important features of SAP FSCM-CR is the ability to tailor how credit checks will behave for each customer. You can configure the check rules that best fit your company needs. Each check rule can consist of several individual checks, also known as check steps. You can define your own check rules as shown in Figure 5.21.

You may configure each individual check rule to perform different steps that represent a hierarchy of importance for checking credit score. Access the individual steps by selecting checks. You can also assign the credit segment and maximum document value to better match your credit check requirements.

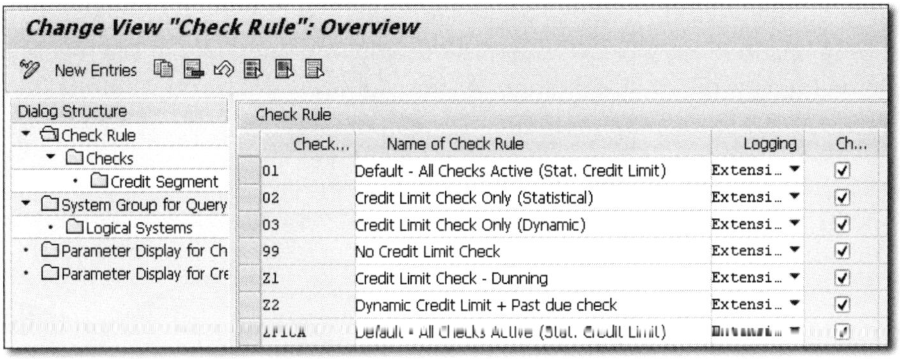

Change View "Check Rule": Overview

New Entries

Check...	Name of Check Rule	Logging	Ch...
01	Default - All Checks Active (Stat. Credit Limit)	Extensi... ▼	✓
02	Credit Limit Check Only (Statistical)	Extensi... ▼	✓
03	Credit Limit Check Only (Dynamic)	Extensi... ▼	✓
99	No Credit Limit Check	Extensi... ▼	✓
Z1	Credit Limit Check - Dunning	Extensi... ▼	✓
Z2	Dynamic Credit Limit + Past due check	Extensi... ▼	✓
ZPICA	Default - All Checks Active (Stat. Credit Limit)	Extensi... ▼	✓

Dialog Structure:
- Check Rule
  - Checks
    - Credit Segment
  - System Group for Query
    - Logical Systems
  - Parameter Display for Ch
  - Parameter Display for Cre

Figure 5.21 Checking Rules Configuration

Events

Configuring credit events is critical to determining how the system will react to a given event. Events respond to basic questions, such as "what to happens when the BP score changes?" or "is the risk class also impacted?" Also, events help determine at what time (or under which condition) a specific event will be triggered either internally in SAP, or in the external systems via the SAP PI interface. Access event configuration via menu path SPRO • FINANCIAL SUPPLY CHAIN MANAGEMENT • CREDIT MANAGEMENT • CREDIT RISK MONITORING • PROCESSES • DEFINE EVENTS AND FOLLOW-ON PROCESSES.

Change View "Events": Overview

New Entries

Dialog Structure:
- Events
  - Follow-On Processes

Activity	Type of Event	XI	Log
Update of Cr... ▼	External Rating Changed ▼	☐	
Business Par... ▼	Blocked in Credit Management ▼	✓	With log
Business Par... ▼	External Rating Changed ▼	✓	
Business Par... ▼	Score Changed ▼	☐	
Business Par... ▼	Credit Limit Changed ▼	☐	
Business Par... ▼	Change to Credit Limit Requ... ▼	☐	
Business Par... ▼	Risk Class Changed ▼	☐	
Master Data ... ▼	Score Changed ▼	☐	
Master Data ... ▼	Credit Limit Changed ▼	☐	
Master Data ... ▼	Rule for Calculating Score ... ▼	☐	
Credit Check ▼	Credit Rejected ▼	☐	
Update of Pa... ▼	Limit Utilization over 100% ▼	☐	

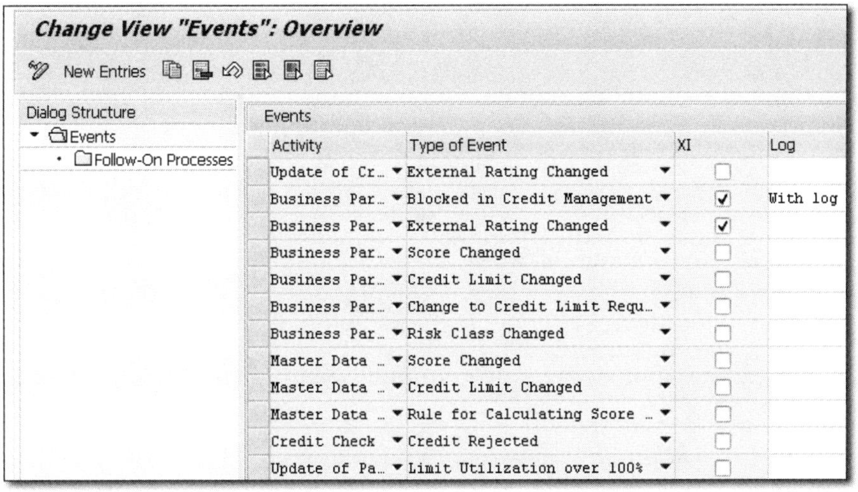

Figure 5.22 Credit Events and Follow-on Processes Configuration

You can create your own events by selecting an activity and a type of event, as shown in Figure 5.22. You can also select PI/XI to indicate that the external systems will receive the event. Additionally, you can select WITH LOG if you want to add traceability to the credit event.

If you select FOLLOW-ON PROCESSES, you can also configure which process are to be follow-on after the credit event triggers. It's very common to assign a workflow event to trigger as the result of a credit event, such as manager approvals.

Integration with Accounts Receivable and Sales and Distribution

In order to integrate SAP FSCM-CR to the rest of the components and external interfaces, you have to implement and configure SAP-delivered BAdIs and customized BAdIs. The BAdI UKM_R3_ACTIVATE (Activate FSCM Credit Management in FI-AR) is the most common SAP FSCM-CR BAdI required for Sales and Distribution integration, but you may need to customize others based on your individual requirements. You should verify the implementation using the corresponding SAP Notes (1096882 and 1554160), as they relate to integration FSCM-CR credit checks with LE Delivery.

Other integrations for SAP FSCM-CR and Sales and Distribution follow a similar configuration as the credit checks denoted throughout this chapter in addition to the credit configuration shown in Figure 5.22.

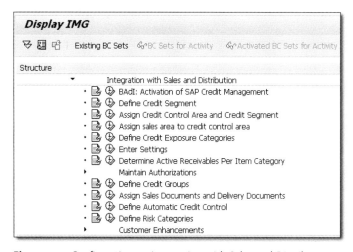

Figure 5.23 Configuration on Integration with Sales and Distribution

Follow the menu path SPRO • FINANCIAL SUPPLY CHAIN MANAGEMENT • CREDIT MANAGEMENT • INTEGRATION WITH ACCOUNTS RECEIVABLE ACCOUNTING AND SALES AND DISTRIBUTION • INTEGRATION WITH SALES AND DISTRIBUTION. You can configure integration according to your own company's requirements.

5.2   Credit Management Operations

From a credit management point of view, important operations include releasing and rejecting blocked documents, credit review, and mass change of customer credit master records.

Releasing Blocked Document

When a sales document is blocked, a warning or error message appears, such as MAXIMUM PERCENTAGE OPEN ITEMS EXCEEDED. If you click on the question mark, you'll find the details of the credit checks performed on the document, the ones it cleared (OK), and the ones it failed to clear (NOK). As shown in the Figure 5.24, the document was subjected to neither a static credit limit check nor any check for user exit 1, 2, or 3. It cleared (OK) the check for dynamic credit limit, document value, critical fields, next check date, and maximum dunning level. It failed (NOK) the check for open items and oldest open item. You could still save the document can and have it reviewed by the credit representative by using Transaction VKM1 or following the menu path SAP EASY ACCESS • LOGISTICS • SALES AND DISTRIBUTION • CREDIT MANAGEMENT • EXCEPTIONS • BLOCKED SD DOCUMENTS. All of the important information required for making the decision to either release or reject the document is available here.

By selecting a document, you can access the customer master record using the menu path ENVIRONMENT • CUSTOMER MASTER, or customer credit master record using the menu path ENVIRONMENT • CUST. MASTER CREDIT of the sold-to party for that document. You can see the other open sales using the menu path ENVIRONMENT • OPEN SALES VALUES • OPEN SALES ORDER, and deliveries or billing documents by using the menu path ENVIRONMENT • OPEN SALES VALUES • OPEN DLVS/BILL DOCS. You can also generate the credit master sheet found using Transaction S_ALR_87012218 or following the menu path ENVIRONMENT • CREDIT MASTER SHEET; this is a particularly useful report to review the credit status of an individual customer. The report gives more information than Transaction FDK43, but with Transaction VKM3, you can review several customers at once. Based on all of the available information, the credit representative may decide to release the document by selecting the checkbox on P.St. column, as seen in Figure 5.25 and then click on the green flag icon to accept, or the REJECT button to reject.

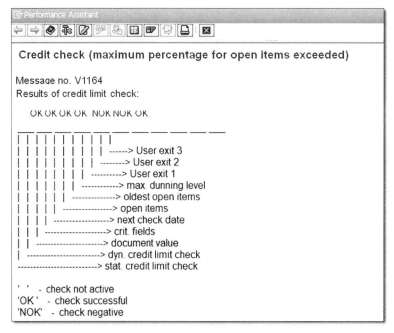

Figure 5.24 Results of the Credit Check

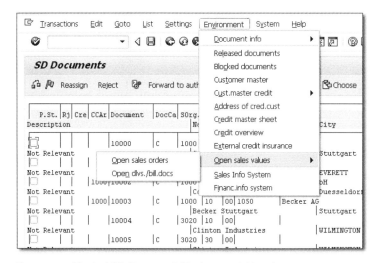

Figure 5.25 Blocked SD Document (Environment Menu)

Credit Review of Individual Customer

Individual customers are reviewed internally at regular intervals to increase or decrease their credit limits and change their risk categories in the credit master record (Transaction FD32). For a credit review, the credit master sheet report is normally sufficient for individual customers. To review a large number of customers, you can use the credit overview Transaction F.31 or the menu path SAP EASY ACCESS • LOGISTICS • SALES AND DISTRIBUTION • CREDIT MANAGEMENT • CREDIT MANAGEMENT INFO SYSTEM • OVERVIEW). The following data is normally useful during credit reviews:

- Total sales
- Days of sales outstanding (DSO)
- Credit utilized
- Payment history
- Due days analysis

Credit Master Record Mass Change

Credit master data maintenance is the joint responsibility of the accounting and sales officials responsible for credit management. In some companies, master data maintenance is a separate function. When NEXT REVIEW DATE is used as a reason to block the orders in credit management, mass maintenance becomes important. It's important to review customer credit ratings and update the customer credit master records before the expiration of the next review date.

The steps for a mass change of the customer credit master record NEXT REVIEW DATE field are as follows:

1. Using Transaction F.34, you can change the NEXT REVIEW DATE field of any number of customers in no time. In the initial screen, select the customers based on the restriction on the following fields of the customer credit master record:
   - CREDIT ACCOUNT
   - CREDIT CONTROL AREA
   - CREDIT REPRESENTATIVE GROUP
   - RISK CATEGORY

> ▹ Last Internal Review

> ▹ Next Internal Review

2. After entering the required values in the input screen, execute the process to go to the screen shown in Figure 5.26.

3. Select all of the customers by pressing [F5] or clicking on the Select All icon.

4. Click on the New Values button.

5. Enter the new date for Next Internal Review in the pop-up window shown in Figure 5.26, and click on Continue.

6. You'll get the message "New values are held and can be saved." Click on the Save icon.

7. For all successful changes, you'll get the message "Control area data <credit control area> Changed," and for failed changes the message will be "Account <customer credit account> is currently blocked by another user."

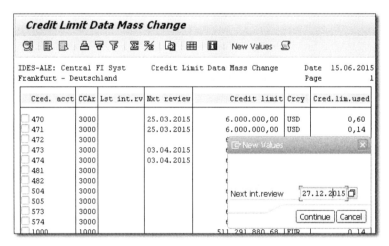

Figure 5.26 Credit Limit Data Mass Change

Mass Changes

For mass changes of fields such as risk category (KNKK-CTLPC), customer credit group (KNKK-GRUPP), or individual limit (KNKA-KLIME), use Transaction MASS, object KNA1, and then table KNKK or KNKA. For mass changes of the Credit Limit (KNKK-KLIMK) field, you can use Transaction SE16N with the SAP edit (&SAP_EDIT) function. For more details on these methods, see Chapter 2.

5.3   Blocking and Unblocking Customers

For an SAP ERP user, it's easier to block a customer for sales, rather than creating orders blocked for credit and then rejecting them for release or deleting them. The customer is unblocked when payment received improves his credit rating, and orders are no longer expected to be blocked for credit during automatic credit checks. This is usually used as an add-on to the credit management process, rather than as substitute for it. Using reports like FDK43, customers with more than 100% credit utilization (or per the credit policy, perhaps 120% credit utilization) are identified and blocked at regular intervals. Unblocking follows the same process. Block and unblock customers using the following transactions:

▶ Transaction XD05 for different company codes and sales areas

▶ Transaction VD05 for different sales areas

▶ Transaction FD05 for different company codes

Because Transaction XD05 is a more comprehensive method of blocking and/or unblocking, we'll use it for the rest of this discussion. As shown in Figure 5.27, go to Transaction XD05 and specify the company code and sales area details in the first screen.

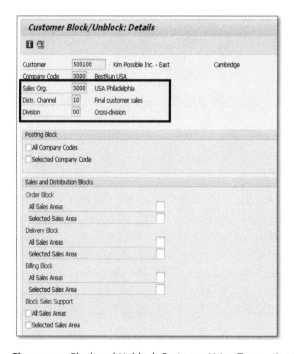

Figure 5.27 Block and Unblock Customer Using Transaction XD05

The POSTING BLOCK applies to the accounting component, and no customization is involved. By selecting (or removing) the appropriate checkbox, you can block (or unblock) it for all company codes, and/or the company code for which you have executed the transaction (in this example, we've executed the transaction for COMPANY CODE 3000, refer to the company code above the highlighted area).

In the Sales and Distribution functionality in SAP ERP, the same method applies to sales support. You can block sales support for either all sales areas or the selected sales area (we've taken 3000-10-00 as our sales area).

For order, delivery, and billing, you can block a customer for the specified sales area or all sales areas. Additionally, you can specify the reason for blocking via a drop-down list. There are three predefined drop-down lists as reasons for blocking the customer for order, delivery, and/or billing. You can modify these three lists in three ways:

▶ Order block: Transaction OVAS or menu path SAP IMG • SALES AND DISTRIBUTION • SALES • SALES DOCUMENTS • SAP DEFINE AND ASSIGN REASON FOR BLOCKING

▶ Delivery block: Transaction OVLS or menu path SAP IMG • LOGISTICS EXECUTION • SHIPPING • DELIVERIES • DEFINE REASONS FOR BLOCKING IN SHIPPING

▶ Billing block: Transaction OVV3 or menu path SAP IMG • SALES AND DISTRIBUTION • BILLING • BILLING DOCUMENTS • DEFINE BLOCKING REASON FOR BILLING

5.4 Solving Common Credit Risk Problems

Let's take a look at a few common credit risk management problems encountered during or after implementation.

▶ **Problem**
Our orders are too large, and when, after entering the order, the user finds that the customer's order cannot be delivered, the user feels resentment. We want the user to know if the customer order will be blocked for credit or not before he actually enters the order. When the user enters the customer code in the order screen, the user should receive the message that the customer is blocked.

Solution: It's not possible to carry out a credit check without actually entering the credit-relevant items. However, customers who have fully utilized their credit limits and whose orders are not likely to be released can be blocked. You can block the customer using either Transaction FD32 or XD05. In Transaction FD32, select the BLOCK checkbox in the status screen. In Transaction XD05, you may block the customer for the order and assign a reason for it. In both the cases, you'll achieve the desired result. The message that the order cannot be completed will appear when you enter the customer code. However, it will not be because of an automatic credit check.

▶ **Problem**

Our customers give us a security deposit at the time of their appointment. They want us to include the amount of this deposit during the credit check. Where should we make the necessary configuration changes?

Solution: This is an accounting functionality, done using Transaction OBXR. The steps are given below:

▷ Double-click on the special GL indicator for the security deposit in the first screen.

▷ Enter the credit-relevant GLs in the second screen.

▷ Click on the PROPERTIES button on the application toolbar.

▷ In the third screen, select the REL.TO CREDIT LIMIT checkbox.

▶ **Problem**

In the customer credit master sheet (S_ALR_87012218), we find an open order value, which blocks the customer's orders in credit management. We've checked and found no open orders. When there are no open orders, how can there be an open order value for credit management?

Solution: Open order, open delivery, and open invoice values are determined based on the entries in table fields S066-OEIKW, S067-OLIKW, and S067-OFAKW, respectively. The error in updating these fields may occur for various reasons. You can find some of those reasons in the list of SAP notes provided in Table 5.3. To update the system after rectifying these mistakes, you can use the program RVKRED77 (in Transaction SE38).

SAP Note	Description
626880	Credit values are not updated
748217	Changing the doc type causes incorrect statistical values

Table 5.3 SAP Notes on Failure to Update Open Order, Delivery, and Bill Values

SAP Note	Description
754372	Third-party: Open credit value is deleted, although ordered
767454	Billing plan: Incorrect credit update
805704	RVKRED77: Correction program updates incorrectly
801834	Billing plan: Incorrect credit update
842927	RVKRED88: Open sales order values are not displayed
860621	Negative open delivery value with batch after billing doc
864105	Simulation credit values: incorrect results in ABAP memory
880557	RVKRED77 + sched agr w/ rel order: mult value of gds for dely
890550	RVKRED77 + sched agrmnt w/ rel: mult value of delvy goods
948824	VL02N: S073 and change docs are incorrect after credit check
950025	VL02N: S073 and change docs are incorrect after credit check
981598	Third-party: Confirmed quantity despite credit block
993714	RFDKLI20: Negative credit values
1025260	RVKRED77: Completed order receives open delivery value
1058456	EK00: Incorrect sales values for credit limit check
1067486	Incorrect credit value when you increase delivery quantity
1070715	Credit value reduced twice with "Deliver Sales Order"
1072322	Open quantity (OLFMNG) not reduced by delivery
1116400	Sales documents are not or only partially updated
1126067	BW + LIS: Incorrect open qty when credit management is active
1297946	RVKRED07: Incorrect credit values due to incorrect election

Table 5.3 SAP Notes on Failure to Update Open Order, Delivery, and Bill Values (Cont.)

▶ **Problem**

Is there any report where we can see the log for open credit values? We're using tables S066 and S067 right now, but it becomes very difficult to track the entries back to the documents that created them. Also, we want information about the user who created the document, and when it was created.

Solution

There's no standard report as such. However, you can follow the steps listed in SAP Note 1042857 (Logging Credit Values) to create your own report for this purpose.

▶ **Problem**

When we release any order from a credit block, we expect the system to carry out another availability check, especially for items that were not fully confirmed at the time of the first credit check. This does not happen in our system. What modification should we make?

Solution

This happens in a standard system. A second availability check takes place after the credit release only when the confirmed quantity (VBAP-KBMENG) is nil. You can, however, use user exit USEREXIT_AVAIL_CHECK_CREDIT in include program MV45AFZF (using Transaction SE38) to perform the availability check in all (or some) scenarios.

▶ **Problem**

We use rush orders that generate delivery automatically. Even when we've activated a credit check for the rush order (SO), deliveries are still created automatically, when there is insufficient credit limit. Why does this happen?

Solution

Refer to SAP Notes 1224912 and 365271. Please note that the simultaneous use of rush orders and update group 15 is not compatible in SAP ERP. This means you'll have to choose one or the other. Because you've ruled out the possibility of a standard setting for rush orders where a credit check is not activated, update group 15 may be the cause of the problem.

5.5   Summary

In this chapter, we discussed how credit management works and how to configure automatic credit control in the Sales and Distribution functionality of SAP ERP. We explored Credit Management functionality in SAP FSCM, and then discussed how to block and unblock customers for accounting posting and for various sales and distribution operations such as order, delivery, billing, and sales activities.

With this knowledge, you should be able to configure your system as per company credit policy and processing procedures. You should also able to block and unblock customers for different sales processes.

In the next chapter, we'll discuss different logistics operations.

This chapter teaches you how to customize delivery document types. You'll review the processes for individual document and mass processing and familiarize yourself with special processes, such as route determination, stock transfer, serialization, and batch determination. You'll also learn about output determination and how to use SAP ERP to help facilitate these processes.

6   Logistics Management

The "distribution" part of sales and distribution is our next focus. This chapter deals with the physical movement of materials: how material is picked as per the order, and how it is packed and shipped as per the determined route. These processes are becoming increasingly automated by default, with the option for manual intervention.

In SAP ERP, these processes are part of the Logistics Execution functionality. We'll discuss the Shipping and Transportation components of the Logistics Execution functionality in this chapter. You'll learn how to customize the processes and functionalities available in SAP ERP for the delivery of material to customers, including internal customers. A plant considers the other plants or groups of the company as internal customers during stock transfer. Plants transfer the stock between each other so that the stock is available to the customers in a make-to-stock scenario. Once this is completed, with or without reference to an order, the customer receives a bill. The sales return process, which is the reverse process of sales, also involves a delivery (return type). You have a substantial opportunity to reduce the total cost of shipping by optimizing your shipments and selecting the correct route and mode of transport.

In this chapter, we'll start with the various elements of the delivery document and goods movement, and then discuss delivery processing for both individual and multiple documents using the delivery due list. From there, we'll move on to picking, managing handling units, packing, and issuing goods, before we examine defining routes and route determination. We'll discuss batch and serial number processing. Finally, we'll list some common errors during post–goods issue (PGI) processing and summarize the chapter.

6.1 Delivery Types and Delivery Item Categories

The delivery primarily consists of a header (stored in table LIKP and others) and items (stored in table LIPS and others). The delivery is like the sales documents discussed earlier, in that it contains both header and item level data, much of which copies over from the sales order. Of course, you can create a delivery without reference to an order. In the next few sections, we'll discuss the following:

1. How to customize a delivery type, which in turn controls the delivery header

2. How to customize delivery item categories, which control the delivery items

3. How to customize automatic item category determination for delivery types

6.1.1 Delivery Types

You define delivery types using Transaction OVKL or following the menu path SAP IMG • LOGISTICS EXECUTION • SHIPPING • DELIVERIES • DEFINE DELIVERY TYPES. After executing the transaction, you'll see a list of existing delivery types. Select any one and click on the COPY AS ([F6]) icon to go to the screen shown in the Figure 6.1. Sales and Distribution uses document categories J (delivery) and T (return delivery for order) for delivery document types. The standard number range maintained for outbound deliveries (LF) is 17 (80000000 to 83999999) for internal assignments. When you don't provide any manual number at the time of document processing, the next available number becomes the delivery document number, 18 (85000000 to 88999999) for external assignments. This means that if you want to manually give a number to the delivery, you can choose any available number from this range. Different customized delivery types can have different number ranges. You can use the form USEREXIT_NUMBER_RANGE in include program MV50AFZ1 to give different delivery number ranges for the same document type, similar to billing documents. The item number increment is the difference between two consecutive items in a delivery. The first item number is automatically zero (0) plus the item number increment.

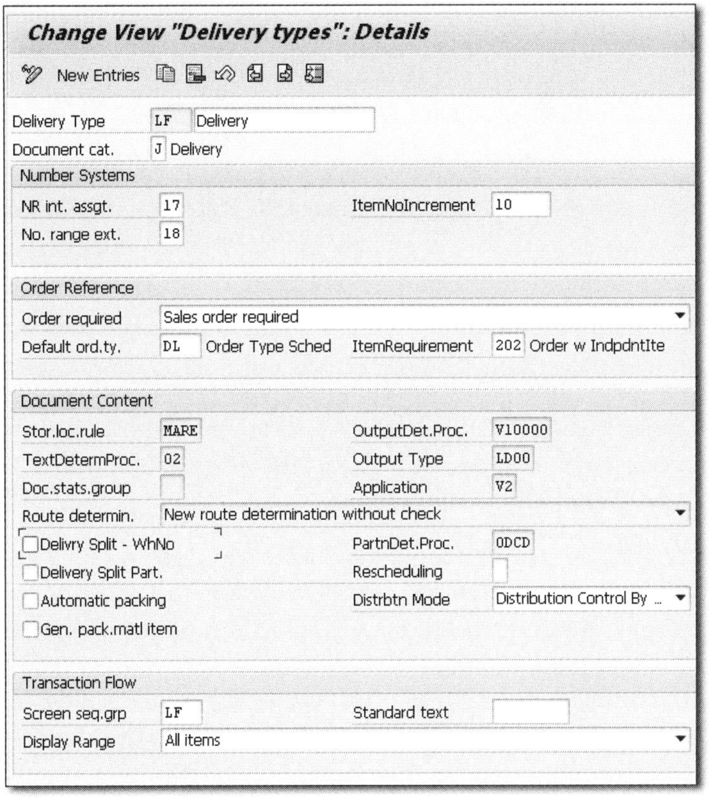

Figure 6.1 Define Delivery Types

Document Types

Sales document type BV (cash sale), which has the Sales and Distribution document category C, and delivery document type BV (cash sale), which has the Sales and Distribution document category J, are two different document types. This may be confusing, because the system automatically creates a delivery document for the sales document for cash sales.

Order reference for the delivery can be mandatory or optional (the ORDER REQUIRED field stays blank). If mandatory, the reference can be further specified as a sales order (X SALES ORDER REQUIRED as shown in Figure 6.1) or a work order from the production planning interface (W), a stock transfer order (B), or another permitted reference. The default order type and item requirement routine (which copies the requirement for deliveries routine) gives you the option of creating a delivery without order reference using Transaction VL01NO. Free samples, for example, are often delivered without orders, and in many industry sectors, it is standard practice to send newly introduced materials to some customers with good relationships.

To create your own routine, use Transaction VOFM. After executing the transaction, to create a new routine, go to COPYING REQUIREMENTS • DELIVERIES and select any existing routine to copy and use to create a new routine. Routine 202 is especially important because it allows you to add new items to deliveries manually. The new items have references to an order. By default, the values for the default order type determine the nature of the new item. However, this functionality is not available once the goods issue (PGI) or goods receipt (post–goods receipt [PGR], as in case of return delivery) for the delivery is complete. After PGI is complete, you can only change the text fields. The other possible operation after PGI is additional output (e.g., printing the delivery header).

In the DOCUMENT CONTENT area of the screen shown in Figure 6.1, some fields are not ready for input (or are disabled). Other transactions determine the values for these fields, and the values assigned in the other transactions or customization settings are only available for display here. The following is a list of such fields, and the transaction and/or menu path where you assign the values to the delivery document.

▶ **Storage Location Rule**
There are three standard rules.

▷ The rule MALA uses the combination of shipping point, plant, and storage condition to automatically determine the storage location for any specific item of a delivery. Storage location is determined as per the setting in Transaction OVL3 or through menu path SAP IMG • LOGISTICS EXECUTION • SHIPPING • PICKING • DETERMINE PICKING LOCATION • ASSIGN PICKING LOCATIONS.

▷ The rule RETA uses the combination of plant, situation, and storage condition for automatic determination of the storage location. When this rule is used, the storage location is determined by the customization in Transaction S_ALR_87006703 or the menu path SAP IMG • LOGISTICS EXECUTION • SHIPPING • PICKING • DETERMINE PICKING LOCATION • STORAGE LOCATION DETERMINATION WITH SITUATION.

▷ The third standard rule, MARE, first tries to find a storage location as per the MALA rule and then tries to find one using the RETA rule.

You can define a new rule using the include program `MV50AFZZ` (Transaction SE38). If you have valid reasons to use `MALA` for some materials and `RETA` for others, this is where to do it.

▶ **Output Determination Procedure**
Use Transaction V/71 or follow the menu path SAP IMG • Logistics Execution • Shipping • Basic Shipping Functions • Output Control • Output Determination • Maintain Output Determination for Outbound Deliveries • Assign Output Determination Procedures • Assign deliveries (header). The output determination procedure assigned here appears in the screen shown in Figure 6.1, in Display Mode.

▶ **Text Determination Procedure**
Use Transaction VOTXN or follow the menu path SAP IMG • Logistics Execution • Shipping • Basic Shipping Functions • Text Control • Define And Assign Text Determination Procedures. Select the Delivery Header radio button and click on Change. Double-click on the Text Assignment Procedure folder on the left of the screen. The complete list of delivery types will appear, and you can assign a text determination procedure as per requirements. The assignment done here appears in the screen shown in Figure 6.1 in Display Mode.

▶ **Output Type**
You can refer the menu path for assigning output determination procedure to the delivery document type (Transaction V/71). In addition to assigning a determination procedure to the delivery document type, you can also specify a default output type, which is displayed in Figure 6.1.

▶ **Document Statistical Group**
Use Transaction OVRK or follow the menu path SAP IMG • Logistics – General • Logistics Information System (LIS) • Logistics Data Warehouse • Updating • Updating Control • Settings: Sales • Statistics Groups • Assign Statistics Groups for Each Delivery Type. The assignment done here appears in the screen shown in Figure 6.1 in Display Mode.

▶ **Application**
This is the same as the application of the default output type. It is `V2` (Shipping).

▶ **Route Determination**
We'll discuss this Section 6.5.

▸ **Partner Determination Procedure**
Use Transaction VOPAN or following the menu path SAP IMG • SALES AND DISTRIBUTION • BASIC FUNCTIONS • PARTNER DETERMINATION • SET UP PARTNER DETERMINATION • SET UP PARTNER DETERMINATION FOR DELIVERY • PARTNER DETERMINATION PROCEDURE ASSIGNMENT (FOLDER).

The fields for which the values are defined as follows:

▸ **Delivery Split – Warehouse Number**
When you select this checkbox, different deliveries will process the items in different warehouses.

▸ **Delivery Split for Additional Partner**
When this checkbox is selected, even for the partner function other than ship-to party (e.g., forwarding agent), if partners are different for different items, the delivery will split.

▸ **Rescheduling**
This indicator determines if rescheduling should take place for backlog entries (option X), when the route is redetermined (Y), or if the new deadline should be set for the delivery (option A). When it's left blank, there will be no rescheduling.

▸ **Automatic Packing**
When you select this checkbox, all items using packing proposals are automatically packed.

▸ **Distribution Mode**
This field controls when the delivery transfers to the distributed warehouse management system. You have to decide if the distribution will happen manually (option 1) or automatically when the delivery is created (option 2). When left blank, the control for distribution depends on the setting for warehouse number.

▸ **Generate Packaging Material Item**
If you select this checkbox, the delivery automatically creates an item for the packaging material.

SAP Fiori Apps for Logistics Management

At the time of writing, there are five important SAP Fiori apps for Logistics Management to keep in mind.

Description	Requirements
The *Track Shipments* transactional app gives your customers shipment information on their mobile devices. It lists shipments, delivery dates, shipment statuses, and tracking info.	SAP ERP 6.0 SP 15 or higher
Use the *Outbound Delivery* fact sheet app to display information about outbound deliveries, such as number of packages, related volume, and weight. You can also check the items already delivered, the delivery status, and the proposed delivery date.	SAP EHP 7 for SAP ERP 6.0 SP 02
The *Goods Issue* fact sheet app displays information on the goods issue business object.	SAP EHP 7 for SAP ERP 6.0 SP 02
The *Inbound Delivery* fact sheet app gives details of an inbound delivery, like the packages, weight, volume, status of the items to be received, and overall delivery status.	SAP EHP 7 for SAP ERP 6.0 SP 02
Using the *Returns Delivery* fact sheet app, you can get details of a returns delivery, such as the packages, weight, and volume for an inbound delivery. Check the status of an inbound return delivery using this app.	SAP EHP 7 for SAP ERP 6.0 SPS

6.1.2 Delivery Item Category

The delivery item category controls the behavior of a delivery item. For example, it determines whether the material in the delivery item will reduce the stock and increase the stock in transit (stock transfer case), or increase the stock (return case), or only reduce the stock (delivery to customer). The item category of an order becomes the item category of a delivery, as per the copy control setting. For a delivery without reference to sales order, the delivery type and item category of the material maintained in the material master record decide the item category.

You customize the delivery item category using Transaction 0VLP or following the menu path SAP IMG • Logistics Execution • Shipping • Deliveries • Define Item Categories for Deliveries. After you execute the transaction, select any item category (e.g., REN) and click on the Copy As ([F6]) icon to go to the screen shown in Figure 6.2. Except for the text determination procedure assigned via Transaction V/73, other fields here help define the delivery item category. Two other fields, Incompletion Procedure and Item Category Statistical Group, are also available in table TVLP. This table stores the item category's configuration setting, but neither is available or required for display in the maintenance view,

V_TVLP (the screen shown in Figure 6.2). Item categories are assigned to these fields elsewhere. Table TVLK stores delivery type settings.

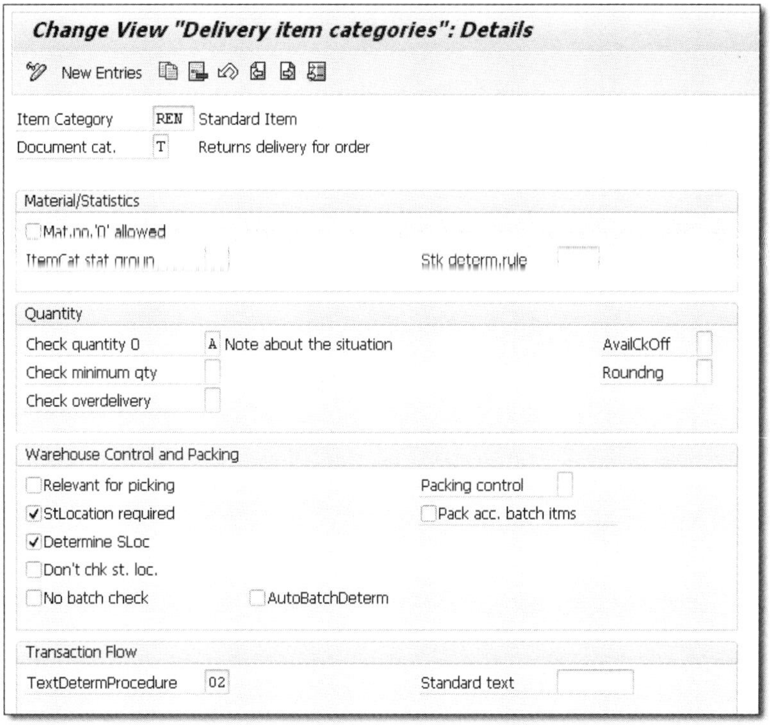

Figure 6.2 Delivery Item Category

Transaction Confusion

Transaction 0VLP, used for customizing delivery item categories, is different from Transaction OVLP, which you use to make item categories relevant for picking.

We will now discuss the fields (and their role) for customization of the delivery item categories.

- ▶ MAT. NO. '0' ALLOWED
  If this checkbox is selected, it's not mandatory for the delivery item to contain a material number (e.g., text item).

- ▶ ITEM CAT. STAT. GROUP
  You can specify the statistics group that the delivery item will use. The statistics

groups are used to update the structures of sales information system (SIS) reports. We'll discuss this in Chapter 9.

▶ STK. DETERM. RULE
The stock determination rule, along with the stock determination group, determines the stock determination strategy.

▶ CHECK QUANTITY 0
In this field, you define if the system will give information (A), an error message during delivery creation (C), or an error message during delivery change (B). If the field is left blank, there will be no dialog box when the delivery quantity is zero.

▶ AVAILCKOFF
The availability check can be switched off by selecting option X or Y, for example, in a make-to-order scenario.

▶ CHECK MINIMUM QTY.
If the delivery quantity is below the minimum delivery quantity specified in the material master record or the customer-material info record, you can customize the system to have no response (blank), to only inform the user (option A), or to issue an error message (option B).

▶ ROUNDNG
You can specify if the quantity of the delivery item with this type of delivery item category will have no rounding (blank), round off (option X), round up (option +), or round down (option –).

▶ CHECK OVERDELIVERY
If the delivery quantity exceeds the order quantity, the system gives an error message (option B) or information (option A), as defined in this field. These will be no response when the field is left blank.

▶ RELEVANT FOR PICKING
You can make the item category relevant for picking via Transaction OVLP, or by selecting this checkbox.

▶ STLOCATION REQUIRED
If this checkbox is selected, the delivery item must have a storage location for the delivery to be complete.

▶ DETERMINE SLOC
When you activate this checkbox, the system attempts to determine the storage location automatically.

- ▶ Don't Chk St. Loc.
  If you select this checkbox, the system will check if the material is created for the storage location (determined automatically or entered manually).

- ▶ No Batch Check
  When this checkbox is selected, the system will not check if the material of the batch is available.

- ▶ AutoBatchDeterm
  If you want the automatic batch determination to occur, select this checkbox.

- ▶ Packing Control and Pack acc. Batch Items
  You can customize these two fields using Transaction VLPP, which will be discussed in Section 6.2.3 of this chapter.

6.1.3   Automatic Determination of Delivery Item Category

Customize the determination of item categories for delivery using Transaction 0184 or following the menu path SAP IMG • Logistics Execution • Shipping • Deliveries • Define Item Category Determination in Deliveries.

Once you've executed the transaction, you'll see the screen shown in Figure 6.3. The system maintains the default item category and allowed item categories for the various combinations of delivery document type, item category group (maintained in material master records), usage indicator, and higher-level item category. During document (delivery) processing, you can change the item category from the default item category to any one of the allowed item categories. So, if the choice of item category needs occasional manual intervention, you now know how to do that.

Customize via Transaction 0VVW or the menu path SAP IMG • Logistics Execution • Shipping • Deliveries • Define Item Category Usage. You can use standard item usages, such as CHSP (batch split), SEIN (delivery item relevant for billing), SENI (delivery item not relevant for billing), TEXT (text item), V (purchase order), FREE (free goods), and others, to create new usages by copying them. You can find the usage indicator for a combination of material and customer in the customer material info record. Because this is a factor in determining delivery item category, you can use it in various business scenarios. For example, you can make a material not relevant for billing for a particular customer (by maintaining a customer material info record). The same material may be relevant for billing to all other customers.

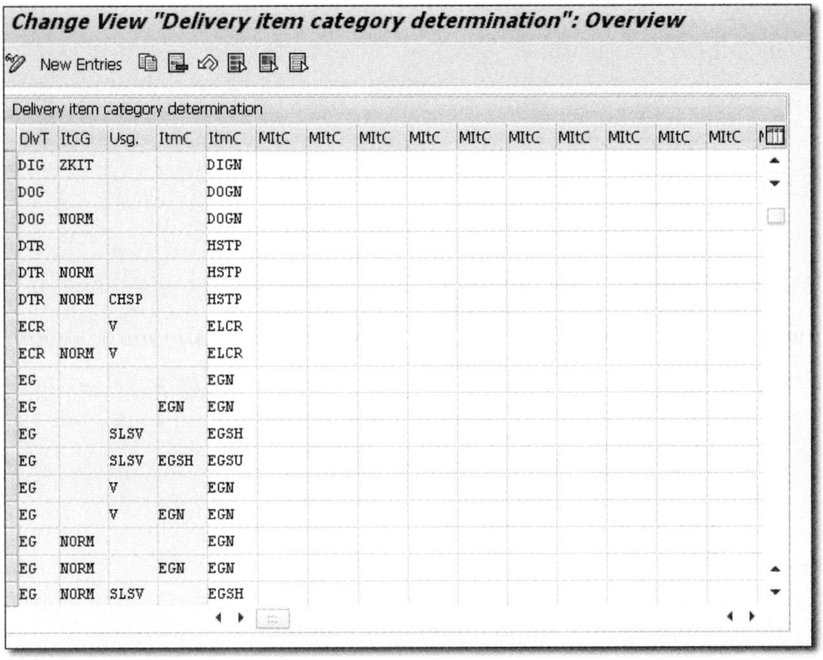

Change View "Delivery item category determination": Overview

New Entries

Delivery item category determination

DlvT	ItCG	Usg.	ItmC	ItmC	MItC	MItC	MItC	MItC	MItC	MItC	MItC	MItC	MItC	MItC	
DIG	ZKIT			DIGN											
DOG				DOGN											
DOG	NORM			DOGN											
DTR				HSTP											
DTR	NORM			HSTP											
DTR	NORM	CHSP		HSTP											
ECR		V		ELCR											
ECR	NORM	V		ELCR											
EG				EGN											
EG			EGN	EGN											
EG		SLSV		EGSH											
EG		SLSV	EGSH	EGSU											
EG		V		EGN											
EG		V	EGN	EGN											
EG	NORM			EGN											
EG	NORM		EGN	EGN											
EG	NORM	SLSV		EGSH											

Figure 6.3 Delivery Item Category Determination

6.2   Delivery Processing Including Delivery Due Lists

In this section, we'll discuss how deliveries are created and how the Warehouse Management functionality in SAP ERP influences delivery processing. You can create a delivery with or without reference to the following documents:

- Sales document (e.g., order or return)
- Stock transfer order
- Subcontract order
- Project

When the delivery is created *with* reference to a sales document, the information copies over to the delivery document that's based on the copy control settings and the routines in use. If it's created *without* reference, the customer master record of the ship-to party, the material master record, and the customer material info records provide default values for the delivery document.

An outbound delivery can be created for a sales order when the following conditions are met, subject to availability:

1. The order is not blocked for delivery due to customization settings or credit blocks at the document or schedule line level.

2. At least one line item in the order is due for delivery.

3. The delivery quantity must not be zero for those item(s) due for delivery.

4. The product status of the material should allow delivery.

5. The order is complete (i.e., not in incompletion log).

Upon the creation of a delivery with reference to an order, the order status automatically updates (as per copy control settings) as partially or fully delivered at the header and item levels. You can add additional items to a delivery, and you can delete items created with reference to the order, depending on customization. During delivery processing, you can perform picking, packing, shipping point determination, and goods issue. In addition, you can also perform route determination, serialization of materials, and batch determination, which we'll cover later in this chapter.

It's possible to split and combine orders during delivery processing. You can split an order into different deliveries if the shipping point, plant, incoterm, or ship-to parties for different items are different in a standard system. You can also define a delivery split profile using Transaction OVDSP; use Transaction VLSP (subsequent delivery split) to split a delivery using the split profile. Similarly, you can process items from different orders in one delivery if the shipping point, plant, incoterm, ship-to party, and sales organization are the same. The combined orders must have value X in the ORDER COMBINATION field of the SHIPPING tab. The system automatically proposes a value for this field based on the value maintained in the customer master record (ORDER COMBINATION field in the SHIPPING tab in the SALES AREA data). During the mass processing of different orders using the delivery due list, the splitting and combination occur automatically.

The delivery due list is an optimization tool available for the mass processing of sales and stock transfer orders. In addition to processing, you can use the list for reporting purposes. Table 6.1 lists the standard delivery due lists available in SAP ERP. You can customize these due lists, or create your own. It's important to remember that the profiles are created and assigned to scenarios, and that Table 6.1 simply lists the default profiles for the existing scenarios that have the same codes.

Transaction	Description	Profile/Scenario
VL10	User-specific delivery due list	VL10
VL10A	Sales orders due for delivery	0001
VL10C	Order items due for delivery	0101
VL10E	Order schedule lines due for delivery	0201
VL10B	Purchase orders due for delivery	0002
VL10F	Purchase order schedule lines due for delivery	0202
VL10G	Documents due for delivery	0003
VL10H	Items due for delivery	0103
VL10I	Schedule lines due for delivery	0203
VL10U	Cross-system deliveries	1001

Table 6.1 Delivery Due Lists for Different Scenarios

Stock Transfer Orders

The purchase orders relevant for outbound delivery are stock transfer orders, which we'll discuss later in this chapter.

Delivery due lists function as work lists for creating multiple deliveries. Work lists are reports or lists that can be further processed, for example, while creating deliveries, as in this case. It's not possible to manually select the orders (or *stock transfer orders* [STOs]) that are to be delivered and the orders that can wait. Companies usually follow very complex rules and/or use manual intervention for this task. You can incorporate all or some of this logic to include some orders for delivery processing while excluding others. Therefore, despite so many standard delivery due lists, you may still want to customize your own. The steps for customizing delivery due lists, and their corresponding transaction codes, are as follows:

1. Maintain the profile for delivery creation (VL10CUC).

2. Create the profile for delivery due lists (VL10CUA or VL10CU_ALL).

3. Exclude specific function codes during list processing (VL10CUE).

4. Assign profiles to scenarios (VL10CUV).

5. Maintain requirements routines for due list processing (VOL1).

6. Modify the default layout if required (OVB9).

Let's now discuss each of these steps in further detail.

6.2.1 Profile for Delivery Creation

To define profiles for creating a delivery, use Transaction VL10CUC or follow the menu path SAP IMG • Logistics Execution • Shipping • Worklists • Maintain Parameters for Creating Deliveries, which you can see in Figure 6.4. Select any existing profile and click on the Copy As ([F6]) icon to go to Figure 6.8. You'll find the following fields here:

▶ **Repeat Blocked**
During processing of a delivery due list, documents not blocked by any other user are processed. The system then attempts to process the documents that it could not process in the first round. In the second attempt, a few documents still may not be available for processing. During delivery due list processing, this process repeats based on the number specified in this field.

▶ **Maximum Lines**
This field should be left as 1.

▶ **Package Type**
This field refers to the grouping of items in the delivery. Option 1 groups the items of a document with same ship-to party in one package, whereas option 2 groups the items of a document together. If you want to use your own logic, you can define the package type in the FORM routine USEREXIT_PREPARE_PACKAGES_CREA, in the include program LV50R_VIEWG09.

▶ **Maximum Number of Tasks**
This field is for when you want to process the delivery due list as parallel multiple tasks. The system will process the delivery due list by dividing the tasks into groups as many times as specified here.

▶ **Selected Items**
If you select this checkbox, only the selected items will process. Otherwise, all items of the documents are processed, even when a few of them may actually match the selection criteria.

▶ **Maximum Delivery Period in Future** (MxDlvCrteDate)
In this field, a value of 30 means that the system will process all of the deliveries due to go out in next 30 days.

▶ **Description**
This field describes the profile.

▶ **Group Parallel**
This field specifies the server group for parallel processing of deliveries. To use this optimization functionality, which distributes the load on the servers, you'll require Basis help.

▸ **No Output Determination, Rescheduling, Shipping Deadlines, SD Picking List and Country-specific Delivery Number**

These five checkboxes, if selected, prevent output determination, rescheduling, additional shipping deadlines, sales and distribution picking lists, and country-specific delivery numbering for those deliveries created by processing the delivery due list. For example, when the last checkbox is selected, it will not generate additional country-specific delivery numbers *only when* deliveries are created using customized delivery due lists.

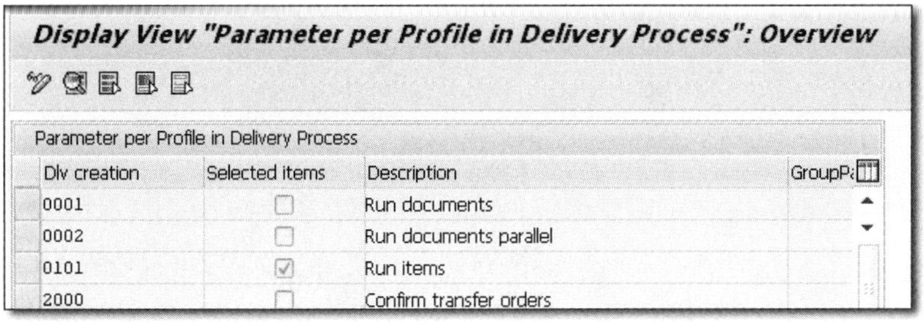

Display View "Parameter per Profile in Delivery Process": Overview

Dlv creation	Selected items	Description	GroupPa
0001	☐	Run documents	
0002	☐	Run documents parallel	
0101	☑	Run items	
2000	☐	Confirm transfer orders	

Figure 6.4 Maintain Parameters per Profile in Delivery Process (Overview)

Change View "Parameter per Profile in Delivery Process": Details

Dlv creation 0001

Parameter per Profile in Delivery Process

Repeat Blocked	100
Maximum lines	1
Package Type	All items for document and ship-to party
Max. no. tasks	
☐ Selected items	
MaxDlvCrteDate	30
Description	Run documents
GrpParallel	
☐ No OutputDet.	
☐ No reschedule	
☐ No ship. sched.	
☐ NoSDPicklist	
☐ NoDelNumber	

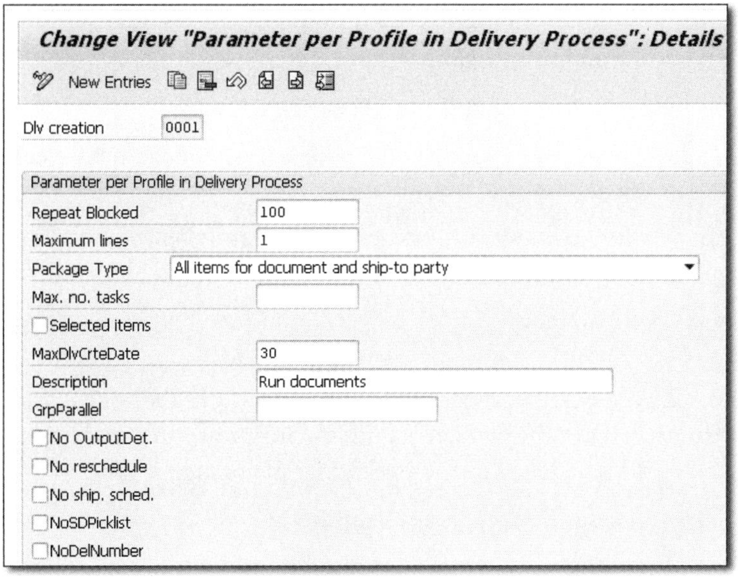

Figure 6.5 Maintain Parameters per Profile in Delivery Process (Detail)

6.2.2   List Profile

Use Transaction VL10CUA or VL10CU_ALL to create the list profile, or follow the menu path SAP IMG • Logistics Execution • Shipping • Worklists • Configure List Profile. You can go to the screen shown in Figure 6.6 when you select any existing entry and click on the Copy As (F6) icon.

As you can see, several fields collectively define the profile. We can group the fields broadly into four different categories:

▶ Fields that provide default values on the selection screen

▶ Fields that influence the layout

▶ Fields that restrict the possible documents for selection

▶ Fields that influence delivery processing

Fields that provide default values on the selection screen include the following:

▶ The Rule DlvCrDate (rule for the default value of the selection criteria for delivery creation date) field can take any of the following six values. That value becomes the default value for the field CalcRuleDefltDlvCrDt on upon executing Transaction VL10*.

  ▷ Blank (everything up to a maximum number of days)

  ▷ 1 (documents due for delivery today)

  ▷ 2 (documents due for delivery today and tomorrow)

  ▷ 3 (documents due for delivery, on or before the last day of the next week, plus those due before today)

  ▷ 4 (documents due for delivery, on or before tomorrow, plus those due before today)

  ▷ 9 (as defined in user exit)

▶ You may maintain the Selection Criteria field either at this customization setting or as a value for the parameter LE_VL10_USER_VARIANT in the user master data record. You can create the default layout by following the menu path Goto • Variants • Save as Variant after executing Transaction VL10*.

Fields that influence the layout include the following:

▶ Open Deliveries
When this checkbox is selected, the system includes the open deliveries created manually for processing.

▶ With Ship-To Party's Name
When you enable this checkbox, the ship-to party's name appears on the screen. However, this reduces system performance.

▶ With Stock Data
When this checkbox is selected, the screen will display the unrestricted stock of the material.

▶ Display Delivery Block with Quantity 0
When this checkbox is selected, the screen displays blocked schedule lines with the quantity zero.

▶ Use Control
When selected, this checkbox allows the display of output in ABAP List Viewer (ALV) format.

▶ Selection Indicator at Header Level
When selected, this checkbox displays the list at the document level that would otherwise display the items.

▶ Traffic Light
The Traffic Light icon that appears in output (when you execute Transaction VL10*) is red when the delivery is already due. If it is due for today or a future date, the value in the traffic light field determines when it will be green or yellow. It will be green when the delivery due date is greater than the value maintained in this field.

▶ Layout
Layout can be sequential (1) or hierarchical sequential (2), depending on how you want it to display.

▶ Key Type
When the layout is a hierarchical sequential list, key type defines the hierarchy. For example, if you select option 1 (Ship-To Party and Source Document), the items of an order are grouped together, and then all orders of a ship-to party are shown below the ship-to party. All of the ship-to parties appear one after another in the list.

▶ Expand
When the layout is hierarchical, you can define whether it will appear as expanded (Yes) or collapsed (No) by default.

▶ Stock Details
Here you can specify whether Transaction CO06, CO09, MD04, or MMBE will display stock.

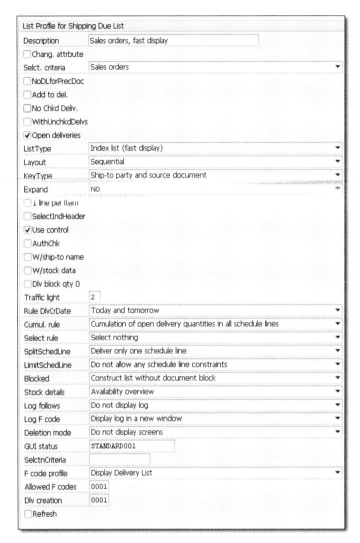

List Profile for Shipping Due List

Description	Sales orders, fast display
☐ Chang. attrbute	
Selct. criteria	Sales orders ▼
☐ NoDLforPrecDoc	
☐ Add to del.	
☐ No Chkd Deliv.	
☐ WithUnchkdDelvs	
✔ Open deliveries	
ListType	Index list (fast display) ▼
Layout	Sequential ▼
KeyType	Ship-to party and source document ▼
Expand	NO ▼
☐ 1 line per item	
☐ SelectIndHeader	
✔ Use control	
☐ AuthChk	
☐ W/ship-to name	
☐ W/stock data	
☐ Dlv block qty 0	
Traffic light	2
Rule DlvCrDate	Today and tomorrow ▼
Cumul. rule	Cumulation of open delivery quantities in all schedule lines ▼
Select rule	Select nothing ▼
SplitSchedLine	Deliver only one schedule line ▼
LimitSchedLine	Do not allow any schedule line constraints ▼
Blocked	Construct list without document block ▼
Stock details	Availability overview ▼
Log follows	Do not display log ▼
Log F code	Display log in a new window ▼
Deletion mode	Do not display screens ▼
GUI status	STANDARD001
SelctnCriteria	
F code profile	Display Delivery List ▼
Allowed F codes	0001
Dlv creation	0001
☐ Refresh	

Figure 6.6 List Profile 0001 for Delivery Due List (Detail Screen)

► LOG FOLLOWS

Here you can specify whether, after processing, the log will appear in the same window (Y), a new window (X), or not at all (blank).

► LOG F CODE

In this field, you can specify whether the log will appear in the same window (Y), a new window (X), or not at all (blank) when the user clicks on the DISPLAY LOG button or follows the menu path after processing.

▶ DELETION MODE
Here you can define if, during the batch input for deleting deliveries, the screens involved will be displayed (A), displayed only when there's an error (E), or not to be displayed at all (N).

▶ ALLOWED FUNCTION CODES
We'll discuss the function code that will be excluded from a profile in Section 6.2.3. In this field, you can specify the default function code for the profile.

Fields that restrict the possible documents for selection include the following:

▶ SELECTION CRITERIA FOR DOCUMENT TYPE SELECTION
Here, you can specify the list of allowed document types (e.g., sales order, purchase order, and delivery) that process with the due list.

▶ DO NOT SELECT DELIVERIES FOR PRECEDING DOCUMENTS
This checkbox prevents both the open delivery and its preceding document (sales order or stock transfer order) from simultaneously appearing in the due list.

▶ ADD TO DELIVERIES
This checkbox allows you to add items to an existing delivery.

▶ DO NOT SELECT CHECKED and SELECT UNCHECKED DELIVERIES
These two checkboxes together determine whether only the checked or unchecked deliveries are to be selected.

▶ OPEN DELIVERIES
Select this checkbox to include open deliveries in the delivery due list, even when their reference document (sale order or stock transfer order) is also present in the list.

Finally, fields that influence delivery processing include the following:

▶ LIST TYPE
Here, you define whether the index list or delivery list generates for processing. The delivery list, which provides more details and hence takes more time, has the added option of manually changing the delivery quantity.

▶ 1 LINE PER ITEM
If this checkbox is selected, there will be one line per item, even when multiple schedule lines exist for the item.

▶ CUMULATION RULE
This rule defines how the open schedule lines add up during delivery creation.

- SELECT RULES
  In this field you define whether all or none or the schedule lines in the specified date range are selected by default.

- SPLIT PER SCHEDULE LINE
  When there are multiple schedule lines per item, the rule specified here determines whether there will be one delivery per order, one delivery per schedule line, or whether the system will combine a backlogged schedule line in one delivery item and generate one delivery item each for future schedule lines.

- LIMITS AT SCHEDULE LINE
  In this field, you decide if the limits that you set in the selection screen are for the delivery due date (1), route schedule (2), and/or planned goods issue date (3), or there are no constraints (blank). When there's more than one constraint, the option is coded as per the constraints included (e.g., option 23 means route schedule (2) + planned goods issue date (3)).

- BLOCKED
  You can display and process all documents due for delivery (blank), or documents that are due, but not blocked by a user (1).

- FUNCTION CODE PROFILE
  The function code profile is a set of standard SAP function codes arranged in sequence. You can create your own profile via the menu path SAP IMG • LOGISTICS EXECUTION • SHIPPING • WORKLISTS • CONFIGURE LIST PROFILE. As shown in Figure 6.6, you control what selection criteria to use for sales order or purchase orders by configuring the SELECT CRITERIA field. You can also control how many days you will display (unlimited, today, and tomorrow as an example) under the field RULE DLRVCRDATE. The two standard profiles, 0001 and 5000, allow you to display the delivery due list for processing.

- PROFILE FOR DELIVERY CREATION
  Here, you assign the profile for delivery creation (defined in the first step) to the list profile (or user profile).

6.2.3   Function Codes Excluded during List Processing

You may run into the requirement to exclude function codes during list processing. This is done via Transaction VL10CUE or the menu path SAP IMG • LOGISTICS EXECUTION • SHIPPING • WORKLISTS • EXCLUDE FUNCTION CODES FROM LIST STATUS, as shown in Figure 6.7. When you select the FCODE ALLOWED checkbox, the system excludes the function code. You should seek the help of an ABAP developer for this step.

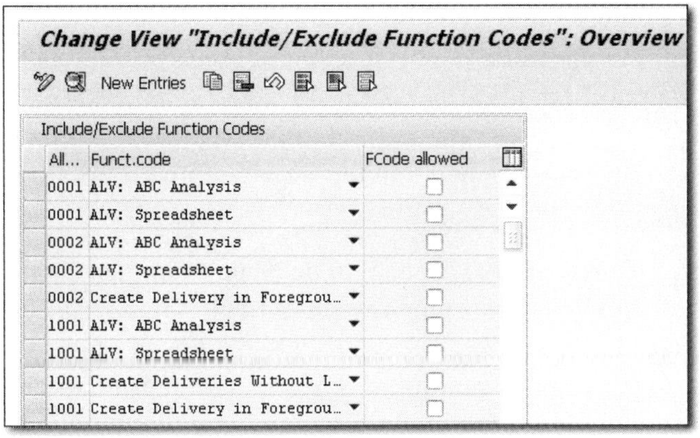

Change View "Include/Exclude Function Codes": Overview

New Entries

Include/Exclude Function Codes

All...	Funct.code	FCode allowed
0001	ALV: ABC Analysis	☐
0001	ALV: Spreadsheet	☐
0002	ALV: ABC Analysis	☐
0002	ALV: Spreadsheet	☐
0002	Create Delivery in Foregrou...	☐
1001	ALV: ABC Analysis	☐
1001	ALV: Spreadsheet	☐
1001	Create Deliveries Without L...	☐
1001	Create Delivery in Foregrou...	☐

Figure 6.7 Include or Exclude Function Codes

6.2.4 Assign Profile to Scenarios

You assign profiles to the SAP-defined scenarios using Transaction VL10CUV or following the menu path SAP IMG • LOGISTICS EXECUTION • SHIPPING • WORKLISTS • ASSIGNMENT OF LIST PROFILE TO DELIVERY SCENARIO. Upon execution, you'll see the screen shown in Figure 6.8.

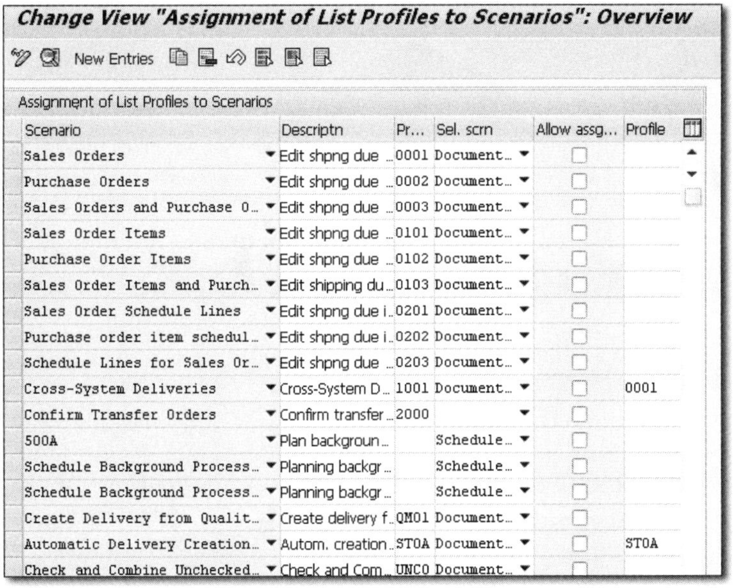

Change View "Assignment of List Profiles to Scenarios": Overview

New Entries

Assignment of List Profiles to Scenarios

Scenario	Descriptn	Pr...	Sel. scrn	Allow assg...	Profile
Sales Orders	Edit shpng due ...	0001	Document...	☐	
Purchase Orders	Edit shpng due ...	0002	Document...	☐	
Sales Orders and Purchase O...	Edit shpng due ...	0003	Document...	☐	
Sales Order Items	Edit shpng due ...	0101	Document...	☐	
Purchase Order Items	Edit shpng due ...	0102	Document...	☐	
Sales Order Items and Purch...	Edit shipping du...	0103	Document...	☐	
Sales Order Schedule Lines	Edit shpng due i...	0201	Document...	☐	
Purchase order item schedul...	Edit shpng due i...	0202	Document...	☐	
Schedule Lines for Sales Or...	Edit shpng due ...	0203	Document...	☐	
Cross-System Deliveries	Cross-System D...	1001	Document...	☐	0001
Confirm Transfer Orders	Confirm transfer...	2000		☐	
500A	Plan backgroun...		Schedule...	☐	
Schedule Background Process...	Planning backgr...		Schedule...	☐	
Schedule Background Process...	Planning backgr...		Schedule...	☐	
Create Delivery from Qualit...	Create delivery f...	QM01	Document...	☐	
Automatic Delivery Creation...	Autom. creation...	STOA	Document...	☐	STOA
Check and Combine Unchecked...	Check and Com...	UNCO	Document...	☐	

Figure 6.8 Assign Profile to Scenarios

It's important to notice the two PROFILE columns (third and sixth) where the profiles are assigned to the scenarios. In the third column, you can specify the list profile created in step two; in the sixth column, you can specify the parameter according to the profile you defined in step one.

6.2.5 Maintain Requirement Routines

You can find the VOFM requirement routine needed for delivery creation using the delivery due list via Transaction VOL1 or the menu path SAP IMG • LOGISTICS EXECUTION • SHIPPING • WORKLISTS • MAINTAIN REQUIREMENTS FOR CREATING WORKLISTS, as shown in Figure 6.9. You can modify routine 104 and replace it with another routine if need be.

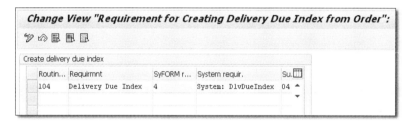

Figure 6.9 Maintain Requirement Routine

6.2.6 Modify Layout

You can define the default layout for the delivery due list using Transaction OVB9 or following the menu path SAP IMG • LOGISTICS EXECUTION • SHIPPING • WORKLISTS • DEFINE LIST LAYOUT OF DELIVERY LISTS. However, this will require help from an ABAP developer.

SAP Note

Refer to SAP Note 113411, Collective Note on VL10, and its related notes for more information on customizing delivery due lists, also known as extended delivery due lists.

6.3 Delivery Processing Integration with Warehouse Management

When the WM functionality in SAP ERP is implemented, the system assigns warehouse numbers to the combination of plant and storage locations. Picking is done by a *transfer order* created within WM. You may create a transfer order automatically during delivery processing via delivery header output type WMTA.

The following are advantages that the WM functionality in SAP ERP offers:

▸ Better utilization of resources (space, employees, and equipment).

▸ Better compliance with first in first out (FIFO) and other accounting principles.

▸ Better inventory management achieved with the additional functionality that warehouse number, storage type, storage bin, and the quant offer. You can find these when you use the WM functionality in SAP ERP. A warehouse number identifies the whole stockyard or warehouse complex at a given location. Storage types physically or logically segregate a warehouse into separate units. Storage bin refers to the exact physical location where materials are stored or can be stored in three-dimensional space. A quant is a group material with the same features (e.g., materials with same batch number). You may manage inventory at the storage bin level in terms of quant.

▸ Use of barcodes and/or radio frequency identification (RFID).

▸ Better management of hazardous materials by segregating them as a separate storage type. You can designate separate storage bins to exclusively store hazardous materials, such as inflammable oils or explosives.

▸ Compliance with employee health and safety standards.

In the future, any improvement made to the picking functionality in SAP ERP will take place via the WM functionality. Picking functionality cannot be enhanced without the WM functionality in place—unless you adopt a third-party logistics (3PL) system; 3PLs are outside of the scope of this book. Let's look at picking next.

6.4   Picking, Handling Unit Management, Packing, and Goods Issue

During delivery processing, the activities carried out are either basic functions or specialized functions. We'll deal with specialized functions, which include batch determination, serial number allocation, creating an inspection lot, stock transfer, and route determination, later in this chapter. In this section, we'll discuss four basic functionalities: picking, handling unit management, packing, and goods issue. These are important from an Inventory Management point of view, especially the goods issue (or receipt).

6.4.1   Picking

Picking is the process of identifying the materials that will be included in a delivery. The steps for customizing the picking functionality are as follows:

1. Define item categories relevant for picking using Transaction OVLP or following the menu path SAP IMG • LOGISTICS EXECUTION • SHIPPING • PICKING • DEFINE RELEVANT ITEM CATEGORIES. Here, you'll find all item categories with individual checkboxes. To select a corresponding item category for picking, simply select a checkbox.

2. The result of picking comes from the Warehouse Management (WM) functionality in SAP ERP. If you do not use WM, you can still report the result of picking back to the delivery item by using the picking confirmation requirement functionality. You define the picking confirmation requirement for each shipping point using Transaction VSTK or following the menu path SAP IMG • LOGISTICS EXECUTION • SHIPPING • PICKING • DEFINE CONFIRMATION REQUIREMENTS. The system will propose all shipping points. You can leave the CONFIRMATION REQUIREMENT column blank if no confirmation is required, or select A if confirmation is required. You can customize the confirmation requirement setting by coding the form USEREXIT_LIPS-KOQUI_DETERMINE in include program MV50AFZ3.

3. Modify picking requirement routine 111 if necessary, using Transaction OVB6 or following the menu path SAP IMG • LOGISTICS EXECUTION • SHIPPING • PICKING • DEFINE PICKING REQUIREMENTS. By default, this routine does not allow picking to take place if there's a credit block, but you may want the picking to be complete for a few special customers. You can modify this by clicking on the pencil icon shown in Figure 6.10. You can reach the screen shown in Figure 6.10 by using Transaction OVB6, selecting the row for routine 111, and clicking on the REQ. MAINTENANCE tab below it. In the intermediate screen, select routine number 111 and click on the SELECT TEXT icon or press F5. You can also use Transaction SE38 and program LV07A111 to go to this screen for inserting modifications.

4. Automatic determination of the picking location is another optimization tool SAP offers you. You can use automatic determination of the picking location via Transaction OVL3 or the menu path SAP IMG • LOGISTICS EXECUTION • SHIPPING • PICKING • DETERMINE PICKING LOCATION • ASSIGN PICKING LOCATIONS when the storage location rule is MALA, or Transaction S_ALR_87006703 or the menu path SAP IMG • LOGISTICS EXECUTION • SHIPPING • PICKING • DETERMINE PICKING LOCATION • STORAGE LOCATION DETERMINATION WITH SITUATION when the rule is RETA.

For the first option, you'll find the storage location for all combinations of shipping point, plant, and storage condition (maintained in that material master record), and the system automatically proposes a storage location at the time of delivery processing. In the second case, the storage location is maintained using a combination of plant, situation, and storage condition and is proposed at the time of delivery processing.

```
ABAP Editor: Display Include LV07A111

Include        LV07A111                    Active

    1
    2    *----------------------------------------------------------------*
    3    *        FORM BEDINGUNG_PRUEFEN_111                              *
    4    *        User checks for subsequent functions from a delivery    *
    5    *                                                                *
    6    *        Picking                                                 *
    7    *----------------------------------------------------------------*
    8
    9   FORM BEDINGUNG_PRUEFEN_111.
   10   * Picking is not allowed if a credit block exists
   11   *   IF statement deleted                              "n_566523
   12   *    document header
   13      IF VBUK-CMGST CA 'B'.
   14   *Read the subsequent function information for the message
   15      PERFORM FOFUN_TEXT_READ USING     GL_FOFUN
   16                              CHANGING FOFUN_TEXT.
   17      MESSAGE ID 'V1' TYPE 'E' NUMBER '849'
   18              WITH FOFUN_TEXT
   19              RAISING ERROR.
   20      ENDIF.
   21   ENDFORM.
   22   *eject
   23
```

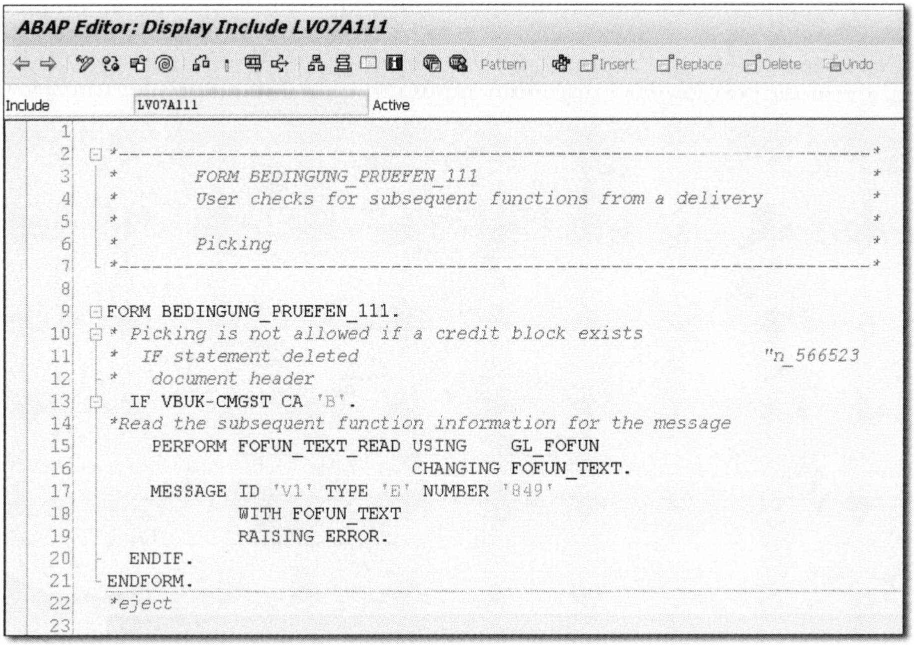

Figure 6.10 Picking Requirement Routine 111

6.4.2 Handling Unit Management

Handling units (HUs) are used for packing, which we'll cover in more detail in the next section. HUs are tangible units that can contain one or more materials and packaging materials. There can also be an HU within another HU, as shown in Figure 6.11. An HU has the following:

▸ A unique identifying number

▸ A specific dimension, weight, and volume

▸ A status (e.g., blocked, loaded)

- Materials and their quantities

- Packaging materials (e.g., corrugated box, pallet, container)

- Packing instructions (necessary for automatic creation of HUs)

- A header level that contains information on means of transport, output determination, procedure, and so on

- An item level containing material, packaging material, and other HUs

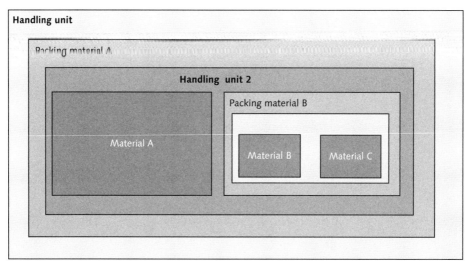

Figure 6.11 Typical Handling Unit

There are two steps for customizing an HU, which are as follows:

1. Define the number range for handling unit using Transaction SNRO (numbering object RV_VEKP) or Transaction VNKP or following the menu path SAP IMG • LOGISTICS EXECUTION • SHIPPING • PACKING • DEFINE NUMBER RANGES FOR HANDLING UNITS.

2. Define the handling unit group 1 to 5 using Transaction VEG1 or following the menu path SAP IMG • LOGISTICS EXECUTION • SHIPPING • PACKING • USE HANDLING UNIT SUPPLEMENTS • HANDLING UNIT GROUP 1 TO 5.

6.4.3 Packing

In customization for packing, you can decide whether the materials must be packed (option A), can be packed (left blank), or must not be packed (option B) during delivery processing. You can make this decision for each possible delivery item category using Transaction VLPP or following the menu path SAP IMG • EXECUTION • SHIPPING • PACKING • PACKING CONTROL BY ITEM CATEGORY, as shown in Figure 6.12.

All delivery item categories appear by default on the screen, and in the PACKING CONTROL column, you can specify whether the material must be packed (A), can be packed (blank), or must not be packed (B) for a particular delivery item category. The pack-accumulated batch becomes relevant only when you've made the handling unit management active for the storage location. When the PACKING checkbox is selected, the system considers accumulated quantities in the main item for packing, not the batch splits.

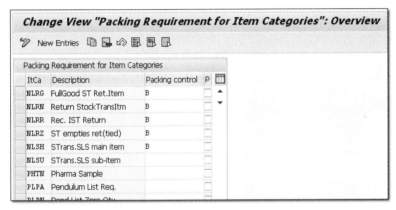

Figure 6.12 Packing Requirement for Item Categories

6.4.4 Goods Issue

The goods issue is the final activity in delivery processing. Once the goods issue (or receipt) is completed, it's not possible to change the delivery (except for changes to a few text fields). Create the goods issue by clicking on the POST GOODS ISSUE button in the task bar of the delivery overview screen (Transaction VL02N) when the delivery is complete. For return deliveries, the tab becomes POST GOODS RECEIPT.

Material and accounting documents are generated in the background when goods are issued. Material documents are those documents used in the Inventory Management functionality in SAP ERP. These documents have headers and items such as sales, delivery, and billing documents. They store the information related to a particular transaction. Some of these documents generate in functionalities other than Inventory Management. PGI is a classic example. Usually, these material documents also update the accounting posting as per customization by generating accounting documents. Accounting documents primarily store the GL accounts that are credited and debited in both transactional currency and company code currency. Transaction VL06G handles mass processing of goods issue, and Transaction VL09 reverses PGI or PGR. For goods issue, receipt, or reversal of these documents, the period (both material and accounting period) that you're posting to should be open. You can open several accounting or fiscal periods using Transaction OB52 (though we don't recommend this practice).

Now that you understand picking, handling units, and goods issues, let's move on to delivery processing integration with the WM functionality in SAP ERP.

Documents

Material documents store the header information in table MKPF and item information in table MSEG. Accounting documents store the header information in table BKPF and item information in table BSEG.

6.5   Routes and Route Determination

You determine routes during order processing. The route determined for an item ordered is automatically copied to the delivery document header. During the data transfer, the route can be re-determined, as per the setting in the delivery item category and copy control.

In the following three sections, we'll discuss how to define a route, how to define a route determination procedure, and then how to customize route schedule determination.

6.5.1   Define Route

Routes consist of the mode of transport (e.g. road, rail, or sea), transportation connecting points (e.g., sea port), and shipping types (e.g., goods train, ship). There are four key steps for defining routes.

1. Define the modes of transport (e.g., road, sea, air) using Transaction 0VTB or following the menu path SAP IMG • SALES AND DISTRIBUTION • BASIC FUNCTIONS •

ROUTES • DEFINE ROUTES • DEFINE MODES OF TRANSPORT, which you can see in Figure 6.13. You can create new modes of transport by selecting any existing entry and clicking on the COPY AS icon. For each new entry, you have to provide a key, description, and mode of transport category. You'll find the list of possible categories for mode of transport in Figure 6.13. Access the list by pressing F4 when your cursor is on the STYPE field.

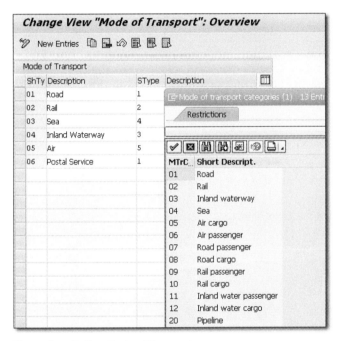

Figure 6.13 Define Mode of Transport

2. Define the SHIPPING TYPES field using Transaction 0VTA or following the menu path SAP IMG • SALES AND DISTRIBUTION • BASIC FUNCTIONS • ROUTES • DEFINE ROUTES • DEFINE SHIPPING TYPES, as shown in Figure 6.14. You can create a new shipping type by selecting an existing entry and clicking on the COPY AS icon. Next, you provide a key, description, mode of transport, and shipping type procedure group. The list of shipping type procedure groups shown is accessible by pressing the F4 key. You create a shipping type with respect to a mode of transport. For example, the shipping type Truck is created for the mode of transport Road.

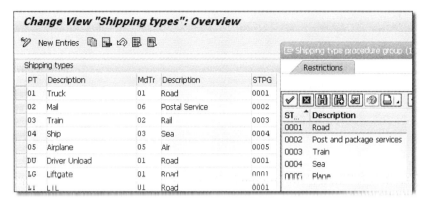

Figure 6.14 Define Shipping Types

3. Define the transportation connection points using Transaction 0VTD or following the menu path SAP IMG • Sales and Distribution • Basic Functions • Routes • Define Routes • Define Transportation Connection Points. Once you've entered the transaction, the system takes you to an overview screen. You can select an existing entry and click on the Copy As icon, or, in this case, simply click on the New Entries button to go to the screen shown in Figure 6.15. While defining the transport connection point, you have to define whether it's an airport, railway station, border crossing, or port (inland/sea).

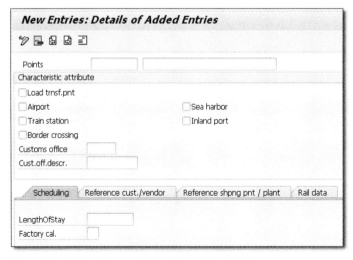

Figure 6.15 Define Transportation Connection Points

You should also specify the custom office name, if applicable. The custom office is where a shipment enters the jurisdiction of another country. There are normally two customs offices: one that belongs to the country the shipment is leaving, and another belonging to the country it's entering.

When you define the transportation connection, you normally specify the customs office of the receiving country. You'll also find the fields for the transportation connection point in the SCHEDULING, REFERENCE CUSTOMER/VENDOR, REFERENCE SHIPPING POINT/PLANT, and RAIL DATA tabs.

4. Define routes and route stages using Transaction 0VTC or following the menu path SAP IMG • SALES AND DISTRIBUTION • BASIC FUNCTIONS • ROUTES • DEFINE ROUTES • DEFINE ROUTES AND STAGES. In the OVERVIEW screen, you can select any existing entry and click on the COPY AS icon to go to the screen shown in Figure 6.16. Here, you can enter the information for defining routes and for route scheduling.

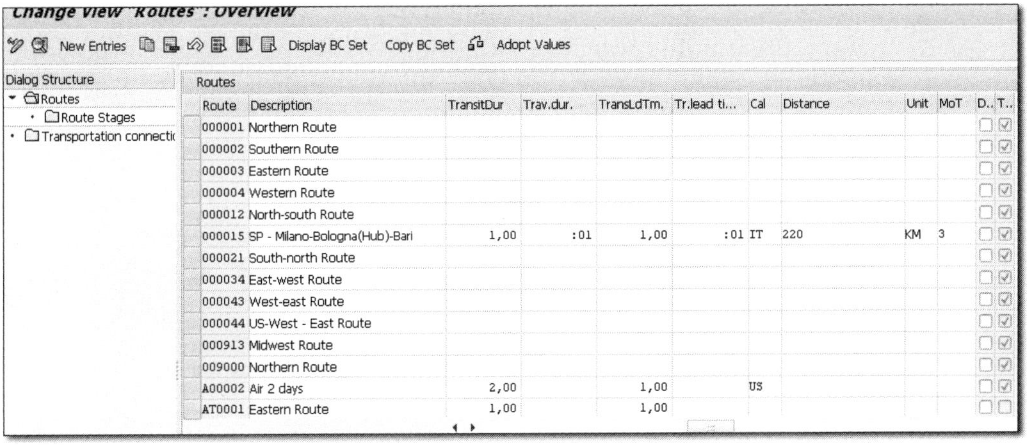

Route	Description	TransitDur	Trav.dur.	TransLdTm.	Tr.lead ti...	Cal	Distance	Unit	MoT	D..	T..
000001	Northern Route										✓
000002	Southern Route										✓
000003	Eastern Route										✓
000004	Western Route										✓
000012	North-south Route										✓
000015	SP - Milano-Bologna(Hub)-Bari	1,00	:01	1,00	:01	IT	220	KM	3		✓
000021	South-north Route										✓
000034	East-west Route										✓
000043	West-east Route										✓
000044	US-West - East Route										✓
000913	Midwest Route										✓
009000	Northern Route										✓
A00002	Air 2 days	2,00		1,00		US					✓
AT0001	Eastern Route	1,00		1,00							

Figure 6.16 Routes and Stages Configuration

6.5.2 Route Determination

Route determination is an optimization tool that SAP ERP offers you. The system automates the selection of routes for delivery processing, determining the route based on the delivery type, shipping point, and various other factors.

The customization steps for route determination are as follows:

1. Define the transportation zones for each country using Transaction OVR1 or following the menu path SAP IMG • SALES AND DISTRIBUTION • BASIC FUNCTIONS • ROUTES • ROUTE DETERMINATION • DEFINE TRANSPORTATION ZONES. Transportation zones can be either departure zones for the shipping point, or receiving zones for the ship-to party.

2. Assign the departure zones to the shipping points using Transaction OVL7 or following the menu path SAP IMG • SALES AND DISTRIBUTION • BASIC FUNCTIONS • ROUTES • ROUTE DETERMINATION • MAINTAIN COUNTRY AND TRANSPORTATION ZONE FOR SHIPPING POINT.

3. Define transportation groups for the materials using Transaction OVSY or following the menu path SAP IMG • SALES AND DISTRIBUTION • BASIC FUNCTIONS • ROUTES • ROUTE DETERMINATION • DEFINE TRANSPORTATION GROUPS.

4. Specify the selected routes according to the criteria in sales processing using Transaction 0VRF or following the menu path SAP IMG • SALES AND DISTRIBUTION • BASIC FUNCTIONS • ROUTES • ROUTE DETERMINATION • MAINTAIN ROUTE DETERMINATION. In the initial screen, you can define all possible combinations of departure country plus departure zone, and destination country plus receiving zone. While adding a new combination, you can further specify the route determination for a specific shipping point and ship-to party by clicking on the ENTER FURTHER COMBINATION button. The pop-up window shown in Figure 6.17 will appear. Once you've defined a combination, you can select it and click on the ROUTE DETERMINATION WITHOUT WEIGHT GROUP (ORDER) folder to specify a route for each possible combination of the shipping condition and transportation group.

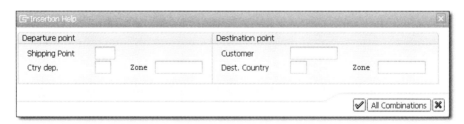

Figure 6.17 Further Criteria for Route Determination

5. Define the delivery types for repeating the route determination and set the indicator in the appropriate delivery types.

6. Define weight groups using Transaction OVS8 or following the menu path SAP IMG • SALES AND DISTRIBUTION • BASIC FUNCTIONS • ROUTES • ROUTE DETERMINA-

TION • DEFINE WEIGHT GROUPS. In addition to a key and description, you'll find the total weight with unit of measurement for each weight group in the MAINTAIN DETAILS FOR WEIGHT GROUPS folder. The total weight refers to the upper limit, and the total weight of delivery determines the weight group for it.

7. Specify the routes you want selected according to the criteria for delivery processing. The transaction and menu path are same as in the previous step, but this time, select the ROUTE DETERMINATION WITH WEIGHT GROUP (DELIVERY) folder. In addition to the criteria mentioned for route determination in order, you can perform further fine tuning according to weight group.

6.5.3 Route Schedule Determination

A route schedule is the periodic processing of deliveries from a shipping point to the unloading points of different ship-to parties. When more than one route schedule exists for a combination of requirements, the system tries to find the closest one to the planned goods issue date and time.

Route schedules can be active for the different shipping points for periodic delivery processing to the unloading point of different ship-to parties. You do this using Transaction S_ALR_87005924. When the route scheduling is active for a shipping point, it can be active or inactive for the specific sales document type (defined in Transaction S_ALR_87005922) or delivery document type (defined in Transaction S_ALR_87005932).

6.6   Outputs in Shipping

In Chapter 3, we discussed the customization of sales output type using the SAP Implementation Guide (IMG) menu path. In this section, we'll discuss how to customize output using Transaction NACE. This is a general method of customizing any output in SAP ERP.

1. Execute Transaction NACE. You'll see the screen shown in Figure 6.18.

2. Select the application for which the output is to be maintained. Table 6.2 lists the applications relevant for the Sales and Distribution functionality in SAP ERP. We've selected application V2, as shown in Figure 6.18.

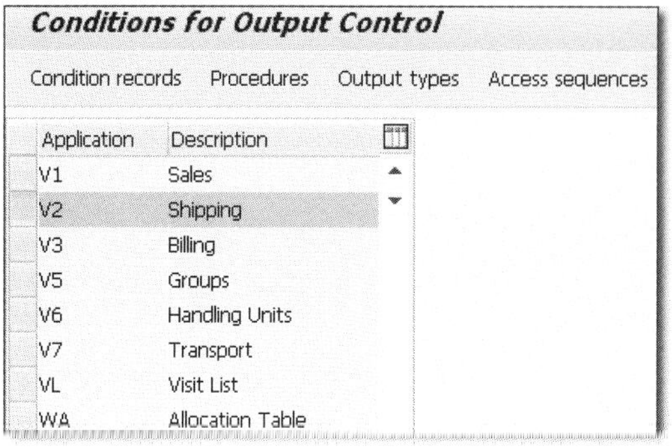

Figure 6.18 Conditions for Output Control

Application	Field Catalog	Condition Table	Output Type Is Assigned	
			To	Using
V1 (sales)	V/86	V/57	Header	V/43
			Item	V/69
V2 (shipping)	V/87	V/60	Delivery header	V/71
			Delivery item	V/73
V3 (billing)	V/88	V/63	Billing type	V/25
V5 (delivery groups)	V/89	V/G2	Group type	V/21
V6 (handling units)	V/90	V/94	Packaging material type	V/22
K1 (sales activity)	V/92	V/66	Sales activity	V/26

Table 6.2 Applications for Output Control

Condition Tables

The transactions listed for condition tables in Table 6.2 are the transactions used to change the condition tables of their respective applications. To create a new condition table, use the previous number (e.g., V/G1 for application V5) and for display, use the next number (e.g., V/67 for application K1).

3. After selecting the application, click on the OUTPUT TYPES button on the APPLICATION menu bar, as shown in Figure 6.18, to get the list of output types specific to the application.

4. Click on the pencil icon or follow the menu path TABLE VIEW • DISPLAY CHANGE to modify or create a new condition type.

5. Click on the NEW ENTRIES button to create a new output type from scratch.

6. Select any existing output type and click on the COPY AS icon to copy it and create a new output type.

7. Enter the relevant data in the GENERAL DATA, DEFAULT VALUES, TIME, STORAGE SYSTEM, PRINT, MAIL, and SORT ORDER tabs. Refer to Chapter 3 for details on creating a new output type.

8. Once the output type is created, you must customize the three folders available in the left dialog structure: MAIL TITLE AND TEXTS, PROCESSING ROUTINES, and PARTNER FUNCTIONS. By selecting a particular output type in change mode and double-clicking on the PROCESSING ROUTINES folder, you can replace the form or smart form. Alternatively, you can modify the standard form attached to the output type as per your requirement.

9. To create new access sequence for the output type, click on the ACCESS SEQUENCES button when an application is already selected (see Figure 6.18).

10. You can create a new access sequence in the NEW ENTRIES tab or by selecting an existing entry and clicking on the COPY AS icon in the change mode. Please refer the discussion in Chapter 4 for condition techniques.

11. The access sequence consists of several individual accesses that contain access numbers. The access number determines the sequence in which each access is to be executed in order to determine the output type, if any. Each access must contain a condition table and may contain a requirement routine, as well as an exclusive indicator.

12. You cannot define the condition tables, or insert fields from the field catalog intended for the condition tables, using Transaction NACE. These steps, which are an important part of the condition technique described in Chapter 4, are done using the transactions listed in Table 6.2.

13. To create a new output procedure, select the application created in the new procedure and click on the PROCEDURES button (refer to Figure 6.18).

14. The list of existing procedures will appear. To create a new procedure, click on NEW ENTRIES, or select any procedure and click on the COPY AS icon in change mode.

15. Select any existing procedure and click on the CONTROL folder. The steps of the procedure already created or copied will display. Each step must have a counter and output type, and may contain a requirement routine and indica-

tor for manual entry. In the same step, different counters determine the sequence in which the output type is processed. The requirements routine checks the requirements for processing the output type. For example, routine 62 in billing output checks if the invoice is posted to accounting.

16. Finally, create the condition records for automatic determination of the output type by selecting the application and clicking on the CONDITION RECORDS tab (see Figure 6.18). Double-click on the condition type to reach the initial screen of Transaction NACR, which maintains condition records for output types. The process of creating, changing, or displaying condition records is very similar to the process we discussed in Chapter 3.

> **Picking Lists**
>
> Other than customizing picking lists, which belong to the application V4, you can configure all other output types using output control Transaction NACE. For a pick list, use Transaction V/38 to maintain output, Transaction OVLT to assign picking lists to shipping points, and Transaction V/53 to assign customized forms and programs to picking lists.

6.7 Batch Determination in Deliveries

Batch determination is fairly straightforward.

However, there are times in batch determination when you may not want to freeze the batch number in an order, but would instead prefer that it be determined during delivery. The system assumes the batch number specified in the order is part of the information from the purchase order. The customer doesn't care what batch number he's given, but if the batch number specified in the order is not available at the time of delivery, then the order cannot be delivered. So you'll want the batch determination to occur in deliveries, and not in orders.

Another situation arises when a newly created delivery references a stock transfer order (see Figure 6.19) and the batch split is to be carried out in the delivery. You can go to the screen for this by double-clicking on any delivery item and selecting the BATCH SPLIT tab.

Batch splitting is basically picking more than one batch in a delivery; you can only utilize this functionality in deliveries. In an order, if you must specify more than one batch number for a material, you can create different items for the same material. During the batch split, the classification system can also select batches. Use the REFRESH, CHANGE, and DISPLAY BATCH DETERMINATION buttons to redetermine, change, or display batches selected with the quantity for the line item. From the batch determination screen, you move quantities to the delivery by clicking on the COPY tab.

Figure 6.19 Batch Split

6.8 Serialized Materials Processing

Serial numbers are very similar to batch management. You can think of it as a situation where each batch of the material has only one unit. You may use the serial and batch numbers together, but in some industries, such as paint, food, and pharmaceuticals, the batch becomes more relevant, while other industries, such as automobiles and durable consumer goods, prefer the serial number.

Not only does the Sales and Distribution functionality in SAP ERP use a serial number, but so do other SAP ERP functionalities, including Plant Maintenance (e.g., equipment), Quality Management (e.g., inspection lot), Production Planning (e.g., production order), and Materials Management (e.g., goods movements).

In the Sales and Distribution functionality of SAP ERP, serial number usage is restricted to the list in Table 6.3.

Procedure	Serialized Business Process
SDAU	Assign serial number in sales order (including inquiry and quotation)
SDCC	Assign serial number during completeness check for delivery
SDCR	Assign serial number during completeness check for return delivery
SDLS	Assign serial number for deliveries
SDRE	Assign serial number for return deliveries

Table 6.3 Allowed Sales and Distribution Business Processes for Serialization

You activate the serialization by entering a valid serial number profile in the material master record of a material. The steps for creating a new serial number profile are as follows:

1. Define the serial number profile using Transaction OIS2 or following the menu path SAP IMG • SALES AND DISTRIBUTION • BASIC FUNCTIONS • DETERMINE SERIAL NUMBER PROFILES, as shown in Figure 6.20.

2. Copy any one of the four default serial number profiles to create a new serial number profile.

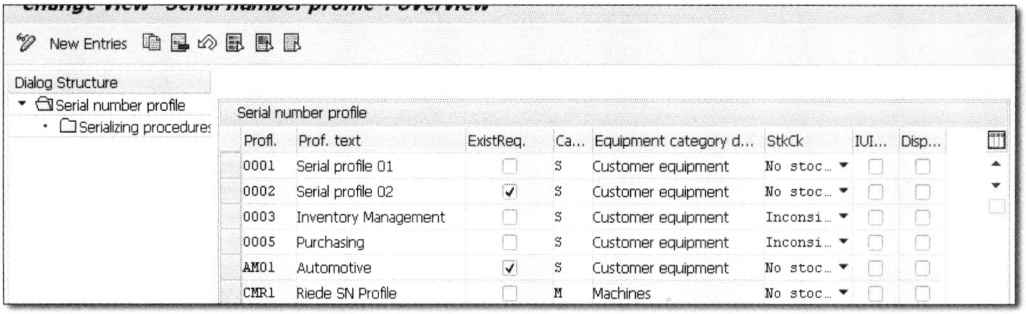

Figure 6.20 Defining Serial Number Profile

3. After creating a new serial number profile, select the new profile (profile 0002) and click on the SERIALIZING PROCEDURES folder, as shown in Figure 6.21.

4. As shown in Figure 6.21, you can assign a different procedure to a serial number profile. Serial number usage (SERUSAGE) is 01 when no serial number is to be assigned, 02 when a serial number can be assigned, 03 when serial number must be assigned, and 04 when serial number is automatically assigned to the business transaction (called a procedure). The equipment requirement (EQREQ)

field is 01 when it's optional, and 02 when it's compulsory for the serial number master record to contain equipment details.

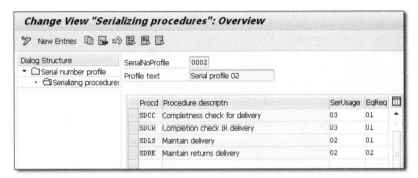

Figure 6.21 Customizing Serialization Procedure

You create serial numbers for materials using Transaction IQ01 or following the menu path SAP EASY ACCESS • LOGISTICS • SALES AND DISTRIBUTION • MASTER DATA • PRODUCTS • SERIAL NUMBERS • CREATE. To mass create serial numbers, you can use Transaction IQ04 or follow the menu path SAP EASY ACCESS • LOGISTICS • SALES AND DISTRIBUTION • MASTER DATA • PRODUCTS • SERIAL NUMBERS • LIST EDITING. The mass maintenance functionality discussed here and elsewhere in the book can create problems for you if it's not well thought out, planned, and executed. Be sure to have a good amount of practice before you should use it in a production environment. You can create serial numbers for materials even when the serial number profile is not present in the material master record. However, to use the serial numbers in a business process, you must maintain a serial number profile in the material master record. This also gives you the option to use the serialization of materials in one plant while not using it in another.

> **Serial and Batch Numbers**
>
> Both serial numbers and batch numbers can have alphanumeric values, but only when they are created manually. When generated automatically, they are simply numbers, which is true for any SAP EPR internal number range.

6.9   Solving Common Delivery Problems

Let's take a look at common delivery problems and their best practice solutions. These errors are not necessarily part of Sales and Distribution or logistics execution functionality, but we list them here primarily because they occur at the time of delivery processing. In many cases, you may not even have the necessary authorization to carry the solution and will require help from others.

▸ **Problem**

You're getting the error message "This delivery 80177150 is currently being processed by another user (ABAP2). Message no. VL 046." But the user ABAP2 is not currently logged into the system. For the last three days, this delivery has given the same error message. You can't do anything, including completing the billing or reversing PGI and deleting it.

Solution

If you verify via Transaction SM04 or table USR41 that the user (ABAP2) is not active, then delete the locked entry by following the menu path TOOLS • ADMINISTRATION • MONITOR • LOCK ENTRIES (Transaction SM12). From the OVERVIEW screen (see Figure 6.22), follow the menu path LOCK ENTRY • DELETE or LOCK ENTRY • DELETE ALL, which deletes all locked entries. We do not recommend the second option (delete all).

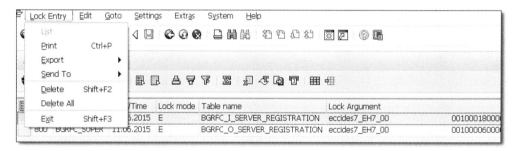

Figure 6.22 Delete Lock Entry

▸ **Problem**

The system blocks a customer's order when it shouldn't. Upon examining the details in the customer credit master sheet (Transaction S_ALR_87012218), you find the open delivery and an open order value. But the customer has no pending/open delivery or order, which you confirmed by running Transactions VA05N, VL06, and VF04.

Solution

Run the report RFDKLI20.

▶ **Problem**

While performing PGI, you receive the error message "Account 23001 requires an assignment to a CO object. Message no. KI 235."

Solution

At the time of PGI, the system creates materials documents and accounting documents in the background. This problem has to do with the accounting document not generating, which prevents the PGI from processing. Using Transaction FS00, check to see if the CO element is assigned to GL 23001. During stock transfer, if the valuations of the material are different in the receiving and supplying plants, the difference in valuation posts to the material difference account. These material difference GL accounts do not always receive proper testing, because the GL, like any other master record, is not transported.

▶ **Problem**

While doing PGI, you receive the error message "Posting only possible in periods 2015/10 and 2015/11 in company code US10. Message no. M7 053."

Solution

The two possible periods (in the Materials Management functionality in SAP ERP) in which postings are possible include October 2015 and November 2015, if the material year is the same as calendar year. The material year can be different than the calendar year. For example, if the material year is April to March, then period 2015/10 means January 2016. 2015/01 is April 2015, 2015/02 is May 2015, and so on. The delivery document's actual GI date determines the posting period of the delivery document. If the actual goods issue date field remains blank, the system takes the current system date as the default value. To overcome this problem, you have to either make the Materials Management period active for the period in which your actual GI date falls, or change your actual GI date to the period that's open in the system.

▶ **Problem**

While performing PGI, you receive the error message "Posting period 005 2015 is not open. Message no. [F5] 201."

Solution

Note the difference in this error message from the previous one. In particular, note the error message number that you receive only in the long message by double-clicking on the error message, or by clicking on the question mark icon in the error log. When the previous error arises due to the material period (also called the MM period), you can trace this problem back to the accounting period (also called the FI period). The solution is similar: either you open the period pertaining to the actual GI date, or you change the GI date to the accounting period open in the system. To open a range of accounting periods for a company code, use Transaction OB52.

▶ **Problem**

While performing PGI, you receive the error message "Deficit of SL Unrestr. prev. 5 M.T: 1100245 2058 0001. Message no. M7 021." You have verified that sufficient stock (more than 15 MT) is available at the particular storage location of the plant.

Solution

The problem relates to the material period (MM period). Normally, two material periods are open in a system. Of the two periods, one is called the current period, and the other is called the previous period. When posting is allowed in the previous period, you can perform the PGI in the previous period. In certain cases, a PGI can cause the stock in the previous period to be negative, and the customization (negative stock not allowed in the previous period) may prevent such PGI. There are two solutions to this problem:

  ▸ You can change the previous period to current. The previous to present period becomes the previous period. For example, if 2015/10 (previous period) and 2015/11 (current period) are currently open, change it to 2015/09 and 2015/10.

  ▸ The second option is to perform the PGI, making the actual GI date fall in the current period.

▶ **Problem**

While performing PGI, you get the error message "Account determination for entry CAUS GBB ____ BSA 7920 not possible. Message No. M8 147."

Solution

The problem is that the customization for automatic account posting is incomplete. Using Transaction OBYC for the chart of account CAUS, transaction key GBB, assign a GL to the general modifier BSA and valuation class 7920.

6.10 Summary

In this chapter, we discussed shipping and transportation as subsequent functions to sales. We discussed the components of a delivery document—mainly headers and items—and how the system determines item category. We discussed picking, handling unit management, packing, and goods issue processes. We discussed individual and collective delivery processing, routes, route determination, and scheduling processes. We also covered batch splitting and processing serialized material.

With this knowledge you can optimize your delivery process in SAP ERP: creating your own customized delivery due list and using it as a work list for creating multiple deliveries, and automating route determination, serialization, and batch determination during shipping. You can configure a system to take care of stock transfers between different plants and tailor the output functionality that SAP ERP offers.

In the next chapter, we'll discuss billing as a subsequent function of delivery and sales. We'll also cover how billing in the Sales and Distribution functionality in SAP ERP is integrated with SAP ERP Financials.

Because we've already covered pricing and copy control, this chapter focuses on integration with SAP ERP Financial, especially as relates to billing and accounts receivable.

7   Billing

A bill, also called an invoice, is a legal commercial document sent to a customer in order to collect the payment for goods and/or services that he received or will receive.

Upon receiving an invoice, the customer verifies its accuracy with respect to the quantity of material received, prices committed, and other commitments (e.g., commitments for quality parameters or incoterm). Your customer expects an accurate, clear, and self-explanatory invoice from you. Various prices, taxes, discounts, and surcharges that you've included in the invoice should not surprise your customer. In addition to price, the invoice should also spell out when you expect payment, whether there is any cash discount if the customer pays before the due date, and which rate of interest he has to pay if he does not make payment on or before the due date. Your customer expects the same level of details for rebates, credit memos, debit memos, and returns. We'll discuss these as we move through this chapter.

Billing is the last stage in the Sales and Distribution functionality in SAP ERP. It primarily consists of the following functions:

▶ Creation of the invoice with reference to a sales order or delivery, or with a general billing interface using external data

▶ Creation of documents for complaint handling (e.g., credit memo, debit memo, and return)

▶ Creation of a pro forma invoice

▶ Creating of a billing plan

▶ Rebate settlement

▶ Cancellation of billing documents

- Copy control and pricing functions
- Issuing of different types of outputs (e.g., printed, EDI, or mail)
- Transfer of data to an accounting document (SAP ERP Financials)

In this chapter, we'll start with a discussion of the principles of billing, and then move on to the configuration of billing types. We'll discuss the customization steps for billing plans and the transfer of data to accounting, with a focus on revenue account determination using condition techniques. Finally, we'll discuss some errors encountered during billing processes and their solutions before summarizing the chapter.

7.1 Bill Processing

Billing, or bill processing, is how you process individual bills. This involves how you create an invoice, what actions to take if the bill is incorrect, and whether reference documents (delivery/order) are processed individually or collectively (that is, with multiple documents combined). We'll now describe the following processes to help you understand how SAP ERP processes a bill:

- How to create individual invoices with reference to an order or delivery
- How to combine different orders or deliveries into a single invoice
- How to split a single order or delivery into several invoices
- How to process billing due list
- How to create an invoice list
- How to cancel an invoice
- How to use a general billing interface for creating an invoice using external data

7.1.1 Creating Individual Invoices

You create invoices using Transaction VF01 or following the menu path SAP EASY ACCESS • LOGISTICS • SALES AND DISTRIBUTION • BILLING DOCUMENT • CREATE.

The initial screen looks similar to the screen shown in Figure 1.1. In the DOCUMENTS column, you can enter one or more deliveries (relevant for billing) or the orders (relevant for billing). You select the invoice type and enter the billing, pricing, and service rendered dates, and then press ⌐Enter⌐ for processing. This data, if not entered, fills in from the default values maintained in the document types being processed and the referenced document. The deliveries (or orders) will create one or more invoices depending on the customization settings and the differences in important data in the referenced deliveries (or orders).

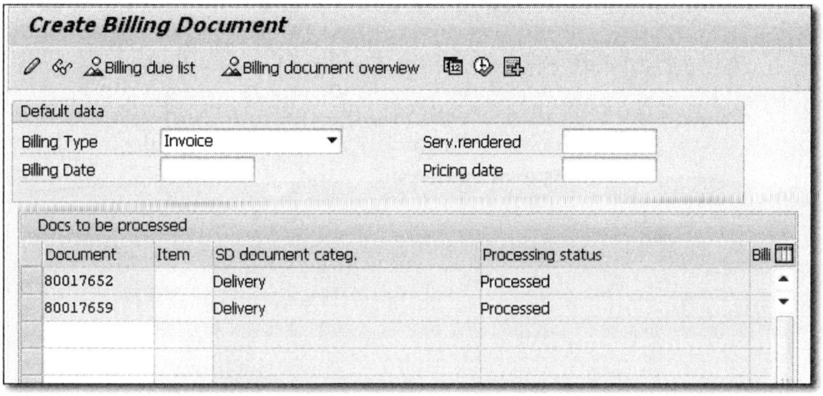

Figure 7.1 Creating Billing Document

You maintain the customization setting in the data transfer routine, as shown in Figure 7.2. For the DATA field, VBRK/VBRP has routine 001 assigned to it. You can change this to 003 (Single Invoice) if you want each reference document to only have one invoice.

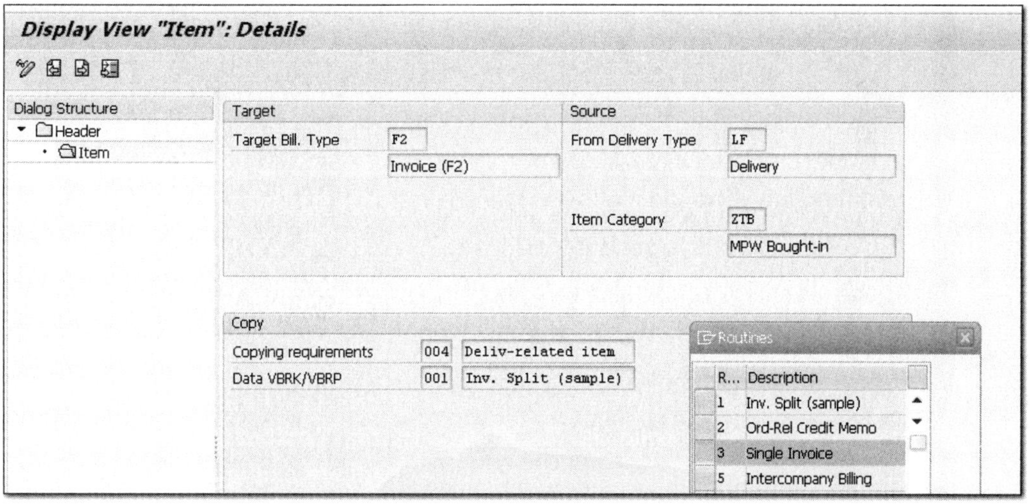

Figure 7.2 Data Transfer Routines for VBRK/VBRP

Data transfer routine `010` is the same as `003`, with Do Not Allow Splitting enabled even when a billing plan is involved. Routine `006` is also similar but is mainly used to restrict the maximum number of items in an invoice, due to company policy or legal requirements. Note that we also used these routines in copy control settings in Chapter 3. Other than this routine, there's no restriction on the number of line items an invoice can have. However, an accounting document cannot have more than 999 line items, so an invoice that creates more than 999 line items in its accounting document cannot be released to accounting. To avoid this error, you have no option but to delete part of the delivery and/or order and then process the invoice.

> **Invoice Maximums**
>
> One line item in an invoice can have more than one line item in an accounting document, depending upon your pricing procedure. Therefore, the maximum possible number of items possible in an invoice has to be less than 999 and will vary from document to document.

Copy control for billing is an important functionality that SAP ERP offers. It reduces the effort and errors involved in creating an invoice with reference to a delivery or order. It is done using Transaction VTFL (delivery related) and Transaction VTFA (order related). To reach the screen shown in Figure 7.2, execute the following steps:

1. Enter Transaction VTFL or follow the menu path SAP IMG • Sales and Distribution • Billing • Billing Documents • Maintain Copying Control For Billing Documents • Copying Control: Delivery Document to Billing Document.

2. Select the row with `F2` in the target column and `LF` in the source column.

3. Double-click on the Item folder.

4. Double click on the item category that you intend to customize. In Figure 7.2 we've done this for the customized item category `ZTB`.

Repeat the procedure for all of the combinations of billing type, delivery type, and item category for individual billings with a reference to delivery. For individual billings with a reference to an order, instead of Transaction VTFL, you should use Transaction VTFA, or follow the menu path SAP IMG • Sales and Distribution • Billing • Billing Documents • Maintain Copying Control For Billing Documents • Copying Control: Sales Document to Billing Document.

7.1.2 Collective Billing Document

By default, if the sold-to party, sales organization, and billing dates are the same, when you process several deliveries (or orders) using either Transaction VF01 or Transaction VF04 (billing due list), they combine to create a collective billing document.

Certain fields, such as the net value or date of creation, should not cause any invoice split. The billing due list is a work list in which all of the documents due for billing appear that can then be processed (billed). The list of such fields can be found in the include program MV60ATOP (shown in Figure 7.3). Other than the fields listed in Table 7.1, the difference in any fields for table VBRK (billing header) during bill processing will cause the invoice to split.

Table Field	Description
VBRK-NETWR	Net value
VBRK-KNUMV	Document condition number
VBRK-VBELN	Billing document
VBRK-ERNAM	Created by
VBRK-ERDAT	Created on
VBRK-ERZET	Time
VBRK-AEDAT	Changed on
VBRK-BELNR	Document number
VBRK-RFBSK	Posting status
VBRK-SFAKN	Cancelled billing document
VBRK-MWSBK	Tax amount
VBRK-FKTYP	Billing category

Table 7.1 Fields That Don't Cause Invoice Splitting

The customization for copy control also determines whether invoices should be combined or split during processing. Copy control routines 003, 006, and 010 will not allow different reference documents to create a collective billing document. In addition to the standard splitting rules, routine 007 will split if the division, distribution channel, department, or receiving points differ.

To avoid unnecessary splitting during collective processing, you can use Transaction VF04 or Transaction VF06 to enter a date for the billing document. To manually enter a billing date in Transaction VF04, follow the menu path SETTINGS • DEFAULT DATA when you're at the selection screen. A dialog box appears where you can enter the billing date. You can enter the billing date in the DEFAULT DATA field and then move on to create a new VOFM data transfer routine for the billing document by copying any standard routine (e.g., 007) and modifying it. Then you can assign the new routine in the copy control setting in the DATA VBRK/VBRP field.

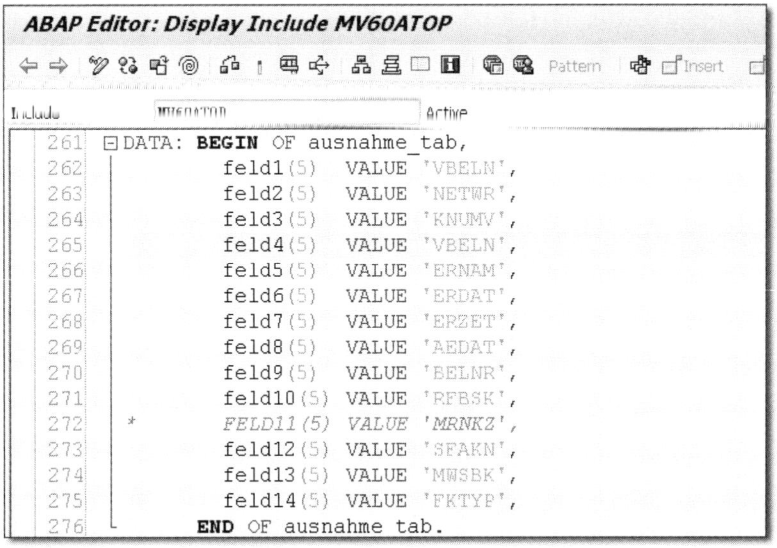

Figure 7.3 Fields Ignored During Invoice Split

In the next section, we'll discuss invoice splitting, including how to avoid unnecessary splitting and how to induce it when required.

7.1.3 Invoice Split

As we've touched on earlier, invoices split based on the following reasons:

▶ The customization done for copy control

▶ The difference in the billing header (VBRK) fields other than those specified in Table 7.1

During invoice processing, if the invoice split takes place, all invoices with their values will be available as a list in the billing document overview screen. You can reach this screen by pressing F5 or clicking on the BILLING DOCUMENT OVERVIEW button, as shown in Figure 7.1. In the billing document overview screen, you can select any two proposed invoices at a time and click on the SPLIT ANALYSIS button in the application toolbar. You can see the cause of the invoice split, as shown in Figure 7.4. If you find the reason for splitting unnecessary, you can take corrective measures. You can use either a user exit or customize the routines used in copy control.

Now that you understand what invoice splitting does, let's discuss the billing due list.

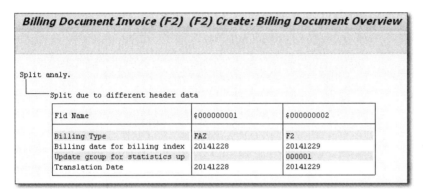

Figure 7.4 Split Analysis

7.1.4 Billing Due List

The billing due list is a generated list of orders, deliveries, or both that are due for invoicing based on certain selection criteria you specify in the selection screen.

Once the list is generated, you have the option of using it as a report or performing further processing. You can generate invoices for the documents due for billing by selecting all or some of the documents and clicking on the any of the following three buttons to create the invoices:

▸ INDIVIDUAL BILLING DOCUMENT

▸ COLLECTIVE BILLING DOCUMENT

▸ COLLECTIVE BILLING DOCUMENT/ONLINE

Before creating invoices, it's possible to simulate them. You can mass process invoices in the background using Transaction VF06. You can also schedule this processing for a time when the server is idle in order to optimize system performance and prevent manual intervention.

7.1.5   Invoice List

The invoice list functionality is another optimizing tool that SAP ERP offers. You combine different invoices (and debit memos) into a single invoice list and send it to the payer for payment. Similarly, you can group all credit memos together.

Invoice lists are created either periodically (e.g., monthly) or on a fixed date (e.g., the first day of every month). All of the individual billing documents become the items in an invoice list. You have the option of giving special discounts to take care of factoring services, for example.

A factoring service is a service rendered by a collecting agency or organization to collect payment, and involves factoring costs. For example, the service could make reminder phone calls on behalf of the client. Standard available output types exist for invoice lists.

7.1.6   Cancellation Invoice

While defining the billing type (Transaction VOFA), you can assign a cancellation billing type that can only be used for that billing type. You can also specify the copying requirement routine, if any, that must be satisfied in order to create a cancellation invoice with reference to the original invoice. You also specify the rule for the reference number and allocation number here. We'll discuss the importance of these fields later in this chapter.

It's important to note that the customization done in the copy control transaction from billing document to billing document (Transaction VTFF) is not relevant when you create a cancellation invoice with reference to an invoice. You can cancel one or several invoices using Transaction VF11 or by going to SAP IMG • Logistics • Sales and Distribution • Billing • Billing Document • Cancel.

> **SAP Notes**
>
> SAP Notes 1259505 (FAQ: New Cancellation Procedure in SD) and 400000 (FAQ: Transaction VF11: Cancellation of SD Billing Documents) are quite useful for learning more about the cancellation functionality.

Having discussed the cancellation invoice, let's move to the general billing interface. Here we'll explain how to create an invoice without a reference.

7.1.7   General Billing Interface

You use the general billing interface to create invoices in SAP ERP with external data. This is like creating an invoice without a reference (to an order or delivery). Program RVAFSS00 imports the data to the interface tables of the function module GN_INVOICE_CREATE. Function module GN_INVOICE_CREATE generates invoices when you use the general billing interface, as opposed to function module RV_INVOICE_CREATE. The fields specified in Table 7.2 must be present in the flat sequential file for creating an invoice (using the general billing interface). The data supplied should adhere to the length and the data type (e.g., numeric or character) requirement for the field.

Field Name	Field Length	Description
MANDT	3	Client
AUART	4	Sales document type
VKORG	4	Sales organization
VTWEG	2	Distribution channel
SPART	2	Division
FKDAT	8	Billing data
KUNAG	10	Sold-to party
MATNR and WERKS or LAND1	18 and 4 or 3	Material number and plant or country
PSTYV	4	Item category
KWMENG	8	Cumulative order quantity

Table 7.2 Mandatory Fields for Creating an Invoice with the General Billing Interface

The record type of the data in the sequential flat file determines the intended table for it. Table 7.3 lists some record types and the interface tables they populate.

Record Type	Interface Table	Purpose
A	XKOMFKGN	Item data
B	XKOMFKKO	Condition data
C	XKOMFKTX	Text data

Table 7.3 Important Interface Tables for Function Module GN_INVOICE_CREATE

When using the general billing interface you should ensure the following:

- Use standard billing type FX, or a copy of it, as the billing type.
- In the copy control transaction for billing (VTFA), maintain the PRICING TYPE FIELD in the item folder as C, D, or G. Pricing should remain unchanged. Use copy requirement routine 013 to ensure that the blocked customers are not billed. The system also removes items with no quantity.
- If pricing is to be transferred from an external system to SAP ERP, set the condition type as modifiable during customization. In other words, the MANUAL ENTRIES field should have the value A, C, or blank.
- Item categories used for external billing should be relevant for pricing and billing.
- Relevant customer and material master records should exist in the system. If the material master record is not expected to exist, then the external data should also contain the information on the material short text, sales unit, currency, and material tax indicator. Be sure the NO_MARA field in the primary record of the sequential file is marked. If you do not expect the customer master record to exist, use the one-time customer master record and transfer additional information such as name, partner functions, and components of address.

Now that you understand the principles of bill processing, let's move on to billing types.

SAP Fiori for Billing

At the time of writing, there are four key SAP Fiori apps applicable for billing to keep in mind.

Description	Requirements
The *Customer Billing Document* fact sheet app displays contextual information on the billing document business objects, such as header/item, business data, and billing document status.	SAP EHP 7 for SAP ERP 6.0 SP 02
Using the *Customer Invoice* transactional app you can display invoices and their status; break invoice amount, shipment, and taxes at the item level; search by customer, document number, purchase order, and sales orders; and sort and filter invoice data.	SAP ERP 6.0 SP 15 or higher
The *Analyze Unbilled Items* transactional app gives you access to follow-on tasks for items past their billing date and still not considered during billing. You can total or filter the amount and number of unbilled items by various criteria.	SAP ERP 6.0 SP 15 or higher

---

Description	Requirements
The *Customer Accounting Document* fact sheet app gives information about the customer accounting document and allows you to navigate to related business objects.	SAP EHP 7 for SAP ERP 6.0

7.2   Billing Types

A bill can be an invoice, a credit memo, or a debit memo.

In accounting, these three types of bills differ significantly in terms of how they are treated. They also differ with respect to the reference documents they need for pricing, output, and various other aspects.

Customizing billing types broadly includes the following steps:

▸ Customizing the standard billing types or creating new billing types

▸ Defining number ranges for billing types

▸ Checking customized billing types

We'll discuss these three broad steps in the following subsections.

7.2.1   Customizing Billing Types

Use Transaction VOFA for customization of billing types or follow the menu path SAP IMG • SALES AND DISTRIBUTION • BILLING • BILLING DOCUMENTS • DEFINE BILLING TYPES • DEFINE BILLING TYPES. After pressing Enter or clicking on the IMG – ACTIVITY icon (clock), you'll see the list of all existing billing document types. To create a new one, select any existing billing type and click on the COPY AS (F6) icon. In Figure 7.5, we've selected F2 and clicked on the COPY AS icon to get to the screen shown.

To create a new billing type, give an alphanumeric key of a maximum of four characters, starting with Y or Z. We'll cover this more in Section 7.2.2, but first, we'll discuss the following:

▸ General control

▸ Cancellation

▸ Account assignment/pricing

▸ Output/partner/texts determination

These are also the headings for different frames in the screen, as shown Figure 7.5.

The General Control area contains the following fields:

▶ Document Category
This field groups different document types of the Sales and Distribution functionality in SAP ERP. A few examples of document categories for invoices are:

▹ M (invoice)

▹ N (invoice cancellation)

▹ O (credit memo)

▹ P (debit memo)

▹ U (pro forma invoice)

▶ Posting Block
Select this checkbox when you don't want the billing document automatically post to accounts. However, you can execute a manual transfer to accounts by executing Transaction VF02 and clicking on the Release To Accounting icon (green flag). A posting block gives you the opportunity to verify the invoice before posting.

▶ Transaction Group
Enter transaction group 7 (billing document) or 8 (pro forma invoices) here, depending on whether posting to accounts is required.

▶ Statistics
When this checkbox is selected, the statistics in sales information system (which we'll discuss in Chapter 9) is updated for the billing documents of this type of billing.

▶ Billing Category
You can use this field to group the billing document types for printing (selection criteria), creation (selection criteria), and transfer to accounting.

▶ Document Type
In this field, you specify the accounting document type for the billing document. The standard accounting document type for a sales invoice (e.g., F2) is RV (billing document transfer).

▶ Negative Posting
Leave this checkbox blank if you don't allow negative posting. If the company code allows negative posting, it should be allowed for the same posting period

(option A) or without any restriction (option B). It's important to note that when a negative posting is not allowed, the invoice can still have a negative value. When the invoice has a negative value, the value posts to the offsetting account as a positive value. The following example will help clarify this concept. Notice that in both cases, there is no negative figure in the accounting document. Only the GLs to be debited (Dr) or credited (Cr) are interchanged.

Example of No Negative Posting
Case 1: Invoice amount: 100 USD
Accounting document: Cr Sale Revenue Account 100 USD
Dr Customer Account 100 USD
Case 2: Invoice amount: -100 USD (negative invoice)
Accounting document: Dr Sales revenue account 100 USD
Cr Customer account 100 USD

▶ BRANCH/HEAD OFFICE
This field determines the partner function transferred to the accounting document. There are three possible values for this field. When the field is left blank, the payer becomes the customer; the sold-to party becomes the branch in the accounting document when the payer and sold-to party are different in the invoice, irrespective of customization in accounting. This rule is the only option when credit management is active in the system. When credit management is not active, you can either transfer the sold-to party (option A) or payer (option B) to the accounting document as a customer, and the system determines the branch as per the setting in SAP ERP Financials.

▶ CREDIT MEMO WITH VALUE DATE
If you leave this checkbox unselected, the credit memo becomes due immediately. When you select it, the fixed value date (VBRK-VALDT) field in the credit memo fills with the baseline date of the invoice for which the memo is issued. The invoice reference field (BSEG-REBZG) of the accounting document line items fills with the accounting document number of the referenced billing document.

▶ INVOICE LIST TYPE
You specify the invoice list type for the billing document type here. Examples of invoice list types are:

  ▶ LG (credit memo list)

  ▶ LGS (cancel credit memo list)

- ▸ LR (invoice list)
- ▸ LRS (cancel invoice list)

▸ REBATE SETTLEMENT
Leave this field blank if your rebate settlement does not use this billing type. However, if it is to be used for rebate processing, depending upon its usage, it can have any of the following indicators:

- ▸ A (final rebate settlement)
- ▸ B (rebate correction document)
- ▸ C (partial settlement for a rebate agreement)
- ▸ D (manual accruals for a rebate agreement)

▸ RELEVANT FOR REBATE
Select this checkbox for the billing types for rebate processing (as specified above) or for the billing type for which the rebate must accrue.

▸ STANDARD TEXT
No longer used.

The CANCELLATION area has the following fields:

▸ CANCELLATION BILLING TYPE
In this field, you can specify the billing type used for cancelling the billing type that you're customizing. Some invoice types (for example, pro forma invoices), however, don't require a cancellation billing type and are never cancelled.

▸ COPYING REQUIREMENTS
Enter the copying requirement type routine that must be fulfilled to create a cancellation invoice with reference to the invoice in this field. The copy control setting, maintained for billing document to billing document using Transaction VTFF, does not apply for copy control from invoice to cancellation invoice. This is true even though both the invoice and cancellation invoice are essentially billing documents.

▸ REFERENCE NUMBER
This field defines the value of the reference key field (BKPF-XBLNR) in the accounting document that the billing document creates. You can enter any of the six figures, listed in Table 7.4, from the billing document to the accounting document (header level). This becomes important for joining tables VBRK and BKPF.

▶ ALLOCATION NUMBER

This field defines the value of the assignment field for the items of the accounting document (BSEG-ZUONR). You can customize the billing type to pass any of the six permitted document numbers. This, along with the reference number, becomes important for reporting purposes, especially cross-component reports where information from Sales and Distribution, as well as the accounting components, will be extracted.

Code	Description
A	Purchase order number
B	Sales order number
C	Delivery number
D	External delivery number
E	Current billing document number
F	External delivery number if available; otherwise delivery number

Table 7.4 Options for Reference Number and Allocation Number

The ACCOUNT ASSIGNMENT/PRICING area contains the following fields:

▶ ACCOUNT DETERMINATION PROCEDURE

Assign the revenue account determination procedure for the billing document type here.

▶ DOCUMENT PRICING PROCEDURE

In the condition technique for pricing, the document pricing procedure, customer pricing procedure, and sales area determine the pricing procedure. You assign the document pricing procedure for the billing type here.

▶ ACCOUNT DETERMINATION RECONCILIATION ACCOUNT

Assign the reconciliation account determination procedure for the billing document type here.

▶ ACCOUNT DETERMINATION CASH SETTLEMENT

You can assign the cash account determination procedure for the billing document type here.

▶ ACCOUNT DETERMINATION PAYMENT CARDS

Assign the payment card account determination procedure for the billing document type in this field.

You can customize the fields found in OUTPUT/PARTNER/TEXTS DETERMINATION in other sections of customization, and depending upon the customization done in those sections, you'll find the value here. You do have the option of specifying the determination procedures for output, partner, and texts for a billing type in the screen shown in Figure 7.5. Normally, you perform the customization step of assigning determination procedures to billing types using Transactions NACE, VOPAN, and VOTXN, respectively, for output, partner, and texts.

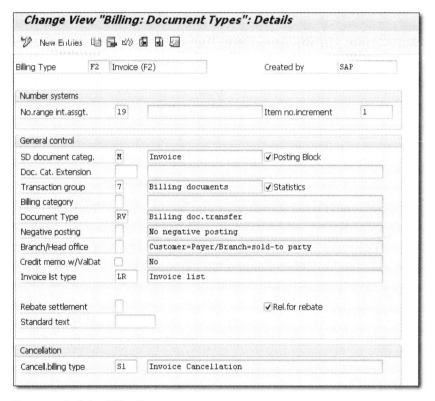

Figure 7.5 Defining Billing Type

7.2.2 Number Ranges for Billing Types

It isn't possible to have an external number range for the billing document. You can have a different or the same number range for different document types. You can maintain the document number ranges created or available by default in the RV_BELEG numbering object in the NUMBER RANGE FOR INTERNAL ASSIGNMENT

CUSTOMIZING field. You can add new number range intervals to the RV_BELEG numbering object by using Transaction SNRO.

Different Number Ranges for Different Plants

You may require multiple number ranges for the same invoice type (e.g., F2) based on the delivery plant or the geographical location of the delivery plants.

The standard SAP system does not provide a solution to such a requirement—but there is a requirement for a user exit in such a case. The ABAP coding takes place in the include program RV60AFZZ at form USEREXIT_NUMBER_RANGE, using US_RANGE_INTERN for this purpose.

Before coding RV60AFZZ, ensure that the following activities are complete:

1. Create a Z-table with the name ZINVNRANGE with the CLIENT (MANDT), DOCUMENT CATEGORY (VBTYP), BILLING TYPE (FKART), PLANT (WERKS), and NUMBER RANGE OBJECT FOR INVOICE (NORANGE) fields, as shown in Table 7.5.

2. For all combinations of billing type and plant combination, assign a number range object in table ZINVNRANGE.

3. Define the number range objects used in table ZINVNRANGE in Transaction SNRO (RV_BELEG object).

The code in the include program RV60AFZZ (shown in Listing 7.1) will ensure that the invoice number of a delivery (or order) belonging to different plant belongs to different number ranges as defined in table ZINVNRANGE.

```
FORM USEREXIT_NUMBER_RANGE USING US_RANGE_INTERN.
DATA: V_VBTYP type VBRK-VBTYP,
 V_FKART type VBRK-FKART,
 V_WERKS type VBRP-WERKS.
DATA: WA_ZINVNRANGE type ZINVNRANGE.
DATA: V_NUMKI type TVFK-NUMKI,
V_ANS(1).
V_VBTYP = xvbrk-vbtyp.
V_FKART = xvbrk-FKART.
V_WERKS = XVBRP-WERKS.
Select single *
from ZINVNRANGE
into wa_ZINVNRANGE
where
vbtyp eq V_VBTYP and
```

```
FKART eq V_FKART and
WERKS eq V_WERKS.
IF SY-SUBRC = '0'.
US_RANGE_INTERN = WA_ZINVNRANGE-NORANGE.
ELSE.
Message I001(ZKK) with 'ENTRY NOT FOUND IN TABLE ZINVNRANGE'.
ENDIF.
ENDFORM.
```

Listing 7.1 Program RV60AFZZ

Different Number Ranges for Different Countries

If you want to base the number range on geographical region (country or province), then assign all of the delivery plants in a region should to the same number range object in table ZINVNRANGE. If there are five plants in three different regions, and you require three different number ranges, the entries in table ZINVNRANGE will be similar to the entries shown in Table 7.5.

> **SAP Notes**
>
> SAP ERP offers the functionality of official document numbering for many countries that require special rules or norms for numbering invoices. Italy, Taiwan, Chile, Peru, Latvia, Argentina, India, and China are some such countries. Refer to the SAP Notes listed here and any other SAP notes that are referenced in those notes for exploring this functionality for a specific country.
>
> ► SAP Note 746162: Using Official Document Numbering for Italy
>
> ► SAP Note 1259078: Official Document Numbering for Latvia
>
> ► SAP Note 605870: Official Document Numbering for India—Program Changes
>
> ► SAP Note 571376: Official Document Numbering—New Customizing Tables (Argentina)
>
> ► SAP Note 385973: China: Various Problems with Official Document Numbering
>
> ► SAP Note 408769: Peru, Chile: New Settings for Official Document Numbering

Client (MANDT)	Doc Cat. (VBTYPE)	Bill Type (FKART)	Plant (WERKS)	Number Range (NORANGE)
300	M	F2	1000	A1
300	M	F2	2000	A1
300	M	F2	3000	A2

Table 7.5 ZINVNARANGE with Sample Entries

Client (MANDT)	Doc Cat. (VBTYPE)	Bill Type (FKART)	Plant (WERKS)	Number Range (NORANGE)
300	M	F2	4000	A2
300	M	F2	5000	A3

Table 7.5 ZINVNARANGE with Sample Entries (Cont.)

Plants 1000 and 2000 will take the same number range (A1), and so will invoices for the deliveries or orders of plant 3000 and 4000 (A2). Invoices for plant 5000 will have a different invoice range (i.e., A3). The entries made in Transaction SNRO (RV_BELEG object) for the A1, A2, and A3 number range objects will determine the exact number that the invoices will take.

7.2.3 Check Customized Billing Types

Use Transaction VCHECKVOFA to check customization of billing types or follow the menu path SAP IMG • Sales and Distribution • Billing • Billing Documents • Define Billing Types • Check Customizing Settings for Billing Document Types. In the initial screen, you have the option of restricting the customization check to some billing type (e.g., Z*) or executing without any restriction for checking all the billing types.

The report checks the following settings:

1. For the pro forma billing type, (VBTYP = U), the field account determination procedure field gets hidden in the screen shown in Figure 7.5. But if you're creating a pro forma invoice type by copying a billing type that's not a pro forma invoice, and you enter a value in the account determination field first and then change the billing type, the error shown in Figure 7.6 (which shows the billing type ZF2) will occur.

2. Billing type N can cancel billing type (VBTYP) M. In customization, if you enter a different cancellation billing type, you'll receive an error message. However, a situation may occur in which you assigned a correct cancellation billing type to a billing type, and then the billing type field of the cancellation billing type can be changed. The change will cause an inconsistency. The billing document type ZF1 shown in Figure 7.6 shows this type of error.

3. Transaction VCHECKVOFA also checks if the cancellation billing document type partner functions are empty, or if those that correspond to the billing type

used are empty. The billing document type ZF3 shown in Figure 7.6 has this type of error.

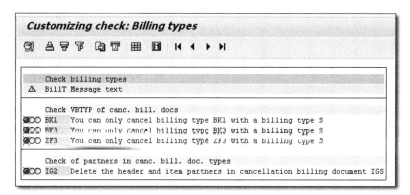

Figure 7.6 Error Messages for Transaction VCHECKVOFA

However, there will be no error for incomplete customization. For example, if a billing type does not maintain any of the following fields, you'll have a problem in bill processing using the particular document type, but Transaction VCHECK-VOFA will not report an error:

- Cancellation invoice type
- Output determination procedure
- Number range
- Document category
- Text determination procedure at header or item level or any other field

Now that you know about billing types and customized ones, let's talk about another important feature: the billing plan.

7.3 Billing Plan

When certain rules dictate that items in a sales order should be billed on different dates, a billing plan becomes necessary.

There are a couple different types of billing plans. When you want to bill a percentage of the total bill amount on different dates aggregating to cent per cent, the billing plan is called *milestone billing*. Billing dates, called *milestones*, can be particular stages in a large project, for example, as for an SAP ERP implementation project using ASAP methodology (see the introduction). The other standard billing plan in SAP systems is *periodic billing*. Periodic billing (e.g., rent) takes place at regular intervals (e.g., monthly) for the entire bill amount (e.g., monthly rent as per the rent contract) for a particular period (e.g., three years as per the rent contract).

During sales order processing, the items relevant for the billing plan automatically determine whether milestone billing or periodic billing applies to the item. In the overview screen for a billing plan, the details to enter for the item differ, depending on whether it's a milestone billing or periodic billing plan.

The steps for customizing a billing plan are as follows:

1. Define billing plan types.

2. Define date descriptions.

3. Define and assign date categories.

4. Maintain date proposals for milestone billing.

5. Assign billing plan types to sales document types.

6. Assign billing plan types to item categories.

7. Define rules for determining dates.

Now that you have an overview of the steps, let's discuss each of these in further detail.

7.3.1 Define Billing Plan Types

As already mentioned, the standard system comes with two predefined billing plans: milestone billing and periodic billing. To modify a milestone billing plan (billing plan type 02), use Transaction OVBO or follow the menu path SAP IMG • SALES AND DISTRIBUTION • BILLING • BILLING PLAN • DEFINE BILLING PLAN TYPES • MAINTAIN BILLING PLAN TYPES FOR MILESTONE BILLING. Use Transaction OVBI to change periodic billing plans (billing plan type 01), or follow the menu path SAP IMG • SALES AND DISTRIBUTION • BILLING • BILLING PLAN • DEFINE BILLING PLAN TYPES • MAINTAIN BILLING PLAN TYPES FOR PERIODIC BILLING.

Both Transactions OVBI and OVBO are for modifying the existing billing plan types. To create a new billing plan type, click on the BACK icon to go to the overview screen, where you can see the existing billing plan type (by default one in both periodic and milestone cases). You can select any existing billing plan type and click on the Copy As icon to go to the screen shown in Figure 7.7 and Figure 7.8, respectively, for milestone (Transaction OVBO) and periodic (Transaction OVBI) billing.

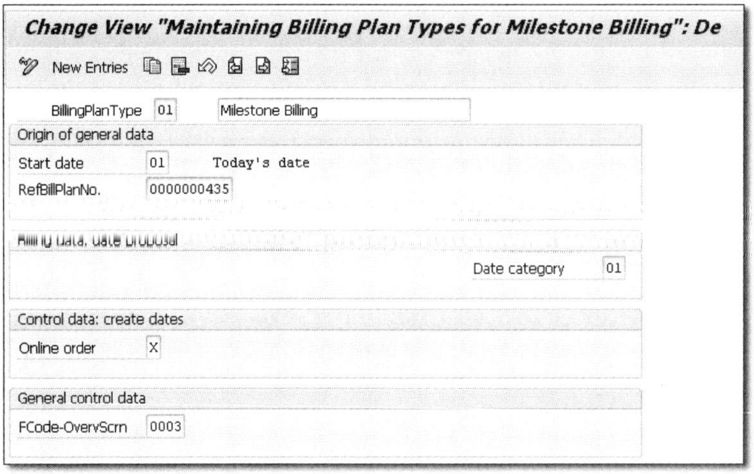

Figure 7.7 Milestone Billing

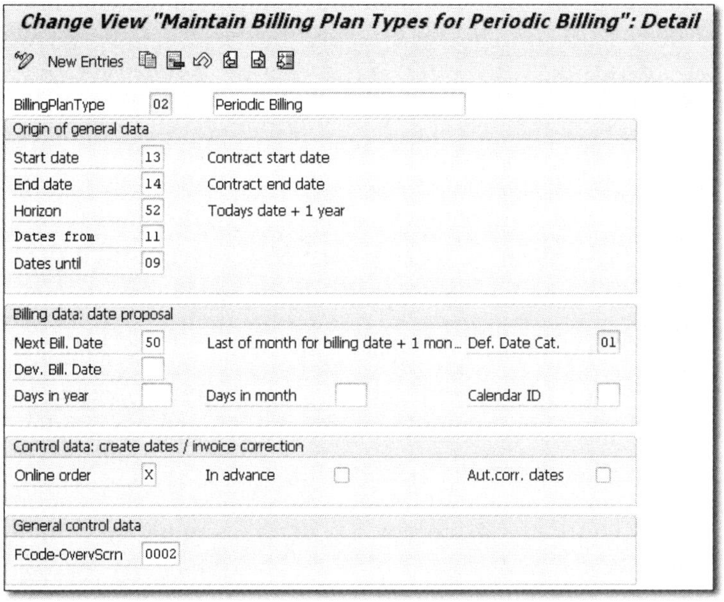

Figure 7.8 Periodic Billing

In the milestone billing customization screen, in addition to the two-character key and description, you fill in three fields in the screen shown in Figure 7.7 in enable mode (white background):

▸ In the START DATE field, you define the rule for the milestone billing plan's starting date.

▸ When the ONLINE ORDER field is blank, you will manually enter the billing plan dates during order processing. Dates are automatically determined according to the date proposal, with (option X) or without (option Y) a dialog box for manual entry to overwrite the proposed dates.

▸ The FCODE FOR OVERVIEW SCREEN determines the maintainable fields in the overview screen. The reference billing plan number and date categories are assigned to the billing plan type in subsequent steps.

Periodic Billing

From the screen shown in Figure 7.8, you can create periodic billing plan types with a two-character alphanumeric key and a description in the BILLING PLAN TYPE field. Except for the DEFAULT DATE CATEGORY field, which you assign to the billing plan in a later step, you customize the other fields in this step.

7.3.2   Define Date Descriptions

Date descriptions differentiate between different dates in a billing plan. You define the date description using Transaction OVBN or following the menu path SAP IMG • SALES AND DISTRIBUTION • BILLING • BILLING PLAN • DEFINE DATE DESCRIPTIONS.

7.3.3   Define and Assign Date Categories

To create date categories, use Transaction OVBJ or follow the menu path SAP IMG • SALES AND DISTRIBUTION • BILLING • BILLING PLAN • DEFINE AND ASSIGN DATE CATEGORIES • MAINTAIN DATE CATEGORY FOR BILLING PLAN TYPE. The initial screen shows all of the existing date categories. Select any existing categories and click on the COPY AS ([F6]) icon to create a new date category. You will see the screen shown in Figure 7.9 when you click on the COPY AS icon. We have selected the standard date category 01 as the reference for creating a new one.

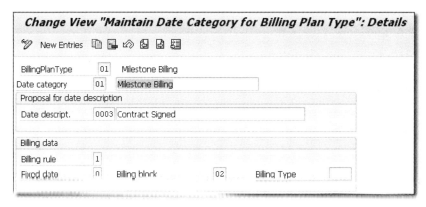

Figure 7.9 Maintain Date Categories for Billing Plan Type

In the customization for date category, you can specify a date description for the category. The billing rule can use any of the options listed in Table 7.6.

Billing Rule	Description
1	Milestone billing on a percentage basis
2	Milestone billing on a value basis
3	Closing invoice in milestone billing
4	Down payment in milestone billing on percentage basis
5	Down payment in milestone billing on a value basis

Table 7.6 Billing Rules

You can also specify values for a fixed date (from the options listed in Table 7.7), billing block (if required), and billing type.

Fixed Date	Description
Blank	Assignment to milestones not possible
0	Fixed date, date not copied from milestone
1	Planned/actual date from milestone
2	Planned/actual date from milestone if before billing date
3	Planned/actual date from milestone if after billing date

Table 7.7 Fixed Date for Date Category

The customization of billing date category controls the billing at the billing date level. The same item can have several billing dates; the bill of each date, depending upon the date category, can vary.

You assign date categories to the billing plan types by following the menu path SAP IMG • SALES AND DISTRIBUTION • BILLING • BILLING PLAN • DEFINE AND ASSIGN DATE CATEGORIES • ALLOCATE DATE CATEGORY. When you double-click on the ALLOCATE DATE CATEGORY option, you see the screen shown in Figure 7.10, in which you will enter the default date category for the existing billing plan in the DD column.

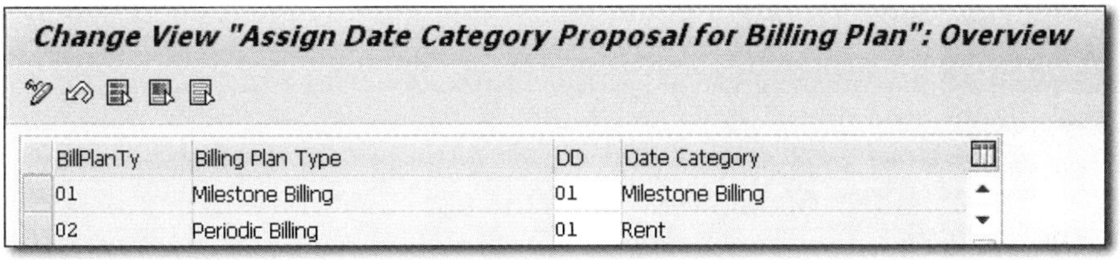

Change View "Assign Date Category Proposal for Billing Plan": Overview

BillPlanTy	Billing Plan Type	DD	Date Category	
01	Milestone Billing	01	Milestone Billing	
02	Periodic Billing	01	Rent	

Figure 7.10 Assign Default Date Category to Billing Plan Type

7.3.4 Maintain Date Proposals for Milestone Billing

To maintain the date proposal for milestone billing, use Transaction OVBM or follow the menu path SAP IMG • SALES AND DISTRIBUTION • BILLING • BILLING PLAN • MAINTAIN DATE PROPOSALS FOR BILLING PLAN TYPES. The date proposal is not relevant for periodic billing. From the initial screen, you click on MAINTAIN DATE with or without entering a reference billing plan. You control the invoice to be raised on different dates with this customization. The dates in the reference billing plan copy over to the invoice and are predetermined as per the rule (see the last step) specified for this purpose.

7.3.5 Assign Billing Plan Types to Sales Document Types

To assign billing plan types to the sales document types, use Transaction OVBP or follow the menu path SAP IMG • SALES AND DISTRIBUTION • BILLING • BILLING PLAN • ASSIGN BILLING PLAN TYPES TO SALES DOCUMENT TYPES. After you execute the transaction, you go to the screen shown in Figure 7.11. The system proposes all of the sales document types existing in the system. For those relevant to the billing plan, you specify the billing plan type in the BILLPLANTY column. This step is not required if you don't use a header billing plan.

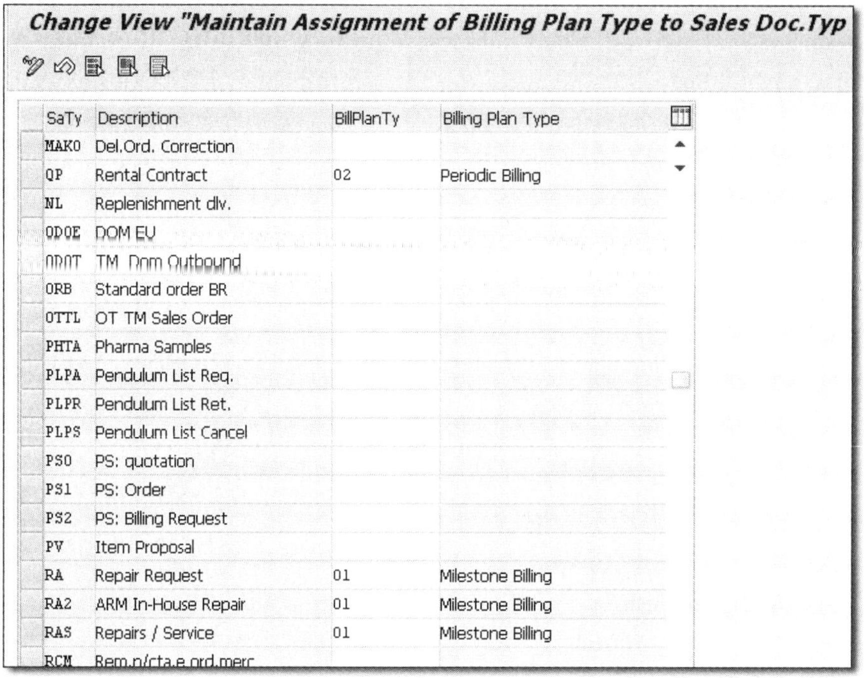

Change View "Maintain Assignment of Billing Plan Type to Sales Doc.Typ

SaTy	Description	BillPlanTy	Billing Plan Type	
MAK0	Del.Ord. Correction			
QP	Rental Contract	02	Periodic Billing	
NL	Replenishment dlv.			
ODOE	DOM EU			
ODOT	TM Dom Outbound			
ORB	Standard order BR			
OTTL	OT TM Sales Order			
PHTA	Pharma Samples			
PLPA	Pendulum List Req.			
PLPR	Pendulum List Ret.			
PLPS	Pendulum List Cancel			
PS0	PS: quotation			
PS1	PS: Order			
PS2	PS: Billing Request			
PV	Item Proposal			
RA	Repair Request	01	Milestone Billing	
RA2	ARM In-House Repair	01	Milestone Billing	
RAS	Repairs / Service	01	Milestone Billing	
RCM	Rem.p/cta.e ord.merc			

Figure 7.11 Assign Billing Plan to Sales Document Type

7.3.6 Assign Billing Plan Types to Item Categories

You define item categories as relevant for a billing plan (option I) using Transaction OVBK or following the menu path SAP IMG • SALES AND DISTRIBUTION • BILLING • BILLING PLAN • ASSIGN BILLING PLAN TYPES TO ITEM CATEGORIES. Upon entering the transaction code in the transaction window, you go to the screen shown in Figure 7.12. You also define the billing plan type applicable for the item categories here. You cannot change the billing plan type assigned to an item category at the time of document processing.

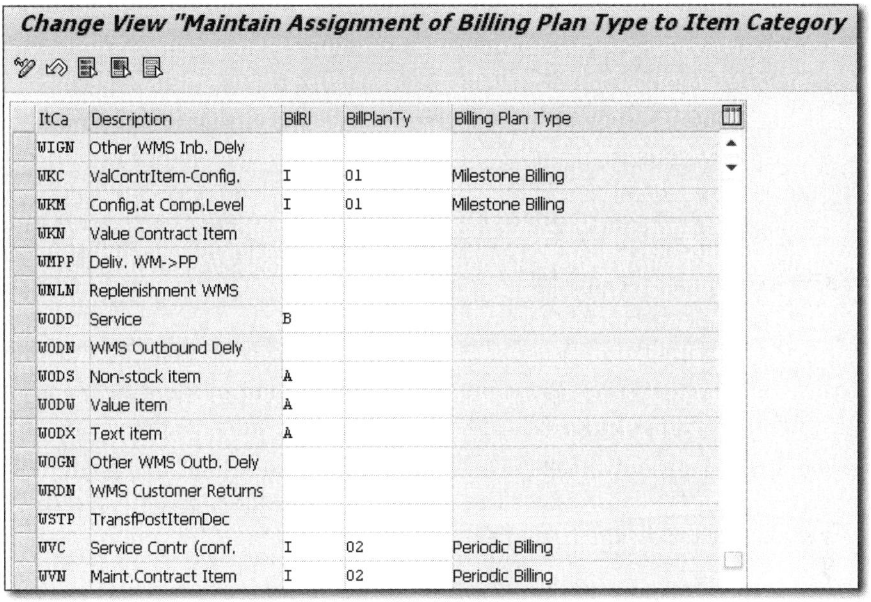

Figure 7.12 Assigning Billing Plan Type to Item Categories

7.3.7 Define Rules for Determining Dates

You can execute the rule for defining date determination using Transaction OVBS or following the menu path SAP IMG • SALES AND DISTRIBUTION • BILLING • BILLING PLAN • DEFINE RULES FOR DETERMINING DATES. When you enter the transaction in the transaction window and press Enter, you go to an overview screen, which lists all of the existing rules. Select any one of them (e.g., 50 – MONTHLY ON FIRST OF MONTH) and click on the COPY AS (F6) icon to go to the screen shown in Figure 7.13. The baseline date forms the basis of date determination. You specify the rule for baseline date determination, which can be any one of the standard options listed in Table 7.8.

Baseline Date	Description
01	Today's date
02	Contract start date
04	Acceptance date

Table 7.8 Baseline Date Options

Baseline Date	Description
05	Installation date
06	Date contract signed
07	Billing date/invoice date
08	Contract start date plus contract duration
09	Contract end date

Table 7.8 Baseline Date Options (Cont.)

In the TIME PERIOD field, you can specify the number of days or months. The unit (e.g., days or months) in the TIME UNIT field is then added to the baseline date. Use the LAST OF MONTH field to change the date from any date to either the first or last day of the month, if required. You can also specify the calendar ID that uses the rule. Select the CONTRACT DATA checkbox if item level dates are to be ignored while calculating the baseline date.

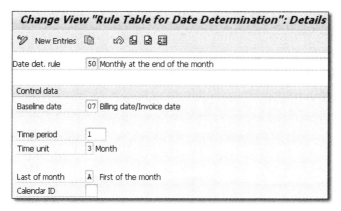

Figure 7.13 Rules for Date Determination

7.4   Revenue Account Determination

Revenue account determination also uses the condition technique. Account determination is the basic customization for transferring billing information to the accounting document. From the accounting point of view, revenue is not generated until the accounting document for the bill is generated, which means no profit, and no payable.

The accounting document generated for the bill may contain several line items pertaining to several general ledgers. This is an important integration of the Sales and Distribution functionality with the Financial Accounting functionality of SAP ERP. The basic steps for account determination are as follows:

1. Include fields relevant for account determination in the field catalog for the account determination table.

2. Select the available account determination table, or create customized ones.

3. Create the access sequence for the account determination table.

4. Customize the account determination type.

5. Customize the account determination procedure.

6. Customize the account key.

7. Assign GLs to account determination types.

Now that we've listed the general steps, let's discuss them in the following subsections.

7.4.1 Field Catalog for the Account Determination Table

The FIELD CATALOG is the list of fields allowed for use in the account determination table. Certain fields such as the CONDITION TYPE (KSCHA), CHART OF ACCOUNTS (KTOPL), ACCOUNT GROUP CUSTOMER (KTGRD), ACCOUNT GROUP MATERIAL (KTGRM), ACCOUNT KEY (KVSL1), SALES ORGANIZATION (VKORG), DISTRIBUTION CHANNEL (VTWEG), and PLANT (WERKS) are by default present in the standard field catalog for the account determination table. You can add new fields to the catalogue using Transaction OV25 or following the menu path SAP IMG • SALES AND DISTRIBUTION • BASIC FUNCTIONS • ACCOUNT ASSIGNMENT/COSTING • DEFINE DEPENDENCIES OF REVENUE ACCOUNT DETERMINATION • FIELD CATALOG: ALLOWED FIELDS FOR THE TABLES.

Existing entries will appear in the initial overview screen. To insert a new field, click on the NEW ENTRY button, and then press the [F4] function key. The screen shown in Figure 7.14 will appear. This screen shows the list of all fields that you can import into the field catalog. Double-click on the field that you want to import and save it.

Table Name	Short Description
Field Name	Short Description
KOMCV	Maintenance
VKORG	Sales Organization
VTWEG	Distribution Channel
KTGRD	Account assignment group for this customer
WERKS	Plant
KTGRM	Account assignment group for this material
KSCHA	Condition type
KVSL1	Account key
SPART	Division
CCINS	Payment cards: Card type
LOCID	Payment cards: Point of receipt for the transaction
LIFNR	Account Number of Vendor or Creditor
MWSKZ	Tax on sales/purchases code
BEMOT	Accounting Indicator
AUGRU	Order reason (reason for the business transaction)
KDUMMY	Dummy function in length 1
PDUMMY	Dummy function in length 1
PSTYV	Sales document item category
KOMKCV	Determination header
KTOPL	Chart of Accounts
VKORG	Sales Organization
VTWEG	Distribution Channel
KTGRD	Account assignment group for this customer
KAPPL	Application
KALSMC	Account determination procedure
RKPREL	CO account assignment exists
LIFNR	Account Number of Vendor or Creditor
LLAND	Country of Destination
AUGRU	Order reason (reason for the business transaction)
KDUMMY	Dummy function in length 1
IX_KOMT1_V	Index number for internal tables
IX_KOMT1_B	Index number for internal tables
CLMTY	Warranty Claim Type
RELTY	Type of Warranty Object
KATEG	Category
KOMPCV	Determination item
WERKS	Plant
KTGRM	Account assignment group for this material
KSCHA	Condition type
KVSL1	Account key
POSNR	Item number of the SD document
STUNR	Step number
KRUEK	Condition is Relevant for Accrual (e.g. Freight)
SPART	Division
CCINS	Payment cards: Card type
LOCID	Payment cards: Point of receipt for the transaction
MWSKZ	Tax on sales/purchases code
BEMOT	Accounting Indicator
PDUMMY	Dummy function in length 1
PSTYV	Sales document item category
J_1ISTCODE	LST CST applicability code
J_1IFORMC1	Form Type
J_1IFORMC2	Form Type
POSKT	Controlling Item Type
REFKT	Reference Type
RETPA	Status for Parts that Have to Be Returned from Claimant

Figure 7.14 Allowed Fields for Account Determination Table

7.4.2 Account Determination Table

SAP ERP predefines six standard account determination tables. To create an account determination table, you can use Transaction V/12 or follow the menu path SAP IMG • SALES AND DISTRIBUTION • BASIC FUNCTIONS • ACCOUNT ASSIGNMENT/COSTING • DEFINE DEPENDENCIES OF REVENUE ACCOUNT DETERMINATION • ACCOUNT DETERMINATION: CREATE TABLES. The customized table should have numbers between 501 and 999. You can create a condition table with or without reference to an existing condition table. If you create it without reference, then the field catalog will appear in the right side of the screen shown in Figure 7.15, and the SELECTED FIELDS area will be empty. You have to select the field in the field catalog and click on the SELECT FIELD button on the application toolbar to move it to the left side.

When creating with reference, you will see the fields in the referenced table in the SELECTED FIELDS part of the screen, so you may have to add only a few fields to them. To delete an already selected field, click on that field and then click on the DELETE icon. Once the fields that will constitute the condition table are finalized and in the SELECTED FIELDS section of the screen, click on the GENERATE icon present in the far left of the application toolbar.

Figure 7.15 Create Condition Table

7.4.3   Access Sequence

Access sequences are assigned to the condition types that a determination procedure has automatically determined using a condition technique.

The menu path for customizing an access sequence is SAP IMG • SALES AND DIS-
TRIBUTION • BASIC FUNCTIONS • ACCOUNT ASSIGNMENT/COSTING • REVENUE
ACCOUNT DETERMINATION • DEFINE ACCESS SEQUENCES AND ACCOUNT DETERMINA-
TION TYPES • MAINTAIN ACCESS SEQUENCES FOR ACCOUNT DETERMINATION. The existing access sequence types will appear in the right side of the initial screen. KOFI
and KOFR are two standard access sequences. You can modify these sequences or
create your own by selecting an existing one and clicking on the Copy As ([🗐])
icon and then giving a new key and description to the access sequence. Once a
sequence is created, double-click on it to go to the screen shown in Figure 7.16.
Here, you list the sequence of condition tables accessed in order to find the
desired condition record (GL account in this case). You can assign the requirement routines for account determination to optimize performance.

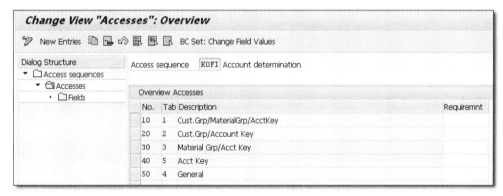

Figure 7.16 Standard Access Sequence KOFI

You can optimize performance using Transaction OVU1 to specify the access
number for a condition type. The setting in Figure 7.17 shows that access 10 of
access sequence KOFI executes for condition type KOFI. This contradicts the customization shown in Figure 7.16. So, for account determination type KOFI, access
number 10 of access sequence KOFI only executes if you expect the previous
accesses 3 and 5 to execute first. To make the customization shown in Figure 7.16
valid, you have to delete the entry shown in Figure 7.17.

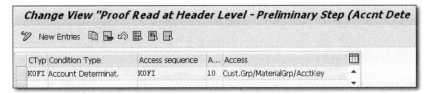

Figure 7.17 Optimize Access (Revenue Account Determination)

7.4.4 Account Determination Type

Here, the condition type is referred to as account determination type. You define it by following the menu path SAP IMG • SALES AND DISTRIBUTION • BASIC FUNCTIONS • ACCOUNT ASSIGNMENT/COSTING • REVENUE ACCOUNT DETERMINATION • DEFINE ACCESS SEQUENCES AND ACCOUNT DETERMINATION TYPES • DEFINE ACCOUNT DETERMINATION TYPES. Double-clicking on the IMG – ACTIVITY icon at the end of the menu path takes you to the screen shown in Figure 7.18. The two standard account determination types are KOFI and KOFK. You create new account determination types by clicking on the NEW ENTRIES button and entering a key and a name. You can also specify the access sequence for the account determination type, if you require automatic determination of GL.

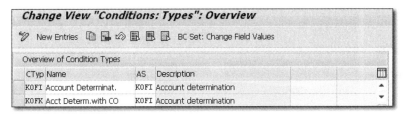

Figure 7.18 Account Determination Types

7.4.5 Account Determination Procedure

An account determination procedure must contain at least one account determination type. The system assigns it to the billing types in order to automatically find the revenue accounts for prices, discounts, taxes, and surcharges (including freight).

To define an account determination procedure and assign it to the billing types, use Transaction S_ALR_87007038 or follow the menu path SAP IMG • SALES AND DISTRIBUTION • BASIC FUNCTIONS • ACCOUNT ASSIGNMENT/COSTING • DEFINE AND ASSIGN ACCOUNT DETERMINATION PROCEDURES. After clicking on the IMG – ACTIVITY icon at the end of the menu path, you have the option of either defining or assigning the account determination procedure. Double-clicking on the DEFINE ACCOUNT DETERMINATION PROCEDURE option takes you to the list of existing procedures. Select any procedure and click on the CONTROL folder at the left to go to the screen shown in Figure 7.19.

You list the account determination types that must be determined once the procedure becomes relevant. The standard account determination routines assigned here are for optimization purposes. You can have your own customized routines assigned here for achieving certain business requirements. If those requirements are not met, account determination stops. Assigning requirements at the procedure level is better than assigning them at the access sequence level.

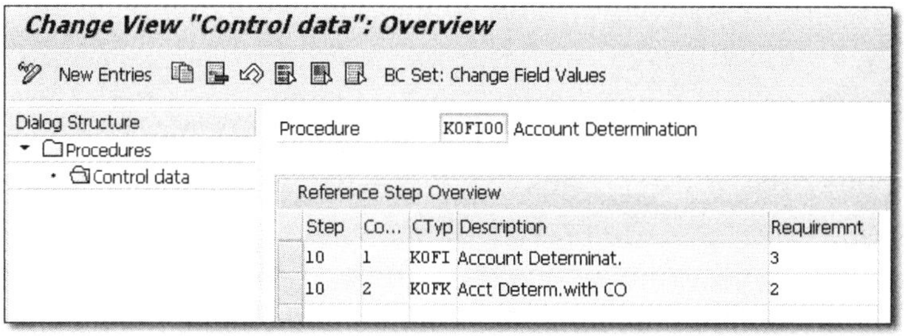

Figure 7.19 Account Determination Procedure KOFI00

After defining the account determination procedure, assign it to the billing type by double-clicking on the option ASSIGN ACCOUNT DETERMINATION PROCEDURE at the end of the CUSTOMIZING menu path. You'll see the overview screen shown in Figure 7.20. For pro forma invoices, the system does not assign an account determination procedure because no accounting document is to be generated for them.

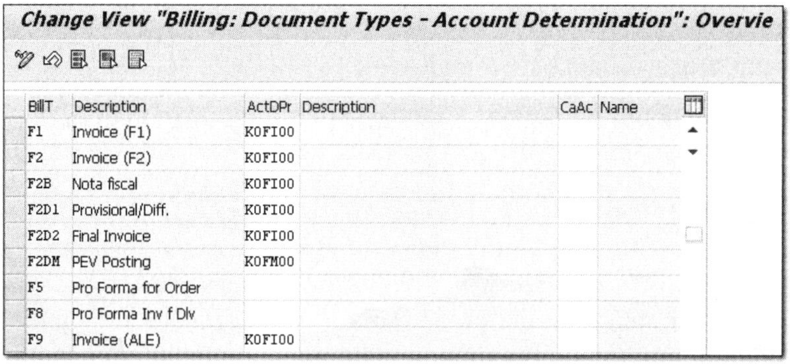

Figure 7.20 Assign Account Determination Procedure to Billing Types

7.4.6 Account Key

Account keys are used to group GL accounts. They also automatically post components of the pricing procedure, such as sales, freight, discounts, surcharges, and taxes to relevant GL accounts. You can copy the standard account keys such as ERL (revenues), ERF (freight revenue), ERS (discounts), EVV (cash settlement), and MWS (tax) to create new account keys.

The menu path for defining and assigning account keys is SAP IMG • SALES AND DISTRIBUTION • BASIC FUNCTIONS • ACCOUNT ASSIGNMENT/COSTING • REVENUE ACCOUNT DETERMINATION • DEFINE AND ASSIGN ACCOUNT KEYS. By clicking on the IMG – ACTIVITY icon, you get the options of defining and assigning. When you double-click on DEFINE ACCOUNT KEY, you receive a list of all existing account keys. You can select any one and click on the COPY AS ([F6]) icon to create a new account key starting with Y or Z and a description.

In the CUSTOMIZING menu path, you can click on ASSIGN ACCOUNT KEYS to assign the account keys to the condition types (not account determination type but pricing condition types) of the pricing procedure. All of the pricing procedures already defined become available in the overview screen with the assignments, if any, already made in Transaction V/08 (Define Pricing Procedure). Figure 7.21 shows the overview screen.

Proc.	Step	Cntr	CTyp	Name	ActKy	Name	Accrls	N
RVAAMX	310	0	PN00	Net Price	ERL	Sales revenues		Sa
	320	0	PMIN	Minimum Price	ERL	Sales revenues		
	805	1	KP00	Pallet Discount	ERS	Sales deductions		
	805	2	KP01	Incomp.Pallet Surch.	ERS	Sales deductions		
	805	3	KP02	Mixed Pallet Disc.	ERS	Sales deductions		
	805	4	KP03	Mixed Pallet Surch.	ERS	Sales deductions		
	810	1	HA00	Percentage Discount	ERS	Sales deductions		
	810	2	HB00	Discount (Value)	ERS	Sales deductions		
	810	3	HD00	Freight	ERF	Freight revenue		
	815	0	KF00	Freight	ERF	Freight revenue		
	820	0	HM00	Order Value	ERS	Sales deductions		
	901	0	B001	Group Rebate	ERB	Rebate sales deduct.	ERU	Re
	902	0	B002	Material Rebate	ERB	Rebate sales deduct.	ERU	Re
	903	0	B003	Customer Rebate	ERB	Rebate sales deduct.	ERU	Re
	904	0	B004	Hierarchy Rebate	ERB	Rebate sales deduct.	ERU	Re
	905	0	B005	Hierarchy rebate/mat	ERB	Rebate sales deduct.	ERU	Re

Figure 7.21 Assign Account Keys to Pricing Procedure

7.4.7 Assign General Ledger to Account Determination Types

Transaction VKOA assigns a general ledger to account determination types (e.g., KOFI). You can also use the general Transaction OBYF and then select application V (sales/distribution), or follow the menu path SAP IMG • SALES AND DISTRIBUTION • BASIC FUNCTIONS • ACCOUNT ASSIGNMENT/COSTING • ASSIGN G/L ACCOUNTS.

The initial screen lists all of the account determination tables. Double-click on any table for which you want to maintain the GL accounts. You'll see the screen shown in Figure 7.22. Note that there is a provision for two GL account numbers. The second GL account is to be to be specified for accruals (e.g., rebate agreements).

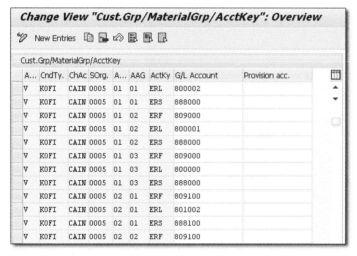

Figure 7.22 Assign GL Account to Account Determination Type

In Figure 7.22, the fourth and fifth columns contain the same heading AAG (account assignment group). The first heading is the account assignment group for customers, and the second one is for account assignment groups for materials. These groups are simply a group of customers or materials that are identical from an accounts posting point of view. For example, you can define all customers from one country (e.g., Mexico) as one account assignment group (for customers), and all trading materials as one account assignment group (for materials). Therefore, the sale of such a material made to such a customer will go to one specific GL account (e.g., Mexico trading account).

These account assignment groups are maintained in the customer master record (Billing Document tab of Sales Area data) and material master record (Sales:Sales Org 2 tab) for individual customers or materials, respectively. You can create new account assignment groups for *materials* using Transaction OVK5 or following the menu path SAP IMG • Sales and Distribution • Basic Functions • Account Assignment/Costing • Check Master Data Relevant For Account Assignment • Materials: Account Assignment Groups. You can create new account assignment groups for *customers* using Transaction OVK8 or following the menu path SAP IMG • Sales and Distribution • Basic Functions • Account Assignment/Costing • Check Master Data Relevant For Account Assignment • Customers: Account Assignment Groups. Defining and assigning customer and material assignment accounts is a prerequisite for account determination — return to Chapter 2 for more information on these.

Now that you understand how revenue accounts are determined, let's discuss the accounts interface for billing.

7.5 Accounts Interface

In this section, we'll discuss various topics related to the Sales and Distribution–Financial Accounting interface in SAP ERP. We'll specifically discuss revenue recognition, reconciliation account determination, cash account determination, and data that's transferred to accounting from invoices.

7.5.1 Revenue Recognition

To use the revenue recognition functionality of SAP ERP, you need explicit permission from the SAP system (see SAP Note 820417). You can get the best practice guide (in PDF format) for implementing revenue recognition functionality in SAP Note 1172799. SAP Note 1323315 is also very helpful for implementing revenue recognition.

You customize revenue recognition for any sales item category using Transaction OVEP or following the menu path SAP IMG • Sales and Distribution • Basic Functions • Account Assignment/Costing • Revenue Recognition • Set Revenue Recognition For Item Categories. The initial overview screen lists all of the existing item categories. Double-click on any item category to view the customization. Customization specifies four fields—Revenue Recognition Category,

Accrual Period Start Date, Revenue Distribution Type, and Revenue Event—for the item category.

The revenue recognition category for an item category can take any of the following six options:

- Blank: The system recognizes revenue for this item category at the time of invoice creation (standard option).
- A: The value of this item category is recognized for the same amounts according to the accrual period.
- B: Revenue is recognized based on business transactions (e.g., goods receipt for delivery-relevant items, sales order creation for items not relevant to delivery).
- D: The value of the item is implemented in equal amounts, in accordance with the accrual period for this item (billing-related).
- E: Billing-related, service-related revenue recognition (IS-M).
- F: Credit and debit memos with reference to predecessor.

The accrual period start date can take any of the following three options:

- Blank: Not relevant.
- A: Proposal based on contract start date.
- B: Proposal based on billing plan start date. For milestone billing plans, this is the billing date of the first milestone. For periodic billing plans it's either the billing plan start date or the date of the first settlement period, whichever is earlier.

The revenue distribution type can take any of the following four options:

- Blank: The total value is linear, and the correction value is not distributed.
- A: The total value is linear, and the correction value is distributed linearly.
- B: The total value is Bill.Plan-Reld, and the correction value is not distributed.
- C: The total value is Bill.Plan-Reld, and the correction value is linearly distributed.

The revenue event is the event that determines revenue recognition. The possible options it can take are as follows:

- Blank: Not event-related
- A: Incoming invoice

- B: Acceptance date
- X/Y/Z: Customer-specific event X/Y/Z, the definitions of which are in the BAdI for the specific event

The configuration done in the Sales and Distribution functionality in SAP ERP is only part of the overall customization done in SAP ERP Financials. So before beginning the customization, be sure to read the relevant SAP Notes mentioned at the beginning of this section, understand the limitations of the revenue recognition functionality, and work with an SAP ERP Financials consultant.

7.5.2 Reconciliation Account Determination

You'll find the customer reconciliation account in the customer master record (ACCOUNT MANAGEMENT tab of COMPANY CODE DATA). The offsetting entry for the revenue accounts posts to this reconciliation GL, so when you make a sale, the accounting entries look like:

- Cr Sales Revenue – 100 USD
- Cr Tax Payable – 5 USD
- Dr Customer Reconciliation Account – 105 USD

You can use a condition technique for reconciliation account determination, similar to the revenue account determination we discussed earlier in this chapter. The steps for customizing the condition technique are available via the menu path SAP IMG • SALES AND DISTRIBUTION • BASIC FUNCTIONS • ACCOUNT ASSIGNMENT/ COSTING • RECONCILIATION ACCOUNT DETERMINATION. At this node of the menu path, you have the following options for customizing the condition technique:

- MAINTAIN CONDITION TABLES (Transaction OV62)
- MAINTAIN FIELD CATALOG (Transaction OV60)
- MAINTAIN ACCESS SEQUENCES (Transaction OV67)
- MAINTAIN CONDITION TYPES (Transaction OV66)
- MAINTAIN ACCOUNT DETERMINATION PROCEDURE (Transaction OV65)
- ASSIGN ACCOUNT DETERMINATION PROCEDURE (Transaction OV68)
- ASSIGN G/L ACCOUNTS (Transaction OV64)
- DEFINE ALTERNATIVE RECONCILIATION ACCOUNTS (Transaction S_ALR_87002480)

7.5.3 Cash Account Determination

You may involve a cash account in a sales invoice (e.g., credit memo). For example, instead of issuing credit memos that are used as payments for other purchases by the customer, you may want to issue a check for the credit memo. In such a situation, you can determine the cash account to be posted by using a condition technique, just like you would for revenue or reconciliation account determination.

The steps for customizing cash account determination are available via the menu path SAP IMG • SALES AND DISTRIBUTION • BASIC FUNCTIONS • ACCOUNT ASSIGNMENT/COSTING • CASH ACCOUNT DETERMINATION. At this node, you can branch into any of the following IMG activities for customizing the condition technique:

▸ MAINTAIN CONDITION TABLES (Transaction OV71)

▸ MAINTAIN FIELD CATALOG (Transaction OV73)

▸ MAINTAIN ACCESS SEQUENCES (Transaction OV74)

▸ MAINTAIN CONDITION TYPES (Transaction OV75)

▸ MAINTAIN ACCOUNT DETERMINATION PROCEDURE (Transaction OV76)

▸ ASSIGN ACCOUNT DETERMINATION PROCEDURE (Transaction OV78)

▸ ASSIGN G/L ACCOUNTS (Transaction OV77)

7.5.4 Data Forwarded to Accounting Document

Various data from billing documents of Sales and Distribution are transferred to the SAP ERP Financials accounting documents. In our discussion of the customization of billing types, we've covered how the following data is determined for accounting documents based on the information available in billing document.

1. Accounting document type

2. Reference number (BKPF-XBLNR)

3. Allocation number (BSEG-ZUONR)

4. Partner function for accounting document

5. Invoice reference (BSEG-REBZG)

Aligning an Accounting Document Number with an Invoice Number

By default, the number range assigned to accounting document types used to create accounting documents for invoices is the *internal number range*. There's no provision for manually entering a number for a bill's accounting document, so the question of making it external does not arise.

However, if you make the number range *the same* as that for a billing document type and select the checkbox for external assignment, then the accounting document number will be same as that of the billing document. Because several billing document types can have the same accounting document type, the number range for the accounting document type should be such that all of the number ranges for billing document types assigned to it fall within its number range. At the same time, the number range cannot overlap with the number range of any other accounting document type. Tracking the billing document and corresponding accounting document (and vice versa) for error handling wastes a lot of time. Also, it becomes very complicated to link the two in an ABAP report when they're different numbers.

7.6   Solving Common Billing Problems

As with previous chapters, let's take a look at common crises that arise during billing.

Note

We've included some common errors or queries that are expected of a junior or middle-level consultant, especially in a post-implementation scenario. Most of the problems that come from super users or junior consultants are of two types: mistakes in configuration or customization. We've avoided these because they would have been repetitions of what we've already covered. We also won't cover errors due to customized reports, user exits, or routines, because they're project specific. You can regenerate most of these problems in a test environment.

▶ **Problem**

We have a large invoice to cancel. It should take few minutes to cancel, but each time we attempt to cancel it, we encounter a timeout and are unable to do so. We can't find any options for executing the transaction for invoice cancellation, Transaction VF11, in the background.

Solution

It isn't possible to execute Transaction VF11 in the background, so when an invoice is too large, or when you include multiple invoices for cancellation, the time-out situation may arise. Your only option is to increase the time limit for the time out by changing the time limit for the parameter RDISP/MAX_WPRUN_TIME using Transaction RZ11.

Go to the screen shown in Figure 7.23 when you enter the parameter RDISP/MAX_WPRUN_TIME in the initial screen of Transaction RZ11, and execute it. To change the existing values, click on the CHANGE VALUES button, and the dialog box also shown in Figure 7.23 will appear. This is where you change the values of the parameter. Be sure to review SAP Note 25528 before attempting this.

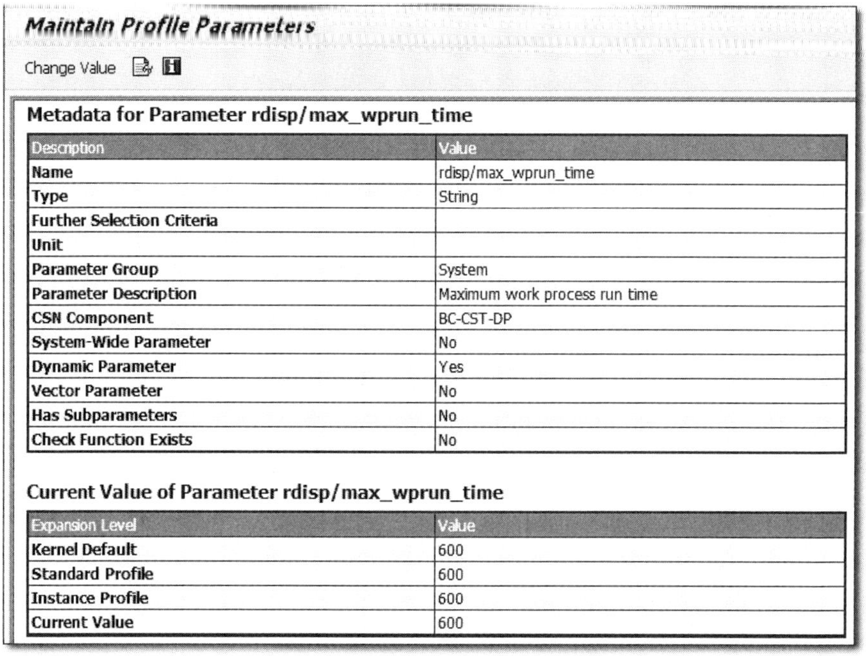

Maintain Profile Parameters

Change Value

Metadata for Parameter rdisp/max_wprun_time

Description	Value
Name	rdisp/max_wprun_time
Type	String
Further Selection Criteria	
Unit	
Parameter Group	System
Parameter Description	Maximum work process run time
CSN Component	BC-CST-DP
System-Wide Parameter	No
Dynamic Parameter	Yes
Vector Parameter	No
Has Subparameters	No
Check Function Exists	No

Current Value of Parameter rdisp/max_wprun_time

Expansion Level	Value
Kernel Default	600
Standard Profile	600
Instance Profile	600
Current Value	600

Figure 7.23 Changing Values of Parameter of rdisp/max_wprun_time

▶ **Problem**

We have few materials that are tax free, so we've made a tax code for 0% tax. This works fine until we have to create the invoice. While releasing it to accounts, we're getting the error shown below. Because there will be no value to be posted to accounts, we haven't assigned it to any GL. Even if we do, how can there be an accounting document with a zero value line item?

> ### Error Message
>
> **Error in account determination: table T030K key CANA MWS U7**
>
> Message no. FF709
>
> **Diagnosis**
>
> In the chart of accounts to be posted to, no accounts are defined for the tax code you used.
>
> **Procedure**
>
> Contact your system administrator.
>
> Define the accounts to which a tax posting are to be made with the tax code entered in CUSTOMIZING for taxes on sales/purchases.
>
> To do this, choose MAINTAIN ENTRIES ($\boxed{\text{F5}}$).

Solution

Access table T030K using Transaction OB40, where you can maintain a GL for tax code U7 Transaction MWS in the chart of account CANA, even when no posting is required. You can do this by executing Transaction FTXP, entering the tax code in the initial screen, and then executing and clicking on the TAX ACCOUNTS button. Selecting the chart of account (e.g., CANA) will take you to a dialog box where you have to maintain the GL accounts for different transaction keys (e.g., MWS). Note that when using Transaction FTXP, you can maintain GL accounts even when the client is not modifiable, which is not the case for Transaction OB40. Because the document value, and therefore the accounting document value, will not be zero, there will be no error in posting to accounting. The tax GL that you've assigned to tax code U7 will, however, have no entry, even after posting. If you open the accounting document using Transaction FB02/03 (or by clicking on the ACCOUNTING button from the VF02/03 overview screen) and click on the TAXES button.

▶ **Problem**

We have a customized report using Transactions S066 and S067. Currently, we are facing serious performance issues for the report. It's taking too much time, and we noticed that these tables contain many line items with zero value (or a negligible amount, e.g., 0.01). How can we improve the performance of the report?

Solution

Run report program RVKRED77 at regular intervals. Be sure to refer to SAP Note 400311 for details.

▸ **Problem**

We've been using the standard pricing condition type PR00 in both the pricing procedure for invoice (billing type F2) and pro forma invoice (billing type F8). In both cases, we've maintained condition records that are automatically determined during billing. We don't want any manual changes during billing. In the customization for the condition type PR00, we've opted for option D (Not Possible to Process Manually) in the MANUAL ENTRIES field. Also, in the copy control from order to invoice (Transaction VTFA), we've opted for option G (Copy Pricing Elements Unchanged and Redetermine Taxes) for the item categories. The same condition type should be modifiable manually in a pro forma invoice without changing the customization for the invoice. Is this possible?

Solution

In the standard SAP system, there's no provision for making a condition type modifiable in certain cases and nonmodifiable in others. To achieve this, you have to use exits. To do it in order, use the user exit USEREXIT_PRICING_PRE-PARE_TKOMP in the include program MV45AFZZ. If the objective is to make the condition type modifiable for certain users and nonmodifiable for others, you can create a customized authorization object as recommended in SAP Note 105621. Then, code the exit in include program MV45AFZZ for an order, or program RV60AFZZ for an invoice. To make the condition type modifiable for the F8 invoice type and nonmodifiable for others, you can input the code in Listing 7.2 in the user exit USEREXIT_PRICING_PREPARE_TKOMP of the include program RV60AFZZ.

```
FORM USEREXIT_PRICING_PREPARE_TKOMP.
DATA: i_T685A TYPE STANDARD TABLE OF T685A WITH HEADER LINE.
IF VBRK-FKART = 'F8'.
 LOOP AT XKOMV.
 IF XKOMV-KSCHL = 'PR00'.
 SELECT * FROM T685A INTO TABLE I_T685A WHERE KSCHL = 'PR00'.
 READ TABLE I_T685A WITH KEY KSCHL = XKOMV-KSCHL.
 I_T685A-KMANU = 'C'.
 MODIFY I_T685A INDEX SY-TABIX.
 MODIFY T685A FROM TABLE I_T685A.
 REFRESH I_T685A.
 ENDIF.
 ENDLOOP.
ELSE.
 LOOP AT XKOMV.
 IF XKOMV-KSCHL = 'PR00'.
 SELECT * FROM T685A INTO TABLE I_T685A WHERE KSCHL = 'PR00'.
 READ TABLE I_T685A WITH KEY KSCHL = XKOMV-KSCHL.
```

```
I_T685A-KMANU = 'D'.
MODIFY I_T685A INDEX SY-TABIX.
MODIFY T685A FROM TABLE I_T685A.
REFRESH I_T685A.
ENDIF.
ENDLOOP.
ENDIF.
ENDFORM.
```

Listing 7.2 USEREXIT_PRICING_PREPARE_TKOMP

▶ **Problem**

We want to send a daily short message service (SMS) to customers for invoices created. We're in touch with a company that provides an HTTP API for sending bulk SMS. Can we use it to send SMS from our SAP server?

Solution

There are a lot of bulk SMS service providers who provide you with HTTP APIs. The advantage to using such services is the cost benefit, whereas the risk is data security. An example of one such provider is clickatell.com, whose API is *http://api.clickatell.com/http/sendmsg?user=xxxxx&password=xxxxx&api_id=xxxxx&to=xxxxxxxxxx&text=Hello+World*.

After registration, most providers give a few free credits to test their service. After receiving the user, password, and api_id (it varies), you can insert those values in place of "xxxxx" in the API string. After "to=" you replace "xxxxxxxxxx" with the mobile number to which you want to send the message. The message in the sample API string is "Hello World." Test it by typing the whole string in the address window (where you type the website address) of any browser and press Enter. If the message reaches the intended number, then the HTTP API is ready for use. You can use the code in Listing 7.3 to enter the parameters of the API in the selection screen and execute to post the message.

```
REPORT ZSMS.
DATA: http_client TYPE REF TO if_http_client.
DATA: wf_string TYPE string,
result TYPE string,
r_str TYPE string.
DATA: result_tab TYPE TABLE OF string.

SELECTION-SCREEN: BEGIN OF BLOCK a WITH FRAME.
PARAMETERS: USER(20) LOWER CASE,
PASSWORD(20) LOWER CASE,
APIID(20) LOWER CASE,
```

```
TO(50) LOWER CASE.

TEXT(160) LOWER CASE,
SELECTION-SCREEN: END OF BLOCK a.

START-OF-SELECTION.
 CLEAR wf_string.
 CONCATENATE
'http://api.clickatell.com/http/sendmsg?user='
 USER
 '&password='
 PASSWORD
'&api_id='
 APIID
 '&to='
 TO

 '&text='
 TEXT
INTO
 wf_string.

CALL METHOD cl_http_client=>create_by_url
EXPORTING url = wf_string
IMPORTING client = http_client
EXCEPTIONS argument_not_found = 1
plugin_not_active = 2
internal_error = 3
OTHERS = 4.

CALL METHOD http_client->send
EXCEPTIONS
http_communication_failure = 1
http_invalid_state = 2.

CALL METHOD http_client->receive
EXCEPTIONS
http_communication_failure = 1
http_invalid_state = 2
http_processing_failed = 3.
CLEAR result.
result = http_client->response->get_cdata( ).

REFRESH result_tab.
SPLIT result AT cl_abap_char_utilities=>cr_lf INTO TABLE result_tab.
LOOP AT result_tab INTO r_str.
WRITE:/ r_str.
ENDLOOP.
```

Listing 7.3 Report ZSMS

Note that, for some service providers, the API may contain an IP address instead of a valid domain name, as shown below:

http://196.5.254.66/http/sendmsg?user=xxxxx&password=xxxxx&api_id=xxxxx& *to=xxxxxxxxx&text=Hello+World*

In such cases, you have to change the IP address to a valid domain name because the SAP server cannot use IP addresses, even though from a browser you won't have any problem. The message should not contain special characters such as *?*, *&* or *=*, because these characters have specific uses in an API string.

Once you are able to post messages from your SAP server, the next step is to trigger the message for different events and customize the message's content, such as invoice creation. You can also schedule the program to run as a background job.

▶ **Problem**

We're seeing the error message "Posting period 005 2200 is not open. Message no. F5201" while trying to release a billing document to accounts. The accounting document is not getting generated.

Solution

After you release the billing document, an accounting document is generated. The accounting document's posting date becomes the same as the billing date of the billing document.

In the system, you allow the users of a particular company code to post accounting documents for a specific time interval, using Transaction OB52. If the billing date and the subsequent posting date of the accounting document don't fall in the permitted periods, then the accounting document will not be generated, and you'll see the above error message. In this case, it seems that, rather than the allowed accounting period, you have to change the billing date, which, as per the error message is the fifth period of the year 2200 (May if the accounting year is the same as the calendar year, August if the accounting year is April to March, as practiced in many countries).

There's probably a typing error. You can rectify it by following the menu path GOTO • HEADER • HEADER from the overview screen of the invoice using Transaction VF02 and changing the billing date as shown in Figure 7.24.

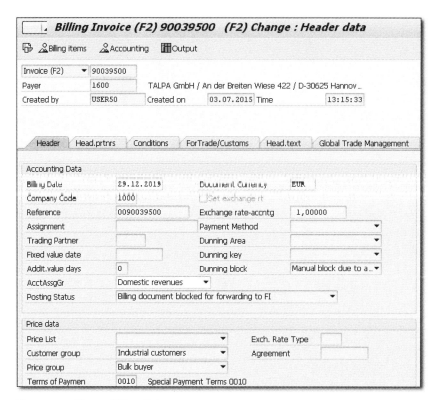

Figure 7.24 Change Billing Date

▶ **Problem**

While saving an invoice, we're receiving the error "Foreign Trade Data is Incomplete." Why is this (especially because it's a domestic invoice)?

Solution

There can be several reasons for this error. Follow the menu path GOTO • HEADER • FOREIGN TRADE/CUSTOMS and click on the INCOMPLETENESS ANALYSIS icon (shown in Figure 7.25) to identify the incomplete data. Also check if, in the order for this invoice, the shipping point has been deleted. The possibility of this being the problem is very high, since you mentioned that it's a domestic sale. Also read SAP Note 354222 (Foreign Trade Data Incomplete for Domestic Business) to understand the problem.

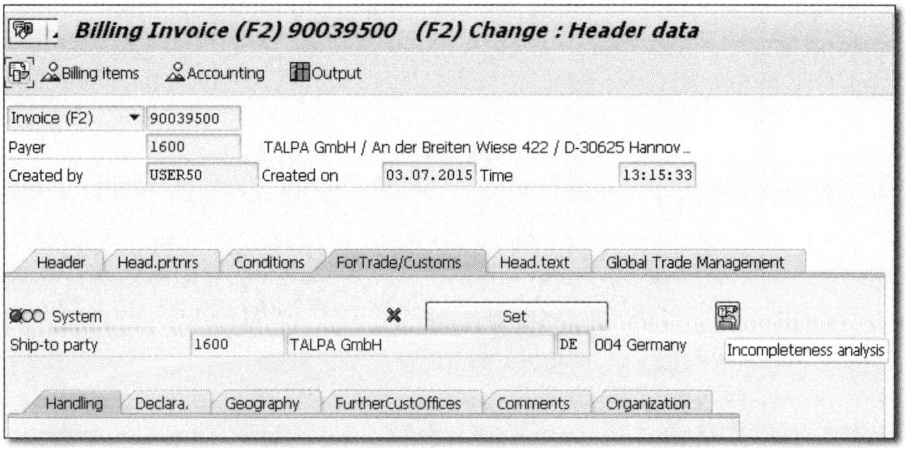

Figure 7.25 Incompleteness Analysis of Foreign Trade Data

▸ **Problem**

We've activated number range buffering in our organization, but for our U.S. subsidiary, this feature creates trouble. There are times when the invoice numbers are not consecutive. We want to deactivate the number range buffering for U.S. invoices, but not for the other countries.

Solution

Use the code in Listing 7.4 in the form USEREXIT_NUMBER_RANGE using US_RANGE_INTERN of the include program RV60AFZZ. Refer to SAP Notes 23835, 424486, and 363901 for details.

```
DATA: LS_T001 LIKE T001.
 DATA: LD_I_INTCA LIKE T005-INTCA.
 CALL FUNCTION 'FI_COMPANY_CODE_DATA'
 EXPORTING
 I_BUKRS = XVBRK-BUKRS
 IMPORTING
 E_T001 = LS_T001.
 CALL FUNCTION 'COUNTRY_CODE_SAP_TO_ISO'
 EXPORTING
 SAP_CODE = LS_T001-LAND1
 IMPORTING
 ISO_CODE = LD_I_INTCA.
 IF LD_I_INTCA EQ 'US'.
 NO_BUFFER = 'X'.
 ENDIF.
```

Listing 7.4 USEREXIT_NUMBER_RANGE

▶ **Problem**

Some sales documents show as open documents in Transaction VA05N. They also show up in the billing due list, and their status is open in tables VBUK and VBUP. But as per the document flow, we find that subsequent documents are created, and their status should have been complete.

Solution

To stop these documents from appearing in the document due list, use the report program SDVBUK00. This program will update the document status. In Transaction SE38, enter the program name (SDVBUK00) and press the ⌨F8⌨ key. You'll go to the screen shown in Figure 7.26.

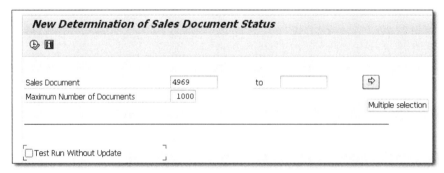

Figure 7.26 New Determination of Sales Document Status

Click on the MULTIPLE SELECTION icon highlighted in the figure and enter all of the documents whose status you want to redetermine. Unselect the TEST RUN WITHOUT UPDATE checkbox. You can do a test run without unselecting it, in which case you'll receive a report, but the document status won't change. When you run the report with this criteria, the statuses of documents are rectify and update. Refer to SAP Note 207875 for more details.

▶ **Problem**

Our accounting department has found an instance where the figures of a billing document in Sales and Distribution do not match the figures in an accounting document. We have not found the reason for this error, or any other document with a similar problem. Is there any way to confirm that there is no such error in our system?

Solution

Run the report SDFI_CONSISTENCY_CHECK by executing the following steps.

▸ Enter Transaction SE38.

▸ In the Program field of the initial screen, enter the program name "SDFI_?CONSISTENCY_CHECK."

▸ Press F8.

▸ The selection screen will appear.

▸ Enter the company code, fiscal year, and period (01 for January, 02 for February, and so on, provided the fiscal year is the same as the calendar year) in which you require the report. You can run this program for few documents by specifying the document number in the selection screen.

▸ Press F8 to run a check. The screen shown in Figure 7.27 will appear.

▸ Select the Difference Amnt column and click on the Summation icon. If the total in the Difference column is zero, everything is likely to be OK.

▸ Select the Totals tab. Figure 7.27 shows the Differences tab. In the Totals tab, GL-related totals are available. In the Differences tab, the totals are document-related.

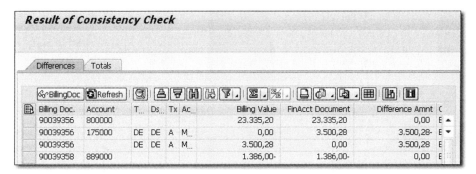

Figure 7.27 Result of Consistency Check for Audit

▸ **Problem**
We've been asked to provide a report on tax codes and the GL assigned to them for automatic posting. Is there any standard report for this?

Solution
You can use the standard report SAPUFKB1 for this purpose, which actually is meant for auditing. Execute the following steps:

▸ Enter the program name SAPUFKB1 in the Program field in the initial screen of Transaction SE38.

▷ Press F8.

▷ In the screen that appears, enter the chart of account (e.g., CANA) and company code (e.g., US01) for which a report is required.

▷ The screen shown in Figure 7.28 will appear. The screen lists all of the possible automatic accounting postings in the system.

▷ Select the %TX – SALES/PUR. TAX checkbox. This option will give you the details about the GL assigned for automatic tax posting.

▷ Press F8.

The report will provide the information you need. If there's a tax code for which a GL is not assigned, you'll be able to see it and rectify it. The same thing can be done for other auto-postings scenarios (e.g., posting to revenue accounts). This is a kind of preventive maintenance.

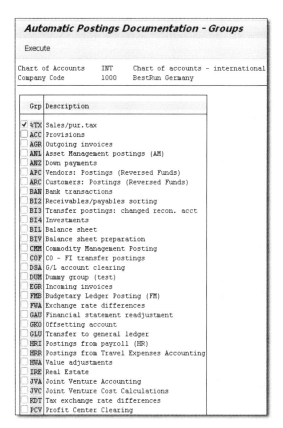

Figure 7.28 Automatic Postings (e.g., Tax Accounts) Audit

▶ **Problem**

We cancelled a credit memo, so we no longer require the credit memo request for it. When we attempt to delete it, however, we get an error message. Because we cancelled the subsequent document (credit memo), why does it show such an error?

Solution

For normal sales processing of an order, delivery, and billing, if you want to cancel the order after creation of the bill, the following steps are required:

- Cancel the invoice using Transaction VF02.

- Reverse the PGI of the delivery using Transaction VL09.

- Delete the delivery using Transaction VL02N.

- Delete the sales order using Transaction VA02.

In this situation, note that the subsequent document for the order (that is, the delivery) doesn't exist. However, the situation for a credit memo or debit memo is slightly different because there's no delivery in between. You cannot delete the invoices (e.g., credit memos) and can only cancel them if required. In this situation, the standard practice is to do either of the following, or both:

- Reject all items of the credit memo request.

- Change the quantity (and hence the value) to zero. Thus, everybody will ignore the zero-value open order.

If neither option suits you, you can do the following to delete the credit memo requests of the cancelled credit memos:

- Go to Transaction SE16N.

- Enter the table name "VBFA."

- Activate the function &SAP_EDIT.

- Select the lines for the credit memo request. The line linking the request to the credit memo and the document that cancelled the credit memo (S2 type invoice) will appear.

- Delete all of the rows for this credit memo request.

- Go to Transaction SE38.

- Run the report program SDVBFA01.

- In the selection screen, enter the credit memo request number.

- Unselect the TEST RUN WITHOUT UPDATE checkbox.

▶ Execute.

▶ In Transaction VA02, you can now delete the credit memo request.

▶ **Problem**
We found several deliveries in a billing due list (VF04) that should not be there. These deliveries are already billed. Is there any way rectify this error?

Solution
Refer to SAP Note 128947. As suggested in the note, run the standard program RVV05IVB using Transaction SE38. In the selection screen, you'll find 14 checkboxes for updating indices, shown in Figure 7.29. In Table 7.9, we've listed the database tables corresponding to the checkboxes. The list in Table 7.9 is in the same sequence as the corresponding checkboxes (see Figure 7.29). So to update the billing due list for deliveries, select the ninth checkbox. The list of deliveries that are to be updated appears in the selection list. Also select the BILLING INDEX checkbox in the DELIVERIES frame, as shown in Figure 7.29. Execute the program by pressing the F8 key.

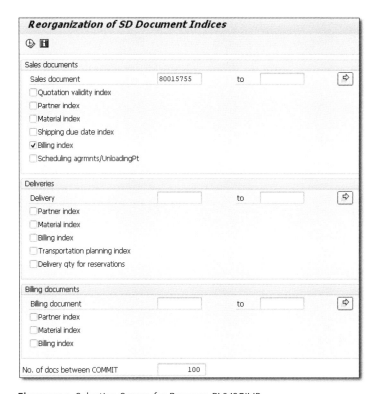

Figure 7.29 Selection Screen for Program RVV05IVB

No.	Table	Table Description	Transaction
1	VAKGU	Sales Index: Quotation Validity	VA25
2	VAKPA	Sales Index: Orders by Partner Function	VA05
3	VAPMA	Sales Index: Order Items by Material	VA05
4	VEPVG	Delivery Due Index	VL04
5	VKDFS	SD Index: Billing Initiator	VF04, VF24
6	VLPKM	Scheduling Agreements by Customer Material	VA25
7	VLKPA	SD Index: Deliveries by Partner Functions	VL05, VL06
8	VLPMA	SD Index: Delivery Items by Material	VL05, VL06
9	VKDFS	SD Index: Billing Initiator	VF04, VF24
10	VTRDI	Shipment Planning Index	VT01, VT04
11	VRSLI	Receipt of Materials from Deliveries	ME2O
12	VRKPA	Sales Index: Bills by Partner Functions	VF05
13	VRPMA	SD Index: Billing Items per Material	VF05
14	VKDFS	SD Index: Billing Initiator	VF04, VF24

Table 7.9 Tables Updated by Program RVV05IVB

▶ **Problem**

We've have found a billing document that has not updated a sales info structure. Is there any way to manually update an info structure?

Solution

Refer to SAP Note 174141. The update programs are as follows:

- ▶ Update SIS for orders (or old orders): RMCVNEUA

- ▶ Update SIS for deliveries (or old deliveries): RMCVNEUL

- ▶ Update SIS for invoices (or old invoices): RMCVNEUF

7.7 Summary

In this chapter, we've discussed how SAP ERP processes invoices. You learned about the steps involved in the configuration of billing types, billing plans, and revenue account determination. In the coverage of accounts interface, you also learned how to use the condition technique for reconciliation and cash account determination. We discussed how to modify revenue reorganization, and you should now understand how the accounting document can take the billing document number. In the last part of this chapter, we listed some of the common errors for billing and their solutions.

In the next chapter, you'll learn about text processing, message control, ABAP tools, and numbering objects.

This chapter covers topics that are useful but which haven't yet been fully covered in this book. Many of these topics are relevant not only for Sales and Distribution, but for other SAP ERP functionalities as well.

8 Cross-Functional Customization

There are several functions that are not specific to the Sales and Distribution functionality, and which you can, in fact, use in other SAP ERP components. For example, batch determination is important not only for sales and distribution, but also for purchasing, inventory management, and production planning; here, we'll cover batch input. In this chapter, we'll cover topics including text processing, message control, ABAP tools, and numbering objects. We've touched on some of these topics in previous chapters, but in this chapter, we'll provide the overview of what you need to understand regarding what they are and how they impact your day-to-day work.

So let's get started.

8.1 Text Processing

The "cockpit" transaction for text processing in Sales and Distribution is Transaction VOTXN, as shown in Figure 1.1. All of the listed text objects contain a radio button in this screen, so you can customize any of these 16 text objects, one at a time. Note that this list has all of the text objects that you encounter in Sales and Distribution, with a few exceptions (e.g., texts used in credit management, accounting text of customer master records). The customization technique used for text processing is primarily a condition technique, which by now you should be quite comfortable with. VOFM routines also play a crucial role in text processing.

Table 8.1 lists all of the text objects you can customize using Transaction VOTXN. Note that for sales, delivery, and billing documents, the text objects for header and item texts are same. It is the text group that differentiates them.

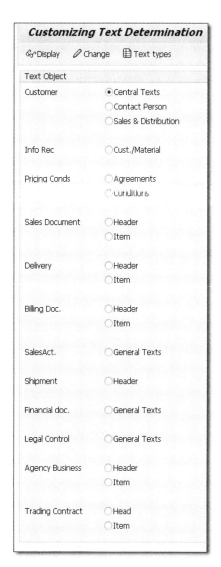

Figure 8.1 Customizing Text Determination

Text Fields in ABAP Report Documents

To use the information stored in the text fields of a document in an ABAP report, you cannot reference it by the table field as you do for other fields. For example, ABAP reports refer to sales document number as VBAK-VBELN. VBAK is the table for sales document header and VBELN, which store the document number in one of its many fields.

Function module READ_TEXT transfers the content of a text to an ABAP report. To read the text of a particular document or record, you have to specify the text name, language, text ID, and text object. You'll become familiar with these terms as you continue in this chapter.

Text Object	Code	Text Group
Customer – Header	KNA1	G (Customer: Header Texts)
Customer – Contact Person	KNVK	I (Customer: Contact Person Texts)
Customer – Sales Area	KNVV	J (Customer: Sales Texts)
Customer/Material Info Record	KNMT	O (Customer/Material Info Record)
Pricing Agreements	KONA	M (Agreements)
Pricing Condition Records	KONP	N (Conditions)
Sales Document – Header	VBBK	A (Sales Document Header)
Sales Document – Item	VBBP	D (Sales Document Item)
Delivery – Header	VBBK	B (Delivery Header)
Delivery – Item	VBBP	E (Delivery Item)
Billing Document – Header	VBBK	C (Billing Header)
Billing Document – Item	VBBP	F (Billing Item)
Sales Activity – General Texts	VBKA	K (Sales Activities)
Shipment – Header	VTTK	L (Transportation Header)
Financial Doc. – General Texts	AKKP	W (Documentary Payment)
Legal Control – General Texts	EMBK	X (Legal Control)
Agency Business – Header	WBRK	P (Agency Business Header)
Agency Business – Item	WBRP	Q (Agency Business Item)
Trading Contract – Header	WBHK	Y (Trading Contract Header)
Trading Contract – Item	WBHI	Z (Trading Contract Item)

Table 8.1 Text Objects Customized Using Transaction VOTXN

Text Limits

The text fields for a document can store any amount of text. Only the first line of the text is visible, however. To view (or change or add) the complete text, double-click on it.

> **Changing Text Fields**
>
> Only the text fields are changeable when the document becomes practically nonmodi-fiable, such as the billing document after posting to accounting, or delivery after PGI. You can use this feature of text fields to store some qualitative information (e.g., the customer informs you that he received the material too early).

Follow these steps to customize text determination, which uses a condition technique:

1. Define the text IDs for text objects
2. Create the text determination procedure.
3. Assign text IDs to the text determination procedure.
4. Define the access sequence if automatic determination is required.
5. Assign the text determination procedure to a document type, customer account group, or as otherwise required for the specific text object and text group.

Let's discuss each of these steps in detail in the follow subsections. Then in Section 8.1.6, we'll discuss the text determination analysis, which analyzes whether and how the system automatically proposes the text.

8.1.1 Text IDs

Text IDs, or text types, are created for specific text objects.

In the screen shown in Figure 8.1, select the radio button next to the text object for which you want to create the text IDs and click on the TEXT TYPES button in the application toolbar. You'll get an information message: "Caution: The table is cross-client." This means changes in any one client of a server are automatically made to all other clients of the server. Typically, except for a production server, all others have multiple clients.

When you press Enter or click on the CONTINUE (checkmark) icon, you go to the screen shown in Figure 8.2. You'll find all of the existing text IDs for text objects here. You can change the description of any text ID to suit your purposes, or create your own IDs by copying one and giving it a new key (starting with Y or Z) and description.

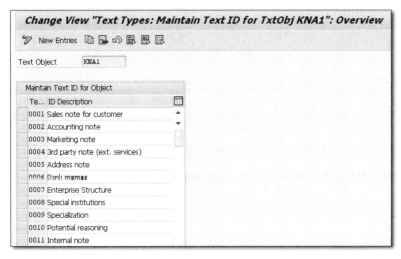

Figure 8.2 Text IDs for the Text Object KNA1 (Customer Master Header)

Text IDs

Text IDs are specific to text objects, not text groups (third column in Table 8.1). This means that a text ID created for sales document header will automatically be available for the delivery header and billing header. The text object for all three are the same: VBBK. The text groups are different.

Languages

You can save text in multiple languages for a text item. You can use this functionality while taking an output (e.g., for an invoice) in different languages. Also, you can create standard text using Transaction SO10 and use it in outputs.

8.1.2 Text Determination Procedure

The text determination procedure (or *text procedure*) is created for a combination of text object and text group.

In Figure 8.1, select the radio button of the object (text object plus group) for which you will create or modify the text determination procedure. Click on the CHANGE (pencil) icon in the application toolbar, and you'll go to the screen shown in Figure 8.3.

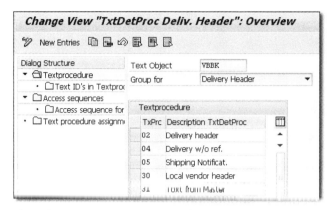

Figure 8.3 Text Determination Procedure

You'll find all of the existing text determination procedures as a list on the right side of the screen. To create a new procedure, select any existing procedure and click on the COPY AS (F6) icon. A new dialog box will appear as shown in Figure 8.4. Select the COPY ALL option, if you want to copy the text IDs already assigned to the reference procedure to the new procedure. You can, alternatively, copy only the text determination procedure and assign text IDs, as we'll explain in the next step.

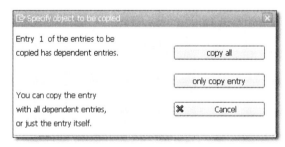

Figure 8.4 Copy Text IDs Along with Text Determination Procedure

Remember that the text determination procedure is for the combination of text object and text group, so the text determination procedure for the sales document header is not relevant for either the delivery header or the billing header.

8.1.3   Assigning Text IDs to a Text Determination Procedure

To modify the text IDs assigned to a text determination procedure, or to assign new text IDs to it, double-click on the text IDs in the TEXT PROCEDURE folder, as shown in Figure 8.5. The text IDs appear in the same sequence they'll appear in for the object (e.g., customer master record). You can also specify whether to reference or duplicate the text, if it is mandatory, and the access sequence for the text ID.

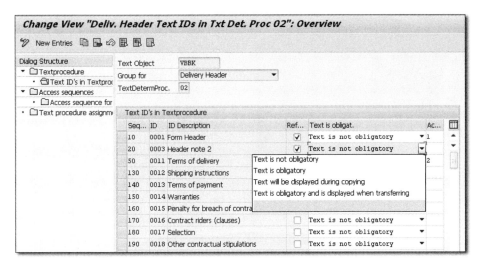

Figure 8.5 Assigning Text IDs to a Text Determination Procedure

As we saw in the other use of condition techniques, in Chapter 4, there's no separate step to assign an access sequence to a text type (equivalent of a condition type). Also note that the sequence is valid for a specific combination of text object (e.g., VBBK), text group (e.g., B delivery header), and text determination procedure (e.g., 02 delivery header).

8.1.4 Define Access Sequence

To create or change the access sequence, double-click on the ACCESS SEQUENCES folder. The list of all existing sequences appears, and you can create a new one by selecting any existing one, clicking on the COPY AS icon ([F6]), and providing a new key and description. By clicking on the COPY ALL icon, you'll copy all of the existing accesses in the reference access sequence, all which are modifiable.

Like the text determination procedure, and unlike the text types, the access sequence is valid for a combination of text objects and text groups. Therefore, an access sequence created for the sales document header doesn't become valid for either the delivery header or the billing header. After creating an access sequence, you can modify, add, or delete the existing accesses. To do this, select any existing access sequence and select the ACCESS SEQUENCE FOR TEXT IDs folder. As shown in Figure 8.6, you can maintain the text IDs, along with their text object, in different accesses. In the PARTNER FUNCTION column, you specify the partner function to be used if the text copies over from the customer master record to a document, and in the LANGUAGE column, you specify the language of choice.

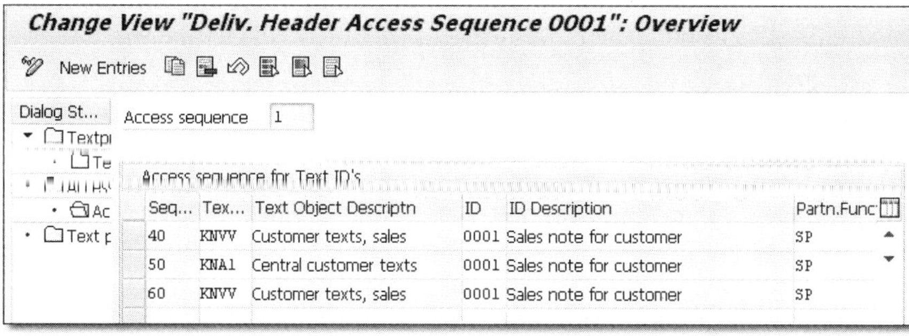

Figure 8.6 Access Sequence 0001 for Text Object VBBK (Sale Doc Header)

8.1.5 Assignment of Text Determination Procedure

Assign the text determination procedures by clicking on the TEXT PROCEDURE ASSIGNMENT folder. As shown in Figure 8.6, it's assigned to the delivery types in case of the text object DELIVERY header (text object VBBK and text group B). The assignment for a customer master record text is not required because automatic determination for it is irrelevant. Manually maintain text fields by going to EXTRAS • TEXTS from the GENERAL, CONTACT PERSON, or SALES AREA screens for general, contact person, and sales area texts, respectively.

You can assign the text determination procedure by selecting the TEXT PROCEDURE ASSIGNMENT folder, shown in Figure 8.7. The system bases assignment on the text object and text group. For a different combination of text object and text group, the assignment of the text determination procedure takes place as per the list shown in Table 8.2. Even when automatic determination is not required, this step is valid for manual text maintenance.

Description	Text Obj. – Text Group	Text Determination Procedure Is Assigned to
Customer – Header	KNA1 - G	Customer account groups
Customer – Contact Person	KNVK - I	Customer account groups

Table 8.2 Assignment of Different Text Objects

Description	Text Obj. – Text Group	Text Determination Procedure Is Assigned to
Customer – Sales Area	KNVV - J	Customer account groups
Cust./Material Info Record	KNMT - O	Customer account groups
Pricing Agreements	KONA - M	Agreement types
Pricing Condition Records	KONP - N	Condition types
Sales Document – Header	VBBK - A	Sales document types
Sales Document – Item	VBBP - D	Sales item categories
Delivery – Header	VBBK - B	Delivery document types
Delivery – Item	VBBP - E	Delivery item categories
Billing Document – Header	VBBK - C	Billing types
Billing Document – Item	VBBP - F	Billing types
Sales Activity – General Texts	VBKA - K	Sales activity types
Shipment – Header	VTTK - L	Shipment types
Financial Doc. – General Texts	AKKP - W	Financial document indicators
Legal Control – General Texts	EMBK - X	Legal regulations plus types
Agency Business – Header	WBRK - P	Billing types (agency business)
Agency Business – Item	WBRP - Q	Billing types (agency business)
Trading Contract – Header	WBHK - Y	Contract types
Trading Contract – Item	WBHI - Z	Contract item categories

Table 8.2 Assignment of Different Text Objects (Cont.)

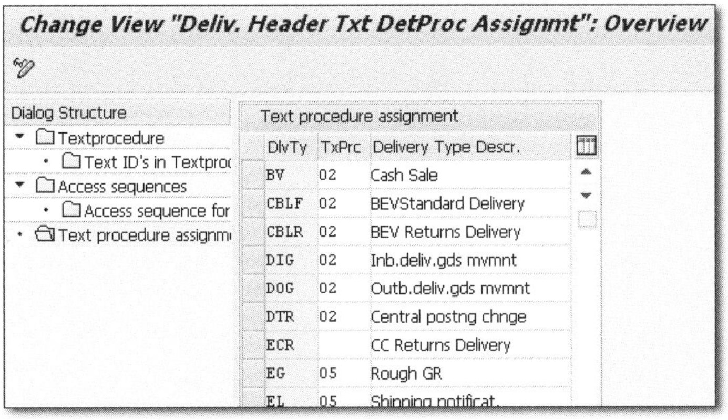

Figure 8.7 Assignment of Text Determination Procedure to Document Types

8.1.6   Text Determination Analysis

During document processing, the texts determined based on the text determination procedure and routines populate from the following possible sources:

▸ Reference document (e.g., from order to delivery)

▸ Customer or material master record

▸ Condition records or info records (e.g., customer or material info record)

If you click on the DISPLAY LOG icon, highlighted in Figure 8.8 in the TEXTS tab of the document header, you can see the details of the text determination analysis. Note that if the text IDs used in the text determination procedure are the same for document header or item in the case of an order, delivery, and billing, the content flows automatically. In this case, the transfer of text doesn't require any determination procedure. Therefore, you can customize text determination procedures for the transfer of data to an order from customer master records, material master records, or condition records, and then use the same text ID in delivery and billing to transfer the content of the text ID to the billing document.

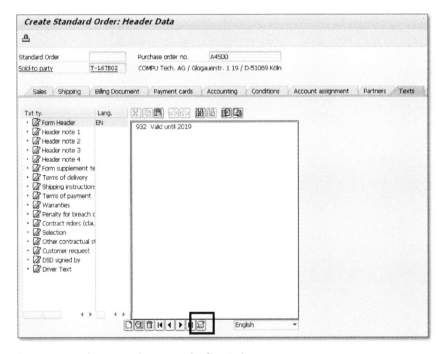

Figure 8.8 Display Log in the Texts Tab of an Order

The analysis shown in Figure 8.9 shows that the text existing in the text type 0001 (or ID) of the KNA1 text object automatically determines the text type 0001 (of the VBBK text object and text group A), as per access sequence 40. This means the text maintained for text type 0001 in the customer master record GENERAL DATA area of the sold-to party in the order is transferred to order header text type 0001. Even though both have the same key (0001), they are completely different because they're part of different text objects: VBBK and KNA1. The other accesses of the access sequence do not execute. For text type 0003, there's no access sequence, which means manual maintenance is required. If any text type defined as mandatory is empty at the time of saving the document, then the system considers the document incomplete. The details will appear in the incompletion log.

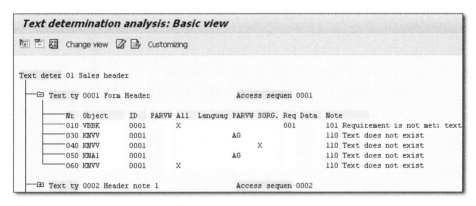

Figure 8.9 Text Determination Analysis

8.2 Message Control

We've already discussed how to use the condition technique in output determination, as well as how to use Transaction NACE for this purpose. In this section, we'll focus on data transfer using *electronic data interchange* (EDI) and *application link enabling* (ALE). EDI uses a set of standards for data exchange between two or more independent systems. Examples of such standards are UN/EDIFACT (recommended by the UN), ANSI ASC X12 (X12) (preferred in the US and Canada), TTRADACOMS of Article Numbering Association (ANA), and ODETTE. In every system there, should be a provision for receiving (inbound process) and sending (outbound process) the EDI document.

The inbound process is for receiving information such as purchase orders from a customer. It does the following:

▶ Receives the EDI transmission

▶ Converts the transmission into an intermediate document (IDoc), which is transferred to the SAP layer

▶ Creates an SAP document (e.g., sales order)

In an outbound process, you send information such as an invoice or an *advance shipment notice* (ASN) to a customer. The following things happen in an outbound process.

▶ An IDoc is generated for the SAP document.

▶ The IDoc is transferred from the SAP system to the operating system.

▶ The IDoc is converted to EDI standards.

▶ The EDI document is transferred to the business partner.

▶ The EDI system reports the status back to the SAP system.

Let's look closer at the steps for customizing the EDI or IDoc interface, and then turn our attention to ALE, which we also use for business data transfer.

8.2.1   IDoc Interface and EDI

In customizing the output type, you maintain the EDI option (option 6) as a medium for output, as shown in Figure 8.10 (Transaction NACE). The program name for this is RSNASTED, and form routine is EDI_PROCESSING.

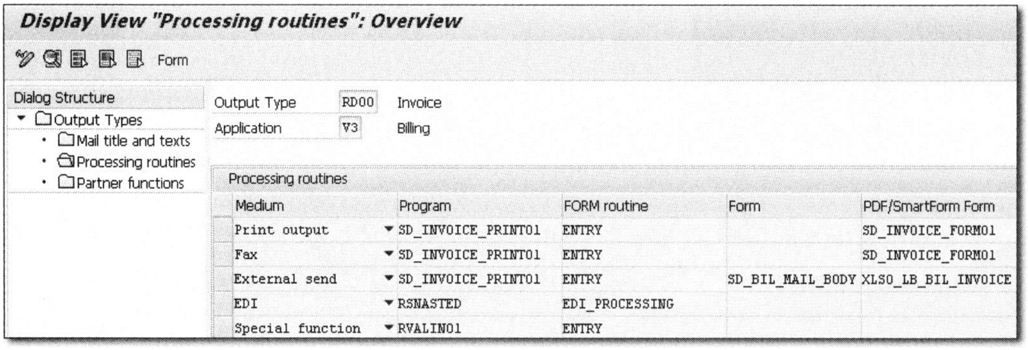

Figure 8.10 Assigning EDI Medium to Output Type

Click on the relevant application (e.g., V3 for billing). Click on the OUTPUT TYPE button on the application toolbar, select the output type (e.g., RD00) that you want to assign to the EDI output, and select the PROCESSING ROUTINES folder (also shown in Figure 8.10). This is an overview screen that allows you to access the detail screen by selecting an individual item. When there's only one medium as the option for an output type, the system will take you directly to the details screen.

When the message control function makes the determination, or when you manually opt for the EDI medium for the output type for a document, the following five things happen:

▸ The form routine EDI_PROCESSING is triggered.

▸ EDI_PROCESSING reads the partner profile.

▸ It determines which function module to use (e.g., IDOC_OUTPUT_ INVOIC for invoices).

▸ The function module generates the IDoc (e.g., EXPINV02). You can use Transaction WE60 to pull up the documentation for an individual IDoc. In the initial screen, enter the IDoc type (e.g., EXPINV02) and select the HTML format to display the data structure of the IDoc, as shown in Figure 8.11.

▸ The IDoc is either sent immediately (option 4) or scheduled for dispatch (as per the option selected in the message control setting) so that it's sent when the system is less busy.

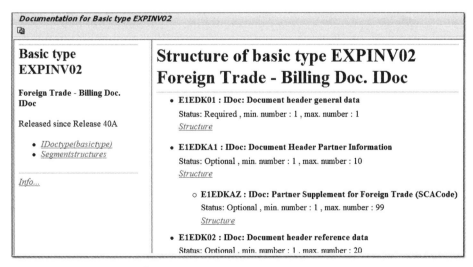

Figure 8.11 Data Structure of IDoc EXPINV02

All of the steps relevant for message control are also relevant for EDI transfer. It's important to remember that it's possible to make an EDI transfer without using message control. We'll now discuss two important activities involved in customizations of EDI transfer: defining the port and defining the partner.

Defining the Port

A port is logical/virtual connecting point for data exchange between different systems (or computers). At least one port is required for the IDoc interface to communicate with each external system. Use Transaction WE21 to define the port for EDI transfer. In the initial screen, click on the folder Files and then click on the CREATE icon, shown in Figure 8.12. Once you provide a port name and description, you can select the radio button IDoc REC.TYPES SAP Release 3.0/3.1 for version. Note that this has nothing to do with the SAP version you may be using.

You can you customize the port using four tabs:

▶ OUTBOUND FILE
In this tab, you can specify the directory path used to send the IDoc to the EDI subsystem and enter a name for the file in the OUTBOUND FILE field. Alternatively, in the FUNCTION MODULE field, you can specify a function module to generate file names.

▶ OUTBOUND: TRIGGER
In this tab, you can specify whether an automatic start is possible. By selecting the AUTO-TRIGGER checkbox, you can start the EDI subsystem by remote function call (RFC). RFC is one of the tools used for communication between an SAP system and another SAP (or non-SAP) system. You have to specify the RFC destination if AUTO-TRIGGER is selected. In the DIRECTORY field, you can enter the path of the command file, and the COMMAND FILE field should specify the name of the file that contains the commands (e.g., shell script for UNIX) to start the EDI subsystem.

Transactions

You can use Transaction SMGW to capture the RFCs running, Transaction ST22 to find the short dumps caused by RFCs (failed RFCs), and Transaction SM59 to maintain the RFC destination.

▶ INBOUND FILE

This tab has the same fields as the OUTBOUND FILE tab (see Figure 8.12). You can specify the directory that stores the incoming IDocs. Specify the name for the incoming IDocs in the INBOUND FILE field or determine them in the FUNCTION MODULE field.

▶ STATUS FILE

This tab has the same fields as the OUTBOUND FILE tab (Figure 8.12). You can specify the directory that stores the status of outgoing or incoming IDocs. Specify the name for status files in the STATUS FILE field or determine them in the FUNCTION MODULE field.

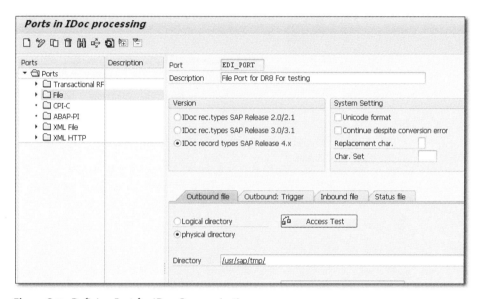

Figure 8.12 Defining Port for IDoc Communication

Defining the Partner

Customers, vendors, employees, forwarding agents, and so on are considered partners of your business in the SAP ERP system. You create master data records for them. In addition, if you communicate with them electronically using an IDoc interface, you must also define them as partners in the IDoc interface or for EDI transfer.

Define partners for EDI transfer via Transaction WE20. This process consists of two broad steps: defining the partner and defining inbound and/or outbound messages for the partner. To define a partner when you enter the transaction and see the screen shown in Figure 8.13, you can perform the following steps:

1. Click on the CREATE icon.

2. Enter the customer code in the PARTNER NUMBER field.

3. Enter the partner type (e.g., KU for customer) in the PARTN. TYPE field.

4. In the POST PROCESSING: PERMITTED AGENT tab, you should specify the employees who will receive the mail (or error message) after processing the IDoc.

5. In the CLASSIFICATION tab, set the partner status to A (active).

6. In the TELEPHONY tab, you can fill the optional fields, including TELEPHONE NUMBER, COUNTRY CODE, NAME, and COMPANY NAME.

7. Once you define the partner (for IDoc communication), the icons below the OUTBOUND PARAMETER and INBOUND PARAMETER frames become active. You can insert a new message type here.

8. Double-click on any existing message type, as shown in Figure 8.14.

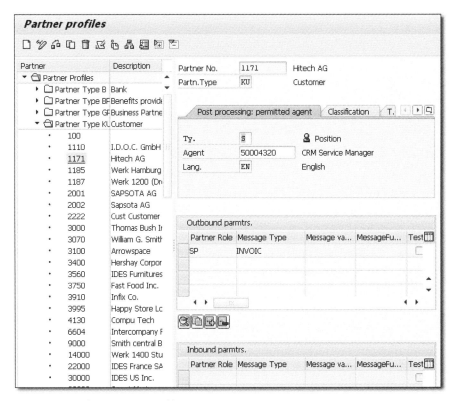

Figure 8.13 Defining Partner Profiles

Figure 8.14 Parameter Profiles for Outbound Messages

9. In the OUTBOUND OPTIONS tab, you can specify the port used to send the IDoc. In the PACKET SIZE field, you can specify the number of the IDoc that will be sent in one RFC. You can also specify whether the IDoc will be sent immediately or at a future scheduled time, as well as the IDoc type (e.g., INVOIC01).

10. We covered the information for the MESSAGE CONTROL tab in our discussion on output processing (Chapter 6). Also, for the POST PROCESSING: PERMITTED AGENT and TELEPHONY tabs, refer the earlier steps in this list. You can leave the fields in the EDI STANDARD tab blank, unless they're required for your EDI subsystem. This customization is done with a Basis system administrator, keeping in mind the system performance.

Transaction WEDI

The area menu transaction code for IDoc interfaces is WEDI. You can use it to retrieve all of the transactions related to IDocs and EDI on the SAP EASY ACCESS menu path.

Having discussed how to customize an IDoc interface for using EDI, let's move on to understand ALE.

8.2.2 Application Link Enabling

We use ALE extensively for integrating SAP components; in contrast, EDI cannot be used for internal data transfer. Both ALE and EDI require an IDoc interface. There is no role in the EDI subsystem that can convert the IDoc into the EDI standard.

The area menu for ALE customization is SALE. When you enter SALE like a transaction in the transaction window and press Enter, all of the customization steps relevant for ALE customization appear. This is helpful because you have a ready-to-use checklist. The basic customization steps for ALE communication are as follows:

1. Basic settings

2. Communication

3. Modeling and implementing business processes

4. System monitoring

> **ALE Modeling**
>
> As a functional expert, you're expected to contribute to the third step of customization for ALE: modeling and implementing business processes. More details on this exceeds the scope of this book.

8.3 ABAP Tools

In this section, we'll discuss the specific ABAP tools that are important for functional experts to know. Our discussion will contain the following topics: Sales and Distribution user exits, debugging, and LSMW.

8.3.1 SD User Exits

ABAP enhancements include user exits, field exits, and BAdIs. In this section, we'll only discuss the user exits available for the Sales and Distribution functionality in

SAP ERP (in other words, user exits in the program MV45AFZZ). Technically, these are neither enhancements nor user exits, since version upgrades do not affect enhancements, and user exits are created using Transaction CMOD or SMOD. What we often refer to as *SD user exits* are actually modifications. In the Sales and Distribution functionality, SAP ERP provides different windows in specific standard include programs (which themselves are a type of ABAP program). In these windows or forms, you can insert your own code to fine-tune the standard transactions, which we've seen in earlier chapters. Here we'll just list few such include programs.

But first, we need to see if these customer codes are inside a standard program and whether it's possible to escape the upgrade process. Upgrading is when you move from one version to a newer version of SAP ERP. Even while using same version (e.g., SAP ERP 6.0), SAP releases several SAP Notes that are implemented collectively, and the system is upgraded. These SAP Notes proactively address new tax requirements, program bugs, and similar issues.

It's natural that new requirements for user exits come up. Governments in different countries tend to innovate when it comes to taxing. Companies also make frequent changes in the Sales and Distribution functionality in SAP ERP to be on track with the market.

Let's look at an example. Suppose you've made some changes in program MV45AFZZ, which contains several user exists. SAP inserts another user exit and delivers it via an SAP note. When you implement that SAP note, the new program will overwrite the program already in system, and your customized coding will be overwritten. This is not what you want to happen.

So when there's a *new* requirement, SAP creates a new user exit in which you can insert customer code. However, instead of adding the exit to any existing include program, SAP creates a new one. Consequently, you'll have many include programs for sales, delivery, billing, and other functions of this functionality:

▸ FV45EFZ1	▸ FV50UZZZ	▸ MV45AFZC	▸ MV45AOZZ	▸ MV50AFZZ
▸ FV45VFZZ	▸ FV50VTZZ	▸ MV45AFZH	▸ MV45ATZZ	▸ MV50BFZ1
▸ FV45VTZZ	▸ MV45AFZ4	▸ MV45AFZU	▸ MV50AFZ1	▸ MV50SFZ1
▸ FV50DFZZ	▸ MV45AFZA	▸ MV45AFZZ	▸ MV50AFZ3	▸ MV50SFZ2
▸ FV50UZXX	▸ MV45AFZB	▸ MV45AIZZ	▸ MV50AFZK	▸ MV50SFZ3

▶ MV50SFZ4	▶ MV75AFZ2	▶ RV60FUS2	▶ V05AZZEN	▶ V51AFZZ1
▶ MV55AFZ1	▶ MV75AFZ3	▶ RV60FUS3	▶ V05AZZLK	▶ VV05HFZ1
▶ MV55AFZ2	▶ MV90VFZZ	▶ RV60FUS4	▶ V05AZZLP	▶ VV05HFZ2
▶ MV55AFZ3	▶ RMCS1US1	▶ RV60FUS5	▶ V05EA1AG	▶ VV05LFZ1
▶ MV60SFZ1	▶ RMCS1US2	▶ RV60FUST	▶ V05EA1RE	▶ VV05LFZ2
▶ MV60SFZ2	▶ RMCS1US3	▶ RV61AFZA	▶ V05EA1RG	▶ VV05TFZ1
▶ MV60SFZ3	▶ RMCS1US4	▶ RV61AFZB	▶ V05EA1WE	▶ VV05TFZ2
▶ MV60SF74	▶ RMCS1Z01	▶ RVCOMF74	▶ V05EZZAG	▶ VV05TFZ3
▶ MV60SFZ5	▶ RMCS5Z01	▶ RVCOMFZZ	▶ V05EZZRG	▶ VV05WFZ1
▶ MV61AFZA	▶ RMCS6Z01	▶ RVKMPNNN	▶ V05EZZWE	▶ VV05WFZ2
▶ MV61AFZB	▶ RV45PFZA	▶ RVKMPUS2	▶ V05HZZMO	▶ VV05WFZ3
▶ MV65AFZ1	▶ RV50BTOP	▶ RVKPRFZ2	▶ V05IEXI2	▶ VV05XFZ1
▶ MV65AFZ2	▶ RV53SFZ1	▶ RVKPRFZ3	▶ V05IEXIT	▶ VV05XFZ2
▶ MV65BFZ1	▶ RV60AFZC	▶ RVKPRFZ4	▶ V05LZZMO	▶ VV05XFZ3
▶ MV65BFZ2	▶ RV60AFZD	▶ RVKREFZ1	▶ V05TZZMO	
▶ MV65BFZ3	▶ RV60AFZZ	▶ RVKREFZ2	▶ V05WZZMO	
▶ MV75AFZ1	▶ RV60FUS1	▶ RVKREFZ3	▶ V05XZZMO	

We've seen the use of various user exits in earlier chapters. In particular, see Chapter 3 (for MV45AFZZ), Chapter 5 (for LVKMPTZZ, LVKMPFZ1, LVKMPFZZ2, and LVK-MPFZZ3), Chapter 6 (for MV50AFZ1, MV50AFZ3), and Chapter 7 (for RV60AFZZ).

8.3.2 Debugging

Debugging is how you find an error in a program.

SAP ERP offers the debugging function /h. While you're still in a transaction, you can type "/h" in the transaction window. When you press Enter, you'll get the message, "Debugging switched on."

When in debugging mode, you move from one screen to another, step by step, examining the effects of each line of the program. The program that runs in the background to take you from one screen to the next is now visible on your screen.

We turned debugging on while in the overview screen of a sales order and clicked on the CONDITIONS tab (Figure 8.15). Use the red arrows on the application toolbar proceed down the program code. Click the straight arrow on the right to exit debugging mode. You can click on the FIELDS OR TABLE button and specify the field name or table name at the bottom of the window. Click on the arrow to go one step at a time. From there, you can see how the value of the specific field or table is populated, modified, or processed during that step in the program.

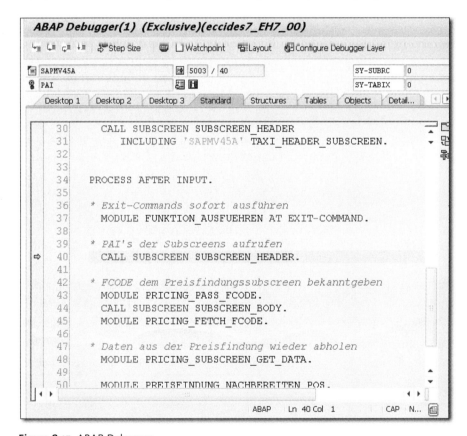

Figure 8.15 ABAP Debugger

New Debugger

The new debugger available with SAP ERP 5.0 or above creates a new session for debugging. It has several new features that you may want to explore once you're comfortable with the basic features.

Because all of the standard programs for standard transactions are also written with ABAP, debugging is also possible for standard transactions, which provides functional experts good insight into the logic that a particular program follows. Even if you don't know the ABAP syntax, you can get help from a technical person during the debugging process.

Debugging

If you're in a situation where the value of a particular field in a document needs to be changed manually, you can do it using debugging. To do so, you need to understand the standard program, table, and structures that store the values temporarily.

8.3.3 Legacy System Migration Workbench

The purpose of the Legacy System Migration Workbench (LSMW) is to transfer legacy data to your SAP system during an SAP project implementation before go-live. Though we've included it in the ABAP tools section, this is a cross-functional tool. With Transaction LSMW, you can record an SAP transaction and use the recording to repeat the transaction.

Let's walk through the post-implementation scenarios where the LSMW can come to your rescue. These five examples will help you understand how to use this tool optimally:

1. You want to change any field of all material master records or all customer master records, or a field in any other master record. There are thousands of master records.

2. Your company has introduced a new material, and today, the day the product launches, 10 units are to be sold to all of the existing 5,000 or so customers.

Mass Creation Orders

LSMW is not suitable for the mass creation orders if the numbers of items differ (that is, if in one order there are 5 items and in another there are 10). For this situation, use the functional module `BAPI_SALESDOCU_CREATEFROMDATA1`, `BAPI_SALESORDER_CREATE-FROMDAT1`, or `BAPI_SALESORDER_CREATEFROMDAT2`. Also note that you have to provide information on schedule lines, if relevant, because they're not created automatically while creating orders using any of the above function modules. The function module `GUI_UPLOAD` uploads data from your desktop to SAP ERP for mass creation of sales orders, credit memo requests, or other order types. An ABAP developer has to write a program using the function modules mentioned for mass creation of orders.

3. In your company, credit memos are blocked for posting by default. Upon creation, all of the credit memos for a month or week undergo verification. A senior manager verifies them using reports, and once they're verified, all documents release as soon as possible. Manually performing this task for thousands of documents will take hours, but with LSMW you can do it in minutes. You may reuse one LSMW recording created for this purpose week after week.

4. Every day, hundreds or thousands of sales orders undergo verification using reports and other information for credit release, and the documents not released are to be deleted. Deleting a few thousand orders will take a few minutes using an LSMW recording.

5. Every month, the prices (condition records) of the materials change. Thousands of condition records require modification.

Now that you understand the importance of LSMW, not only during implementation but also as a post-implementation optimizing tool, let's do an actual recording. We'll record a simple sequence of changing the field value of the SEARCH TERM 2 (KNA1-SORT2) field of a customer master record using Transaction VD02. We'll then use the recording to change this field in several customer master records. Let's walk through each step in the following subsections.

1. **Create project, subproject, and object for LSMW recording.**
   In this step, you create a new project, subproject, and object for LSMW. You can use an existing project or sub-project for a new object. These three elements identify a LSMW recording. The combination for an LSMW must be unique. SAP provided LSMW to transfer data from legacy systems to SAP ERP during an implementation project, so the project name can be the name of the SAP implementation project. The subproject name can be Z_MASTER_DATA for master data transfer. The object can be Z_CUST_MASTER for transferring customer master data to SAP ERP. Once the data is transferred from the legacy customer master data to SAP ERP, you can use the same project, subproject, and object to create a master data record in SAP ERP by providing the input for it in an Excel file.

   To start a recording, you need to create a project, subproject, and object to specify the recording. These values are important for using the recording in the future as well. By executing Transaction LSMW (you may get a welcome note), you go to the screen shown in Figure 8.16, where you can specify the project, subproject, and object. You can use any existing project and subproject to create a new object. After you enter these values in their respective fields, click on the CREATE icon. You'll get a dialog box to give the description for any or all of the three elements. Press ꜰ8 or click on the clock icon to reach the next screen, which lists all of the steps of the LSMW. By default, the MAINTAIN OBJECT ATTRIBUTES radio button will be selected. Press ꜰ8 or click on the clock icon to go to the screen shown in Figure 8.17.

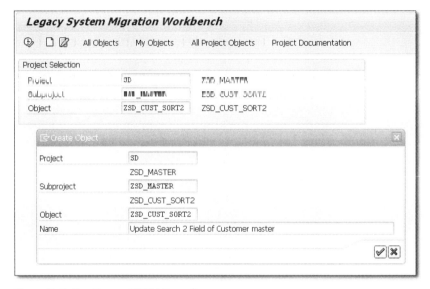

Figure 8.16 Creating an LSMW Recording

2. **Maintain object attributes.**

   In this step, you specify how the system provides data for the LSMW for input into SAP ERP. BAPIs, direct input, and batch input sessions are three other possible forms of data entry. We'll restrict our discussion to the batch input session method.

   In the screen shown in Figure 8.17, click on the DISPLAY/CHANGE button to make the screen ready for input, and select the BATCH INPUT RECORDING radio button. If you select the OVERVIEW icon to the right of it, you'll pull up a list of all existing recordings in the project you're in. You can create a new recording by clicking on the CREATE icon. In the dialog box that appears, give a name and description for the recording. In the next dialog box, enter the transaction code that you want to record and execute (e.g., VD02 to change the SEARCH 2 fields of existing customers).

This takes you to the initial screen of the transaction code. The initial screen will look slightly different than the initial screen of Transaction VD02, which is executed directly (not for the LSMW recording). The tabs that appear in Transaction VD02 for a customer master record will appear as the checkbox, when the same transaction is executed for the LSMW recording. Because you know that the SEARCH TERM 2 field is in the ADDRESS tab, select the ADDRESS checkbox only. Because the SORT2 field is also part of the central address management, select that check box as well. Specify the customer and the sales area (combination of sales organization, distribution channel, and division) and press Enter. You'll go to the ADDRESS tab of general data area, where you can enter some the new values for the customer in the SEARCH TERM 2 field, and then press Enter.

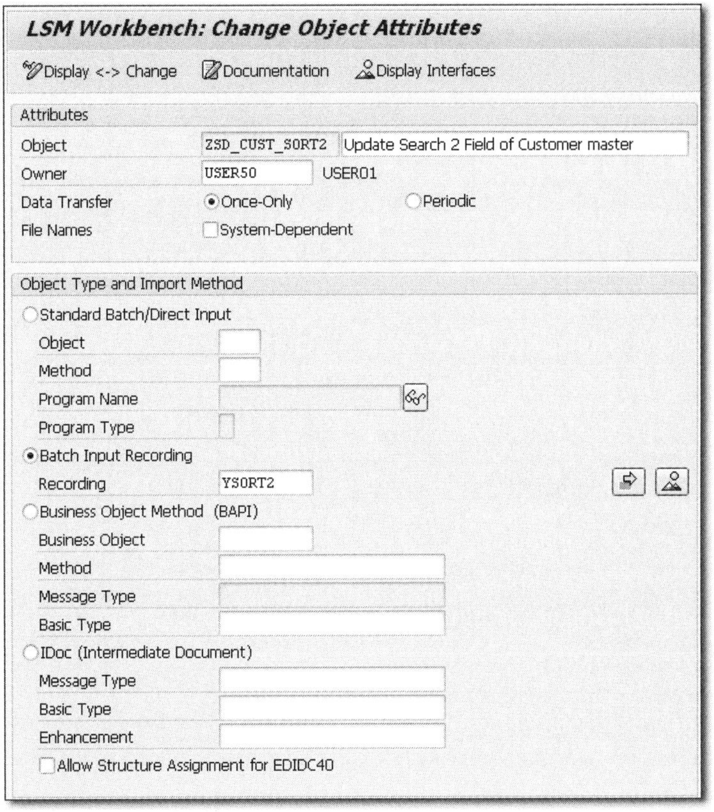

LSM Workbench: Change Object Attributes

Display <-> Change   Documentation   Display Interfaces

Attributes

Object	ZSD_CUST_SORT2	Update Search 2 Field of Customer master
Owner	USER50	USER01
Data Transfer	⦿ Once-Only	◯ Periodic
File Names	☐ System-Dependent	

Object Type and Import Method

◯ Standard Batch/Direct Input

Object

Method

Program Name

Program Type

⦿ Batch Input Recording

Recording   YSORT2

◯ Business Object Method (BAPI)

Business Object

Method

Message Type

Basic Type

◯ IDoc (Intermediate Document)

Message Type

Basic Type

Enhancement

☐ Allow Structure Assignment for EDIDC40

Figure 8.17 Maintain Object Attributes

You'll go to a screen similar to the one shown in Figure 8.18. If you click on the DEFAULT ALL button, you'll receive an information dialog and the field names. All of the fields in the ADDRESS tab will appear in the recording, and you should delete the fields, other than SORT2, by selecting the field in the screen and clicking on the DELETE SCREEN FIELD button. Make sure to save the setting, and then click on the back arrow to return to the previous screen. The list of existing recordings, along with the one you just created, will be there. Be sure to save, and then click on the back arrow, which will take you to the screen in Figure 8.17. You can arrow back to reach the screen where the LSMW steps are listed, which are no longer relevant for the batch input recording. The second radio button will be selected. Press [F8] or click on the clock icon to go to the next step.

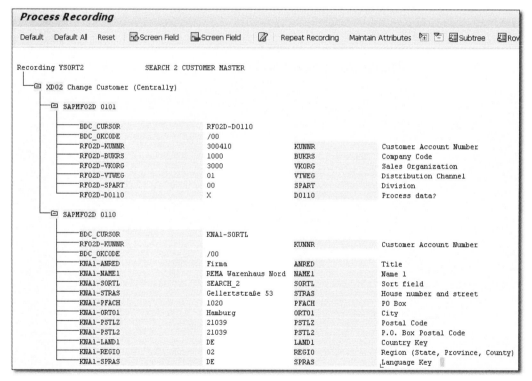

Figure 8.18 LSMW Recording

3. **Maintain source structures.**
In this step, you only give a name to the source structure; you'll define the

fields of the structure in the next step. After selecting the second radio button, you'll see a new screen. To change the mode, click on the CREATE icon, and you can specify the name of the structure and its description in the pop-up screen. Save the setting and click on the back arrow to go back to the initial screen.

4. **Maintain source fields.**

In this step, you define the fields for which you'll provide information. For example, while creating a customer master record, you might have to provide the values for 50 fields (e.g., customer group, default delivery plant, and so on). In some fields (e.g., sales organization may be only one and all customers can have only one value) you might assign a fixed value.

After selecting the radio button, you can create and assign fields to the structure already created. In change mode, select the source structure that you want to create fields for and click on the TABLE MAINTENANCE icon. In the table, you can enter the fields for the input file, whether the field will be a number or a character, and the number of characters allowed for the field. Save the setting and click on the back arrow.

> **Text Files**
>
> When you're in the screen that opens by clicking on the TABLE MAINTENANCE icon, you can upload a text file from your local system (e.g., desktop) to create fields. In this case, you'll see the following information dialog: "The file with the field definition must be structured as follows: Field Number (optional), Name, Description, Type, and Length. The columns must be separated by tabs."

If only one field (as in our example) or multiple fields require modification, you can create the fields one by one by clicking on the CREATE icon and filling the fields in the dialog box that appears.

5. **Maintain structure relations.**

In this step, the relationship between the source and a target structure is established, usually automatically. An error occurs if there's a difference in their fields or if they have same name.

This step occurs automatically if you've specified the name of the recording and completed the previous step correctly. Upon execution, you'll get to the screen shown in Figure 8.19, but in disabled mode. Click on the CHANGE DISPLAY icon and save, and then click on the back arrow.

Figure 8.19 Assign Structure to Batch Input Recording

6. **Maintain field mapping and conversion rules.**

In this step, you maintain how each field in the target structure will receive the input value from the source structure. You also specify whether data will move with or without any conversion. Once you've clicked on the back arrow in the previous step, you can click on the clock icon or press F8 (Figure 8.20). All of the fields in the recording that aren't deleted are available in display mode. Click on the CHANGE DISPLAY icon and select the field (e.g., KUNNR). An external data file provides the value, which in this example we defined as YSORT2.

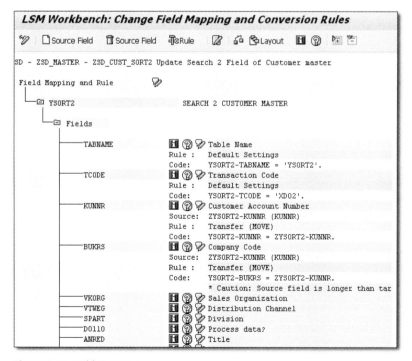

Figure 8.20 Field Mapping

YSORT2 contains two fields: KUNNR and SORT2. We've assumed that all of the customers are in same sales area. Click on the CREATE SOURCE FIELD button so that all of the fields in the source structure are available for selection. From here, you can click on the field that provides the data to the record. In this example, we want the KUNNR field (CUSTOMER) to provide data to the KUNNR field. You can see that one field is part of the external data file, which is the source, and the other is the target field. Both names can be different, although usually they are given the same name. In this example, we've also given the same name, YSORT2, to the batch input recording and the data structure to avoid confusion.

Once you select the field, the source field name will appear next to the target field. For this example, we're simply transferring (moving) a source field to a target field without any modification.

For the next three fields (sales organization, distribution channel, and division) we'll use the fixed values based on these assumptions. To fix the value, select the field, click on the RULES button, and select the CONSTANT radio button. You'll get a dialog box to specify the constant, where you can enter the value for the constant (e.g., 7000 for sales organization). Repeat the step for all fields, and be sure to save. From there, simply arrow back to reach the next step.

7. **Maintain fixed values, translations, and user-defined routines.**
The next step, which is optional, is to maintain the fixed values, translations, and user-defined routines. Normally, with the two rules we discussed in the previous step (move and constant), you can manage data uploads. For example, in a legacy system you had stored the minimum order quantity in material master records in terms of kilograms, and in SAP ERP want to maintain the same in terms of cartons equal to 10 kg. The data is to be converted suitably using these functionalities. By taking advantage of user-defined routines, you can achieve very complex conversions with the help of ABAP developer.

Reusing Among Objects

When you specify certain values, translations, and routines for an object in this step, you can use them for any other object created in the same project.

With this or the previous step, the LSMW object is ready for use.

8. **Specify files.**
In this step, you specify the physical location of the file that will provide the input data. It can be on your local system or on a system that your local system can access. For example, the path to your desktop file can be *C:\Documents and*

Settings\Admin\Desktop\upload.txt. The upload.txt is the actual file that provided the information to be uploaded in correct format.

The next step is to specify the files. Simply click on the SPECIFY FILE button in the initial screen for the LSMW recording and specify the file you want to use. You'll reach the screen shown in Figure 8.21 in disabled mode. Click on the CHANGE DISPLAY icon, and execute the following steps to upload data from a text file from your PC:

▷ Click on LEGACY DATA.

▷ Click on the CREATE icon. The dialog box shown in Figure 8.21 appears.

▷ In the FILE field, specify the path where you have stored the files that contain all of the data. In this case, we're using KUNNR and NEW value.

▷ Name the file (e.g., ZSORT). Note: This has nothing to do the file name of the data file to be uploaded.

▷ If you want the first row of the file to specify the heading (e.g., KUNNR, SORT2), select the FIELD NAMES AT START OF FILE checkbox.

▷ Save and then click on the back arrow to reach the initial screen.

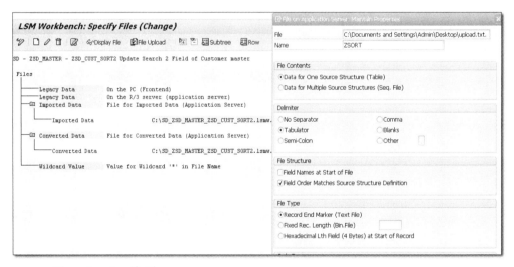

Figure 8.21 Specify File

Modifying Paths and Files

You may occasionally have to change the path and the files specified in this step. To do this, double-click on the file name (in enable mode). The dialog box shown in Figure 8.21 will appear.

9. **Assign files.**

This step is typically to display or check that the file you specified in the previous step receives the correct assignment. File assignment is automatic. Just execute, click on CHANGE DISPLAY icon, save, and click on the back arrow.

10. **Read data.**

In this step, the system reads the data from the file (upload.txt file in step 8). If you change any data in the source file after this step, the change will not go to SAP ERP system.

The next step is to read the data. Select the READ DATA radio button, which takes you to a screen where you can restrict the data that is read. Normally, the whole file is read, so don't put any restriction on it. Leave all of the fields blank, and unselect all of the checkboxes. The data stored in the text file on your PC will be read, and you'll see the information on the screen as shown in Figure 8.22. The screen shows that we stored new values for SEARCH TERM 2 for nine customers. If this is not true, you can verify that text file. It may contain some blank spaces if the number is just one more than the records (or rows) you've stored.

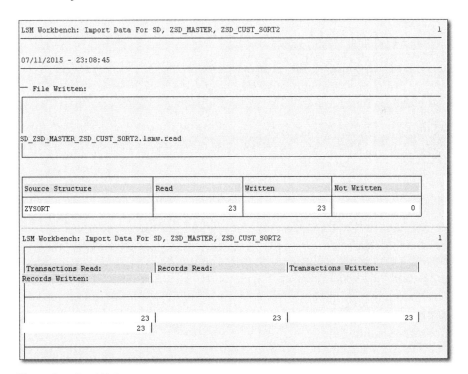

Figure 8.22 Read Data

11. **Display read data.**

This step allows you to manually check that everything read by SAP ERP in the previous step is correct. Errors can occur for various reasons. For example, let's say you're using tab-separated text files for data input and, instead of one tab, there are two between two fields (e.g., SALES ORG and DISTRIBUTION CHANNEL). This will result in the value intended for the DISTRIBUTION CHANNEL field going to the next field (which may be DIVISION) and produce an error.

Displaying the read data is optional. On execution, all of the data read in the previous step displays. Click on any row to go to the screen shown in Figure 8.23. The system provides an intermediate screen where you can restrict the number of displayed rows. Simply press Enter to ignore that screen. Be sure to check a few records carefully, because if the wrong target field populates the SOURCE field, it can lead to serious problems.

Figure 8.23 Display Read Data

12. **Convert data.**

In this step, you execute actual data conversion, as per different routines, rules, or other objects that you may have used in the LSMW. For example, data read as 100 may become 10 after conversion, which may be what you want.

The next step is to convert the data. In addition to the data from the external file, the system also reads the fields that maintain constant values. After executing this step, you can restrict the number of transactions. Each record (or row) in the data file will run the transaction (in our case VD02) once. So the transaction here actually means the number of rows in your data file. Click on the EXECUTION (clock) icon, and you'll retrieve the information on the number of rows and records processed. It should tally with your earlier number, which in this case, is nine.

13. **Display converted data.**

   In this step, you can display the data after conversion for any possible error. Once you see that the data has been converted, you can move to the next step, which is optional. It's similar to displaying the read data. Here, in addition to the data received from the external source, you can see the fields with constant values. Click on a few records to ensure that the data will populate the target fields correctly.

14. **Create batch input session.**

   The batch input session is the step when the transaction (VD02 in our case) is executed some number of times, depending upon the input file. This may take few minutes or several hours, depending on the amount of data input. Various functionalities are available, such as to skip a step if an error occurs, to stop the session if an error occurs, and so on. In this step, you actually customize how the session will run; for example, whether it will be executed in the background. After completing this step, you will reach Figure 8.24. You can reuse the batch input file and folder by selecting the KEEP BATCH INPUT FOLDER(S)? checkbox. Once executed, you'll receive the confirmation message, "1 batch input session with X transaction created," where X is the number of records or rows in your data file.

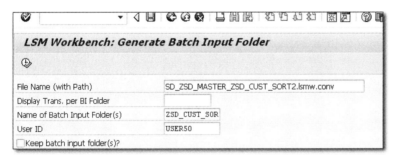

Figure 8.24 Generate Batch Input File

15. **Run batch input session.**

   Next, you need to run the batch input session. Select the batch input session created in the previous step and click on the PROCESS button. You'll see a dialog box asking you to specify if the processing should occur in the foreground or background. We recommend the DISPLAY ERROR ONLY option for practical reasons (for performance and to display errors and escape when an error occurs).

Finally, you get a confirmation message: "Processing of batch input session completed." In the session overview window, you can see the number of successful (green checkmark column) and failed (red zig-zag arrow column) transactions (or records, or rows).

8.4   Numbering Objects

Before we discuss number ranges and numbering objects, let's start with a warning: *do not transport numbering objects.*

It's a standard practice to develop and test the customization in development and quality servers before transporting it to production for use. This general principle does not apply to numbering objects. The SAP system does give you the option to create a transport request for numbering objects. In the production environment, use of a number range will be different from that in development. Suppose you created a numbering object and number range in development for a sales order and transported it to production: in the next month, you may have 100 orders created in production and only 10 in development. Suppose you made some changes in the object and again transported it after one month: the last number used for the number range will be 10 in production. The usage level (10) in development will overwrite the actual use (100) in production. This will happen for all of the number ranges in the numbering object. So, when you try to create an order after transportation, it will show an error, and the order will not be saved. If the numbering object also contains number ranges for delivery or billing documents, you might also have a similar problem while creating those documents.

The cockpit transaction for number objects is Transaction SNRO or menu path SAP Easy Access • Tools • ABAP Workbench • Development • Number Ranges, as shown in Figure 8.25. You'll receive more than a thousand standard numbering objects, which fulfill various purposes. The most important number range object of the Sales and Distribution functionality in SAP ERP is RV_BELEG (number ranges for sales and distribution documents). Each number range object contains several number ranges, identified by a string of two characters. You can customize each number range by specifying a first (from number) and a last number. You also specify whether it's assigned externally. The system automatically updates usage information for number ranges that are not external. The current last number is displayed (in modifiable mode); a number range to be used for the documents in the Sales and Distribution functionality in SAP ERP (e.g., sales, delivery, and billing documents) must be present in the RV_BELEG numbering object (or number range object). Similarly, all of the standard numbering objects have a specific purpose. You can add, delete, and modify number ranges in numbering objects. The number ranges of a numbering object should not overlap, so you don't have same number for order, delivery, and billing. You can have the same number for a billing document and accounting document. The number range object for accounting document is RF_BELEG.

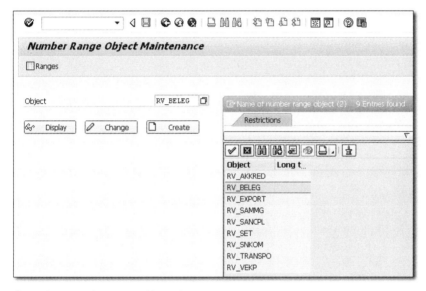

Figure 8.25 Number Range Object Maintenance

Numbering Object

In several places, we have specified the numbering object in addition to the transaction for maintaining the specific number range. Therefore, it's easier for you to maintain them from the single cockpit transaction (SNRO). For example, the transactions for maintaining RV_BELEG (sales document number ranges) and RF_BELEG (accounting document number ranges) are VN01 and FBN1, respectively. You can maintain both using Transaction SNRO.

When you're in the screen displayed in Figure 8.25, you can perform the following actions:

1. Maintain number ranges by clicking on the Ranges button in the application toolbar.

2. Display all of the existing number range objects by clicking on the Overview icon in the application toolbar.

3. Create a new number range object by clicking on the Create icon.

4. Change an existing number range object by clicking on the Change icon.

5. Display an existing number range object by clicking on the Display icon.

In the next two sections, we'll discuss how to maintain number ranges and how to create new number range objects.

8.4.1 Maintain Number Ranges

When you're in the number range object maintenance screen (Figure 8.25), enter the numbering object (e.g., RV_BELEG) in the Object field and click on the Ranges button to go to the tools for number ranges (see Figure 8.26).

Figure 8.26 Tools for Number Ranges

Here you have the following options:

1. Obtain an overview of the existing number ranges by clicking on the Overview icon in the application toolbar.

2. Display the existing number ranges by clicking on the Intervals button. You'll go to a screen similar to the one shown in Figure 8.27. All of the columns in that screen will be in display-only mode.

3. Change the number ranges by clicking on the Change Intervals button. You'll go to the screen shown in Figure 8.27.

4. Change the status of the current number by clicking on the Change NR Status button. You'll go to a screen similar to the one shown in Figure 8.27.

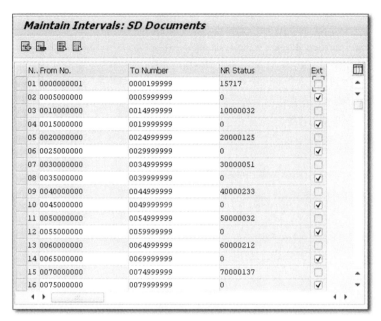

Figure 8.27 Maintain Number Range Intervals

When you reach the screen shown in Figure 8.27, you can do the following:

1. Change the FROM NUMBER if the number range is not yet in use.

2. Change the TO NUMBER if the new interval does not overlap any other range. You will receive an error message if it overlaps any other range.

3. Select or unselect the EXT checkbox if the number range is not yet in use. Selecting the checkbox will make an existing internal number range external. Unselecting it will convert an existing external number range to an internal number range.

4. Add a new number range by clicking on the INSET LINE icon in the application icon. You should provide a new two-character key for the number range and specify the start and end number of the range. You'll receive an error message if the new interval overlaps any existing one. You also specify whether it should be an external number range.

5. Delete an existing number range by selecting the number range and then clicking on the DELETE icon in the application toolbar if the current number is zero.

> **Function Modules**
>
> You can also use the following function modules for maintaining number range objects using an ABAP program.
>
> ▶ NUMBER_RANGE_OBJECT_MAINTAIN
> ▶ NUMBER_RANGE_OBJECT_CLOSE
> ▶ NUMBER_RANGE_OBJECT_DELETE
> ▶ NUMBER_RANGE_OBJECT_INIT
> ▶ NUMBER_RANGE_OBJECT_LIST
> ▶ NUMBER_RANGE_OBJECT_READ
> ▶ NUMBER_RANGE_OBJECT_UPDATE

> **Number Range**
>
> Even when a number range has been used, you can change the current number to zero and then delete it. There will be no error message.

8.4.2 Create Number Range Objects

You can create number ranges objects to provide number ranges to customized, country-specific official document types, or when there are too many number ranges in the number range objects for the Sales and Distribution RV_BELEG numbering object. There can be a maximum of 1296 number ranges. To create number range object, follow these steps:

1. From the initial screen, enter a proposed new name for the numbering object in the OBJECT field.

2. Click on the CREATE icon in the screen shown in Figure 8.25, which takes you to the NUMBER RANGE OBJECT screen (Figure 8.29).

3. Provide a short and a long description.

4. Customize the INTERVAL CHARACTERISTICS, CUSTOMIZING SPECIFICATIONS, and GROUP SPECIFICATION fields. If the group specifications are maintained, you can also maintain the text specifications.

We'll discuss the importance of each field in the fourth step in the following four sections.

Interval Characteristics

In this step, you can customize the behavior of the number ranges that will be created within this numbering object.

▸ The SUBOBJECT DATA ELEMENT field provides a subobject for the object (numbering object). For example, you can use VKORG (sales organization) as a subobject. In that case, you may use the same number range (e.g., 01) for several sales organizations. The initial screen for maintaining number ranges looks like Figure 8.28, instead of Figure 8.26, when VKORG is used as a subobject. A number range created in this numbering object is only valid for the subobject for which it is created.

Figure 8.28 Initial Screen for Maintenance of a Numbering Object with the Subobject Sales Organization

▸ The NUMBER LENGTH DOMAIN field determines the maximum number of digits or characters that the number range object can contain (e.g., NUM10 for numeric 10-digit numbers, CHAR10 for alphanumeric 10-character keys).

▸ The WARNING % field determines the percentage of unused numbers, relative to the total number in a number range (of this object), at which users start receiving warning messages.

▸ The TO-YEAR FLAG checkbox determines if the number range repeats itself every (fiscal) year. Select this checkbox to create the number range object for an accounting document. To use the numbering object in the Sales and Distribution functionality in SAP ERP, do not select this checkbox. During the number range maintenance, in addition to what we've specified in previous sections, there is another TO YEAR column. This column appears between the NUMBER RANGE CODE/KEY and the FROM NUMBER columns.

▸ Select the NO INTERVAL ROLLING checkbox to prevent the numbering object's number range from repeating itself once it reaches the upper limit.

Customizing Specifications

If you select CUSTOMIZING tab in Figure 8.29, you can specify whether a customized transaction will maintain this object, the usage level at which the warning issues, and whether (and how much) buffering is required.

▸ The NUMBER RANGE (NR) TRANSACTION field contains the name of the customized transaction for the new numbering object. You can also use Transaction SNRO for maintenance.

▸ Select the MAIN MEMORY BUFFERING dropdown if you require buffering. To deactivate it, review SAP Note 23835.

▸ The NO. OF NUMBERS IN BUFFER field determines the number of numbers blocked in buffering. Sometimes you'll find an invoice number or delivery number skipping a fixed amount of numbers (e.g., 5 or 10). Rectify this error by temporarily deleting the number specified in this field. To remove buffering, use the menu path EDIT • SET-UP BUFFERING • NO BUFFERING.

Buffering

By default, SAP delivers the `RV_BELEG` and `RF_BELEG` numbering objects with buffering, but you can deactivate buffering using the procedure explained in SAP Notes 23835 and 424486. This becomes a necessity if you observe invoice numbers, or any other document numbers, that are not continuous. There might be some unused numbers. In some cases, you're legally required to have these documents continuously numbered. For example, you might find that the generated invoice numbers are `1001`, `1005`, `1010`, and so on, instead of, `1001`, `1002`, `1003`, and so on. This is usually due to buffering.

Group Specification

The fields in the GROUP tab in Figure 8.29, are optional. You can create a number range object without specifying them. Here you'll find the customized Z-tables created for storing the number ranges.

▸ The group table must be a table with FLD NORANGEELEMENT as a key element (e.g., Customized Z-table). The table with the `KTOKD` field of table `T077D` can be specified for a numbering object that is to contain number ranges for customer master records.

▸ The SUBOBJECT field in group table specifies any other key field.

▸ In the FLD NORANGEELEMENT field, you specify the key field for the number range object. For example, in the customer master record, the customer account group determines the relevant number range object. If the number range you're creating numbers customers in customer master records, fill it with KTOKD (customer account group).

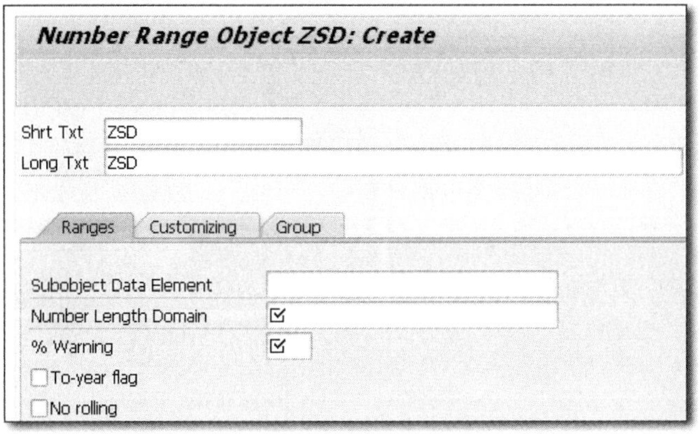

Figure 8.29 Creating Number Range Objects

- The FIELDS INT./EXT. NO.RANGE NO. fields contain a number range for internal and external number ranges. (For example, in the customized table you can specify the NUMKI and NUMKE fields of table T134 as internal and external number range numbers).

- FLD. NORANGENO (Field for Number Range Number) is the field in the group table (see the first item of this list) that stores the number range numbers.

- The DISPLAY ELEMENT TEXT checkbox, when selected, displays the preceding five fields with text during number range maintenance.

8.5 Summary

We started the chapter taking the steps to customize condition techniques for text processing. You can now automatically bring correct text to your documents. For message control, we discussed how to customize IDoc interfaces and use EDI and ALE for communication.

In the section on ABAP tools, we discussed Sales and Distribution user exits and debugging, and listed the steps for LSMW. With this knowledge, you should be able to identify the appropriate user exit for using customized coding by ABAP developers. You can now also use LSMW optimally and debug ABAP programs for errors.

Finally, you learned how to maintain different number ranges and how to customize numbering objects so that you can create and maintain any number range objects and number ranges in SAP ERP.

Now, let's move on to the next chapter, where we'll discuss reports and analysis.

This chapter will cover the reporting and analysis tools available for Sales and Distribution—including enhancements brought by SAP HANA—and how to use them optimally.

9   Reporting and Analysis

Reporting and analysis help users extract information they need and present it in a way that's easy to understand and utilize.

In this chapter, we'll start off by looking at standard reports, since only after you familiarize yourself with standard reports and analyses can you develop your own. The following three sections will teach you the three approaches to creating your own report; you'll learn how to create an ABAP query, how to use the Sales Information System for reporting, and how to create BI queries. We've provided very simple examples, so you'll be able to follow along and ultimately be able to create reports by yourself, starting with simple cases and gradually working toward tougher ones.

After learning this information, you'll be better prepared to team up with technical resources to create better reports. At the end of the chapter, we will look at operative reporting using SAP Business Explorer, SAP HANA, and SAP BW.

9.1   Useful Standard Reports

You can broadly divide SAP standard reports into four categories: lists, work lists, analyses, and display documents.

The standard reports and analyses offer you a variety of features and tools to help you meet your individual reporting and analysis requirements. You should have two basic objectives for studying standard reports:

1. The more you know about the standard reports and their features, the more reporting requirements you'll be able to fulfill with the standard reports. Therefore, there will be less of a need to develop customized reports.

2. While designing the customized report, this information will help you design better reports.

In the next two sections, we'll discuss different categories of standard reports.

9.1.1 Classification of Standard Reports

It's important to be able to identify the differences between the four types of reports so that you can choose which is best for you.

Lictc

A list is typically considered a report. There is a selection screen where you can specify your requirements. For example, you may be interested in listing the OR-type orders (first restriction) created between 01.01.2015 and 01.31.2015 (second restriction). To create this, use Transaction SDO1, as shown in Figure 1.1, and take the following steps:

1. Enter the OR value in the DOCUMENT TYPE field.

2. Enter "01.01.2015" in the first window in the CREATED ON field.

3. Enter "01.31.2015" in the second window in the CREATED ON field.

4. Leave other fields (CREATED BY and ORGANIZATIONAL DATA) blank. By doing so, you allow the list to contain sales orders matching your selection or restriction criteria from any sales area (combination of sales organization, distribution channel, and division). Documents created by any user will display.

   By clicking on the EXECUTE icon (far left in the application toolbar) or pressing the F8 key, you'll see your list, as shown in Figure 9.2.

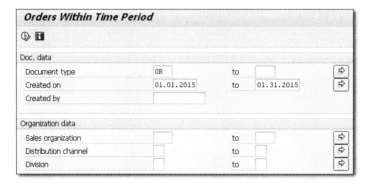

Figure 9.1 Initial Selection Screen (Transaction SDO1)

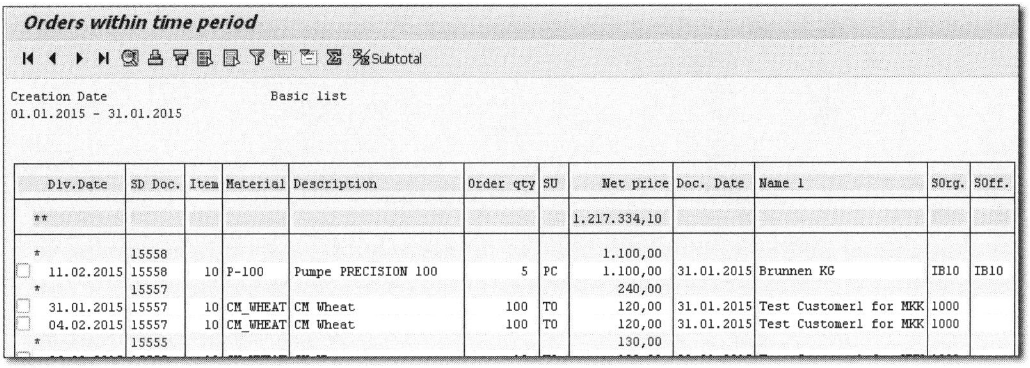

Figure 9.2 List of Orders within Time Period (Transaction SDO1)

There are several standard reports in the Sales and Distribution functionality of SAP ERP. Table 9.1 lists the most common ones, with a brief description.

Transaction	Description
VA55N	Item Proposal – List by Material
VD59	List Customer-Material-Info
VA45N	List of Contracts
VB(8	List Rebate Agreements
VB35	Promotion List
VB25	List of Sales Deals
VA15N	Inquiries List
V.03	Incomplete Inquiries
VA25N	Quotations List
V.04	Incomplete Quotations
VA05N	List of Sales Orders
SDO1	Orders within Time Period
V.02	Incomplete Orders
VA35	List of Scheduling Agreements
V.05	Incomplete Scheduling Agreements
VA45N	List of Contracts
V.06	Incomplete Contracts

Table 9.1 Standard List Transactions

Transaction	Description
V.00	Incomplete SD Documents
V_UC	Incomplete Outbound Deliveries
VF05	List of Billing Documents
VF25	List of Invoice Lists

Table 9.1 Standard List Transactions (Cont.)

Work Lists

The purpose of lists is simply to illustrate or display information. Work lists, on the other hand, allow you to process the information.

The initial step for work lists is the same as for the list transaction. You can specify the selection criteria and execute the task by pressing F8. The list of orders, deliveries, billing documents, or any other document of the Sales and Distribution functionality that matches your selection criteria appears in the list. Once the list appears, you can select the documents you want to further process (i.e., post goods issue or release credit blocks per the specific work list transaction).

You may restrict some work list transactions to being lists by authorization management. Delivery due lists and billing due lists, for example, create multiple deliveries and billings, respectively. Someone who has to create hundreds of deliveries and/or billings daily will find them very useful. You can try a few examples of work lists in Table 9.2.

Transaction	Description
VL10A	Sales Orders Due for Delivery
VL10B	Stock Transfer Orders Due for Delivery
VL10G	Documents Due for Delivery
VL06G	List of Outbound Deliveries for Goods Issue
VKM1	Blocked SD Documents (Credit Management)
VF04	Process Billing Due List
VF24	Edit Work List for Invoice Lists
VFX3	List Blocked Billing Documents
VF31	Output from Billing Documents

Table 9.2 Examples of Work Lists

Analyses

Analyses, or functional analyses, are available in the various transaction screens for specific analyses. There are several important types of analyses available in the Sales and Distribution functionality in SAP ERP.

A *pricing analysis* can be called from sales and billing documents. In pricing analysis, the pricing procedure used for the particular item and the condition types it contains are displayed on the left side of the window, as shown in Figure 9.3. For each condition type, you'll find the accesses made in the folder with same name as the condition type. There are subfolders with the same name as the different accesses. The analysis displays whether the condition record was found for a particular access. The access details are displayed on the right side of the screen, including details of the access made for the particular document.

You go to Figure 9.3 by clicking on the ANALYSIS button at the bottom of the ITEM CONDITION screen. When a user complains about the wrong price being determined in a document item, you can use pricing analysis to find the cause of the error. The error can be due to an incorrect condition record, a wrong access sequence, or an error in a pricing procedure. It can also be due to an error in the customer master record of the sold-to party and/or material master records of the material used in the item. This can result in the selection of the wrong pricing procedure. The rectification will also prevent the error from reoccurring in a similar situation.

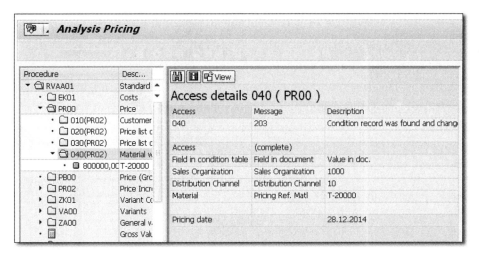

Figure 9.3 Pricing Analysis

You may perform an *account determination analysis* for orders and billing documents. As shown in Figure 9.4, you can access the screen for account determination analysis by going to ENVIRONMENT • ANALYSIS • ACCOUNT DETERMINATION from the sales order overview screen. For a billing document, the menu path is ENVIRONMENT • ACCOUNT DETERMINATION ANALYSIS • REVENUE ACCOUNT from the initial or overview screen. In both cases, the GL to which the postings are made are shown. The screen also shows the details about the other elements of the condition technique, including the determination procedure, condition type, access sequence, and access details used for account determination for a particular item of the document.

The ACCOUNT DETERMINATION ANALYSIS screen often comes into play during error analysis. If the user tells you that proper GLs are not posting in a particular document, you can find the cause of the error. The error may be due to the determination of the wrong account determination procedure, incorrect sequencing in the access sequence, or an error in some other step. Once you find the error, you can rectify it so that the error will not occur in the future for similar documents.

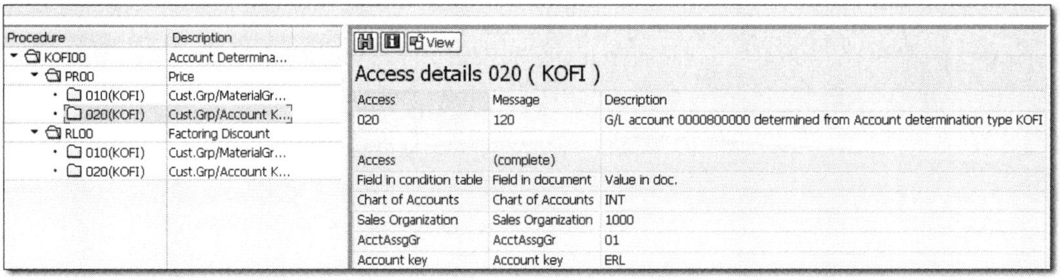

Figure 9.4 Account Determination Analysis

Output determination analysis and *output processing analysis* are available for all of the output objects (e.g., order – header, order – item, delivery – header, delivery – item, etc.) for which the output type is available. In output determination analysis, you receive information about how the particular output was determined (or failed to be determined). In output processing analysis, the sequence shows how the output processes. You can use output determination analysis following these menu paths for the output objects:

▶ **Sales order – header**
   EXTRAS • OUTPUT • HEADER • EDIT from the order overview screen

▶ **Sales order – item**

EXTRAS • OUTPUT • ITEM • EDIT from the order overview screen selecting the particular item

▶ **Delivery – header**

EXTRAS • DELIVERY OUTPUT • HEADER from the delivery overview screen

▶ **Delivery – item**

EXTRAS • DELIVERY OUTPUT • ITEM from the delivery overview screen selecting the particular item

▶ **Billing – header**

GOTO • HEADER • OUTPUT from the billing overview screen

Following these menu paths, you'll see a screen similar to the background of Figure 9.6. From that screen, you can follow the menu path GOTO • DETERMIN. ANALYSIS to go to the screen shown in Figure 9.5.

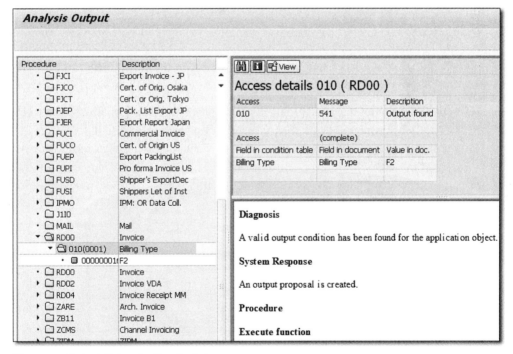

Figure 9.5 Output Determination Analysis

Output processing analysis shows the sequence of events that took place during output processing. It shows the error (or warning), if any occurred during processing.

You can follow the same menu path as for output determination analysis, but you should select PROCESSING LOG, rather than DETERMIN.ANALYSIS, in the final step.

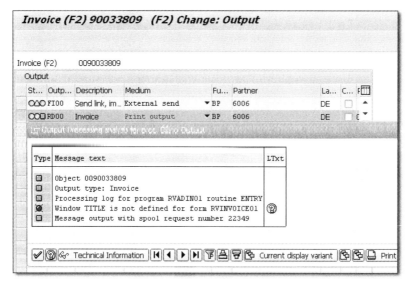

Figure 9.6 Output Processing Analysis

Incompleteness analysis is also called *incompletion log*. It's available for several functions, including sales orders, deliveries, foreign trade, and so on. We've highlighted the INCOMPLETENESS ANALYSIS icon in the FOREIGN TRADE/CUSTOMS tab of the ITEM DETAILS screen for a delivery item in Figure 9.7. When you click on this icon, you see the dialog box shown in Figure 9.7.

Figure 9.7 Incompleteness Analysis (Foreign Trade)

Display Documents

Most documents can be opened in display mode. A separate transaction code and authorization management for the display option make it very useful, especially in a production environment. Consultants normally have restrictive authorization for display-only in production servers. Changes to any document in the production client by a person other than the actual user is not advisable.

You can call all of the analyses discussed so far from the display mode of the document. Many of the lists and work lists discussed so far are also available from the transaction to create, change, or display a document. For instance, you can execute the list of billing documents (Transaction VF05) by going to ENVIRONMENT • LIST BILLING DOCUMENTS from the overview screen of any billing document using Transaction VF03. Individual documents frequently use the following functionalities:

- **Status overview**
  The status of a document stored in tables VBUK (header) and VBUP (item) can be displayed for an individual document.

- **Changes**
  You can display changes to a particular document or master data record by going to ENVIRONMENT • CHANGES.

- **Document flow**
  The DOCUMENT FLOW icon is present in most SAP documents, such as orders, deliveries, and invoices. It's available on the application toolbar in the overview screen. It's possible to display the document flow at both the header and item level. To display document flow at the item level, select the item first and then click on the DOCUMENT FLOW icon, or follow the menu path ENVIRONMENT • DISPLAY DOCUMENT FLOW ORDERS AND INVOICES. For deliveries, go to ENVIRONMENT • DOCUMENT FLOW. In all of these cases, access the menu path from the overview screen.

- **Accounting document overview (for billing document)**
  To display the accounting document in the invoice's initial or overview screen,

you can click on the ACCOUNTING button in the application toolbar, which will get you the dialog box shown in Figure 9.8. You can also follow the menu path GOTO • ACCOUNTING OVERVIEW from the overview screen. The dialog box contains a list of documents from the following components:

▶ Accounting

▶ Profit Center Accounting

▶ Controlling

▶ Profitability Analysis

▶ Fund Management and other components, if applicable

If you double-click on any accounting document, the document is displayed.

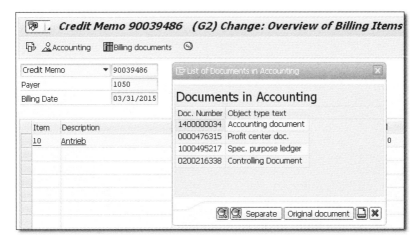

Figure 9.8 List of Documents in Accounting for Billing Document

▶ **Stock overview**
You can call a stock overview (Transaction MMBE) from a delivery for an individual item by going to ENVIRONMENT • STOCK.

▶ **Master record display**
You can display the customer master records and material master records from the individual document. For individual items, you can use the following menu paths for material master records.

▶ Order: ENVIRONMENT • DISPLAY MATERIAL

▶ Delivery: ENVIRONMENT • MATERIAL MASTER DATA

To display customer master records, you can use the following menu paths:

- ▶ Order: ENVIRONMENT • PARTNER • DISPLAY SOLD-TO PARTY/SHIP-TO PARTY/ PAYER/BILL-TO PARTY/CREDIT ACCOUNT
- ▶ Delivery: ENVIRONMENT • SHIP-TO PARTY

9.1.2 Features Available in Standard Reports

Several features are available in different standard reports. We'll now discuss a few of them.

- ▶ **Drill-down**

  In most standard reports, if you click on any document number in a list, you'll go to that individual document. This feature is called drill-down. There can be several levels in a drill-down report. These reports are very useful to account auditors, who often need to check the details of individual figures (e.g., sales revenue) that go into balance sheets or profit and loss accounts.

- ▶ **Changing layout**

  We'll discuss this in depth in Section 9.2.6. By changing the layout, you customize your output for the report to display only the fields that you're interested in.

- ▶ **Search**

  The SEARCH icon allows you to search in a list. In a large list, if you want to find out where a particular word or figure (e.g., 7803) occurs, doing it manually will take a lot time.

- ▶ **Sort**

  You can select a column in a list and click on the ASCENDING or DESCENDING SORT icon to sort the list.

- ▶ **Filter**

  You can use the FILTER icon to reduce the list as per the filter condition. For example, let's say you have a list of documents from several sales organizations. In a filtering condition, you can define, "sales organization = 1000." The list will now display only the documents of sales organization 1000.

- ▶ **Total and subtotal**

  Any numeric field can be summed up by selecting the column and clicking on the TOTAL icon. When at least one column is summed up, you can use the SUB-TOTAL icon by selecting any field and clicking the SUBTOTAL icon. The fields that are already summed up will now show the subtotals. Each unique entry in the column that has been subtotaled will have a subtotal value in the column.

▸ **Print**
Use the PRINT icon to print the list.

▸ **Report in Excel/Lotus**
You can display and directly modify many standard reports directly using Lotus Notes or Microsoft Excel.

▸ **Exporting to other applications**
You can send the report to other applications, such as Excel, Word, or HTML documents. You can also save it on the local system or send it by mail.

▸ **Graphical presentation**
You can present the report graphically using standard 2D and 3D diagrams, such as pie charts or bar diagrams.

9.2 Developing Reports Using Queries

To create a simple query (also called an SAP or ABAP query), execute Transaction SQVI, which is shown in Figure 9.9. You can also access it by executing Transaction SQ01 and then clicking on the QUICK VIEWER button.

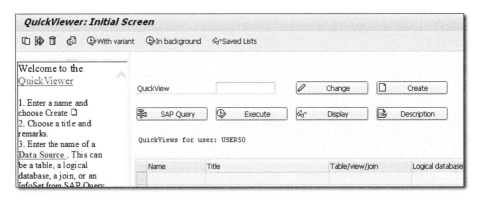

Figure 9.9 Initial Screen for SAP Query

As an example, we'll use a simple case of creating a query and attaching it to a Z-transaction. Suppose one of your accounts auditors wants to see a list of customers in your SAP system, but not in the Sales and Distribution functionality; for example, customers created for sales of assets would fall under this category. There can be few such customers in your system. You might require the report to find customers with incomplete master data records. Customers created with Transaction FD01 won't have the sales area view and won't be available to the Sales and Distribution functionality. The accounting department uses these customers. All customers created in SAP systems create an entry in table KNA1, and those created for the Sales and Distribution functionality create an entry in table KNVV, in addition to table KNA1. Therefore, you can download the two lists and compare them using the CUSTOMER CODE (KUNNR) field, which is present in both tables.

But what if you require the report on a monthly, or even daily, basis? The method in this case is to create an ABAP report. However, we'll show you a second viable option of doing the same thing using a query. The general steps for creating a query are as follows:

1. Create the query.

2. Decide on a data source.

3. Insert the tables you want in Basis mode.

4. Join tables.

5. Select the list and selection fields.

6. Modify the look of the list in layout mode.

7. Create a Z-transaction for the query.

Now let's look at each of these steps in greater detail.

9.2.1 Create Query

When you're in the screen shown in Figure 9.9, enter a name in the QUICKVIEW field (in this case, ZOSS) and click on the CREATE button. You'll see a dialog box similar to the one shown in Figure 9.10.

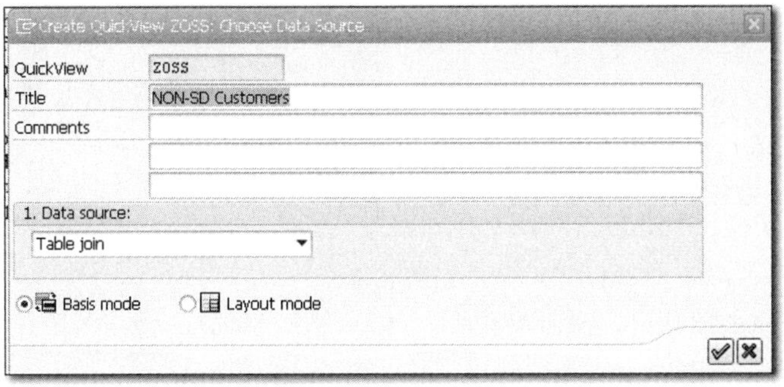

Figure 9.10 Selecting Data Source (Table Join)

9.2.2 Data Source

When you reach the dialog box shown in Figure 9.10, you can decide on the data source you want to use in the query. The data source can be any of the following four options:

▸ **Table or table view**

Because the table or table view can be displayed using Transactions SE16 or SE16N, this option is not practical. But remember, there are some useful standard table views, such as VBRK-VBRP, which is a table join of VBRK (billing documents – header) and VBRP (billing document – items)

▸ **Logical database**

There are more than 200 standard logical databases. When you select this option, you're asked to provide the name of the logical database. You can click on the DISPLAY button next to the field to provide a logical database, which takes you to Figure 9.11. The logical database (DDF, in this example) stores all of the master data and transaction-related accounting data (tables BKPF and BSEG). Logical database queries tend to execute very quickly.

Display Logical Database DDF

☜ 🗗 ♧   📃Source code   Selections 📋Sel.Texts   📘Documentation

| Management | Structure | Search help | Currency/quantity fields |

Node name	Table / Type	Node ty...	Short text
▾ KNA1	KNA1	Table	General Data in Customer Master
• ADDR1_VAL	ADDR1_VAL	Table	Address Data
• KNAS	KNAS	Table	Customer Master (VAT Registration Nos Gen. Sel.)
• KNKA	KNKA	Table	Customer Master Credit Management: Central Data
• KNKK	KNKK	Table	Credit Management Cust. Mstr: Control Area Data
• KNBK	KNBK	Table	Customer Master (Bank Details)
▾ KNB1	KNB1	Table	Customer Master (Company Code)
• KNB4	KNB4	Table	Customer Payment History
• KNB5	KNB5	Table	Customer Master (Dunning Data)
• KNC1	KNC1	Table	Customer Master (Transaction Figures)
• KNC3	KNC3	Table	Customer Master (Special G/L Transaction Figures)
▾ BSID	BSID	Table	Accounting: Secondary Index for Customers
• ADMI_FILES	ADMI_FILES	Table	Archive Files
• BSIDEXT	BSIDEXT	Table	Secondary Index & Additions Section (bsega)
▾ BKPF	BKPF	Table	Accounting Document Header
▾ BSEG	BSEG	Table	Accounting Document Segment
• WITH_ITEM	WITH_ITEM	Table	Witholding Tax Info.per W/Tax Type and FI Line Itm
• GSEG	GSEG	Table	Offsetting Items for B-Segment in Reporting

Figure 9.11 Logical Database DDF (Customer Database)

▸ **SAP query InfoSet**

You may reuse any query InfoSet already created via a table join.

▸ **Table join**

We've opted for this option. We'll discuss it in more detail now.

9.2.3   Insert Tables

When you're in the screen shown in Figure 9.10, you can provide a comment, which will be useful for those reviewing your query in the future. Select the TABLE JOIN option as the data source and then select the BASIS MODE radio button, which will take you to Figure 9.12. You can also use the menu path EDIT • INSERT TABLE to insert a table. A dialog box appears when you follow the menu path or click on the INSERT TABLE icon (second from the left in the application toolbar). In the dialog window, as shown in Figure 9.12, enter the name of the table you want to use and press ⌈Enter⌉, and the table will be inserted. You can repeat the steps to insert more than one table.

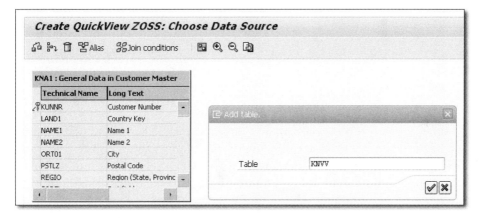

Figure 9.12 Insert Table

9.2.4   Join Tables

Once the tables are inserted, the default joins appear. It's important to understand what tables you're going to join and how to join them. There are two types of joins: *left-outer join* and *inner join.* Default joins are always inner joins. If you select and right-click on any join, you'll get the option to change or delete the join (shown in Figure 9.13).

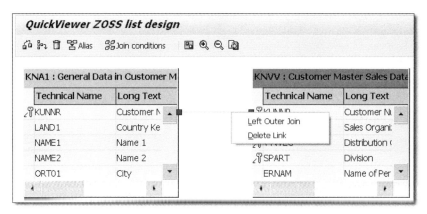

Figure 9.13 Left-Outer Join Tables KNA1 and KNVV

We've opted for this example to stress the difference between the two types of join and the important role they play in a query. If you select the default, the inner join, and use the KUNNR field to join tables KNA1 and KNVV, you'll see the list of customers present in tables KNA1 and KNVV. The inner join will result in a list of the customers present in both tables KNA1 and KNVV. This is not the list of customers that we want. If you use the left-outer join, the list will show all customers in table KNA1. The fields to be populated from table KNVV will remain blank for customers that have entries in table KNA1 but not in table KNVV. So you have to opt for the left-outer join.

You can have more than one inner join between two tables. As shown in Figure 9.14, the AUTHORIZATION GROUP field also joins tables KNA1 and KNVV. To create a join, identify the fields that are to be joined, which must satisfy certain conditions such as the same length and same type (e.g., a character field cannot be joined with a numeric field). The fields to be used as joining conditions should be present in both tables. In simple terms, an inner join is like an AND condition. That is, the system will select all of the records in the first table *and* second table with a common value for the joining field. So in our example, when the system found that some customers, who are used as a joining field (KUNNR), are not present in table KNVV, they are not selected.

Similarly, a left-outer join can be called an OR condition. That is, the system will select all of the records present in the first *or* second table, subject to other restrictions in selection criteria. So when we used customers as the joining fields, the system selected all of the customers (present in table KNA1), even when some of them were not present in the second table (KNVV) for the left-outer join.

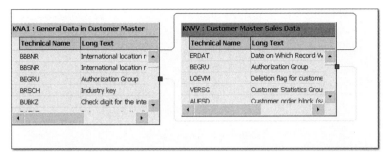

Figure 9.14 Two Inner Joins

Click on the column next to the field name and drag the cursor to the field in the next table, as shown in Figure 9.14. Two inner joins means two AND conditions. In this case, if the customer code and authorization group field value in a record in one table is same as in other table, it will be listed. Press Ctrl + F to search a field in an inserted table. Once you've inserted and joined all of the required tables, click on the back arrow to reach the screen shown in Figure 9.15.

9.2.5 Selection and List Fields

When you reach the screen shown in Figure 9.15, you can decide on the fields you want to use in the selection or initial screen of the report (query). You also decide on the fields for the list here. Let's look at the two ways of doing this.

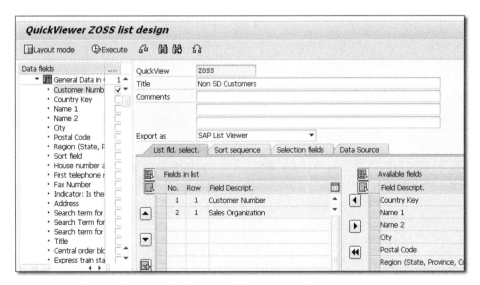

Figure 9.15 Selecting the List and Selection Fields in Basis Mode

403

Using Tabs in the Panel on the Right

As you can see in Figure 9.15, there are various tabs to use as selection and list fields. Click on the LIST FLD. SELECT. tab, and select the fields required in the list from AVAILABLE FIELDS. Next, click on the arrow pointing left (highlighted in Figure 9.15), which will shift the selected fields into the fields in list category.

Click on the SELECTION FIELDS tab, where you'll see all of the fields for tables KNA1 and KNVV in the AVAILABLE FIELDS list again. Select the fields you want and click on the left arrow. The fields will shift to the SELECTION FIELDS list.

Using the Table Join Folder

As you select fields for the selection and list screens, you'll notice checkmarks appearing in the selected fields in the TABLE JOIN folder. In the TABLE JOIN folder, all of the inserted tables appear. Click on the small triangle next to the table name to display or hide fields, and select the checkbox next to the field and in the LIST FIELDS column to make the field appear in the list. Clicking on the checkbox below the SELECTION FIELDS allows the field to appear in the selection screen.

Once you've inserted the tables and selected the fields for the selection and list fields, the system may still require you to add another table. To change the data source, click on the DATA SOURCE tab shown in Figure 9.16. If you're interested in the table join, clicking on the CHANGE JOIN button will take you to the screen shown in Figure 9.13.

Figure 9.16 Data Source Tab to Change Join

9.2.6 List Screen Layout

We've already discussed that two important aspects of report layout are sequence and sorting. You have several options for designing the list screen's layout. In this section, we'll discuss a few of them. When you're in the screen shown in Figure

9.15, click on the LAYOUT MODE button in the application toolbar to go to the screen shown in Figure 9.17.

Let's discuss a few basic elements of field design: sequence of fields, sorting, description of list fields, and column width. You can decide the order in which fields appear by following these steps when you're in Basis mode (Figure 9.15).

1. Select a field (row) and click on the up or down arrow to change its location.

2. The selection fields appear in the same order as presented in the SELECTION FIELDS tab.

3. For the LIST fields, they're transposed, meaning the field on the top (number 1) appears in first column and the field below it (number 2) appear to the right of the first one, and so on.

If the list (or output) is to appear presorted, you can take the following steps to sort the items:

▸ Select the SORT ORDER tab shown in Figure 9.16.

▸ Select the field (or fields) on which the list is to be sorted.

▸ Click on the left arrow.

▸ Click on the ASCENDING or DESCENDING ORDER option for sorting.

In layout mode (Figure 9.17), the list fields' descriptions appear at the top of the screen. You can click on any field and modify the description to make it more meaningful, but any description longer than the field length is not possible. Therefore, you may need to increase the field length or column width first, which we'll explain next.

You can modify the default column width (or field length of the list field or output length), as shown in the bottom-left of the screen in Figure 9.17. In this case, the output length of the SALES ORGANIZATION field (KNVV-VKORS) increases from 4 (which is the standard length) to 29. This is to replace the standard description (SOrg) with a longer description (SALES ORGANIZATION CODE). This is important because the list's user may not understand what SOrg is, and sometimes, the more information you can provide, the better.

Now you can save the setting. A warning message may appear, and after saving the query, click on the EXECUTE button in application toolbar (Figure 9.15). This will take you to the selection screen of the query, as shown in Figure 9.18. We've selected the Customer Code (KUNNR) field of table KNA1 and the Sales Organization (VKORG) field of table KNVV. As you know, we had opted for left-outer join to list customers present in table KNA1 and not present in table KNVV. The inclusion of the KNVV-VKORG field in the selection screen will create a special situation. We're only interested in a list that doesn't have any entries in the table KNVV, and left-outer join will make the KNVV-VKORG field blank.

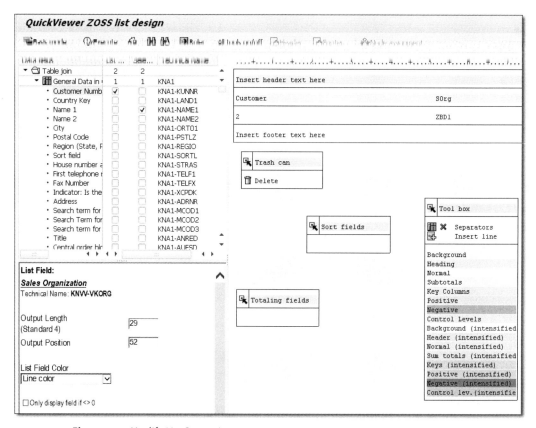

Figure 9.17 Modify List Screen Layout

So if we fix the value of the KNVV-VKORG field (Sales Organization) to blank and then execute the report, we'll get the list we want. Note that we've left the first field blank, which means it can have any value. We've fixed the value of the second field to blank. Because the Sales Organization field is a key field (mandatory) in table KNVV, it isn't possible to have an entry in table KNVV without a value for this field. To select a single value for a selection field, you can take the following steps:

1. Click on the MULTIPLE SELECTION icon, which looks like an arrow pointed to the right, on the far right, against the selection field.

2. A dialog box, shown in Figure 9.18, with the heading MULTIPLE SELECTION FOR XXX will appear, where XXX is the field for which you're making the selection.

3. Click on the SELECTION OPTIONS icon, which we've highlighted in Figure 9.18. This presents you with the SELECT BY INITIAL VALUE dialog box.

4. Select the SELECT: EQUAL TO option and press ⎡Enter⎤.

5. Click on the COPY icon in the bottom-left part of the MULTIPLE SELECTION dialog box.

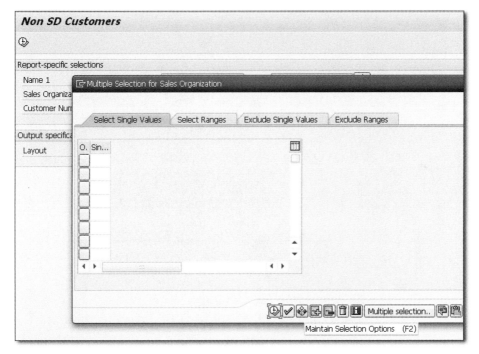

Figure 9.18 Selection Screen of the Query

Save the input setting by clicking on the SAVE AS VARIANT icon. This will take you to the screen shown in Figure 9.19, where you can create a variant. In this first screen, you can provide a name starting with Y or Z for the variant. In the second field, include a description. By selecting the PROTECT VARIANT checkbox, you're preventing others from tampering with the variant while using it. When selected, the ONLY FOR BACKGROUND PROCESSING checkbox makes the variant unavailable in the list of variant icons that appears next to the EXECUTE icon in the application toolbar. You can disable the FIELDS OF field for entry, and hide it, as we've done for Sales Organization.

We've also neglected to select the SAVE FIELD WITHOUT VALUES checkbox for Sales Organization to preserve the settings we made in the steps for the single value selection. This way, nobody using this variant will need to perform those steps again. We opted for background processing, because we'll be using it in a Z-transaction. Finally, save and click on BACK, which takes you out of execution mode, and save the query.

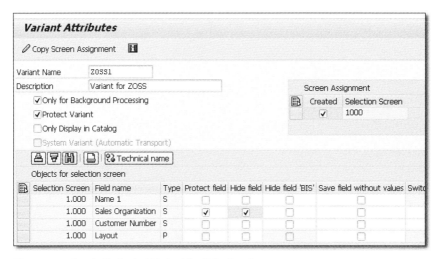

Figure 9.19 Create Protected Variant for Selection Screen

9.2.7 Create a Z-Transaction for the Query

Custom transactions are created for a specific user's convenience. However, a query created by one user is automatically available for use by other users of the system. Also, you can manage authorization—in other words, you can manage which users are allowed to use the transaction for the query, and which are not.

You create customer transactions using Transaction SE93. In the initial screen, enter a code (e.g., ZOSS) and click on the CREATE icon, which will take you to the dialog box shown in Figure 9.20. Here, you can enter a meaningful description and select the PROGRAM AND SELECTION SCREEN (REPORT TRANSACTION) radio button. Press ⌐Enter⌐ and you'll go to the screen shown in Figure 9.21.

In this screen, the proposed transaction code and description will appear by default. For the program name, execute the query in Transaction SQVI. Follow the menu path SYSTEM • STATUS when you're in the selection screen, as shown in Figure 9.18. Copy the entry that you find in the program field to the program field in the screen shown in Figure 9.21. If the program name starts with an exclamation mark, such as !QFKSYSTQV000014ZOSS==========, replace the ! with an A. In the variant field, enter the name of the variant with which you saved the variant in Figure 9.19.

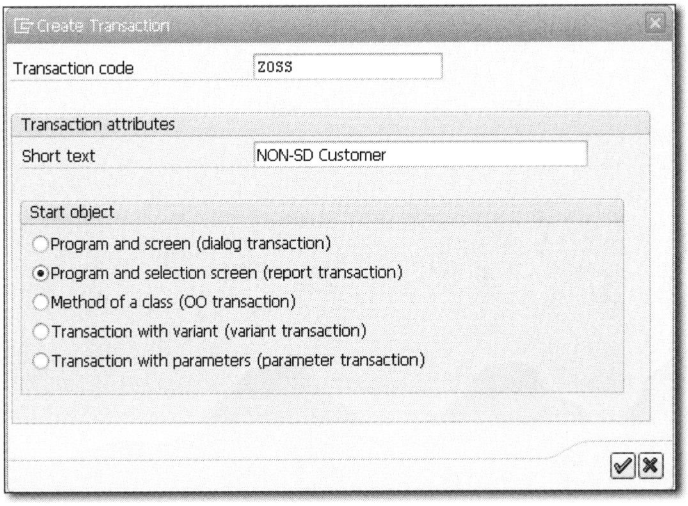

Figure 9.20 Create Transaction (ZOSS) for Query

Save the setting for creating a transaction, and you'll receive a transport request. If you're creating the query in the production client, and the transaction is in development, you have to transport the request with a dummy program name. In production, replace that with the program name of the query. Now when you execute the transaction (e.g., ZOSS), the query developed for it will run. You'll go to the selection screen of the query.

Figure 9.21 Create Report Transaction with Variant

9.3   Sales Information System

The Sales Information System (SIS) is part of the more general Logistics Information System (LIS). SIS consists of different standard and variable analyses, planning information, the early warning system, and the info library. It also consists of customization and archiving tools that pertain to the Sales and Distribution functionality in SAP ERP.

SIS uses the data that originates during the transactions in Sales and Distribution. In addition to transactional data, SIS reports and analyses also use various master data (e.g., customer, material, employee and so on). Be warned, however: the information generated in SIS is not considered reliable for statutory or legal reporting, because it may not be perfect. You need to continuously monitor it for any possible errors in updating of SIS info structures, which we'll discuss in Section 9.3.3. The SIS reports and analyses use the resources of the SAP ERP server, so they affect the overall performance of the SAP ERP system. Many undesirable or unused info structures are like parasites on your system, so you should, in general, delete the info structures that are active in the production server but in use for extracting reports or analyses.

In this section, we'll discuss four general topics concerning the SIS. We'll start with the standard analyses and then move on to flexible analyses and tools available for customizing these analyses. Finally, we'll discuss how to check the consistency of info structures.

9.3.1 Standard Analyses

Several standard analyses are available in the Sales and Distribution functionality in SAP ERP. These analyses are based on individual info structures. The info structures are updated in real time, so they provide reliable, real-time analysis. The same info structure may be in use in several analyses. We'll discuss these analyses in the next few sections.

Customer Analyses (S001)

Customer analyses use the info structure S001 for analyzing orders, invoices, credit memos, and returns for one, or several, customers. The other selection criteria are the sales area (sales organization, distribution channel, and division), material, and date range. Whether the date range is weekly or monthly depends on the update group.

The result or list of the analysis can be drilled down like the list in Figure 9.22. You display the list by clicking on the DISPLAY DRILLDOWN button in the selection screen of the analysis. Table 9.3 lists some customer analyses with their transaction codes. The drill-down structure is different for different analyses. The default fields of the output list are also different. Figure 9.23 shows the output list of MCTA (customer analysis). Press F8 when you complete the selection criteria to see the list or result. You can perform the following operations when you're in the list: drill-down, change the layout to insert hidden columns, and change the column width. You can also opt for Customer Code + Customer Name by following the menu path SETTINGS • CHARACTERISTIC DISPLAY • KEY AND DESCRIPTION. Other features of standard reports, such as graphical display, export to other applications, and so on, are also possible.

Transaction	Description
MC+I	SIS: Customer Credit Memos – Selection
MC+A	SIS: Customer Returns, Selection
MC+E	SIS: Customer, Sales – Selection

Table 9.3 Customer Analyses

Transaction	Description
MC(A	SIS: Customer, Incoming Orders – Selection
MCTA	SIS: Customer Analysis – Selection

Table 9.3 Customer Analyses (Cont.)

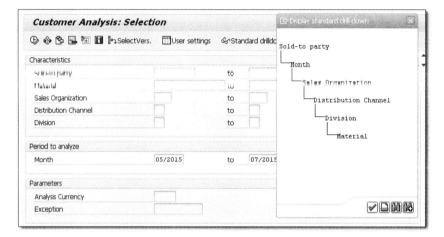

Figure 9.22 Customer Analysis Selection Screen and Drill-Down List

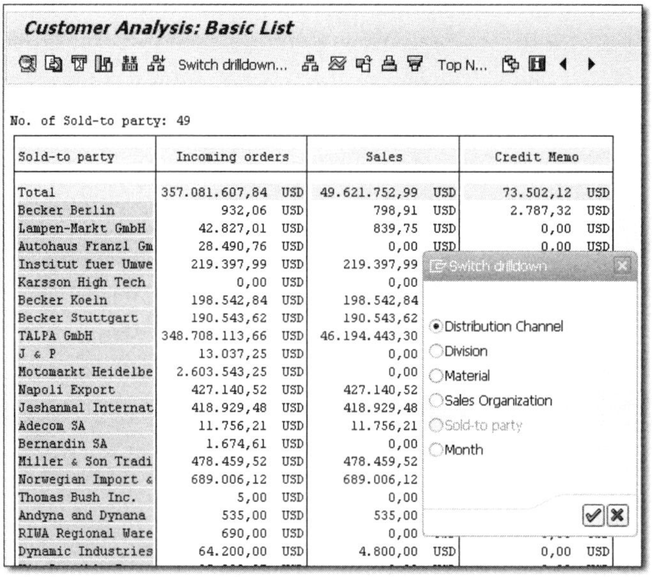

Figure 9.23 List for MCTA (Customer Analysis) with Switch Drilldown Dialog

Sales Office Analyses (S002)

Find the sales office analyses in info structure S002. These analyses are useful for information at the sales group and sales office levels. Note that material is not a part of this structure, so it isn't available in the selection, list, or drill-down. Table 9.4 lists some sales office analyses.

Transaction	Description
MC-E	SIS: Sales Office – Sales Selection
MC-I	SIS: Sales Office Credit Memos Selection
MC-A	SIS: Sales Office Returns, Selection
MC(M	SIS: Sales Office, Incoming Orders Selection
MCTG	SIS: Sales Office Analysis Selection

Table 9.4 Sales Office Analyses

Sales Organization Analyses (S003)

The sales organization is part of all of the standard analyses. This group of analyses would be better named "sales district analyses." These analyses are based on info structure S003, and the sales district, customer, and material are key fields in addition to the sales area elements. Table 9.5 lists some of these analyses.

Transaction	Description
MC+Y	SIS: Sales Org. Returns, Selection
MC(I	SIS: Sales Org. Incoming Orders Selection
MC+6	SIS: Sales Org. Credit Memos Selection
MC+2	SIS: Sales Org. Invoiced Sales, Selection
MCT	SIS: Sales Org. Analysis – Selection

Table 9.5 Sales Organization Analyses

Material Analyses (S004)

Material analyses, listed in Table 9.6, use info structure S004. Note that the division is not part of this info structure.

Transaction	Description
MC+U	SIS: Material Credit Memos, Selection
MC+M	SIS: Material Returns, Selection
MC+Q	SIS: Material, Sales – Selection
MC(E	SIS: Material, Incoming Orders – Selection
MCTC	SIS: Material Analysis – Selection

Table 9.6 Material Analyses

Shipping Point Analyses (S005)

The shipping point analyses, listed in Table 9.7, use info structure S005. SHIPPING POINT/RECEIVING POINT, ROUTE, FORWARDING AGENT, and DESTINATION COUNTRY are the key fields in the info structure. The list contains the net and gross weights and labor requirements for outbound and/or return deliveries.

Transaction	Description
MC(U	SIS: Shipping Point Deliveries Selection
MC-0	SIS: Shipping Point Returns, Selection
MCTK	SIS: Shipping Point Analysis Selection

Table 9.7 Shipping Point Analyses

Sales Employee Analyses (S006)

Sales employee analyses, listed in Table 9.8, use info structure S006. In addition to sales area elements, sold-to party, and material, the sales employee is a key field in this info structure.

Transaction	Description
MC-U	SIS: Employee – Credit Memos, Selection
MC-M	SIS: Employee – Returns, Selection
MC-Q	SIS: Employee – Sales, Selection
MC(Q	SIS: Employee, Incoming Orders Selection
MCTI	SIS: Sales Employee Analysis Selection

Table 9.8 Sales Employee Analyses

We do not consider shipment, sales support, and customer potential analyses part of the SIS. They are part of the broader grouping of the LIS. Nevertheless, you can use them as and when you require them.

9.3.2 Flexible Analyses

In addition to the standard analyses, you may need customized analyses to meet your requirements. These customized analyses are called *flexible analyses*. There are two general parts to creating flexible analyses: creating the customized info structure (or evaluation structure) and creating the customized analysis (or evaluation).

Create Customized Info Structures

When the available standard info structures cannot provide the information that you or your user want, you may want to create your own info structures.

See the steps involved in creating customized info structures:

1. Decide on characteristics and key figures. In an info structure or evaluation structure, Transaction MSC7 selects the characteristics and key fields. Examples of characteristics fields include the sales organization, sold-to party, material, billing type, and sales group. You can include the credit memo quantity, credit memo for returns value, and quantity, debit memo value, and so on, as key figures.

2. Decide on a reference info structure or table. In Transaction MSC7, you need to decide on the reference info structure (e.g., S001) or standard tables (e.g., VBRP). The menu path for Transaction MSC7 is SAP EASY ACCESS • LOGISTICS • SALES AND DISTRIBUTION • SALES INFORMATION SYSTEM • FLEXIBLE ANALYSES • EVALUATION STRUCTURE • CREATE. In the initial screen, shown in Figure 9.24, the database table or the info structure should contain all of the fields you've identified for characteristics and key figures.

3. Press ⌷Enter⌷ after entering the name, description, and reference info structure or table.

4. You'll see a screen similar to the one shown in Figure 9.25. Click on the CHARACTERISTICS button in the application toolbar. Two dialog boxes, as shown in Figure 9.25, will appear. The SELECTION list provides you with the entire list of fields available for selection as characteristics. Click on the COPY + CLOSE icon after selecting all of the fields you want. If there are more fields you want to select, click on the COPY button at the bottom of this dialog box.

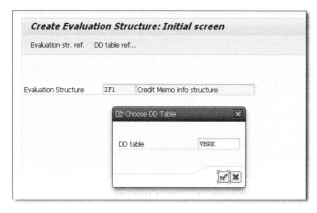

Figure 9.24 Create an Evaluation Structure with Reference to a Database Table

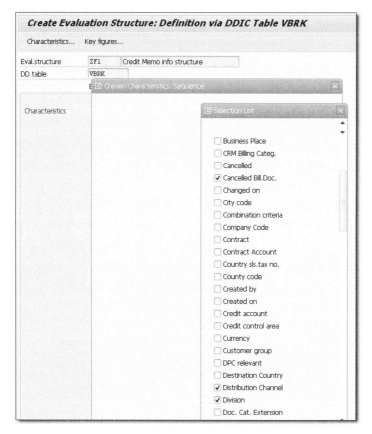

Figure 9.25 Choose Characteristics Fields

5. When all of the fields are copied to the CHOSEN CHARACTERISTICS: SEQUENCE dialog box, click on the COPY button.

6. All of the fields will be copied over to the main screen and will appear in the CHARACTERISTICS box on the left side.

7. Repeat this process to insert key fields. That is, click on the KEY FIGURES button on the application toolbar and select and COPY AVAILABLE FIELDS.

8. Once you have selected all of the fields you want, as shown in Figure 9.26, follow the menu path EVALUATION STRUCTURE • GENERATE to generate the evaluation structure.

9. The system will ask you if transportation is required. Select YES if you're generating the list in a development client for use in production after testing. Once the evaluation structure is created, you can display and change it using Transactions MCS9 and MCS8, respectively.

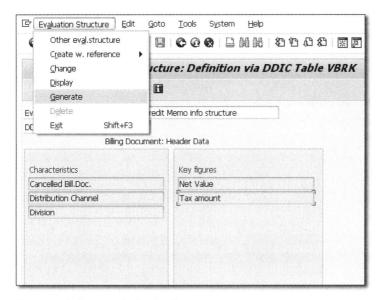

Figure 9.26 Generate Evaluation Structure

Create Customized Analyses

After creating an evaluation structure, the next activity is to create a flexible analyses. You need to create your analysis when the standard analyses don't fulfill your reporting requirements. For example, suppose batch is a very important element in your reporting, and no standard analyses give you this information. You can use flexible analysis for it. (Of course, remember that there are performance issues involved, and batch is typically not included in such analyses for performance reasons.)

But when a typical user looks at any standard analyses, he often says, "We also want XXX next to the last column in this." XXX can be material group description, employee name, or country code. For this, you'll end up creating a customized analysis (and a customized info structure). Create a customized analysis using Transaction MCSA or following the menu path SAP EASY ACCESS • LOGISTICS • SALES AND DISTRIBUTION • SALES INFORMATION SYSTEM • FLEXIBLE ANALYSES • EVALUATION • CREATE. The steps to create a customized analyses are as follows.

1. In the initial screen, specify the evaluation structure to be used for the evaluation.

2. Enter a key and description for the valuation.

3. Press [Enter]. You'll go to a screen similar to the one shown in Figure 9.27.

4. Click on CHARACTERISTICS button in the application tool bar. All of the characteristics fields of the info structure are available for selection here.

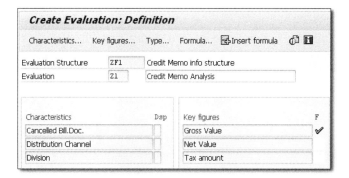

Figure 9.27 Define Evaluation for Flexible Analysis

5. Select all or some of the fields in the SELECTION LIST dialog box.

6. Click on the COPY + CLOSE button of that dialog box.

7. Click on the COPY button of the CHOSEN CHARACTERISTICS: SEQUENCE dialog box.

8. Repeat the same steps for inserting key figures.

9. Once all of the fields are available in the main screen, as shown in Figure 9.27, you can move on to layout modification.

10. To decide how the characteristics that should appear in the selection screen of the analyses, select a CHARACTERISTICS field.

11. Click on the TYPE button in the application toolbar.

12. A dialog box, shown in Figure 9.28, will appear. Customize the appearance as per your requirements.

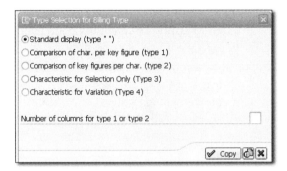

Figure 9.28 Type Selection for Characteristics Field

13. You can perform some simple operations with the key fields by clicking on the ADD FORMULA button in the application toolbar. The dialog box shown in Figure 9.29 will appear.

14. Give a name to the field (or column) that will display the formula's result. In this example, we have used gross value.

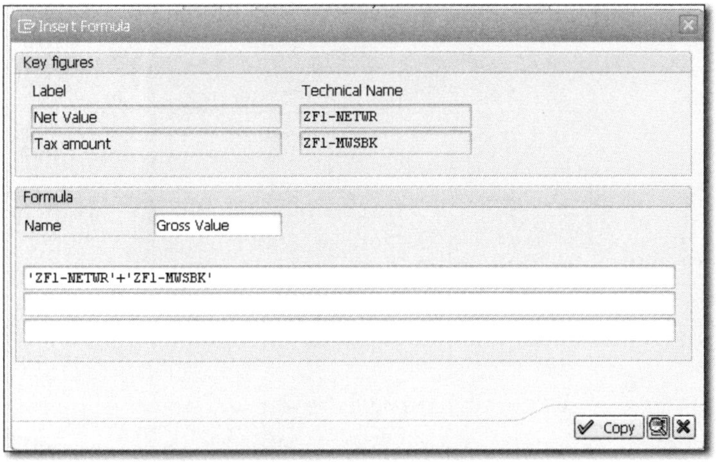

Figure 9.29 Use of a Formula

15. All of the key figures with their technical names will appear on the top part of the screen (see Figure 9.29). You can use these fields in the formula.

16. Click on Copy after the field's formula is complete.

17. The field will appear along with the F field selected, as shown in Figure 9.27.

18. Save, and a dialog box will appear. You can create a transport request if required by clicking on the Yes button.

19. You can display and modify the evaluation using Transactions MCSC and MCSB, respectively.

Execute Flexible Analyses

To use the evaluation, execute Transaction MCSG or follow menu path SAP Easy Access • Logistics • Sales and Distribution • Sales Information System • Flexible Analyses • Evaluation • Execute.

1. Enter the name of the structure and the evaluation in the initial screen.

2. Press F8, and the initial screen of the analyses will appear, which will display the fields for selection/restriction as per customization. Enter the values for which a result list is required.

3. Press F8, which will take you to the results list shown in Figure 9.30.

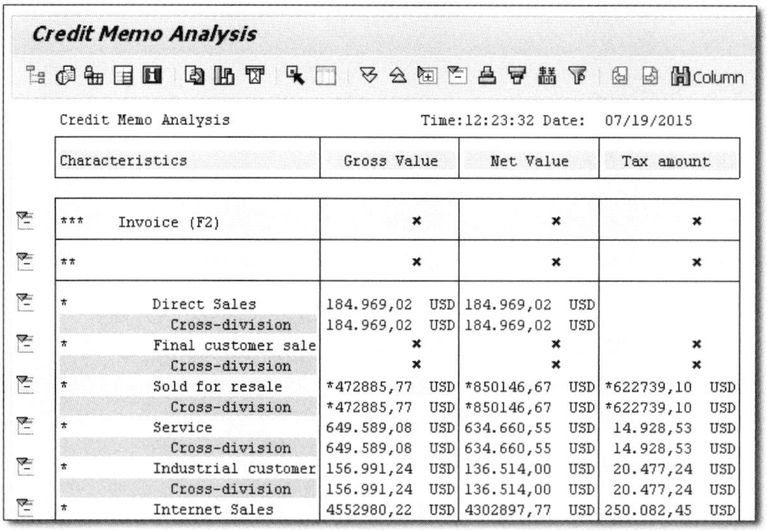

Credit Memo Analysis	Gross Value		Net Value		Tax amount	
Characteristics						
*** Invoice (F2)	✗		✗		✗	
**	✗		✗		✗	
* Direct Sales	184.969,02	USD	184.969,02	USD		
Cross-division	184.969,02	USD	184.969,02	USD		
* Final customer sale	✗		✗		✗	
Cross-division	✗		✗		✗	
* Sold for resale	*472885,77	USD	*850146,67	USD	*622739,10	USD
Cross-division	*472885,77	USD	*850146,67	USD	*622739,10	USD
* Service	649.589,08	USD	634.660,55	USD	14.928,53	USD
Cross-division	649.589,08	USD	634.660,55	USD	14.928,53	USD
* Industrial customer	156.991,24	USD	136.514,00	USD	20.477,24	USD
Cross-division	156.991,24	USD	136.514,00	USD	20.477,24	USD
* Internet Sales	4552980,22	USD	4302897,77	USD	250.082,45	USD

Credit Memo Analysis   Time:12:23:32 Date: 07/19/2015

Figure 9.30 Execution of Flexible Analysis

9.3.3 General Checks for Info Structures

You can create a user-created info structure using Transaction MCSCHECK. You can use that info structure to check the standard info structures, which obviously will have no errors most of the time. However, in one of the checks (the Field Catalog check), even a standard info structure may show an error. This is primarily due to the changes at the customer end during the creation of a customized info-structure.

The initial screen for Transaction MCSCHECK has several frames. On the top is the SELECTION frame, where you can specify the info structure that requires checking. You also specify the application, which is 01 for Sales and Distribution, and the client.

There are five groups of checks that you can use with this tool. They also happen to be the frame headings for the checks they group. Each check has its own checkbox, so you can select any number of checks at a time. We describe the different kinds of checks in the subsections below.

When selected, the checkboxes in the LIS CONTROL TABLES frame check the info structure for any error in the LIS control tables it uses:

► The CONTROL TABLES field checks the assignments and interdependencies of the control tables for the selected information structures. For example, an info structure without any LIS control table associated with it will show an error if this checkbox is selected.

► The FIELD CATALOGS field checks all field catalogs, irrespective of the selected information structure.

► The UNITS field checks whether the units used in the selected info structure are consistent.

The checkboxes in the info structure frame check the info structure for various properties. Info structures that show errors or warnings during these checks are likely to result is erroneous reports when you use them in flexible analyses:

► STATUS LIS/DICTIONARY checks that the statuses in the information structure and the database table are the same.

► FIELDS LIS/DICTIONARY checks the fields in the information structure and the database table. If you select this checkbox, the field's properties (e.g., numeric or character, length, etc.) in info structure and database tables should match.

▶ Select theAssignments to Info Structures checkbox to check the assignment to information structures with different types.

▶ The Stock Values checkbox checks stock values.

The checkboxes in the Updating frame check whether there is or can be any problem in updating the info structure. If an info structure is not correctly updated, it cannot generate a correct report:

▶ The Update Program checkbox, when selected, gives you information on update programs.

▶ The Update Indicators (e.g., V1, V2, and V3) are selected when you select this checkbox.

▶ The Update Group/Event checkbox checks the consistency of table entries.

▶ Select the Characteristics/Key Figures checkbox to check if the update program can fill the info structure with data for characteristics and key figures.

▶ The Formulas/Requirements checkbox checks if the formula and/or requirement routines assigned to update rule exist in an active state.

The Standard Analysis frame checkboxes are more for informational purposes than to check info structures for errors. For example, you can find the list of standard and flexible analyses that may be using a particular standard info structure (first check):

▶ When selected, the Existing Standard Analyses checkbox gives you a list of all existing standard analyses of the selected info structure. For example, the five standard analyses for info structure S001 are Customer Analysis (0001), Customer Analysis: Incoming Orders (2001), Customer Analysis: Returns (2002), Customer Analysis: Invoiced Sales (2003), and Customer Analysis: Credit Memos (2004).

▶ The Compare Key Figures IS and STA checkbox compares the key figures in info structures and standard analyses. In case of differences, an error occurs.

▶ The Standard Default Settings field checks and reports the default user-specific settings for characteristics, key figures, and parameters.

Select the Existing Flexible Analyses checkbox when you want to see the list of existing flexible analyses for the selected info structure. You can use this information, for example, to find the info structure not used in any flexible analyses and either use it, or delete it.

After selecting the entire required check, press [F8] to execute the program. By default, you should select all possible checkboxes. You'll receive a report like the one shown in Figure 9.31. This report will show the possible errors in the customized info structure (or standard info structure) for which the report was executed. The errors (and warnings) are rectified to prevent errors in flexible analyses that use the info structure. The following SAP notes discuss some of the specific errors in customizing info structures, and how to solve them.

▸ SAP Note 202631 (SIS: No Update of Individual Key Figures)

▸ SAP Note 430718 (LIS: Incorrect Unit Update; e.g., 10 USD + 10 EUR = 20 EUR)

▸ SAP Note 434615 (LIS Objects: Field Length; e.g., > 10 Not Possible)

▸ SAP Note 509000 (LIS: Incorrect Display of Values/Quantities in Std. Analysis)

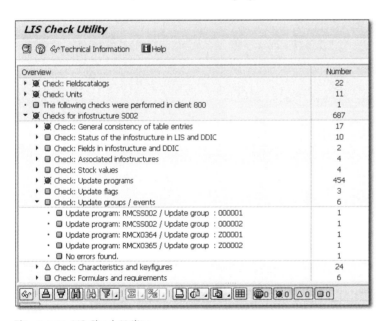

Figure 9.31 LIS Check Utility

9.3.4 Checks for SIS Info Structures

In addition to the general checks discussed in the previous section, there are also checks performed for info structures created in the Sales and Distribution functionality in SAP ERP. These checks check the assignment of update groups using Transaction MCVCHECK01, shown in Figure 9.32. Note that a check takes place for both header and item levels simultaneously. However, in online mode, to avoid ABAP run-time errors, it should be run with restrictions. Running the check in the background ([F9]) for one sales organization at a time is the best solution to avoid an ABAP dump.

There are two different transaction codes (MCVCHECK02 and MCVCHECK03) for checking assignments at the header and item levels, respectively. Transaction MCVCHECK02 is same as MCVCHECK01, except that the CHECK ON HEADER LEVEL checkbox is selected. Transaction MCVCHECK03 is same as MCVCHECK01, except that the CHECK ON ITEM LEVEL checkbox is selected. You should have no problem using these transactions for a consistency check, especially for online execution. These two transactions are also very helpful in helping you understand the output report.

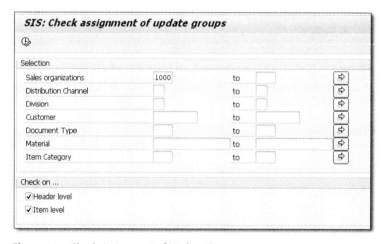

Figure 9.32 Check Assignment of Update Groups

The CHECK FOR UPDATE GROUPS checkbox performs the following checks at the header and item levels.

The header level has the following checks and lists:

- All document types without an update group assigned to them.

- All customers with the Customer Statistics Group (KNVV - VERSG) field empty. The field is maintained in the customer master record (SALES tab of SALES AREA data).

- All of the combinations of document type and customer for which the system is unable to determine an update group.

For the valid combinations at the header level, the item level check performs the following checks at the item level. The missing entries show as warning messages (the yellow triangle shown in Figure 9.33).

▶ All document types without an update group assigned to them.

▶ All customers with the CUSTOMER STATISTICS GROUP field empty.

▶ All of the item categories without an update group assigned to them.

▶ All materials with the MATERIAL STATISTIC GROUP (MVKE-VERSG) field blank. The field is maintained in the SALES: SALES ORG.2 tab of the material master record.

▶ All combinations of the above four for which the system cannot determine the update group.

LIS Check Utility

Technical Information   Help

Overview	Number
▼ △ Sales Organization 1000	999.999
▼ △ Sales Organization 1000 Distribution Channel 01 Division 00	9.890
▶ △ Document Type 01	29
▶ △ Document Type AA	29
▶ △ Document Type AE	29
▼ △ Document Type AEBO	29
▼ △ Cust. no. 0000001006 > STAFO: INITIAL	4
• △ No assignment in Customizing transaction OVRO	1
• △ Statistics group Customer : INITIAL	1
• ▢ Statistics group Document Type : 01	1
▶ △ Cust. no. 0000001185 > STAFO: INITIAL	4
▶ △ Cust. no. 0000001187 > STAFO: INITIAL	4
▶ △ Cust. no. 0000049983 > STAFO: INITIAL	4
▶ △ Cust. no. 0000091500 > STAFO: INITIAL	4
▶ △ Cust. no. 0000091600 > STAFO: INITIAL	4
▶ △ Cust. no. 0000300215 > STAFO: INITIAL	4
▶ △ Document Type AEBQ	29
▶ △ Document Type AF	29
▶ △ Document Type AG	29

Figure 9.33 Output (Online) of Assignment Check for Update Groups

When you create the output in the background (refer Figure 9.34), all data is available. Note that, for online processing, some limitations exist. For example, note the number 999999 in Figure 9.33. This is the upper limit for online processing. Also, because in a production client this process takes a lot of time and slows down the system, you should perform it at night or on the weekend (or when the system is under a relatively light load) as a background job.

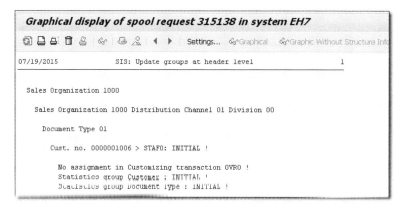

Figure 9.34 Background Processing of Assignment Check for Update Groups

9.4   Business Intelligence and Reporting

The business information warehousing software provided by SAP enables you to extract data from both SAP and non-SAP systems, and to present it in a clear and manageable format. The performance is very fast, and when large amounts of data needs analysis, SAP BW outperforms all other options for reporting discussed in this book.

The key feature of the business intelligence software offered by SAP is that it has its own database. It extracts data from other systems (including SAP ERP) and stores that data in its own database. This also explains the reason for better performance than *online transaction processing* (OLTP) systems like SAP ERP. In contrast, SAP BW is known as an *online analytical processing* (OLAP) system.

SAP provides an add-on called *Business Content* (BI Content), which is a collection of preconfigured reports and objects. The objects of BI Content include the following:

- ► **Extractor programs**
  These programs move information from the SAP ERP system to SAP BW. Function module RSAX_BIW_GET_DATA_SIMPLE is one of the extractor programs available in SAP ERP.

- ► **DataSources**
  DataSources deliver via BI Content. They are activated in the SAP ERP (or other source) system directly, or they can be activated remotely from the SAP BW

system. These DataSources structure data in the staging area in the source system. For example, DataSource 2LIS_11_VASTH extracts the sales order header status from the standard SAP ERP table VBUK. Different fields of this table, such as BILLING STATUS (FKSTK), DELIVERY STATUS (LFSTK), ORDER NUMBER (VBELN), and so on, move to the DataSource fields with the same code (e.g., FKSTK, LFSTK, and so on).

▶ **Process chains**
These are the sequences of operations predefined in the source system (SAP ERP). A process chain can consist of several steps. Some steps are processed only when some previous ones are successfully completed.

▶ **InfoObjects**
An InfoObject is a characteristic, a key figure, a unit, or a time characteristic. For example, document currency is a unit and an InfoObject (0DOC_CURRCY). Document type is a characteristic and an InfoObject (0DOC_TYPE).

▶ **InfoSources**
These consist of various InfoObjects. The standard InfoSource 2LIS_01_S260 (sales order), for example, consists of most of the fields that you find in a sales order and stored in SAP ERP tables VBAK (header) and VBAP (items).

▶ **InfoCubes**
InfoCubes take source data from one or more InfoSources. For example, InfoCube 0SD_C05 (Quotations/Orders) takes source data from InfoSources 2LIS_01_S264 (SD – Quotation), 2LIS_01_S260 (SD – Sales Order), 2LIS_12_VCSCL (Schedule Line Delivery), and 2LIS_12_VCITM (Delivery Item Data). These are used for generating queries that are actual reporting tools.

▶ **ODS objects**
These are database tables in the SAP BW system. They take source data from one or more InfoSources. Other ODS objects can also be sources of information for them. For example, ODS object 0SD_003 (Aggregation Header Level for Sales Order) takes source information from InfoSources 2LIS_11_VAHDR (Sales Document Header Data) and 2LIS_11_VASTH (Sales Document Header Status), as well as ODS objects 0SD_001 (Aggregation Order Item) and 0SD_002 (Returns Items). ODS objects store the data at the document level (e.g., information from individual sales orders) and can be overwritten for changes in the source system.

▶ **Variables**
Variables are what make a BI report dynamic. For example, when a plant is a variable, you can restrict the output to display records for only a particular

plant. There are several types of variables, including formula variable, text variable, and so on.

▶ **Data mining models**

You can access the standard SAP-delivered data mining models using Transaction RSDMWB or following the menu path SAP Easy Access • Information System • Business Information System • Enhanced Analytics • Data Mining. Data mining models look for patterns and correlations in a significantly large amount of data.

▶ **Queries**

These are the actual reports. We'll discuss some of these later.

▶ **Workbooks**

Workbooks are also reporting tools. One workbook can contain several queries, for example, `0LES_C02_Q0001` (Shipment Costs by Material).

▶ **Crystal Reports**

These are also highly structured reporting tools. You can create these reports using not only an SAP BW database, but also other sources.

▶ **Web templates**

These are predesigned web pages used for reporting. They can use the information available on an SAP BW server to provide information interactively to users. The web templates delivered with BI Content are modifiable through the Web Application Designer (WAD).

▶ **Roles**

Different queries, workbooks, and other reporting tools are available to different users as per the roles assigned to them. For example, the standard role sales manager (`0ROLE_0007`) would monitor various aspects of sales, such as incoming orders, returns, weekly deliveries, costs, and so on.

Let's look at some of the standard queries (or reports) that BI Content offers. The technical name of the query is in parentheses.

▶ Monthly incoming orders and revenue (`0SD_C01_Q0002`)

▶ Returns per customer (`0SD_C01_Q010`)

▶ Product profitability analysis (`0SD_C01_Q022`)

▶ Top customers (`0SD_C01_Q023`)

▶ Incoming orders analysis (`0SD_C01_Q024`)

▶ Distribution channel analysis (`0SD_C01_Q026`)

- Proportion of returns to incoming orders (0SD_C03_Q003)

- Average delivery processing times (0SD_C04_Q0004)

You form queries based on InfoCubes. The first six items in the previous list are based on InfoCube 0SD_C01. The next two are based on 0SD_C03 and 0SD_C04. Section 9.5.5 lists the other InfoCubes for order fulfillment, as well as InfoSources that provide data to the InfoCube.

InfoCube	Technical Name	InfoSources
Quotations/Orders	0SD_C05	2LIS_01-_S264
		2LIS_01_S260
		2LIS_12_VCSCL
		2LIS_12_VCITM
Shipment Cost Details	0LES_C02	2LIS_08TRFKZ
Shipment Cost Overview	0LES_C01	2LIS_08TRFKP
Customer	0SD_C01	2LIS_01_S001
Delivery Data of Shipment Stages	0LES_C13	2LIS_08TRTLP
Delivery Service	0SD_C05	2LIS_01_S261
Delivery	0SD_C02	2LIS_01_S005
Service Level on Order Level	0SD_C13	
Service Level on Quantity Level	0SD_C11	
Service Level on Item Level	0SD_C12	
Shipment Stage	0LES_C12	2LIS_08TRTS
Shipment Header	0LES_C11	2LIS_08TRTK
Backlogs	0SD_C14	
Sales Overview	0SD_C03	2LIS_01_S260
		2LIS_01_S261
		2LIS_01_S262
		2LIS_01_S263

Table 9.9 InfoCubes that Source Information from Tables in SAP ERP Sales and Distribution

An InfoSource contains the InfoObjects populated by the standard SAP table fields. For example, InfoObject 0SOLD_TO (Sold-To Party) of 2LIS_01_260 (Sales Order InfoSource) populates from the value in the KUNNR field.

9.5   Operative Reporting Tools

In the previous sections you learned how queries and the SIS system can help you to produce daily reports. Now, let's discuss how you can create business intelligence reports using a handful of other SAP tools that will help you to customize your reports: SAP Business Explorer (BEx) Analyzer and BEx Query Designer, SAP HANA reporting tools, and SAP BW objects. We'll provide instructions on how to use each tool.

9.5.1   SAP BEx Analyzer

SAP Business Explorer (BEx) is one of the most important BI tools, and is currently used by millions of end users around the world. Its primary use is to slice and dice the data in the SAP BW database, and to create individual reports and queries to meet your reporting needs. SAP BEx tools in SAP BW are installed on your workstation via the SAP GUI and BI add-ons. To open SAP BEx, use Windows Explorer to search for the word "Analyzer." Clicking on it will launch Microsoft Excel and the SAP BEx Analyzer, which, as an add-on, shows up in Excel, as seen in Figure 9.35.

Figure 9.35 BEx Analyzer MS Excel Add-in

SAP BEx is the tool in which queries will be executed. It also has a Web-based user interface, and consists of two components for our purposes: the BEx browser and the BEx Analyzer.

9.5.2   SAP BEx Query Designer

An important tool for daily reports is the SAP BEx Query Designer, which you can use to analyze any BI dataset using your own queries. You can evaluate the data of any InfoProvider in a query, where you can combine InfoObjects, their related characteristics, and key figures, or even reuse structures and other query elements.

To create a simple query in the SAP BEx Query Designer, follow these steps:

1. Search for or start the SAP BEx Query Designer. If your machine runs Windows 7, click START • ALL PROGRAM • BUSINESS EXPLORER • QUERY DESIGNER. For Win-

dows 8 or later, search for "Query Designer." You will reach an authentication screen, as seen in Figure 9.36. Enter your credentials and log in.

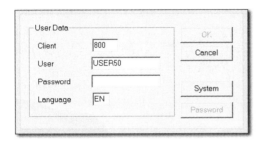

Figure 9.36 Query Designer Logon Screen

2. You will now see the initial screen of the SAP BEx Query Designer. You must create each query based on an InfoProvider. Look for the INFOPROVIDER column on the left, right beside a section for CHARACTERISTICS RESTRICTIONS, in which you can enter any restrictions or initial filters to your query. The third column, DEFAULT values, is where you will enter any type of defaults selected to this query. Once you make your selection, you'll see the ROW/COLUMNS tab shown in Figure 9.37.

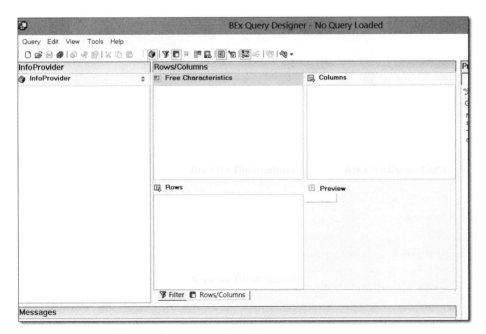

Figure 9.37 Rows/Columns Tab in SAP BEx Query Designer

3. To create a new query, select it from the menu QUERY • NEW. You'll receive a prompt to select an InfoProvider. Search for it using wildcards and partial names, including a search by description or its technical name.

In this case we use ZSD_ISQ001. The InfoProvider is now shown at the right side of the screen, along with the KEY FIGURES and DIMENSIONS, as shown in Figure 9.38.

4. Select ROWS/COLUMNS tab, and drag and drop any of the dimensions required at the row and column levels.

In this case we have selected SALES DOCUMENT and SHIP-TO PARTY because we want to have a final list of sales documents and information about the destination. Additionally, it's required to analyze the order's net value and the cumulative order quantity for each ship-to and sales document combination. Figure 9.38 shows how the SALES DOCUMENTS and SHIP-TO PARTY are now dragged into the ROWS section, and NET VALUE and CUMULATIVE key figures to the COLUMNS section.

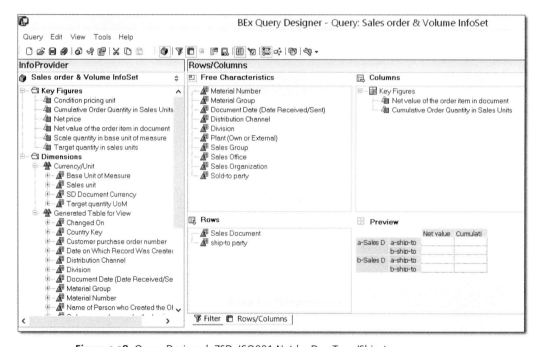

Figure 9.38 Query Designed: ZSD_ISQ001.Net by Doc Type/Ship-to

5. Save using your own query nomenclature. You can always modify your query by adding new characteristics at the Row section and key figures to the Column section.

Figure 9.39 shows how your report will look. The preview section shows the report with the selection of characteristics and key figures, and will react based on the selected combination.

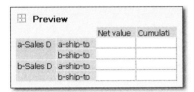

Figure 9.39 Query Preview Section

6. To run your query, open SAP BEx Analyzer and authenticate to your BI box. Next, open your query (or perhaps it will open automatically in MS Excel). If you need to make adjustment to the query, such as adding a new characteristic, you will see the results of the previous query in the SAP BEx Analyzer. If nothing changes, you may have to log out and log back in and then refresh the data in the query. This may be necessary due to the memory used by the query.

Update on SAP BEx Tools

If you run extensive queries or workbooks from version SAP BW 3.5 or earlier, note that SAP NetWeaver 7.4 no longer supports these. You can still execute the queries previously defined via the analytic manager from SAP BW 7.4. You may still need a full migration. SAP recommends the Cookbook for Migration to BEx 7.0 (SAP Note 1807522).

9.5.3   SAP HANA Reporting Tools

During the introductory chapter, we talked about the latest EHP 7 and how Sales and Distribution in SAP ERP has been influenced new functionality and enhancements.

One of these enhancements is SAP HANA-optimized BI Content for Sales and Distribution, which SAP delivered to leverage BI capabilities running in SAP HANA. This technology reduces the data storage amount via new data units called Data-Store objects (DSOs). So how do SAP HANA-optimized BI Content objects directly enhance Sales and Distribution reporting?

Before we get there, we need to understand what an SAP HANA-optimized Info-Cube is. In simple words, it's the traditional InfoCube used in any SAP BW installation—but now optimized for the SAP HANA in-memory database. SAP HANA-optimized BI Content has certain requirements to run Sales and Distribution extractions, among them having SAP BW 7.4 SP 05 or later, running on an SAP HANA database, and following the layered scalable architecture LSA++ (LSA++ being an optimized architecture for SAP BW powered by SAP HANA). If you have SAP HANA, then you will be able to use the BI elements described previously. Otherwise, you can use the optimized BI Content. In addition, if your system currently has InfoCubes activated, you may need to convert them into the new SAP HANA environment. Newly created InfoCubes are created already optimized for SAP HANA, so no conversion is required.

A list of the most commonly used DSOs in Sales and Distribution is shown in Table 9.10. The data flow begins from the extraction of the Sales and Distribution table into the DataSources, which in turn flows to the InfoSources, DSOs, and MultiProviders.

DataSources	Description	InfoSource	DSO	MultiProvider
2LIS_11_VAHDR	Sales Document Header Data	/IMO/SD_IS10	/IMO/SD_D10	(/IMO/SD_M10)
2LIS_11_VAITM	Sales Document Item Data	/IMO/SD_IS11	/IMO/SD_D11	(/IMO/SD_M10)
2LIS_11_VASTH:	Sales Document Header Status	/IMO/SD_IS18	/IMO/SD_D51 /IMO/SD_D52	(/IMO/SD_M50)
2LIS_11_V_ITM	Sales-Shipping Allocation Item Data	/IMO/SD_IS16	/IMO/SD_D16	(/IMO/SD_M10)
2LIS_12_VCHDR	Delivery Header Data	/IMO/SD_1/*/IS20	/IMO/SD_D20	(/IMO/SD_M10), (/IMO/SD_M20)
2LIS_11_VAKON	Order Condition Data			
2LIS_12_VCITM	Delivery Item Data	/IMO/SD_IS21	/IMO/SD_D21	(/IMO/SD_M10), (/IMO/SD_M20)

Table 9.10 Data Flow in Key Common DSOs for Sales and Distribution

DataSources	Description	InfoSource	DSO	MultiProvider
2LIS_11_V_SSL	Sales Document: Order Delivery	/IMO/SD_IS17	/IMO/SD_D50 /IMO/SD_D53	
2LIS_13_VDHDR	Billing Document Header Data	/IMO/SD_IS30	/IMO/SD_D30	(/IMO/SD_M10), (/IMO/SD_M30)
2LIS_13_VDITM	Billing Document Item Data	/IMO/SD_IS31	/IMO/SD_D31	(/IMO/SD_M10), (/IMO/SD_M30)
2LIS_11_VACON	Order Condition Data	/IMO/SD_IS14	/IMO/SD_D14	(/IMO/SD_M40)
2LIS_13_VDKON	Billing Condition Data	/IMO/SD_IS34	/IMO/SD_D34	(/IMO/SD_M40)
SAP HANA Information Model				
	Backorders overview		/IMO/SD_D50	(/IMO/SD_V01) – Virtual Provider (/IMO/SD_M51)

Table 9.10 Data Flow in Key Common DSOs for Sales and Distribution (Cont.)

1. In order for SAP HANA-optimized BI Content to receive Sales and Distribution records, you need to configure some basic settings: among them, transfer currency codes, units of measure, fiscal year variants, and exchange rates from your SAP source system.

   Therefore, you must make sure the transfer of global settings and exchange rates need to be completed a prerequisite. Use Transaction OVRB to determine the statistical currency in each sales organization. Follow the configuration steps below to activate the SAP BW extraction-LO database delta extractions.

2. Identify the source for SAP HANA-optimized BI Content and select the DataSource to activate (e.g., 2LIS_11_VAHDR for a sales order).

3. Activate your selected data source using Transaction RSA5. Navigate the menu to find your selected database and select ACTIVATE DATASOURCES, as shown in Figure 9.40.

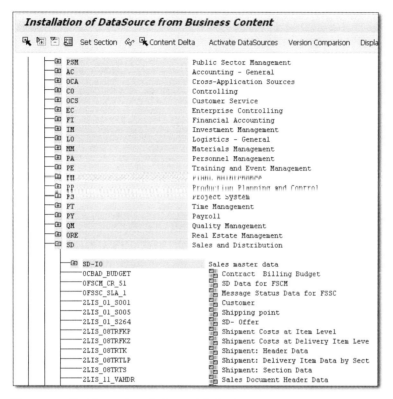

Figure 9.40 DataSource Installation and Activation

4. Using Transaction RSA6, verify that the database is correctly activated. This transaction not only displays currently active DataSources, but it also lets you make modifications to meet your needs. These enhancements are available at the functional side and through the extraction structure.

5. Activate your DataSources using Transaction LBWE, as shown in Figure 9.41. In the Logistics Customizing Cockpit, you can maintain the data structure using Maintenance and selecting your specific fields from the DataSource.

6. Generate the DataSource by selecting the required fields from the different communication structures available in each DataSource, as shown in Figure 9.42.

7. In the SAP BW system, type in Transaction RSA1 and navigate to locate the DataSource. This will show the SAP BW workbench, where you can navigate to find 2LIS_11_VAHDR. If it's not found, you need to replicate the metadata by hovering over the Sales and Distribution folder and then right-clicking on it, as shown in Figure 9.43.

LO Data Extraction: Customizing Cockpit

Source data	Structure	DataSource	Update	Update Mode
▼ 🌢 Logistics applications				
▶ 🌢 02 : Purchasing			Job Control	🖉 Direct Delta
▶ 🌢 03 : Inventory Controlling			Job Control	🖉 Direct Delta
▶ 🌢 04 : Shop Floor Control			Job Control	🖉 Direct Delta
▶ 🌢 05 : Quality Management			Job Control	🖉 Direct Delta
▶ 🌢 06 : Invoice Verification			Job Control	🖉 Direct Delta
▶ 🌢 08 : Shipment			Job Control	🖉 Direct Delta
▼ 🌢 11 : SD Sales BW			Job Control	🖉 Direct Delta
▼ ⚙Extract structures				
▶ ⊙⊙⬚ MC11VA0HDR: Extraction SD Sales BW: Document Header	🖉 Maintenance	🖉 2LIS_11_VAHDR	🖉 Active	
▶ ⊙⊙⬚ MC11VA0ITM: Extraction SD Sales BW: Document Item	🖉 Maintenance	🖉 2LIS_11_VAITM	🖉 Active	
▶ ⊙⊙⬚ MC11VA0KON: Extraction SD Sales BW: Document Condition	🖉 Maintenance	🖉 2LIS_11_VAKON	🖉 Active	
▶ ⊙⊙⬚ MC11VA0SCL: Extraction SD Sales BW: Document Schedule Line	🖉 Maintenance	🖉 2LIS_11_VASCL	🖉 Active	
▶ ⊙⊙⬚ MC11VA0STH: Extraction MD Order Header Status	🖉 Maintenance	🖉 2LIS_11_VASTH	🖉 Active	
▶ ⊙⊙⬚ MC11VA0STI: Extraction MD Order Item Status	🖉 Maintenance	🖉 2LIS_11_VASTI	🖉 Active	
▶ ⊙⊙⬚ MC11V_0ITM: Extraction SD Sales BW: Document Item Allocation	🖉 Maintenance	🖉 2LIS_11_V_ITM	🖉 Active	
▶ ⊙⊙⬚ MC11V_0SCL: Extraction SD Sales BW: Allocation Schedule Line	🖉 Maintenance	🖉 2LIS_11_V_SCL	🖉 Active	
▼ ⊙⊙⬚ MC11V_0SSL: Extraction MD Sales: Order Delivery	🖉 Maintenance	🖉 2LIS_11_V_SSL	🖉 Active	
▶ ☆ Events				
▼ 🌢 12 : LE Shipping BW			Job Control	🖉 Direct Delta
▼ ⚙Extract structures				
▶ ⊙⊙⬚ MC12VC0HDR: Extraction LE Shipping BW: Document Header	🖉 Maintenance	🖉 2LIS_12_VCHDR	🖉 Active	
▶ ⊙⊙⬚ MC12VC0ITM: Extraction LE Shipping BW: Document Item	🖉 Maintenance	🖉 2LIS_12_VCITM	🖉 Active	
▶ ⊙⊙⬚ MC12VC0SCL: Extraction LE Shipping BW: Schedule Line Deliver	🖉 Maintenance	🖉 2LIS_12_VCSCL	🖉 Active	
▼ 🌢 13 : SD Billing BW			Job Control	🖉 Direct Delta
▼ ⚙Extract structures				
▶ ⊙⊙⬚ MC13VD0HDR: Extraction SD Billing Document BW: Document Hea	🖉 Maintenance	🖉 2LIS_13_VDHDR	🖉 Active	
▶ ⊙⊙⬚ MC13VD0ITM: Extraction SD Billing Document BW: Document Iter	🖉 Maintenance	🖉 2LIS_13_VDITM	🖉 Active	
▶ ⊙⊙⬚ MC13VD0KON: Extraction SD Billing Documents BW: Document Cc	🖉 Maintenance	🖉 2LIS_13_VDKON	🖉 Active	

Figure 9.41 Data Extraction Customizing Cockpit

LO Data Extraction: Customizing Cockpit

Source data	Structure	DataSource	Update	Update Mode
▼ 🌢 Logistics applications				
▶ 🌢 02 : Purchasing			Job Control	🖉 Direct Delta
▶ 🌢 03 : Inventory Controlling			Job Control	🖉 Direct Delta
▶ 🌢 04 : Shop Floor Control			Job Control	🖉 Direct Delta
▶ 🌢 05 : Quality Management			Job Control	🖉 Direct Delta
▶ 🌢 06 : Invoice Verification			Job Control	🖉 Direct Delta
▶ 🌢 08 : Shipment			Job Control	🖉 Direct Delta
▼ 🌢 11 : SD Sales BW			Job Control	🖉 Direct Delta
▼ ⚙Extract structures				
▶ ⊙⊙⬚ MC11VA0HDR: Extraction SD Sales BW: Document Header	🖉 Maintenance	🖉 2LIS_11_VAHDR	🖉 Active	
▶ ⊙⊙⬚ MC11VA0ITM: Extraction SD Sales BW: Document Item	🖉 Maintenance	🖉 2LIS_11_VAᴵ	**DataSource Generation**	
▶ ⊙⊙⬚ MC11VA0KON: Extraction SD Sales BW: Document Condition	🖉 Maintenance	🖉 2LIS_11_VAᴷ		
▶ ⊙⊙⬚ MC11VA0SCL: Extraction SD Sales BW: Document Schedule Line	🖉 Maintenance	🖉 2LIS_11_VAˢ		
▶ ⊙⊙⬚ MC11VA0STH: Extraction MD Order Header Status	🖉 Maintenance	🖉 2LIS_11_VASTH	🖉 Active	
▶ ⊙⊙⬚ MC11VA0STI: Extraction MD Order Item Status	🖉 Maintenance	🖉 2LIS_11_VASTI	🖉 Active	
▶ ⊙⊙⬚ MC11V_0ITM: Extraction SD Sales BW: Document Item Allocation	🖉 Maintenance	🖉 2LIS_11_V_ITM	🖉 Active	
▶ ⊙⊙⬚ MC11V_0SCL: Extraction SD Sales BW: Allocation Schedule Line	🖉 Maintenance	🖉 2LIS_11_V_SCL	🖉 Active	
▶ ⊙⊙⬚ MC11V_0SSL: Extraction MD Sales: Order Delivery	🖉 Maintenance	🖉 2LIS_11_V_SSL	🖉 Active	
▶ 🌢 12 : LE Shipping BW			Job Control	🖉 Direct Delta

Figure 9.42 Data Extraction Customizing Cockpit: DataSource Generation

Figure 9.43 Data Warehouse Workbench: Replicate Metadata

8. Now SAP BW has replicated the DataSource, we need to activate the extraction structure using Transaction LBWE, by selecting INACTIVE. You can select the update mode required as shown in Figure 9.44 by navigating to DIRECT DELTA, QUEUED DELTA, or UNSERIALIZED V3 UPDATE.

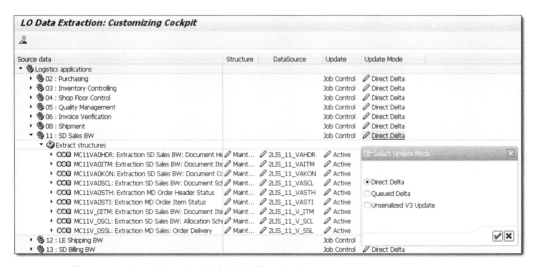

Figure 9.44 Data Extaction Cockpit: Update Options

9. Use Transaction LBWG to delete any content on the Sales and Distribution setup tables, and use application 11 for SAP BW Sales and Distribution. This is important so that your data sources excludes undesired content.

10. You now can perform an extraction using Transaction SBIW or following the menu path SETTINGS FOR APPLICATION-SPECIFIC DATASOURCES (PI) • LOGISTICS • MANAGING EXTRACT STRUCTURES • INITIALIZATION • FILLING IN THE SETUP TABLE • APPLICATION-SPECIFIC SETUP OF STATISTICAL DATA • SERVICE MANAGEMENT • PERFORM SETUP. In the initial screen, make sure you enter a number of run and a future date, and enter other parameters, such as company code and sales organization. You should see a screen similar to Figure 9.45.

Figure 9.45 Reconstruction Display Message: Number of Messages

11. Your internal table now contains Sales and Distribution data. Check the content and use Transaction SE16 with the table name MC11VA0HDRSETUP. As you can see in Figure 9.46, the content may not seem to make any sense. This is not a problem, because this is just a verification step.

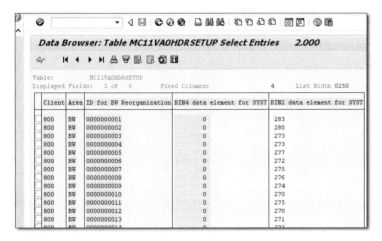

Figure 9.46 Content on Table MC11VA0HDRSETUP

12. Using Transaction RSA1 in the SAP BW system, make sure you create the infopack for the delta initialization, as shown in Figure 9.47. This will trigger the delta initialization and initial run. Enter a name and save when prompted. Select INITIALIZE DELTA PROCESS and INITIALIZATION WITH DELTA TRANSFER in the UPDATE tab. Select SCHEDULE tab and schedule your extraction as required, either immediately or as a background process. Hit the START button to begin the schedule.

13. You can also verify and extract the DataSource contents using Transaction RSA3. Enter "2LIS_11_VAHDR" and execute. You will see a pop up screen with the total number of data records selected. You can display the information by selecting ALV GRID button. To start the extraction, select EXTRACTION button.

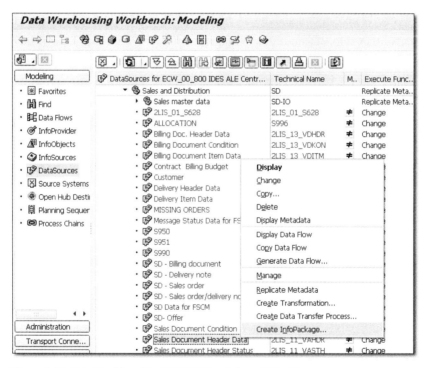

Figure 9.47 Data Workbench in SAP BW Box, Infopack Creation

9.5.4 SAP BW Modeling

If your company has the latest release of SAP BW, you may want to perform the extraction using SAP BW modeling. Let's now discuss how to perform a simple extraction using SAP BW modeling.

1. Using Transaction RSA1, locate the application components and replicate the data sources. Right-click and select REPLICATE METADATA, as described in Figure 9.48.

2. Create the info package in for the DataSource (in this case, 2LIS_11_VAHDR) and make sure it's activated. This will allow to see all the data selected in the extract in the PSA table.

3. Create the DSO for the DataSource and load the data. In Transaction RSA1, select InfoProvider on the right side of the screen and select the related InfoProvider. Right-click to create a new DSO, making sure to enter a name and description as required. Verify that the DSO has successfully activated. Now, you'll upload all the data by using the data transfer process in the activated the DSO.

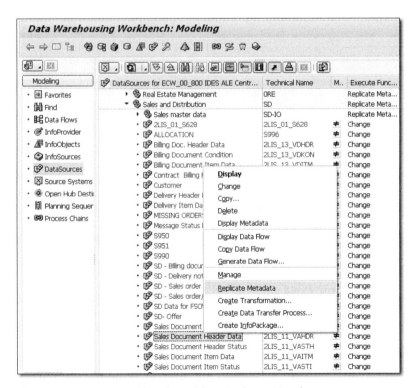

Figure 9.48 SAP BW Workbench Modeling: Replicate Metadata

9.5.5 List-Optimized Daily Reports

The most recent enhancement pack, EHP 7 (SAP_APPL 617), brought new changes to some of the basic Sales and Distribution listing and reporting functionality. Basic listings, such as Transactions VA05 or VA15, have been running in SAP since early versions of Sales and Distribution with minimal enhancements, and it's only with EHP 7 that they've been refreshed and re-introduced as more flexible and friendlier Sales and Distribution listings.

For example, the business function Sales and Distribution, Optimization of Lists (LOG_SD_REPORT_OPT) comes with this enhancement package. This business function list all optimized reports available, and you can pick the report that best suits your needs for sales and invoicing. The Sales and Distribution list-optimized enhances individually at the selection fields or output generated, or both. Figure 9.49 show how the traditional order list VA05 is now optimized in the main screen selection criteria to provide further searching and functionality.

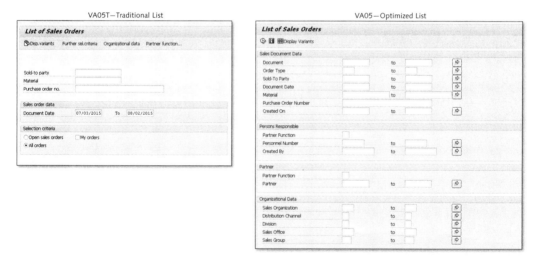

Figure 9.49 Traditional vs. Optimized VA05 Order List Comparison

Table 9.11 show the most important reports that have now been optimized for Sales and Distribution along with the main changes introduced.

Optimized Transaction Code	Description	Report	BAdI	Changes
VA05	List of Customer Orders	SD_SALES_DOCU-MENT_VIEW Enhancement spot: ES_SD_SALES_DOCUMENT_VIEW	BADI_SDOC_WRAPPER BADI_SDOC_VIEW_CUSTOM_FUNC	New initial selection screen, output screen, and enhancement concept.
VA15	List of Inquiries	SD_SALES_DOCU-MENT_VA15 Enhancement spot: ES_SD_SALES_DOCUMENT_VA15	BADI_SDOC_WRAPPER BADI_SDOC_WRAPPER_MASS BADI_SDOC_VIEW_CUSTOM_FUNC BADI_SDOC_VIEW_CUSTOM_FUNC_INT	New initial selection screen, output screen, and enhancement concept.
VA25	List of Quotations	SD_SALES_DOCU-MENT_VA25 Enhancement spot: ES_SD_SALES_DOCUMENT_VA25	BADI_SDOC_WRAPPER BADI_SDOC_WRAPPER_MASS BADI_SDOC_VIEW_CUSTOM_FUNC BADI_SDOC_VIEW_CUSTOM_FUNC_INT	New initial selection screen, output screen, and enhancement concept.
SD01	Orders Within Time Period	SD_SALES_DOCUMENT_SDO1	BADI_SDOC_WRAPPER BADI_SDOC_WRAPPER_MASS BADI_SDOC_VIEW_CUSTOM_FUNC	Output.
VA45	List of Contracts	SD_SALES_DOCUMENT_VA45	BADI_SDOC_WRAPPER BADI_SDOC_WRAPPER_MASS BADI_SDOC_VIEW_CUSTOM_FUNC BADI_SDOC_VIEW_CUSTOM_FUNC_INT	Output.

Table 9.11 Sales and Distribution-Optimization of Lists and Reports

Additional reports apply specifically to billing and credit management. Table 9.13 shows the main optimized transaction codes.

Optimized Transaction Code	Description	Report
VF05	List of Billing Document	Module pool SAPMV65A
VF04	Maintain Billing Due List	Report SDBILLDL
V.21	Log of Collective Run	Report SDSAMPRO
VF24	Process Invoice Worklist	Report SDINVLDL
VKM1	Blocked SD Documents	
VKM2/ VKM3	Released SD Documents	
VKM4	SD Documents	
VKM5	Deliveries	

Table 9.12 Optimized Transaction for Billing and Credit Management

In Customizing for Sales and Distribution, you can activate and deactivate each transaction (report) separately and independently, accordingly to your needs.

1. Access Transaction SFW5 to switch on business functions. Under ENTERPRISE_ BUSINESS_FUNCTIONS search for the new business function `LOG_SD_REPORT_OPT` for Sales and Distribution, Optimization of Lists. Make sure it's activated, as shown in Figure 9.50.

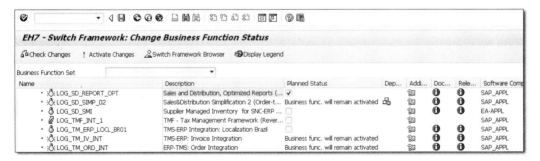

Figure 9.50 EHP 7 Switch Framerwork: Sales and Distribution Business Function

2. Decide which optimized list will adjust better to your company needs. As an example, to activate the optimized version of Transaction VA05 in Customizing, follow the path Transaction SPRO • SALES AND DISTRIBUTION • SALES • LISTS • OPTIMIZED LISTS • ACTIVATE OPTIMIZED REPORTS. Figure 9.51 show the list of optimized report selected: VA05, V.21, V23, VF05, and VKM1. It's important to select ACTIVE to be able to run the new version. This confirmation is revers-

ible—meaning that you can always go back to the traditional transactions instead of the optimized ones.

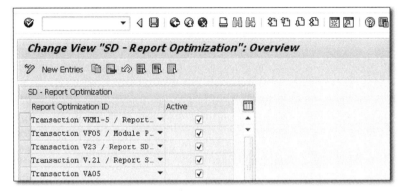

Figure 9.51 Sales and Distribution Report Optimization Activation

3. If your requirements call for a more customized solution, you then have to implement the appropriate BAdIs by following the path Transaction SPRO • SALES AND DISTRIBUTION • SALES • LISTS • OPTIMIZED LISTS. See Table 9.13 for a list of these BAdIs.

BAdI	Description	Main Adjustments
BADI_SDOC_WRAPPER	Line by line	Customer-specific fields as columns for the results list. The data for the output list is processed individually.
BADI_SDOC_WRAPPER_MASS	Mass Access	Mass calculation of the data results using mass processing.
BADI_SDOC_VIEW_CUSTOM_FUNC	Pushbutton	To add additional functions for the results list. Dix functions are displayed as pushbuttons at maximum; the rest are part of the dialog box.

Table 9.13 Main BAdIs to Adjust the Optimized Lists

BAdIs

Once you have activate each of the optimized reports, you won't be able to run your customer-specific variants and layouts, including your enhancements from the previous version. If you need to transfer some of those customized elements, you need to activate the BAdIs indicated above.

For additional information and further technical details, consult SAP Note 1780163.

9.6   Summary

In this chapter, we introduced you to SAP standard reports. We used a simple example for demonstrating the steps of an ABAP query. We also discussed the standard analyses available in the Sales Information System and the steps needed to create a flexible analysis for your own requirement. We concluded with coverage of operative reporting using SAP Business Explorer, SAP HANA, and SAP BW.

With this knowledge, you should be able to help users take advantage of the functionalities that standard reports and analyses offer for Sales and Distribution. You can motivate users to make the best use of standard SIS and BI reports, and you can create your own reports using the steps we detailed for SIS and BEx queries.

The chapter discusses the functionality in the SAP CRM module that specifically applies to Sales and Distribution. It highlights the key configuration in customer quotes, sales orders, marketing, and the Customer Interaction Center.

10   Sales and Distribution and SAP CRM

As part of the SAP Business Suite, SAP CRM focuses on your most valuable asset: your customers. It's common (and in fact, recommended by SAP) for customers to install SAP CRM in a separate box from their ERP system—primarily to maintain high system performance, especially in those company operations with high transactional volume.

A common misconception of SAP CRM and CRM software in general is that they are one and the same. In the market today, we can find different manufacturers and other vendors that offer CRM software in competition with the offering from SAP SE. However, SAP CRM offers the greatest degree of functional and integrative robustness to SAP ERP—and to your customers. Because it's customer-centered by nature, SAP CRM provides you with a 360-degree view of customers by means of analytics and reporting, in order to better detect customers' needs along the lines of sales, services, and marketing.

In the following sections of this chapter, we will provide you with a better understanding of SAP Customer Relationship Management (CRM) and how it interacts with SAP ERP Sales and Distribution. We will start by defining CRM concepts and definitions, and then review the highlights of the SAP CRM integration with Sales and Distribution (SD), along with the rest of SAP ERP.

So what kind of overlap is there between SAP ERP Sales and Distribution functionality and SAP CRM software? Are they complementary? Are there advantages of moving to SAP CRM?

There are several advantages to having an SAP CRM system, especially when compared to the regular Sales and Distribution order-to-cash process. Table 1.1 makes a comparison among the two solutions.

Sales and Distribution	SAP CRM
Focused on the process: order, delivery, billing, accounts receivable.	Focused on customer and their needs; processes are handled in SAP ERP.
Sales/orders and services are traditionally found in different departments or different system platforms.	Orders, order entry, and services are centralized.
Globalization within an SAP ERP deployed system.	Globalization within a similar platform across countries.
Information and workflow limit are limited to a given department and the people involved in such activities. Limitations are based on system architecture.	Centralized information. Unifying database and platform with one customer-facing application. No architectural limitation.
Oriented to fine-tune processes.	Oriented to attain higher customer satisfaction.
Forecasts based on previous sales.	Customer's behavior and forecast, including customer's predictions.

Table 10.1 Comparison Sales and Distrbution and SAP CRM Functionality Highlights

SAP CRM natively interacts with Sales and Distribution and other SAP ERP modules and components, such as SAP ERP Financial Supply Chain Management and Accounts Receivable, etc. To illustrate this interaction, Figure 10.1 describes how a sales order replicates, and how the information flows from the SAP CRM system into Sales and Distribution in order to obtain inventory, delivery, and post-of-goods issued status. The sales order process in Sales and Distribution and the statuses of each subsequent step feeds into SAP CRM for display purposes. For billing, you have two choices regarding a newly created invoice's location: in Sales and Distribution or in SAP CRM.

To implement SAP CRM, your company needs to decide who will be the master of records and who will replicate master data objects among Sales and Distribution and SAP CRM. The master of records is the system of record where daily data creation and maintenance will take place. The customer master, typically SAP ERP, copies over to the SAP CRM business partners.

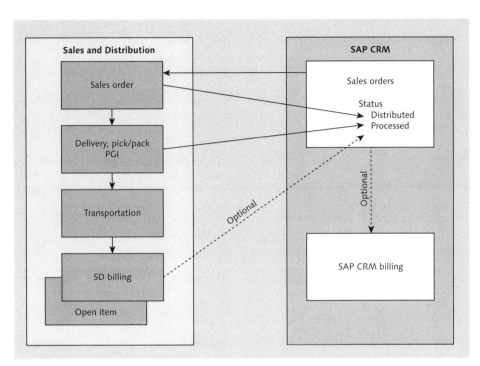

Figure 10.1 Integration Cycle for Sales and Distribution and SAP CRM

You may deploy SAP CRM via a web interface; the interface offers a friendly graphical interaction, standardized across the SAP CRM components. You can personalize this interface, and it's highly adjustable. Today, the SAP CRM WebClient solution is mostly used by end users in their daily operations, and that's likely to continue in the near future, even as SAP plans for further developments in this area. SAP CRM WebClient is a secure web page: access via the SAP ERP security team is required, with a user ID and password.

Now that you understand SAP CRM concepts and how they integrate with Sales and Distribution at a broad level, let's discuss some basic steps to configure this integration in key areas of SAP CRM. We will discuss configuration around Sales, Marketing, and Service, the three main components of SAP CRM, which will help you to optimize your implementation.

10.1 Sales

SAP CRM Sales is the component that most closely parallels the Sales and Distribution functionality. It's here that you'll find the highest degree of SAP CRM-SD integration, including in sales orders, opportunities, pricing, and quotations.

As opposed to sales in Sales and Distribution, SAP CRM uses a different status on sales orders. An SAP CRM sales order document can act as an inquiry, quotation or firm order; the line-item status determines the Sales and Distribution-equivalent order type. Therefore, in SAP CRM you have one document to handle throughout the sales process, rather than several documents, as is the case with the SAP ERP counterpart. The system verifies availability and credit during the order creation—yet another integration with Sales and Distribution.

10.1.1 SAP ERP Order and Quotation Created in SAP CRM WebClient

Let's walk through integrating an SAP ERP quote with SAP CRM WebClient. This section covers a very common scenario. Though we cover the basic configuration in this scenario, other SAP CRM configuration tasks may still apply. Refer to your SAP CRM consultant or configuration guide for further details.

1. Identify which Sales and Distribution document types you will use for your implementation; these are the standards QT for quotation and OR for standard order. Follow menu path IMG • SALES AND DISTRIBUTION • SALES • SALES DOCUMENTS • SALES DOCUMENT HEADER • DEFINE SALES DOCUMENT TYPES or use Transaction VOV8. It's important to understand that SAP CRM will identify QT (quote type) in Sales and Distribution as AG; similarly, the Sales and Distribution order type OR will be order type TA in SAP CRM.

2. Identify which set of item categories you'll use for the SAP CRM integration or Transaction VOV7.

3. Based on your company requirements, you may need to copy the SAP CRM opportunities into a Sales and Distribution quotation. Control this by means of the copying control: SALES DOCUMENT TO SALES DOCUMENT via Transaction VTAA. Include the list of item categories and schedule lines relevant to SAP CRM.

4. In your SAP CRM system, make the following configuration settings to enable and define SAP CRM profile and the RFC connectivity relationship: SAP CRM IMG • CUSTOMER RELATIONSHIP MANAGEMENT • TRANSACTIONS • SETTINGS FOR

SALES TRANSACTIONS • DEFINE PROFILE FOR ERP SALES TRANSACTIONS. Hit ⌈Enter⌉. Create a new profile or change an existing profile, and type in the RFC destination.

5. Highlight the newly created profile or the existing one, and select ASSIGN DOCUMENT TYPES TO ERP PROFILE • NEW ENTRIES (in this case, profile SALESPRO, as shown in Figure 10.2). Here you can enter the list of Sales and Distribution documents. Make sure you save your entries.

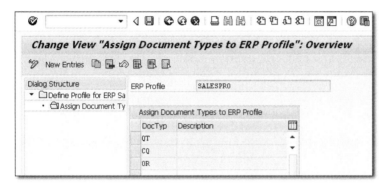

Figure 10.2 SAP CRM Profile: Assign Document Types to SAP ERP Profile

6. Assign the newly created profile SALESPRO to your SAP CRM business roles via Transaction CRMC_UI_PROFILE in SAP CRM. Select the business role that will handle the SAP ERP quotes and orders (in this case, BP_SLS_EMPL). Select ASSIGN FUNCTION PROFILES on the right-hand menu and make a NEW ENTRY to associate the ERP_SALES_ORDER with the profile SALESPRO, as shown in Figure 10.3. You may want to repeat these steps as required to handle SAP ERP sales orders and quotes.

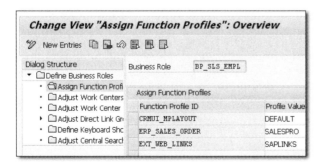

Figure 10.3 SAP CRM: Profile Assignment for SAP ERP Sales Order Quotes

7. You may consider activating the business roles to display as second level entries in the navigator bar, or as links displayed in the work center pages. To do this, stay in the same SAP CRM Transaction CRMC_UI_PROFILE, as shown in Figure 10.4. Select ADJUST WORK CENTER GROUP LINKS in the left menu. Locate Group ID SLS-ERP-CR and/or search (Group ID SLS-ERP-SR) for the SAP ERP quotation and the SAP ERP sales order. You may consider repeating these steps for each group and business role.

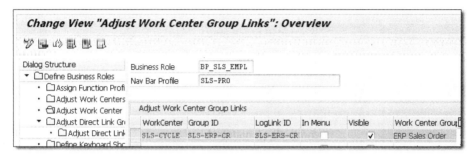

Figure 10.4 SAP CRM: Business Roles Adjustment Work Center Group Link

10.1.2 Adding Sales Functionality to SAP CRM WebClient

If you have some basic experience with SAP CRM WebClient, you probably already noticed that only limited Sales and Distribution sales functionality is available. If you prefer to execute a pricing report or a list of expiring customer quotations in SAP CRM WebClient, take advantage of the SAP ERP sales functionality that SAP has included via the Transaction Launcher, as described in Table 10.2. If you need to activate some of these SAP ERP transaction codes, you need to meet certain pre-requirements, including defining the TRANSACTION LAUNCHER LOGICAL SYSTEMS and URLs. If, in addition, you would like to create URL-based launch transactions, you need to define the URL IDs and PARAMETERS. In both of these activities, you need the support of a Basis consultant or a related expert.

Source	Transaction	Description
SAP ERP	V.15	Display Backorders
SAP ERP	VD03	Display Customer Sales
SAP ERP	VA01	Create Sales Order
SAP ERP	VA21	Create Quotation

Table 10.2 SAP ERP Transactions Included in SAP CRM WebClient

Source	Transaction	Description
SAP ERP	V/LD	Execute Pricing Report
SAP ERP	SDQ1	Expiring Quotations
SAP ERP	S_ALR_87012219	Credit Management: Early Warning List

Table 10.2 SAP ERP Transactions Included in SAP CRM WebClient (Cont.)

1. You can activate the SAP ERP functionality using Transaction CRM_UI_ACTIONWZ or following the SAP CRM menu path IMG • CUSTOMER RELATIONSHIP MANAGEMENT • UI FRAMEWORK • TECHNICAL ROLE DEFINITION • TRANSACTION LAUNCHER • CONFIGURE TRANSACTION LAUNCHER. In order to configure the Transaction Launcher, you need to follow the steps in each screen, as indicated by Table 10.3. You may want to repeat each step, as ERPS transactions must be executed in your SAP CRM WebClient.

Screen	Field	Value
Initial		Initial screen
1	Launch Trans. ID	YBP_ERP_TX_SDQ1
	Component Set	ALL
2	Description	ERP Transaction SDQ1
	Class Name	Give your own name of the class, or pick one.
	Stateful	Unchecked
	Raise Veto	Unchecked
3	Object Type	a-BOR Transaction
	Object Action	Execute
	Transaction Type	BOR Transaction
	Logical System	Logical system (for SAP ERP or SAP CRM) defined for the transaction launcher
	BOR Object Type	TSTC
	Method Name	DISPLAY
4	Parameter	Object Key
	Value	Transaction SDQ1
5	Parameter	Blank
6		Complete button

Table 10.3 Configuration Steps for the Wizard

2. Figure 10.5 shows the second screen of the Transaction Launcher. Here, you can enter your own description and class name to match your requirements. Enable the STATEFUL checkbox and the transaction will open a new screen that remains open until the agent closes it. Otherwise, if unchecked, the launched transaction closes automatically when the agent indicates the end. Check RAISE VETO if you would like to receive an error message when closing the launched transaction.

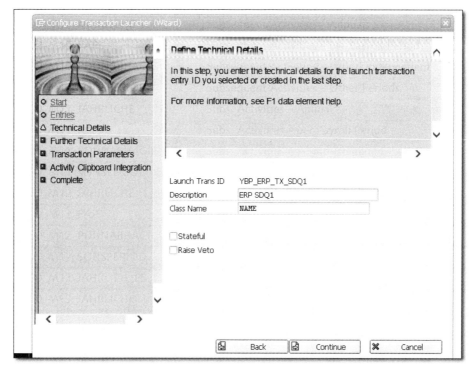

Figure 10.5 Transaction Launcher Wizard

In the following section, we will discuss an important aspect of almost any company: marketing.

10.2 Marketing

SAP CRM Marketing allows you to analyze and optimize your company's marketing strategy and campaign execution. Additionally, SAP CRM Marketing is the component that helps with planning, budgeting, and executing the vast majority of your marketing needs. Furthermore, within this module, SAP has embedded seven main components of the marketing cycle, as shown in Table 10.4.

SAP CRM Marketing Solutions	Key Functions	Integrates with...
Marketing Planning and Budgeting	The marketing plan is the upper echelon of the marketing component. It defines strategic products, timelines and budget. The marketing plan also holds the hierarchy to allocate one or more campaigns, target groups, and even other subcomponents of the marketing plan.	SAP ERP Project System (PS) and MS Project System.
List Management	External lists provide data mapping from the source data into SAP CRM data fields, in addition to providing checks for duplicates, data cleansing, and address validation.	External lists to maintain customer master records and data cleansing. The data export to SAP BW.
Segmentation	SAP CRM provides the segment builder. Customer segments are specially designed to aggregate customers with similar needs and attributes into a customer campaign. It allows you to group customers using marking attributes including income, age, location, or even their hobbies, for marketing campaign purposes.	Data sources are marketing attributes and BI queries, including SAP ERP or other external sources.
Campaign Management	Campaign management helps you to set up a campaign from beginning to end, which includes market analysis, campaign execution, and analytics. Campaign management also allows you to use the graphical interface to provide a clearer overview of the process flow. The campaign management component also allows you to monitor ongoing campaigns and make adjustments.	SD condition technique controls campaign determination. At the sales order, marketing projects (campaigns, one or multiple trade promotions) incorporate into the sales pricing at the item level, depending on your Customizing settings in SAP CRM and SAP ERP.

Table 10.4 SAP CRM Marketing Key Functionality and Sales and Distribution Integration

SAP CRM Marketing Solutions	Key Functions	Integrates with...
Trade Promotion Management (TPM)	TPM will help you manage in-store retail promotions. One of the major advantages of TPM is that it allows you to trace your promotions in detail, so you can demonstrate how many product quantities are sold in each related retail location, covering pay-for-promotion scenarios.	SD configuration for TPM relates to enhanced rebate processing. In Sales and Distribution, rebate agreements are assigned to a condition type group, and then each is assigned to one or more condition types. In the Extended Rebate Processing and Agreement Types W/VAKEY is checked. These are the Customizing settings required for the settlement of SAP ERP rebate agreements via SAP CRM claims management. Find them under Business Configuration (BC) Sets. The name of the BC Set is BIL_ERP_CF_INT1.
Lead Management	SAP CRM leads are especially useful after you've launched your campaigns. This tool allows you to fully manage leads across your marketing channels. They are a repository that allocates follow-up contact from your customers.	Lead management will also help you to qualify leads automatically, and even send them via workflow for qualification.
Marketing Analytics	SAP CRM Marketing Analytics help you support marketing plan optimization, corrective actions, and improvements. Marketing Analytics will allow you to discover market channels, customer behavior, segments, products, market trends, and profitability, among other things.	BI and SAP HANA-optimized BI Content for Sales and Distribution and SAP CRM.

Table 10.4 SAP CRM Marketing Key Functionality and Sales and Distribution Integration (Cont.)

Now that you understand what kind of functionality SAP CRM Marketing offers, and how SAP CRM is a customer-oriented tool, let's discuss another important SAP CRM functionality: service.

10.3 Service

In today's critical environment, where services sell more rapidly than ever, you need a tool to support your operation and to track services all the way through the process.

SAP CRM Service supports all facets of your customer service organization. Along with a better user experience, it can even expedite issues resolution, because it features real-time support and integrated complaint management.

SAP CRM Services provides solutions to all phases of the customer engagement cycle, as described in Table 10.5. The table also highlights the integration with Sales and Distribution.

SAP CRM Service Solution	Key Functions	Integrates with...
Contract & Entitlement Management	SAP CRM service contract management allows your company to manage service agreements and service contracts quotations within the same functionality, including service contracts, parts-and labor, and usage-base agreements. You'll commonly find service contracts as a service-level agreement (SLA), which establish the response time and availability for the customer's entitlements.	Service contracts replicate into the Sales and Distribution contracts module for further processing, pricing and billing.
Service Order Management	The service orders in SAP CRM handle service repairs, maintenance, or installations where a technician is needed. SAP CRM Service Order Management also supports service quotations that outline pricing and delivery conditions. The SAP CRM service order verifies and controls warranties and entitlements.	The service order replicates in SAP ERP under the Sales and Distribution module.

Table 10.5 SAP CRM Service Cycle

SAP CRM Service Solution	Key Functions	Integrates with...
Installed Base Management	Installed base (iBase) is a term commonly used in a service environment to allocate all pieces of equipment installed on a company site. We commonly refer to the individual pieces of equipment that are not directly part of the installed base as individual objects. One customer could have more than one iBase for the service installation, such as a Building and floors. SAP CRM iBase provides a tracking solution to trace customers' installed products via a graphical hierarchical display.	Account and contact management allows you to manage and control the IBase and its history, in order to maximize opportunities.
Warranty and Claim Management	This solution allows you to manage the entire warranty and claims process, including warranty registration, return merchandise authorization (RMA) via the warranty claim, receipt, and inspection. In addition, you will be able to retrieve warranty entitlement during service-related business and track the entitlement services provided to your customers as warranty cost assignment.	SD RMA, pricing
Complaints and Returns	Complaints and Returns provides the tools your company needs to manage customer complaints. A complaint usually follows the creation of credits and debits, free-of-charge replacements, and RMAs, among others.	SAP ERP supports the return process, especially the financial impact. Returns and complaints replicate into SAP ERP Sales and Distribution for further processing.
In-House Repairs	In-house repairs provide you with a tool to assist with the repair process from the RMA authorization, receiving the broken product, and even shipping the repaired product back to your customers.	In-house repairs also replicates into SAP ERP and Sales and Distribution for further processing of the credit/debit memo, or free shipping.

Table 10.5 SAP CRM Service Cycle (Cont.)

SAP CRM Service Solution	Key Functions	Integrates with...
Service Analytics	Each of the Service components provide reports, including iBases, service orders and contracts, entitlement management, resource planning, case management, complaints and returns, and in-house repairs, among others.	BI integration

Table 10.5 SAP CRM Service Cycle (Cont.)

10.4 Interaction Center

The SAP CRM Interaction Center is a tool that provides a user-friendly environment to facilitate communication between your company and your customers via multiple channels, as shown in Figure 10.6. The SAP CRM Interaction Center allows communication via email, fax, telephone, postal letter, and, in the current release, Web chat, providing your company's customers with a multi-channel interaction center.

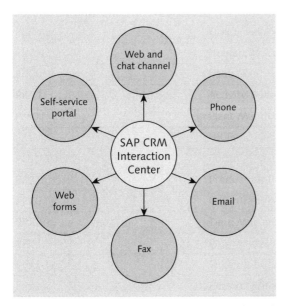

Figure 10.6 SAP CRM Interaction Center Multi-Channel Display

Instead of the traditional call center, centralized in one physical location, the Interaction Center agents can now work virtually anywhere in the world. The main goals of the Interaction Center are to increase customer loyalty and profitability.

You may have noticed that all of the communications described in Figure 10.6 are stored centrally in Interaction Center. This is a key advantage for increasing your customers' loyalty and satisfaction. Very few customers would be pleased to hear that you never received their e-mail or fax, or that it's stored in a system that you don't have access to. The Interaction Center centralizes your customer information in a unified platform.

1. Sales and Distribution integrates with the Interaction Center in different ways. A common requirement is based on a quick launch of the SAP ERP sales order. An agent or sales representative needs to have quick access to the customer's sales orders via the Interaction Center. In this case, the steps outlined below will allow you to activate sales orders in the Interaction Center profile. Each component or function in the Interaction Center has its own profile that is also a valid point for Sales and Distribution integration. If you would like to activate the following functionality, you must have the authorization in SAP CRM, via Transaction PFCG. Additionally, you should verify the role assignments via the SAP CRM Transaction SU01.

2. Update the Transaction Profile to include the SAP ERP sales order by following the menu path CRM • CUSTOMER INTERACTION CENTER • INTERACTION CENTER WEBCLIENT • BUSINESS TRANSACTION • DEFINE BUSINESS TRANSACTION PROFILES. Highlight the business transaction profile required (in this case Z_EMPLOYEE) and then select DEPENDENT BUSINESS TRANSACTIONS. Enter the SAP ERP transactions as new, such as TA for sales orders and AG for quotes, as shown in Figure 10.7. Now select CONTENT MANAGEMENT TEMPLATES FORM from the left menu to maintain object type BUS2000115 as new entries. Finally, save your entries.

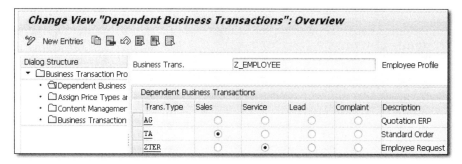

Figure 10.7 Define Business Transaction Profile: Maintain Transaction Types

3. It's now necessary to assign a new navigation bar entry to a new navigation bar profile. Define a new navigation bar profile for the Interaction Center Web-Client scenarios of SAP best practices for SAP CRM • CUSTOMER RELATIONSHIP MANAGEMENT • INTERACTION CENTER WEBCLIENT • DEFINE BUSINESS ROLE. Create a new business role, or highlight an existing one, such as YBP_ICA_SLS. Make sure the SAP ERP sales order is not set to INACTIVE, under ADJUST WORK CENTERS.

4. If you want your sales representative to actively jump into the SAP ERP sales order from the Interaction Center, you must define RFC destinations in SAP ERP. Define a new entry by following the menu path CRM • INTERACTION CENTER WEBCLIENT • BUSINESS TRANSACTION • ERP SALES ORDER • DEFINE PROFILES FOR ERP SALES ORDER. Under ERP SALES ODER PROFILE, select YERP_ORDER and enter the RFC DESTINATION. Save your settings. Now select the ASSIGNMENT DOCUMENT TYPE on the left menu. Enter TA for sales orders and AG for quotations in SAP ERP.

5. Now assign the profiles defined for each function to the WebClient profile. The WebClient identifies and summarizes each profile required under the different scenarios that your company has specified. Follow the menu path SAP CRM • INTERACTION CENTER WEBCLIENT • DEFINE BUSINESS ROLE. You will highlight the YCP_ICA_SLS business role, and select ASSIGN FUNCTION PROFILES. Figure 10.8 describes this assignment. Make a new entry for function profile ID ERP_SALES_ORDER and profile value YERP_ORDER.

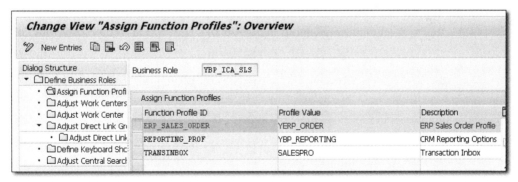

Figure 10.8 Maintain Business Roles for the Interaction Center: Function Profile ID

10.5 Summary

In this chapter, we walked you through the SAP Customer Relationship Management (CRM). You learned how SAP CRM integrates into SAP ERP, and especially how the orders, quotes, and service orders replicate into SAP ERP.

We discussed the main configuration required to integrate with Sales and Distribution, following the best business practices for SAP CRM, along with the key components of the SAP CRM module, including quotes and sales, service, and the Interaction Center.

11 Summary and Conclusion

Throughout this book, we discussed the practical issues and tools that will help you address your own sales and distribution issues and processes. We also discussed the fundamental concepts and techniques used in customization for putting the Sales and Distribution functionality in SAP ERP to optimal use. Let's briefly revisit the important topics and information covered in each chapter.

Introduction

We started the first chapter by establishing the groundwork for a Sales and Distribution configuration: we took a quick look at SAP ERP and gave an idea of how the newest releases and recent technologies impact Sales and Distribution, including SAP HANA, SAP Fiori, and BI-optimized reporting. We then introduced you to popular implementation methodologies and other resources to fast-track your Sales and Distribution implementation.

Organizational Structure and Master Data

In Chapter 1, we introduced you to the organizational units in Sales and Distribution, including how they are defined or imported. We also learned how to check organizational units for consistency after the configuration is done. We discussed sales organizations, divisions, distribution channels, sales offices, sales groups, storage locations, warehouse numbers, shipping points, loading points, and transport planning points.

Chapter 2, Master Data, discussed customer master data: how to reduce the master data maintenance requirement by defining common divisions and common distribution channels, how the system defines the customer account group, and how to customize any field of the customer master data record.

You also learned about the material master sales view. We briefly explained the fields of the three sales views in material master date (SALES: SALES ORG. DATA 1, SALES: SALES ORG. DATA 2, and SALES: GENERAL/PLANT DATA), and you learned how to customize some fields (including PRODUCT HIERARCHY, MATERIAL STATUS, MATERIAL GROUPS 1, 2, 3, 4 and 5, and MATERIAL COMMISSION GROUPS). We explained how to define batches and how to optimize batch management using system messages, layout, DMS, batch numbers, and classification.

Sales

In Chapter 3, Sales, the first three sections discussed how to optimize sales order processing through customized document types, item categories, and schedule line categories. In the next two sections, we discussed different types of routines and how you can use them in copy control. We also discussed using copy control as an optimization tool to create a document with reference to another document with a minimum of error and effort.

You also learned about the use of condition techniques in partner determination, free goods, material determination, material listing and exclusion, batch determination, and output determination. This was a sort of preview for the detailed discussion of condition techniques waiting for you in the next chapter.

We also discussed the special functionalities SAP ERP offers for sales processes, including outline agreements and incompletion logs. You learned about how the sales process differs in some special business processes, such as consignment sales and third-party sales. We discussed how to process returns, credit memo requests, debit memo requests, and other complaint handling tools.

We touched on the common integration point of Sales and Distribution with Materials Management. You learned about the availability check, transfer of requirements, available to promise, and stock transfer processes, and in the last section, we covered the important elements of Global ATP and how to customize it for processing sales availability.

Pricing

Chapter 4 focused on condition techniques. We introduced you to the condition technique, and showed you how to use it for price determination. We even discussed some suggestions for optimization in the first three sections of this chapter. In the fourth section, you learned about the customization requirements for using rebate agreements optimally, and in the fifth section, we took you through the steps for creating your own pricing reports. Finally, we discussed the steps to customize the SAP interface for external tax software, such as Sabrix, Taxware, and Vertex. Finally, we discussed how to spot—and solve—some common pricing problems.

Credit Risk Management

Chapter 5, Credit Risk Management, discussed how to manage the risk associated with credit. We discussed the settings for automatic credit checks and reviewed how to block and unblock customers for different sales operations. The chapter also covered different forms of payment and their automatic determination in sales, and how integration with SAP FSCM Credit Management impacts this process. In the last section of the chapter, we took a look at some problems and their solutions.

Logistics Management

In Chapter 6, Logistics Management, we discussed how to optimize a delivery document by customizing delivery types and delivery item categories. You learned about the various operations carried out as part of delivery processing (including picking, packing, and goods issue). We also discussed processing deliveries in the warehouse in handling units and using a delivery due list.

The following sections included coverage of how to optimize using the route, route determination, and scheduling functionalities. You learned the steps required for stock transfers between different plants, and were introduced to output, in general, and the customization and automatic determination of shipping output, in particular.

We also discussed batch management and how to optimize batch determination in a delivery document. We then discussed processing serialized material, how it can contribute to your business, and how to configure it in SAP ERP. Finally, we reviewed a few of the problems often encountered during delivery processing, and their solutions.

Billing

In Chapter 7, Billing, we reviewed the principles of bill processing and discussed how to create a single or multiple invoice with and without a billing due list. You learned how to split, cancel, or combine them into an invoice list as well. We also discussed how you can use the general billing interface optimally. In the second section, you learned how to optimize billing documents, and we discussed the complaint handling process and billing plan.

The final sections discussed the interface of Sales and Distribution with Accounting. You learned about the use of the condition technique in automatic determination of revenue GLs, reconciliation accounts, and cash accounts. We also covered how to make the accounting document number the same as the billing document number and the data transferred from billing to accounting documents and revenue recognition functionalities. The chapter closed up by reviewing common problems and their solutions.

Cross-Functional Customizing

Chapter 8 discussed how to make the best use of the text IDs available for the Sales and Distribution functionality in SAP ERP. You learned how to customize the IDoc Interface for EDI and ALE communication, and how to create a Web interface. We also discussed how to optimize batch where-used lists and the batch information cockpit for reporting. In the ABAP tools section, we reviewed the LSMW, and finished with coverage of how to make the best use of numbering objects and number ranges.

Reporting and Analysis

In Chapter 9, we reviewed the standard reports and analyses available in SAP ERP and SAP BW 7.4 (optimized business content) for the Sales and Distribution functionality in SAP ERP. You learned how you can create your own reports and analyses using the Sales Information System (SIS), and BEx queries. Lastly, you learned about the optimized new transactions available in EHP 6 and EHP 7.

Integrating Sales and Distribution with SAP CRM

In this chapter, you learned how the overlap between Sales and Distribution and SAP CRM interacts and key integration points between them. Quotes, sales orders, and marketing are the main SAP CRM items we discussed.

A skilled craftsperson needs the best available tools, and now you've seen what a powerful array of configuration tools Sales and Distribution provides you, we hope your new skills bring you ever-growing levels of success.

Appendices

A   Customization of Local Layout

You can customize the local layout to suit your preferences, screen size, processing speed, and various other factors so that you are most comfortable working with it. Begin customizing your local layout by pressing [Alt] + [F12] or by clicking on the CUSTOMIZE LOCAL LAYOUT icon, highlighted in Figure A.1. This icon is available from any SAP screen—in fact, even from the login screen before you have logged on! After clicking the icon, you'll see a list of objects that can be customized, as shown in Figure A.2.

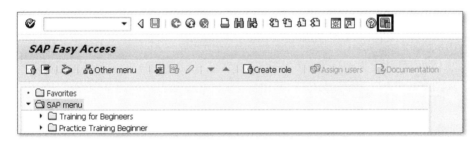

Figure A.1 Icon for Customizing Local Layout

We'll discuss the customization and tools available in the list shown in Figure A.2 in next two sections. In first section, Options Settings, we'll discuss the features available with the first item of the drop-down list. In the second section, Other Customization Options, we'll discuss eleven other features available on the drop-down list.

Figure A.2 Menu for Customizing Local Layout

A.1 Options Settings

Let's examine the first drop-down menu's items.

A.1.1 Visual Design

In the Visual Design area, shown in the left of Figure A.3, you can control the color of the screen, the color contrast between different screen elements, font size, and other features that typically constitute design via pre-delivered themes or by manually modifying them. You may notice that some of the options available under each menu vary based on the selected theme; for example, you can change the contrast and colors under the Enjoy Theme.

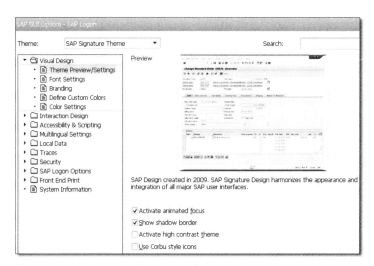

Figure A.3 Visual Design: Streamline Theme

By default, the SAP GUI uses the SAP Signature Theme. Other options are available under predetermined themes: Classic design or Enjoy Theme, which some people favor, since they relate to SAP graphics in older versions. Though the Signature Theme is considered superior for the latest SAP GUI releases, there is no reason you can't use older display modes.

You can change the themes' color setting by placing the cursor on Color Setting and modifying the colors using the SAP Signature Default Color, SAP Gold, SAP Green, SAP Purple, and SAP Red, as shown in Figure A.4. You can now click the OK or Apply button. You can also create our own custom colors by selecting

DEFINE CUSTOM COLORS, where you may modify the DEGREES of the colors and then SAVE AS.

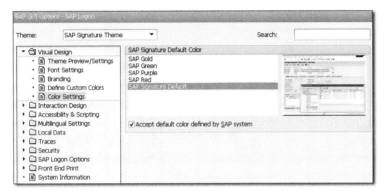

Figure A.4 Visual Desing: Color Settings

By selecting FONT SETTINGS on the right side menu, you can enter your own font and size with FIXED WIDTH-FONT SETTINGS and PROPORTIONAL FONT SETTINGS. Save and apply your preferred settings. You may need to restart your SAP GUI to see the actual changes.

A.1.2   Interaction Design

The INTERACTION DESIGN settings adjust visualization options, keyboard settings, audio feedback, and several other options to better adapt the SAP GUI experience to your personal choices or company branding.

Figure A.5 show the VISUALIZATION 1 options, where the cursor's appearance is controlled, from narrow to wide. An important setting is found under the CON-TROLS box: select SHOW KEYS WITHIN DROPDOWN LISTS to see drop-down lists that include the actual internal SAP key code.

Change other controls as necessary under the NOTIFICATIONS, CONTROL SETTINGS, and SOUND SETTINGS, applying and saving your adjustments.

If you select NOTIFICATIONS on the right screen, you will see a new screen with TOOL-TIP and MESSAGES boxes. The MESSAGES box has four checkboxes. When you select the first checkbox (BEEP AT MESSAGES), you'll hear a beep for any message info, war-nings, or errors. Select the next three checkboxes for messages to appear as a pop-up window (dialog box), in addition to the bottom of the screen in the message area for success/information message, warning, and error messages, respectively.

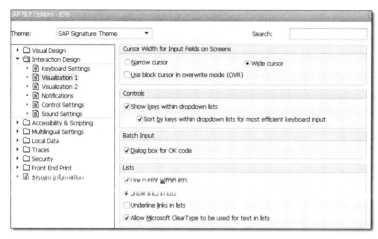

Figure A.5 Interaction Design: Visualization 1

A.1.3 Accessibility and Scripting

By default, the ACCESSIBILITY option is disabled, as shown in Figure A.6. To activate it, select USE ACCESSIBILITY MODE, which will give you access to two more check marks for read-only and display symbols.

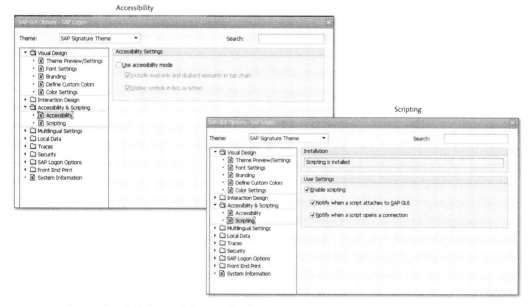

Figure A.6 Scripting and Accessibility Screens

Scripting

You should select the ENABLE SCRIPTING checkbox, but unless you have a good reason, leave the other two (NOTIFY WHEN A SCRIPT ATTACHES TO SAP GUI and NOTIFY WHEN A SCRIPT OPENS A CONNECTION) deactivated, since these will hamper performance. By default, these two checkboxes are not selected.

A.1.4   Multilingual Settings

In this section, you can specify the settings for multiple languages in SAP GUI. An important setting is how to select the IME On/OFF keys, which is shown in Figure A.7. You can select from SHIFT +SPACE, CTRL + SPACE, or NONE.

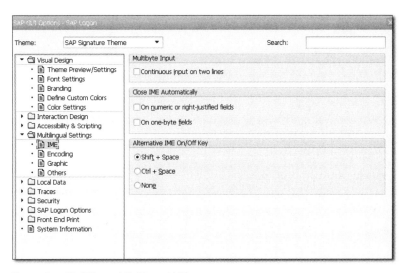

Figure A.7 Multilingual Settings: IME

A.1.5   Local Data

When the HISTORY STATUS radio button is not selected, previous entries to any SAP field are not stored. We recommend that you select either the ON or IMMEDIATELY option. The data is stored locally, so you won't interfere with any other user's performance. EXPIRATION, MAXIMUM PERMITTED FILE SIZE, and NO. OF ENTRIES fill when you select ON or IMMEDIATELY.

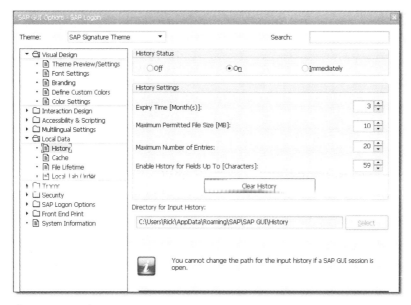

Figure A.8 Local Data, History Screen

You can also clear the data manually from the CLEAR HISTORY button. The location where the data will be stored is specified in the DIRECTORY for LOCAL DATA ORDER. If you select CACHE on the right side menu, you can control the cache size maximum, cache size, and file size. Additionally, you'll be able to control the cache file, how often it is deleted, and its location by selecting FILE LIFETIME and LOCAL TAB ORDER.

A.1.6 Trace

You use the TRACE tab to generate the trace file for analysis of an error relating to the frontend, as shown in Figure A.9.

Activate the trace when you want to run an error analysis and deactivate it afterward. When enabled, the trace option will hamper your system performance. Even when you don't know how to trace the error, you must know how to record it so that you can send it to your contacts who can help you find and fix it. The generated text file records all of the required information between the points at which your trace was active, and when you deactivated it.

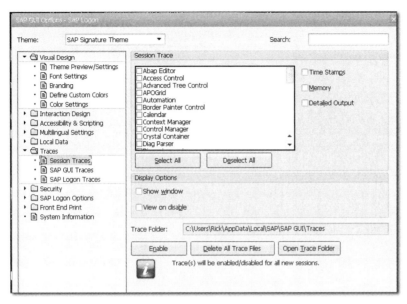

Figure A.9 Traces Window: Session Traces

Figure A.10 shows one such file. The files that constitute the frontend can become damaged, corrupted, or infected quite often if your firewall or network security is not sufficient. Usually, however, it's is easier to reinstall the SAP GUI than to retrace the error.

Figure A.10 Trace File

A.1.7 Front End Point

This option allows you to trace the front-end printing and print log files. If you select the CONFIGURATION FRONT END PRINTING button, a new screen opens in a separate window and offers its own help for configuration.

A.2 Other Customization Options

In this section, we'll discuss the customizing tools available at the local frontend SAP GUI, and how to utilize them optimally.

A.2.1 Clipboard

The four functions for copy and paste are SELECT ([Ctrl]+[Y]), CUT ([Ctrl]+[X]), COPY ([Ctrl]+[C]), and PASTE ([Ctrl]+[V]). With these four operations, you can copy data to and from SAP and non-SAP screens. For example, you can use this feature when you have a list of customers on an SAP report screen that is to be taken to presentation software.

A.2.2 Generate Graphic

You can use the GENERATE GRAPHIC option to generate a screenshot that resembles Figure 1.11. Screenshots can be used for creating user manuals (softcopy).

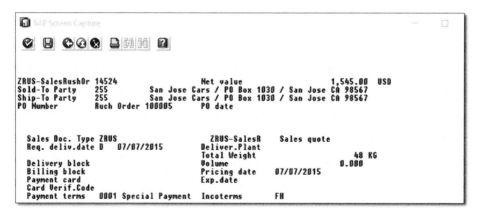

Figure A.11 SAP Screen Capture for Transaction MB52 Initial Screen

A.2.3 Create Shortcut

Creating a shortcut to a transaction code (e.g., VA01) or an area menu (e.g., VA00) will save you time every day. To create a shortcut, click on the CREATE SHORTCUT button on the right side of the SAP GUI menu. After you select the NEW icon, you'll see the screen shown in Figure A.12, in which we show how to create a shortcut for the area menu VA00 and save it on the desktop. You can create several such shortcuts. By clicking on the shortcut, you'll log on directly to the corresponding transaction or area menu.

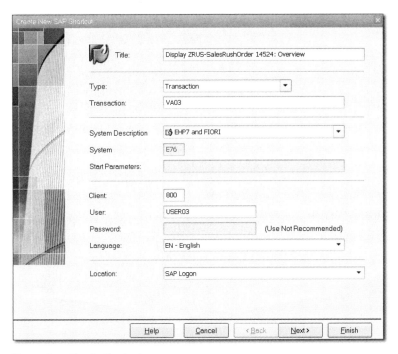

Figure A.12 Create Shortcut

A.2.4 Default Size

When you select the DEFAULT SIZE option, if the window is not maximized already, it will resize itself to a pre-set default size. This feature is useful when you have a large screen and your default size is less than the screen size.

Double-Scroll Bar

This is a typical problem when the screen resolution is less than 1024 x 768 for New Visual design (or less than 800 x 600 for Classic design). For example, a scroll bar will appear to navigate between one item and another in a sales order overview screen (VA02 or VA03), and there will be a scroll bar outside the screen. In such a situation, you'll never able to reach the third item (or any other) of the order. This is when the font size is normal. Refer to SAP Note 26417, which specifies the system requirements for SAP GUI.

A.2.5   Hard Copy

This is the option to make a printout of the current SAP screen. You do this by pressing [Alt]+[F12] to bring up the drop-down list shown in Figure A.2 from any SAP screen. Then, click on the HARD COPY option. This is quite useful for creating user manuals very quickly, with a sequence of screen shots (hardcopy).

A.2.6   Quick Cut and Paste

The QUICK CUT AND PASTE option becomes activated when you click once, and is deactivated if you click again. When this feature is active (see Figure A.2), a checkmark will appear next to the option QUICK CUT AND PASTE. When it's active, you can select and copy texts with a left-click and paste with a right-click. This a very good example of an optimizing tool.

A.2.7   Spell Checker

You'll be surprised by SAP spellcheck, because it will not show errors for your brand names or some of your customer's names, which you'd normally expect. This is the case because the data in the SAP database for materials and customers is taken into consideration, in addition to the dictionary, for spellcheck.

A.2.8   SAP GUI Help

SAP GUI HELP is a complete guide on SAP GUI. It gives you detailed help on how to use and customize the GUI and analyze errors pertaining to SAP GUI.

A.2.9 About

You can use the ABOUT option to retrieve details about the SAP GUI version that you're using, as shown in Figure A.13. You would use this to ensure that you're running the latest version of the GUI (or as suggested by your Basis system administrator).

Figure A.13 About SAP GUI

Automatic Updates

For automatic updates to your SAP GUI, use the method suggested in SAP Note 535308: How to Apply a SAP Frontend Patch.

B   List of SAP Area Menus

Transaction	Description
0KWM	Configuration Menu for Activity-Based Costing
AC00	Service Master Data
ACCR	Accruals/Deferrals
ACE	Accrual Engine – Periodic Accruals
ADWPS_MEB	Maintenance Event Builder
ASMN	Asset Accounting
AUTH	Infosystem Authorizations
BALA	Distribution in Applications
BALD	ALE Development
BALE	ALE Administration
BALM	Master Data Distribution
BALT	IDoc/ALE Test Environment
BANK	SAP Banking
BCA_US_F9MINFO	Information System Bank Customer Accounts
BCA_US_F9MN	Customer Accounts
BCA0	Business Partner Application Development Customizing
BGMN	Guarantees
BM00	Batch Management
BPR1	Activity-Based Costing
BUMR	BP Relationships: Task Menu
BUPA_BIP_MENU	Business Information Provider Menu
BUPT	Business Partner: Task Menu
C000	Overhead Cost Controlling Information System
CA00	Routings
CA01	Cross-Application
CAC0	Master Recipe – Access Via Production Version
CACSBDT	Task Level Menu Commission Contract
CACSBDTB	Task Level Menu for Contract Bundle

Transaction	Description
CACSBDTD	Document Task Level Menu
CACSBDTI	Commission Case Task Level Menu
CACSMN	Commission System
CATI	Time Recording
CATP	Time Sheet
CATS	Time Sheet
CBGL00	Global Label Management
CBIH	Industrial Hygiene and Safety Information System
CBIH00	Industrial Hygiene and Safety
CBP	Constraint Based Planning Workbench
CBWA00	Waste Management
CBWABDT	Waste Management: BDT Settings Complete
CBWAMD	Waste Management: Master Data
CC00	Engineering Change Management
CE00	CAPP-Based Calculation of Standard Values
CEMN	Cost and Revenue Element Accounting
CF00	Production Resources/Tools
CFM	CFM – Corporate Finance Management
CFM_BF	Corporate Finance Management: Basic Functions
CFM_CR	Credit Risk Analyzer
CFM_MR	CFM – Market Risk Analyzer
CFM_PA	CFM – Portfolio Analyzer
CFM_TM	Transaction Manager
CFM_TM_PARABB_GDDD	Parallel Valuation Areas
CFM_TM_PARABB_WP	Parallel Valuation Areas
CFM_TM_ZINSANPASSUNG	Interest Rate Adjustment
CG00	Product Safety
CIC8	CIC Customizing Menu
CICS	Customer Interaction Center
CICT	CIC Customizing Menu
CIF	Core Interface Advanced Planner and Optimizer

Transaction	Description
CIF-EA	Core Interface Advanced Planner and Optimizer
CK00	Product Cost Planning
CK90	Mixed Costing
CKML	Actual Costing/Material Ledger
CL00	Classification
CL00N	Classification
CLOI	Production Optimization Interface
CM00	Capacity Planning
CMC0	Process Planning
CML_FZM4	Drilldown Reporting
CML_PARABB_GDDD	Parallel Valuation Areas_CML
CMPP	Workforce Planning
CMRP	Material Requirements Planning
CMS_CUS_BDT	BDT Development
CMS_CUS_IMG	CMS IMG
CMS_CUS_OMS_BDT	Collateral Objects
CMS_CUS_RE_BDT	BDT Development
CMS_MAIN	Main Menu
CMS_OMS_BDT_MAIN	Collateral Objects
CMS_RE_MAIN	Real Estate Add-On
CN00	Notification
CO_CPROJECTS	Collaboration Projects
CO_CRM	CRM Service Processes
CO00	Shop Floor Control
CO30	Standard Trigger Points
COC0	Process Orders
COCB	Process Management
COFI_REP	Reports for Cost and Revenue Element Accounting (New)
COM_MDF_MENU	Master Data Framework
COND_AV	Condition Maintenance

Transaction	Description
COND_MM	Portfolio Management
CONV00	Conversion of Original Application Files
COPA	Profitability Analysis
CPE_PRICEQUOT	Price Quotations for Commodity Pricing Engine
CPMN	Activity-Based Costing
CR00	Work Centers
CRC0	Resources
CR00	Work Center for Quality Inspection
CS00	Bills of Material
CU00	Variant Configuration
CV00	Document Management
CVI0	Document Distribution
CWVT	Merchandise Distribution
CX00	Consolidation
CX000	SEM BCS – Business Consolidation
CX00BCS	Business Consolidation
CX01	Consolidation Customizing
CY00	Engineering
CY00_PPENG	Integrated Product and Process Engineering (iPPE)
DGP0	Dangerous Goods Management
DICCM	Configuration Control
DICTIONARY	SAPterm – Maintenance for Terminology and Glossary
DUMB	Premium Reserve Fund Transfer in Regulatory Reporting
DZ00	R/2-R/3 Link
ECCS	Consolidation
EHSAMED	Occupational Health
EHSBAS	Basic Data and Tools
EHSH	Report Selection: Occupational Health
EHSH_1	Report Selection: Occupational Health
EHSHSM	Hazardous Substance Management

Transaction	Description
EIS	Report Selection for SAP-EIS
ENH_ELR	Logging
ENH_REBATE	Extended Rebate Processing
ENH_REBATE_INFO	Extended Rebate Processing – Info
EW00	EMU Local Currency Changeover
EXPORT	Export from the Data Pool
F000	Financial Accounting Information System
F8BZ	Payment Program Configuration for Payment Requests
F9L,	Settings for Additional BCA Development
F9LBDT	Development in BDT Environment
F9M1	Bank Customer Accounts: Settings
F9M3	Relationships BP-BP: Settings
F9M4	Setting Payment Transactions
F9MBENCH	Benchmark Customer Accounts
F9MINFO	Information System Bank Customer Accounts
F9MINFO_IHC	Information System In-House Cash
F9MN	Customer Accounts
F9MPAYM	External Payment Transactions
FAGLINFOSYSTEM	Information System (New)
FARI	SAP Business Framework: Open FI
FBDF	BDF Reporting
FBICRC001	Intercompany Reconciliation: Open Items
FBICRC002	Intercompany Reconciliation: Accounts
FBICRC003	Intercompany Reconciliation: Open Items
FBME	Banks
FBOE	ABAP Workbench
FCHK	Check Management
FCMM	Preparations for Consolidation
FCMN	Consolidation
FCRD	Credit Cards

Transaction	Description
FDCU	Loans Customizing Menu
FDMN	Customers
FERC	Regulatory Reporting
FGM0	Special Purpose Ledger
FGRP	Report Painter
FGRW	Report Writer
FI_GL_ACAC	Manual Accruals
FI_GL_CAE_IPM	Accruals for Rights Management
FI_GL_SOA	Provisions for Awards
FIA1	Asset Accounting Information – ALT
FIAA	Asset Accounting Information System
FIAP	Reports for Accounts Payable Accounting
FIAR	Reports for Accounts Receivable Accounting
FICOMAIN	Financial Conditions
FIGL	Information System
FIGX	Flexible General Ledger
FI-LA	Lease Accounting
FILC	Consolidation
FISL	Programs for the Special Purpose Ledger
FITE_INFO	Travel Expenses Info System
FITE_TREE	Reports: Travel Expenses
FITP_INFO	Travel Planning Information System
FITP_TREE	Travel Planning Reports
FITV_INFO	Travel Management Info System
FITV_TREE	Travel Management
FKMN	Accounts Payable
FKTC	Regulatory Reporting Austria – Control Table Maintenance
FLQCUST	Liquidity Calculation Settings
FLQMAIN	Liquidity Calculation

Transaction	Description
FMCA	Reports for Funds Management
FMCB	Cash Budget Management
FMFGE	Additional Functions for US Federal Government
FMUSA	Functions for the US Federal Government
FMUSA2	Functions for the US Federal Government
FNBU	Darwin: Loans Accounting Menu
FNMD	Loans: General Loans
FNME_AENDERUNGSANZEIGER	Change Pointer
FNME_CML	Loans
FNME_NEU	Loans: New
FNME_US	Loans Including U.S. Requirements
FNMEC	General Loans
FNMH	Loans: Mortgages
FNMK	Consumer Loan
FNMO	Loans: Policy Loans
FNMP	Rollover
FNMS	Loans: Borrower's Note Loans
FNUB	Data Transfer: Treasury
FO00	Real Estate Management
FO03	Rental
FO04	Settlements
FO05	Rent Adjustment
FOAR00	Application: Task Menu
FOBE	Rent Adjustment: calculate Amount Transferrable
FOFI	Rental Accounting
FOFI_CP	Rental Accounting Correspondence
FOFV	Real Estate Third-Party Management
FOIO	RE Contract: Development
FOIOSCS	RE Contract: Development/Customizing/Service Charges
FOIC	Real Estate Controlling

Transaction	Description
FOIMGRE	Current Settings
FOIS	Real Estate Information System
FOIS_FI	Rental Accounting Information System
FOIS_SC	Info System Service Charges, Heating Expenses
FOIS_SC1	Master Data for Service Charge Settlement
FOJ0	Real Estate General Contract
FONA	Service Charge Settlement
FOST	Real Estate Management Master Data
FOTI00	Tenant Information: Task Level Menu
FOWB00	Real Estate Management
FRMN	Credit Management
FRMN1	Credit Management
FSBP	Business Partner
FSBP_FINSERV_ALL	SAP Business Partner
FSBPT	Business Partner: Tools
FSBPT_1	Application Development SAP Business Partner for Financial Services
FSBPT_2	Application Development SAP Business Partner for Financial Services: Tools
FSCM	Financial Supply Chain Management
FSCM-BD	Biller Direct
FSCM-COLM	Collection Management
FSCM-CR-AR	Integration Credit Management and FI-AR
FSCM-DM	Dispute Management
FSCM-DM-PW2	Periodic Processing in Accounting
FSCM-IHC	In-House Cash
FSMN	General Ledger
FTBPOB	Business Partner: Development of Partner-Object Relationship
FTBPT	Business Partner: Tools
FTBT	Business Partner
FTBT_ALT	Real Estate Business Partner

Transaction	Description
FTBT_CML	Business Partner (CML)
FTBT_NEU	SAP Business Partner
FTBUP1	Business Partner: Conversion Phase 1
FTBUP2	Business Partner: Conversion Phase 2
FTBUT	Business Partner: Development of Conversion Tool Control
FTR_C_MENU	Transaction: Task Menu
FTW0	Data Retention Tool
FWMY	Securities
FZM4	Treasury Management Information System
FZM4_PERFORMANCE	Performance
FZMN	Treasury Management Basic Functions
FZP0	Partner Management
GCU0	Configuration Menu: Special Purpose Ledger
GFTR_C_MENU	General Transaction Management: Task Menu
GJQ0	CRP Customizing Menu
GJVC	Joint Venture Accounting Configuration
GJVP	Joint Venture Accounting
GLFLEXCUS	Flexible General Ledger
GLFLEXMEN	Flexible General Ledger
GLFLEXSPL	Document Splitting
GMGMT	Grants Management
GRANT_BDT	Grant Master Development Menu
GRANT_CUSTOMIZE	Grant Master Customizing Menu
HR REPORTING TOOLS	HR Reporting Tools
HR_99	International Payroll Information System
HR_AR	Information System
HR_AT	Information System
HR_AU	Information System
HR_BE	Information System
HR_BR	Information System

Transaction	Description
HR_CA	Information System
HR_CH	Information System
HR_CN	Information System
HR_DE	Information System
HR_DE1	Information System
HR_DK	Information System
HR_ES	Information System
HR_FR	Information System
HR_GB	Information System
HR_HK	Information System
HR_ID	Information System
HR_IE	Information System
HR_IT	Information System
HR_JP	Information System
HR_KR	Information System
HR_MX	Information System
HR_MY	Information System
HR_NL	Information System
HR_NO	Information System
HR_NZ	Information System
HR_PA_BR	Administration BR
HR_PA_CA	Administration Canada
HR_PA_JP	Administration Japan
HR_PA_MY	Administration Malaysia
HR_PA_TW	Administration Taiwan
HR_PA_US	Administration United States
HR_PH	Information System
HR_PT	Information System
HR_SE	Information System
HR_SG	Information System
HR_TH	Information System

Transaction	Description
HR_TW	Information System
HR_US	Information System (US)
HR_VE	Information System
HR_ZA	Information System
HR00	Human Resources
HR21NADM	Reporting: Time Data Administration
HR21NCAT	Time Sheet
HR21NINW	Reporting: Incentive Wages
HR21NPEP	Reporting: Shift Planning
HR21NTIM	Reporting: Time Management
HR22NADM	Tools: Time Data Administration
HR22NINW	Time Management Tools: Incentive Wages
HR22NTIM	Tools: Time Management
HRAP1	Recruitment – Reports
HRBEN0000	Benefits
HRBEN00REPTREE	Benefits Reporting Tree
HRCLM0000	Claims (Asia)
HRCMP	Compensation Management Reports
HRCMP0000	Compensation Management
HRECM	Enterprise Compensation Management
HRHCP1	Data Collection, Personnel Cost Planning, and Simulation
HRHCP2	Cost Plans, Personnel Cost Planning, and Simulation
HRHCP3	Tools for Personnel Cost Planning and Simulation
HRHCP4	Settings for Personnel Cost Planning and Simulation
HRHCP5	Information System
HRJP	Administration Japan
HRMGE0000	Management of Global Employees
HROM	Organizational Management
HRPA	Personnel Administration – Reports

Transaction	Description
HRPBC	Position Budgeting and Control
HRPE	Personnel Development – Reports
HRPM	HR Funds and Position Management
HRPT	HR-FPM Tools
HRTR	Travel Expenses Information System
HUM	Handling Unit Management
HUM_CHANGE	Create and Change Handling Units
HUM_DISPLAY	Display Handling Units
HUM_GOODS_MOVEMENT	Goods Movement Postings
HUM_INVENTORY	Handling Unit Physical Inventory
HUM_MD	Master Data
HUM_MD_NACHRICHTEN	Output Conditions
HUM_MD_PV	Packing Instructions
HUM_MD_PV_FINDUNG	Packing Instruction Determination Records
IA00	Work Scheduling
IC00	Work Centers
IDADVAT	Acquisition Tax Accruals
ID-FIGL-PP-CL-REP-GL-ACCBAL-CL	G/L Account Balance Reports (Chile)
IDFISA-FSMN-VATRETURNS-MX	VAT Returns (Mexico)
IE00	Management of Technical Objects
IECS	Management of Technical Objects
IF00	Production Resources/Tools
IHC	In-House Cash
IHC_CM	Financial Status
IHC_GUI	IHC: GUI Functions
IM00	Investment Programs
IMA0	Appropriation Requests
IMFA	Investment Management
IMFR	Appropriation Requests
INFO_PC	Product Cost Controlling
INFO_PC01	Product Cost Planning

Transaction	Description
INFO_PC03	Product Cost by Period
INFO_PC04	Product Cost by Sales Order
INFO_PC05	Costs for Intangible Goods
INFO_PC06	Product Cost by Order
INFO_PC07	Actual Costing/Material Ledger
INFO_PC2	Order-Related Production
INFO_PC2A	Order-Related Production
INFO_PC3	Make-to-Order Production
INFO_PC3A	Make-to-Order Production
INFO_PC4	Repetitive Manufacturing
INFO_PC5	Base Object Costing
INFO_PC8	Product Costing
IP00	Maintenance Planning
IPCS	Service Agreements
IPLM	Preventive Maintenance
IR00	Work Centers
IS00	Area Menu for Solution Database
ISCS	Solution Database
ISE0	Funds Management
ISISMN	Insurance Applications
ISNL	Funds Management
ISP4	Posting
ISSR_BASIC	Regulatory Reporting for Insurance Supervisory Authority
ISZZ	Solution Database
IW00	Maintenance Processing
IWCS	Service Processing
J1IL	India Localization – Excise Statutory Requirements
J1ILN	India Localization Menu
J1IN-FIAP-WITHHOLDINGTAX-IN	FI-AP Withholding Tax (India)
J1IN-FIAR-WITHHOLDINGTAX-IN	FI-AR Withholding Tax (India)

Transaction	Description
JB01	Data Pool
JB02	Profitability Analysis
JB04	Market Risk Analysis
JB0B	Product Control
JB12	Default Risk and Limit System
JB14	Prototype Functions
JB19	Asset/Liability Management
JB3Y	Securities
JB4X	Money Market
JB5X	Foreign Exchange
JB6X	Derivatives
JBBE	Valuation Setting
JBBM	Positions
JBD_VAR_TRANS_OLD	SEM-PA: Obsolete Transaction for Variable Transaction (Old) Area
JBDM	Loans
JBMA	EURO Changeover
JBMVT	Variable Transaction: Task Level Menu
JBMVTWORK	Variable Transaction: Task Level Menu
KAMN	Internal Orders
KCCF	Executive Menu
KCLA	External Data Transfer
KCMB	Executive Information System (EIS)
KCMD	Business Planning (EC-BP)
KE50	Profit Center Accounting
KEMN	Profitability Analysis
KKAM	Product Cost by Sales Order
KKMN	Reference and Simulation Costing
KKOB	Costs for Intangible Goods and Services
KKPM	Product Cost by Period
KKSM	Product Cost by Order

Transaction	Description
KLFZ	Facilities: Initial Menu
KPRO	Knowledge Provider Administration
KSMN	Cost Center Accounting
LD00	Line Design
LE_AID-BI	Auto-ID Backend Integration
LE_ANALYSIS	Analysis Tools
LE_INB	Goods Receipt
LE_INB_DELV	Goods Receipt with Inbound Delivery
LE_INB_TRQ	Goods Receipt w/o Inbound Delivery
LE_IO_TRA	Transportation
LE_IS	Information Systems
LE_IS_INB	Goods Receipt Office
LE_IS_OUTB	Shipping
LE_IS_TRA	Transportation Planning
LE_IS_WM	Warehouse
LE_MASTER	Master Data
LE_OUTB	Goods Issue
LE_OUTB_DELV	Goods Issue with Outbound Delivery
LE_OUTB_TRQ	Goods Issue for Other Transactions
LE_R2R3	R/2-R/3 Link
LE_TRA	Transportation
LE_TRA_DISP	Logistics Execution and Transportation Planning
LE_TRA_EXEC	Transportation
LE_TRA_FREIGHT	Shipment Costs
LE_WM_INT	Internal Warehouse Activities
LE01	Logistics Execution
LES	Logistics Execution
LLVS	Warehouse Management
LO01	Logistics – General
LPRO	Material Forecast
LSO_PVMN	Learning Solution

Transaction	Description
LSO_PVMN1	SAP Learning Solution – Reports
LTRM_MEN	Task and Resource Management
LVAS	Value-Added Services (VAS)
LXDOCK	Cross-Docking
LYM	Yard Management
MB00	Inventory Management
MC00	Logistics Information System (LIS)
MC6A	Sales and Operations Planning
MC6B	Flexible Planning
MCA1	Workflow Information System (WIS)
MCB1	Inventory Controlling (INVCO)
MCC1	Inventory Information System
MCC2	Inventory Information System
MCE0	Purchasing Information System (PURCHIS)
MCE9	Purchasing Information System
MCG1	MCG1
MCH0	Retail Information System (RIS)
MCI0	Plant Maintenance Information System (PMIS)
MCJE	Plant Maintenance Information System
MCK0	Service Management Information System (SMIS)
MCP0	Shop Floor Information System (PP-IS)
MCPI	Production Information System
MCT0	Sales Information System (SIS)
MCT2	Sales Information System
MCU0	Transportation Info System (TIS)
MCV0	Quality Management Information System
MCVQ	Quality Management Information System
MCVQ_INFO_1	Info System: Quality Control Key Figures
MCVQ_INFO_2	Info System: Quality Control Evaluations
MD00	Materials Requirements Planning – External Procurement

Transaction	Description
MDLP	Master Production Scheduling
MDPP	Demand Management
MDRP	Distribution Resource Planning
ME00	Purchasing
MEASURE_BDT	Measure BDT Development Menu
MEL0	Service Entry Sheet
MEMGMT_CONFIG	Device Configuration
MENU_TEST_ECKE	Corner
MEREP_TESTTOOL	Test Tool Center
MF00	Repetitive Manufacturing
MF00_OLD	Repetitive Manufacturing
MI00	Physical Inventory
MM00	Material Master
MM01	Materials Management
MR00	Invoice
MRBE	Valuation
MRM0	Logistics Invoice Verification
MS00	Long-Term Planning
MST0	Mass Maintenance Tool
OCA0	Cross Application
OCH0	Batch Management
OCNG	Graphic Customizing
OFTC	Funds Management Configuration Menu
OFTD	Cash Management Configuration Menu
OFTF	Cash Budget Management Configuration
OHPS	Organizational Management Configuration (Basis System)
OIS0	Funds Management Configuration Menu
OKCM	Configuration Menu
OLI0	Configuration Menu for Master Data in Plant Maintenance

Transaction	Description
OLIA	Configuration Menu for Maintenance Processing
OLIP	Configuration Menu for Planning in Plant Maintenance
OLMS	Master Data Configuration Menu
OLPA	Settings: Sales & Operations Planning
OLQB	QM Customizing in Procurement
OLS1	Sales and Distribution Configuration Menu – Volume Based Rebate
OLVD	Customizing for Sales and Distribution: Shipping
OLVF	SD Customizing: Billing
OLVS	Customizing for Sales and Distribution: Master Data
OMO6	Maintain Applications
OMP0	Configuration Menu for Demand Management
OP01	Logistics Customizing
OPA1	Internal Orders
OPPL	OPPL
ORK0	General CO Configuration Menu
ORKA	Configuration Menu for Internal Orders
ORKL	Cost and Revenue Element Accounting: Configuration Menu
ORKS	Cost Center Accounting: Configuration Menu
OVPS	Document Management Configuration Menu
OWS0	Active Ingredient Management
OWV0	Customizing Pricing
P01A_M01	Company Pension Scheme Germany
P02F_M01	Pension Fund: Switzerland
PA00	Personnel Administration
PACA	Payment Cards: Task Menu
PACK	HR-CH: Pension Fund
PAW0	PAW – Performance Assessment Workbench
PB00	Recruitment

Transaction	Description
PC00	Payroll for all Countries
PC00_M01_JAHRLICHE	Subsequent Activities (Annual)
PC00_M01_PAP	Subsequent Activities – per Payroll Period
PC00_M01_PDUNABHAGIG	Subsequent Activities – Period-Independent
PC00_M01_SONSPERIOD	Subsequent Activities – Other Periods
PC00_M02	Payroll for Switzerland
PC00_M02_JAHRLICHE	Annual Subsequent Activities
PC00_M02_PAP	Subsequent Activities – per Payroll Period
PC00_M02_PDUNABHAGIG	Period-Independent Subsequent Activities
PC00_M02_SONSPERIOD	Subsequent Activities for Other Periods
PC00_M03_JAHRLICHE	Annual Subsequent Activities
PC00_M03_PAP	Subsequent Activities – per Payroll Period
PC00_M03_PDUNABHAGIG	Period-Independent Subsequent Activities
PC00_M03_SONSPERIOD	Subsequent Activities for Other Periods
PC00_M04_JAHRLICHE	Subsequent Annual Activities
PC00_M04_PAP	Subsequent Activities – per Payroll Period
PC00_M04_PDUNABHAGIG	Period-Independent Subsequent Activities
PC00_M04_SONSPERIOD	Subsequent Activities Other Periods
PC00_M05_JAHRLICHE	Annual Subsequent Activities
PC00_M05_PAP	Subsequent Activities – Per Payroll Period
PC00_M05_SONSPERIOD	Subsequent Activities for Other Periods
PC00_M06_JAHRLICHE	Annual Subsequent Activities
PC00_M06_PAP	Subsequent Activities per Payroll Period
PC00_M06_PDUNABHAGIG	Period-Independent Subsequent Activities
PC00_M06_SONSPERIOD	Subsequent Activities – Other Periods
PC00_M07_JAHRLICHE	Subsequent Activities – Annual
PC00_M07_PAP	Subsequent Activities – per Payroll Period
PC00_M07_PDUNABHAGIG	Subsequent Activities – Period-Independent
PC00_M07_SONSPERIOD	Subsequent Activities – Other Periods
PC00_M08_JAHRLICHE	Annual Subsequent Activities
PC00_M08_PAP	Subsequent Activities – per Payroll Period

Transaction	Description
PC00_M08_PDUNABHAGIG	Period-Independent Subsequent Activities
PC00_M08_SONSPERIOD	Subsequent Activities for Other Periods
PC00_M09_JAHRLICHE	Annual Subsequent Activities
PC00_M09_PAP	Subsequent Activities – per Payroll Period
PC00_M09_PDUNABHAGIG	Subsequent Activities – Period-Independent
PC00_M09_SONSPERIOD	Subsequent Activities – Other Periods
PC00_M10_JAHRLICHE	Subsequent Activities – Annual
PC00_M10_PAP	Subsequent Activities – per Payroll Period
PC00_M10_PDUNABHAGIG	Subsequent Activities – Period Independent
PC00_M10_SONSPERIOD	Subsequent Activities – Other Periods
PC00_M11_JAHRLICHE	Subs. Activities – Annual
PC00_M11_PAP	Subs. Activities – per Payroll Period
PC00_M11_PDUNABHAGIG	Subs. Activities – Period-Unrelated
PC00_M11_SONSPERIOD	Subs. Activities – Other Periods
PC00_M12_JAHRLICHE	Annual Subsequent Activities
PC00_M12_PAP	Subsequent Activities – per Payroll Period
PC00_M12_PDUNABHAGIG	Period-Independent Subsequent Activities
PC00_M12_SONSPERIOD	Subsequent Activities for Other Periods
PC00_M13_JAHRLICH_PS	Subsequent Activities – Annual
PC00_M13_JAHRLICHE	Subsequent Activities – Annual
PC00_M13_PAP	Subsequent Activities – per Payroll Period
PC00_M13_PAP_PS	Subsequent Activities – per Payroll Period
PC00_M13_PDUNABHA_PS	Subsequent Activities – Period-Independent
PC00_M13_PDUNABHAGIG	Subsequent Activities – Period-Independent
PC00_M13_PIND	Subsequent Activities – Period Independent
PC00_M13_PS	Payroll for Australian Public Sector
PC00_M13_SONSPERI_PS	Subsequent Activities – Other Periods
PC00_M13_SONSPERIOD	Subsequent Activities – Other periods
PC00_M14_AWS	AWS Accounting for Malaysia
PC00_M14_FAP	FAP Accounting for Malaysia
PC00_M14_JAHRLICHE	Subsequent Activities – Annual

Transaction	Description
PC00_M14_OCWB	Off-Cycle Workbench
PC00_M14_ODS	On-Demand Payroll for Malaysia
PC00_M14_PAP	Subsequent Activities – per Payroll Period
PC00_M14_PDUNABHAGIG	Subsequent Activities – Period-Independent
PC00_M14_SONSPERIOD	Subsequent Activities – Other Periods
PC00_M15_JAHRLICHE	Payroll for Italy
PC00_M15_PAP	Payroll for Italy
PC00_M15_PDUNABHAGIG	Payroll for Italy
PC00_M15_SONSPERIOD	Payroll for Italy
PC00_M16_JAHRLICHE	Annual Subsequent Activities
PC00_M16_PAP	Subsequent Activities – per Payroll Period
PC00_M17_JAHRLICHE	Payroll Venezuela
PC00_M17_PAP	Payroll Venezuela
PC00_M17_PDUNABHAGIG	Payroll Venezuela
PC00_M17_SONSPERIOD	Payroll Venezuela
PC00_M19_JAHRLICHE	HR-PT: Subsequent Activities – Annual
PC00_M19_PAP	HR-PT: Subsequent Activities – per Payroll Period
PC00_M19_PDUNABHAGIG	HR-PT: Subsequent Activities – Period-Independent
PC00_M19_SONSPERIOD	HR-PT: Subsequent Activities – in Other Periods
PC00_M20_JAHRLICHE	Subsequent Activities – Annual
PC00_M20_PAP	Subsequent Activities – per Payroll Period
PC00_M20_PDUNABHAGIG	Subsequent Activities – Period-Independent
PC00_M20_SONSPERIOD	Subsequent Activities – Other Periods
PC00_M22_JAHRLICHE	Subsequent Activities – Annual
PC00_M22_PAP	Subsequent Activities – per Payroll Period
PC00_M22_PDUNABHAGIG	Subsequent Activities – Period Independent
PC00_M22_RETIRE	Retirement Accounting for Japan
PC00_M22_SONSPDSI	Subsequent Activities Other Periods – Social Insurance
PC00_M22_SONSPERIOD	Subsequent Activities – Other Periods
PC00_M22_SYOYO	Shoyo Accounting for Japan

Transaction	Description
PC00_M22_YRENDADJ	Year-End Adjustment for Japan
PC00_M23_JAHRLICHE	Subsequent Activities – Annual
PC00_M23_PAP	Subsequent Activities – per Payroll Period
PC00_M23_PDUNABHAGIG	Subsequent Activities – Period-Independent
PC00_M23_SONSPERIOD	Subsequent Activities – Other Periods
PC00_M25_AWS	AWS Accounting for Singapore
PC00_M25_FAP	FAP Accounting for Singapore
PC00_M25_JAHRLICHE	Annual Subsequent Activities
PC00_M25_MID	Mid-Month Accounting for Singapore
PC00_M25_ODS	On-Demand Payroll for Singapore
PC00_M25_PAP	Subsequent Activities – per Payroll Period
PC00_M25_PDUNABHAGIG	Subsequent Activities Irrespective of Periods
PC00_M25_SONSPERIOD	Subsequent Activities for Other Periods
PC00_M26_JAHRLICHE	Subsequent Activities – Annual
PC00_M26_PAP	Subsequent Activities – per Payroll Period
PC00_M26_PDUNABHAGIG	Subsequent Activities TH – Period-Independent
PC00_M26_SONSPERIOD	Subsequent Activities TH – Other Periods
PC00_M27_JAHRLICHE	Subsequent Activities – Annual
PC00_M27_PAP	Subsequent Activities – per Payroll Period
PC00_M27_PDUNABHAGIG	Subsequent Activities – Period-Independent
PC00_M27_SONSPERIOD	Subsequent Activities – Other Periods
PC00_M28_JAHRLICHE	Subsequent Activities – Annual
PC00_M28_PAP	Subsequent Activities per Payroll Period
PC00_M28_PDUNABHAGIG	Subsequent Activities – Period-Independent
PC00_M29_JAHRLICHE	Payroll Argentina
PC00_M29_MONATLICHE	Payroll Argentina
PC00_M29_PAP	Payroll Argentina
PC00_M29_PDUNABHAGIG	Payroll Argentina
PC00_M29_SONSPERIOD	Payroll Argentina
PC00_M32_JAHRLICHE	Payroll for Italy
PC00_M32_MONATLICHE	Payroll for Italy
PC00_M32_PAP	Payroll for Italy

Transaction	Description
PC00_M32_PDUNABHAGIG	Payroll for Italy
PC00_M32_SONSPERIOD	Payroll for Italy
PC00_M34_JAHRLICHE	Subsequent Activities – Annual
PC00_M34_PAP	Subsequent Activities – per Payroll Period
PC00_M34_PDUNABHAGIG	Subsequent Activities – Period-Unrelated
PC00_M34_SONSPERIOD	Subsequent Activities – Other Periods
PC00_M37_JAHRLICHE	Payroll for Italy
PC00_M37_MONATLICHE	Payroll for Italy
PC00_M37_PAP	Activity per Period
PC00_M37_PDUNABHAGIG	Payroll for Italy
PC00_M37_SONSPERIOD	Payroll for Italy
PC00_M41_BON&OFFS	Bonus & Other Off-Cycles
PC00_M41_JAHRLICHE	Subsequent Activities – Annual
PC00_M41_PAP	Subsequent Activities – per Payroll Period
PC00_M41_PDUNABHAGIG	Subsequent Activities – Period-Independent
PC00_M41_RETIRE	Retire Regular Payroll
PC00_M42_ADV_OCRN	Advance Payment Using Off-Cycle Reason
PC00_M42_ADV_REP	Advance Payment Using Report
PC00_M42_AWS	Bonus Accounting
PC00_M42_JAHRLICHE	Subsequent Activities – Annual
PC00_M42_PAP	Subsequent Activities – Per Payroll Period
PC00_M42_PDUNABHAGIG	Subsequent Activities – Period-Independent
PC00_M42_SONSPERIOD	Subsequent Activities – Other Periods
PC00_M43_PAP	Subsequent Activities – per Payroll Period
PC00_M44_OTHPER	Subsequent Activities in Other Periods
PC00_M44_PAP	Subsequent Activities per Payroll Period
PC00_M44_PERIND	Period Independent Subsequent Activities
PC00_M44_YEARLY	Annual Subsequent Activities
PC00_M48_13M	13th Month Pay
PC00_M48_ADV_NDED	Advance Payment without Deductions
PC00_M48_ADV_WDED	Advance Payment with Deductions

Transaction	Description
PC00_M48_BN	Bonus Payment
PC00_M48_JAHRLICHE	Subsequent Activities – Annual
PC00_M48_PAP	Subsequent Activities – per Payroll Period
PC00_M48_PDUNABHAGIG	Subsequent Activities – Period-Independent
PC00_M48_SONSPERIOD	Subsequent Activities – Other Periods
PC00_M99_PAP	Subsequent Activities per Payroll Period
PC01	Payroll Germany
PC02	Payroll Switzerland
PC03	Payroll Austria
PC04	Payroll Spain
PC05	Payroll Netherlands
PC06	Payroll France
PC07	Payroll Canada
PC08	Payroll Great Britain
PC09	Payroll Denmark
PC10	US Payroll
PC11	Payroll Ireland
PC12	Payroll Belgium
PC13	Payroll Australia
PC14	Payroll Malaysia
PC15	Payroll Italy
PC16	Payroll South Africa
PC17	Payroll Venezuela
PC19	Payroll Portugal
PC20	Payroll Norway
PC22	Payroll Japan
PC23	Payroll Sweden
PC25	Payroll Singapore
PC26	Payroll Thailand
PC27	Payroll Hong Kong
PC28	Payroll China

Transaction	Description
PC29	Payroll Argentina
PC32	Payroll Mexico
PC34	Payroll Accounting for Indonesia
PC37	Payroll Brazil
PC40	Payroll India
PC41	Payroll Korea
PC42	Payroll Taiwan
PC43	Payroll New Zealand
PC44	Payroll Finland
PC48	Payroll Philippines
PC99	International Payroll
PC99_TOOLS	Payroll Tools
PCA0	Production Campaign
PCA1	Profit Center Accounting
PCF	Cost Object
PCI	Process Manufacturing
PCIA	Process Manufacturing
PEPMEN	Task Level Menu for the PEP
PIMN	Human Resources Information System
PK00	Kanban
PKC1	Activity-Based Costing Information System
PM01	Plant Maintenance
PMMN	HR Funds and Position Management
PORTFOLIO	Portfolio Management
PP01	Production Planning
PP70	Organizational Management
PP72	Time Management: Shift Planning
PP74	Personnel Cost Planning
PP7S	Organizational Management
PPMM	Personnel Planning
PPPE	Personnel Development

Transaction	Description
PPSFC_INFO	Shop Floor Control
PR00	Travel Expenses
PS00	Project System
PS01	Project Information System
PS02	Project System: Basic Data
PS03	Project Planning
PS04	Project Budgeting
PS05	Project Execution
PS06	Project Cost Controlling
PS07	Project System: Financials
PS08	Project System: Dates
PS09	Project System: Resources
PS10	Project System: Material
PS11	Project System: Progress
PS12	Project System: Project
PS13	Project System: Documents
PS14	Project System: Claims
PS15	Project System: Collaboration
PS81	Individual Overviews
PS91	Project Information System (Commercial Part)
PSC_MENU	Production Sharing Accounting
PSC4	Consistency Checks
PT00	Time Management: Time Data Administration
PT00_THOMAS	Time Management: Administration
PVMN	Training and Event Management
PVMN1	Training and Event Management – Reports
PW00	Incentive Wages
PW00_THOMAS	Incentive Wages
PWB	Print Workbench
Q000	Quality Management
QA00	Quality Inspection

Transaction	Description
QA00_INFO	Info System: Quality Certificates
QE00	Quality Planning
QE00_INFO_1	Info System: Inspection Planning
QE00_INFO_2	Info System: Basic Data
QE00_INFO_3	Info System: Logistics Master Data in QM
QM00	Quality Notifications
QM00_INFO	Quality Notifications: Info System
QM01	Quality Management
QST00	Stability Study
QT00	Test Equipment Management
QT00_INFO	Info System: Test Equipment Management
QT01	Inspection Processing
QZ00	Quality Certificate
QZ00_INFO	Info System: Quality Certificates
RCC00	Risk Object: Configuration Menu
RCL1	Reconciliation Ledger
RCPMGT	Recipe Management
RECAMENUAPPL	Flexible Real Estate Management: Application Menu
RECAMENUDEV	RE-FX (Extension): Development Menu
RECAMENUDEVCUSTTECH	RE Extension: Technical Customizing (S Tables)
REORG	Reorganization Tools in Market Risk and ALM
RKS1	Cost Center Accounting
ROLLE	Area Menu for Role Reports
RS00	SAP Business Information Warehouse
RS00_ADM	Administration
RS00_BEX	Business Explorer
RS00_BW	SAP Business Information Warehouse
RS00_BW_ONLY	SAP Business Information Warehouse (only BW)
RS00_DM	Data Mining
RS00_EI	Enhanced Analytics

Transaction	Description
RS00_MOD	Modeling
RS00_PLAN	Business Planning and Simulation
RS00_TOOL	Tools
RSW1	Standard Analyses
RTP_US_BDT	Retirement Plan Development BDT
S_TEST_WORKBENCH	Test Workbench Menu
S000	SAP R/3 System
S000_CO	Controlling
S000_CO_PC	Product Cost Controlling
S000_CO_PC_OBJ	Cost Object Controlling
S000_EC	Enterprise Controlling
S000_FI	Financial Accounting
S000_HR	Human Resources
S000_IM	Investment Management
S000_INFO_LO	Logistics Information System
S000_INFO_RW	Accounting Information System
S000_LO	Logistics
S000_OLD	SAP R/3 System
S000_PSM	Public Sector Management
S000_RW	Accounting
S000_TR	Treasury
S001	ABAP Workbench
S002	System Administration
SAP_ICC_BRASIL	Brazil
SAP_ICC_THAILAND	Menu: Check Handling Thailand
SAP_ICC_TURKEY	Turkey
SAP_ICC_VORNUM_BELEGE	Pre-numbered Forms
SAP1	Report Selection
SAP2	Info Catalog
SAPF	Forms
SASAP	Accelerated SAP

Transaction	Description
SBEA	BEAC Corporate Flight System
SBPT	Business Communication
SCC	Subcontracting with Chargeable Components
SCPI	Supply Chain Planning Interfaces
SD01	Sales and Distribution
SD01-01	Information System
SD01-02	Information System
SD01-03	Report Selection
SD01-06	Information System
SD01-07	Information System
SD01-08	Information System
SD01-09	Information System
SDAL	Sales Activity: Address Reports
SDWO	ABAP Workbench
SI00	SAP Knowledge Warehouse
SI00_DOCU	SAP Knowledge Warehouse – Documentation
SI00_OLD	SAP Knowledge Warehouse
SI00_TRAIN	SAP Knowledge Warehouse – Training
SLIS	Special Purpose Ledger: Information System
SM01	Customer Service
SOA_COPY	Business Documents Administration
SOFF	SAPoffice
SP00	Spool and Related Areas
SRZL	Test
SSUO	Structure Graphic: Settings
STTO	Test Workbench
STUN	Performance Monitoring
SWFT	Workflow: Test Suite
SWLD	SAP Business Workflow
SWUX	SAPforms Administration
TAXREPORT_PORTUGAL	Tax Reports – Portugal

Transaction	Description
TBMN	Forex Hedges
TCMK	Funds Management
TCMN	Funds Management
TDMN	Cash Management
TDMN_DIST	Distribute TR Cash Management Data
TFMN	Cash Budget Management
TIMN	Derivative Financial Instruments
TM_HEDGE_MANAGEMENT	TM Hedge Management
TM_IMPAIRMENT	Impairments
TMMN	Money Market
TP00	Travel Planning
TP00_LFD	Current Settings for Travel Planning
TRLM	Limit Management
TRMA	Treasury
TRTC	Cash Management
TRTD	Loans
TRTG	Money Market
TRTM	Market Risk Management
TRTR	Derivatives
TRTV	Foreign Exchange
TRTW	Securities
TV00	Travel Management
TV01	HR Master Data: Travel
TVM1	Market Risk Management
TXMN	Foreign Exchange
TYMN	Treasury Information System
UCUST	Convert Treasury Partner to SAP Business Partner
UPS00	ALE Distribution Units (UOS)
VA00	Sales
VBK0	Material Grouping/Bonus Buy
VC00	Sales Support

Transaction	Description
VECN	Information System for Profitability and Sales Accounting
VF00	Billing
VI00	Shipment Costs
VI01	ROZ/IPD Reporting
VI02	Freight Costs
VI03	Display Freight Costs
VI04	Create Freight Costs
VI05	List Shipment Costs: Change Worklist
VI06	Master Data/Contracts
VI07	Controlling/Settlements
VI08	Reports on Real Estate Management
VI09	Selection Versions
VI10	Master Data
VI11	Contracts
VI12	Overviews
VI13	Controlling RE Objects
VI14	Service/Heating Cost Settlement
VI15	Taxes
VI16	CO Third Party Management
VICP	Correspondence
VIFI	Rental Accounting
VKP0	Pricing
VL00	Shipping
VL30	Inbound Delivery
VLE1	Putaway with Warehouse Management
VLK1	Picking with Warehouse Management
VLK2	Picking with Wave Picks
VLK3	Picking w/o Warehouse Management
VS00	Sales Master Data
VT00	Transportation

Transaction	Description
VX00	Foreign Trade/Customs
VX0C	Foreign Trade
VXDG	Foreign Trade: Documentary Payments
VXDP	Foreign Trade: Cockpit
VXGK	Foreign Trade: Prohibitions and Restrictions
VXIE	Maintain Foreign Trade Data
VXKD	Foreign Trade: Communication/Printing
VXME	Foreign Trade: Periodic Declarations
VXMO	Foreign Trade: CAP – Restitution
VXPR	Foreign Trade: Preference Handling
VXSE	Foreign Trade: Service for Foreign Trade and Customs
VXSL	Foreign Trade: Sanctioned Party List Screening
W10E	Goods Receipt
W10F	Store Retailing
W10M	Retailing
W10T	SAP Retail
W10T_LO	Logistics Retail
WA00	Allocation
WAK0	Promotion
WASSO	Association Management
WB00	Subsequent Settlement, Purchasing – Vendor Rebate Arrangements
WB20	SAP Global Trade Management
WB20N	SAP Global Trade Management
WBST	Inventory Management
WBVK	Subsequent Settlement: Sales
WCM	Work Clearance Management
WCMCP	Category Manager Workbench (Consumer Products) Prototype
WDIS	Material Requirements Planning
WEDI	IDoc and EDI Basis

Transaction	Description
WEKF	Purchase Order
WETI	Labeling
WFIL	Store Order Online
WGCL	Class. System, Retail
WI00	Physical Inventory
WK00	Subsequent Settlement, Purchasing – Customer Arrangements
WKON	Condition/Arrangement
WKUN	Customer
WL00	Vendor
WM00	Material
WMF0	Season Management
WOB0	Plant
WOF0	Plant
WORKFLOW_SUPPORT	Business Workflow Support: Diagnosis and Help Transactions
WP00	Planning
WPDC	SAP Retail Store – PDC Processing
WPOS	POS Interface
WQ00	Value Scales and Quota Scales
WRP0	Replenishment
WRP1	Multi-Step Replenishment
WRPFMM	Replenishment: Forecast, MM-Inventory Management
WRPFSOP	Replenishment: Forecast, Replenishment-Inventory Management
WRRLE	Extended Remuneration List Creation
WRTL	Retail Ledger
WS00	Assortment
WSCM	Category Manager Workbench
WSIS	Information System
WSMP	Merchandise Planning

Transaction	Description
WSRS_ADM	SAP Retail Store – Administration
WTAD	Additionals
WTY_FOLDER_MAIN	Warranty Claim Processing
WVEB	Valuation
WVER	Shipping
WVKF	Sales Order
WVM0	Customer Replenishment
WVTU	Sales Support
WW01	Cost Center Accounting
WWG1	Material Groups and Material Group Hierarchy
WWG2	Material Groups
WWMI	Product Catalog
WWVT	Merchandise Distribution
WXP0	Merchandise and Assortment Planning
WZR0	Agency Business
WZR01	Agency Business

C   The Authors

Ricardo Lopez is a PMP project manager with SD certification by SAP America. He's a senior manager with a solid background coordinating and managing major OTC projects and devising plans and schedules. Ricardo has experience in directing worldwide SAP OTC implementations for a wide range of clients worldwide. Ricardo holds SD certification 4.x by SAP Americas and has more than eighteen years of consulting experience across applications such as Sales and Distribution, SAP FSCM/Biller Direct, Credit and Dispute Management, and SAP Fiori. He has participated in more than 18 full go-live cycles, and 20 template roll-outs around the globe. He currently lives in the New York City area.

Ashish Ranjan Mohapatra has worked with SAP software for 15 years. As team leader and assistant project manager for implementation projects, he has developed a thorough understanding of the Sales and Distribution functionality in SAP ERP and implementation and configuration pain points. As head of the business process department, Ashish expanded his knowledge of other SAP software, including Materials Management, Financials and Accounting, Production Planning, and Quality Management. Ashish is an SAP SD Certified Consultant and a management graduate from the Indian Institute of Management, Ahmedabad.

Index

▶ Explores the key sales and distribution functions and tasks

▶ Teaches how to use SD in daily processes, including sales, pricing, delivery, transportation, and billing

▶ Guides you in troubleshooting common problems and pitfalls

▶ Up to date for ERP 6, EHP7

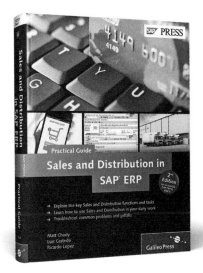

Matt Chudy, Luis Castedo, Ricardo Lopez

Sales and Distribution in SAP ERP—Practical Guide

It's time to deconstruct your tasks in SD. In this book, you'll find the most common duties you'll need to perform in the SD component explained in a simple manner, with helpful screenshots and lists of transaction codes you'll use. Start the journey with master data setup, and then move on to explore sales, shipping, and billing tasks. Push your skills to new heights by mastering reporting and financial supply chain activities.

520 pages, 2nd edition, pub. 11/2014
E-Book: $59.99 | **Print:** $69.95 | **Bundle:** $79.99

www.sap-press.com/3672

Interested in reading more?

Please visit our website for all new
book and e-book releases from SAP PRESS.

www.sap-press.com